INSTRUMENT PILOT'S GUIDE

by

L.W. REITHMAIER

SECOND EDITION

1975

AERO PUBLISHERS, INC.

329 Aviation Road Fallbrook, Cal. 92028

COPYRIGHT©
1969 and 1974
By
AERO PUBLISHERS, INC.

All rights reserved. This book, or parts thereof, must not be reproduced in any form without permission of the publisher.

Library of Congress Cataloging in Publication Data

Reithmaier, Larry W
    Instrument pilot's guide.

    First published in 1969 under title: Pilot's handbook of instrument flying.
    Includes index.
    1. Instrument flying. I. Title.
TL711.B6R43 1974   629.132'52   74-30480
ISBN 0-8168-7305-4

Printed and Published in the United States by Aero Publishers, Inc.

PREFACE

HOW TO USE THIS MANUAL

The purpose of this manual is to present a source of aeronautical knowledge for:
- the student instrument pilot to prepare for the FAA instrument rating written examination.
- the background information needed for the instrument pilot flight training program.
- reference material for the rated instrument pilot to "keep current".

An attempt has been made to eliminate useless theory which has traditionally characterized most pilot training manuals. Each chapter attempts to show the student the information that he must know well. Only sufficient background information is presented to understand properly the required knowledge. It is emphasized that this book is NOT a flight maneuvers manual. The chapter on basic flight control through the use of instruments, however, is quite complete in order to present the interrelationship of airspeed, power control, and trim.

It is recommended that this manual be studied from beginning to end in the sequence given, prior to taking the practice written examination.

The material presented in this manual is based on the assumption that the student has at least a private pilot's certificate. For this reason, the basics of how an airplane flies, airplane limitations and performance, dead reckoning navigation, and use of the navigation computer, are not included.

Although this book is a complete study guide, it is recommended that the student obtain the following publications in their current editions:
- Airman's Information Manual
- Federal Aviation Regulations, Parts 61 and 91
- Instrument navigation charts
- Instrument approach procedure charts

ACKNOWLEDGEMENTS

Various photographs and other material were utilized as provided by the Cessna Aircraft Company, Piper Aircraft Corporation, Bendix Radio Division, King Radio Corporation, Collins Radio Company, Kollsman Instrument Corporation, McDonnell Aircraft Corporation, Federal Aviation Administration, U.S. Navy and the National Weather Service.

TABLE OF CONTENTS

Chapter		Page
1	Introduction to Instrument Flying	7
2	Flight Instruments and Systems	8
3	Learning Instrument Flying	13
4	Radio and Navigational Aids	26
5	Flight Procedures Using Radio	35
6	The Instrument Approach	56
7	Airways and Air Traffic Control (ATC)	78
8	Air Traffic Control (ATC) Procedures	81
9	Aviation Weather for the Instrument Pilot	87
10	Available Weather Data	102
11	Weather Briefing	116
12	Flight Planning	121
	Appendix	125
	The ATC Transponder	126
	Airspace and Airports	129
	Complex Instrument and Navigation Systems	137
	Category II Instrument Approach	141
	Automated Radar Terminal System (ARTS III)	141
	Federal Aviation Regulations	142
	Sample Written Examination	159
	Excerpts from Airman's Information Manual	182
	Greenwich Mean or "Z" Time	186
	Frequently Used Word Contractions	186
	Flight Test Guide—Instrument Pilot	194
	Index	203

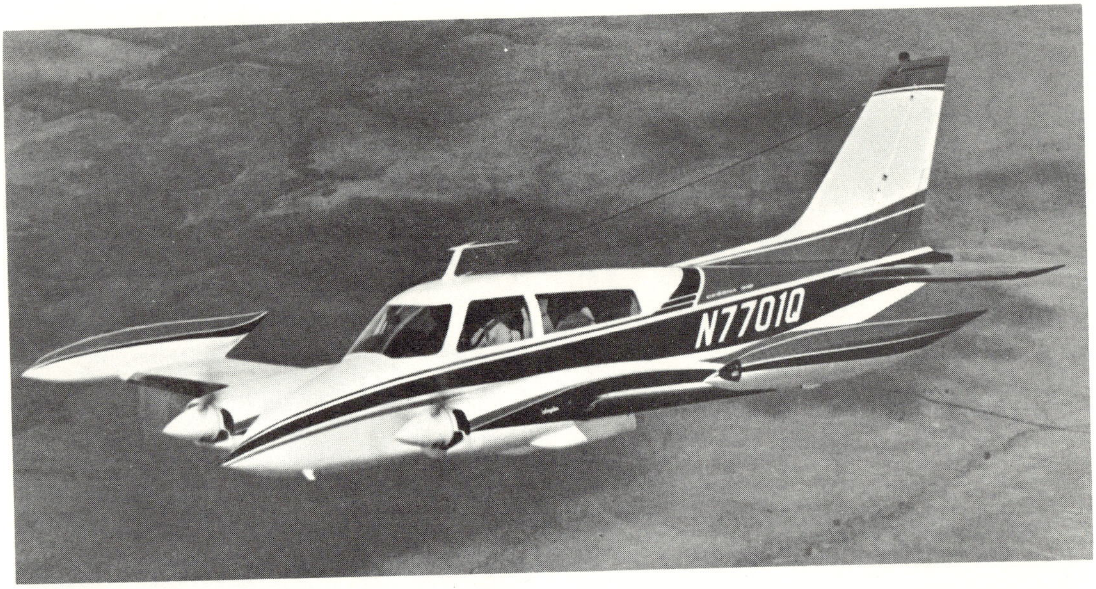
N7701Q

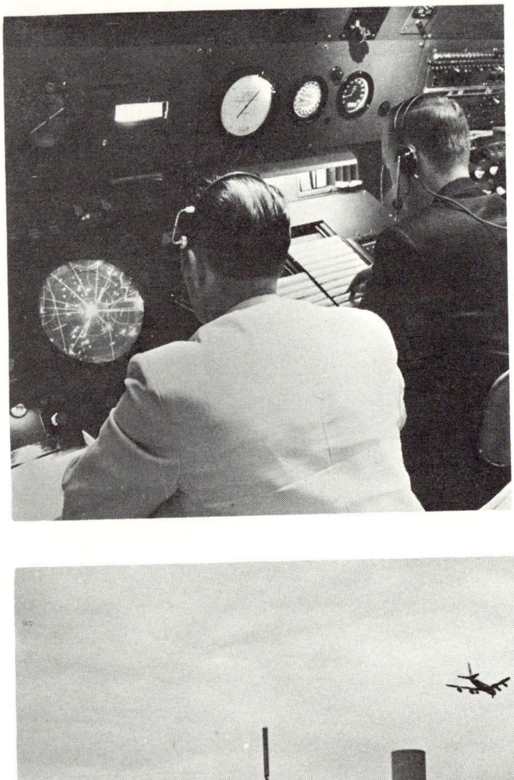

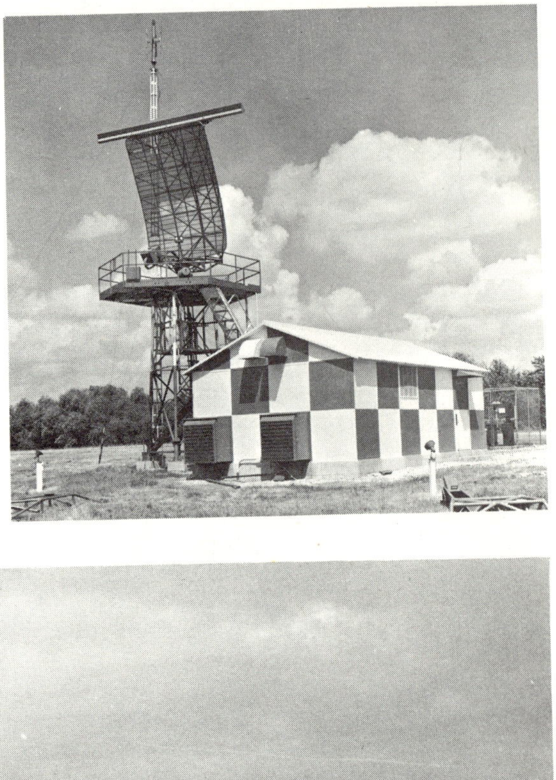

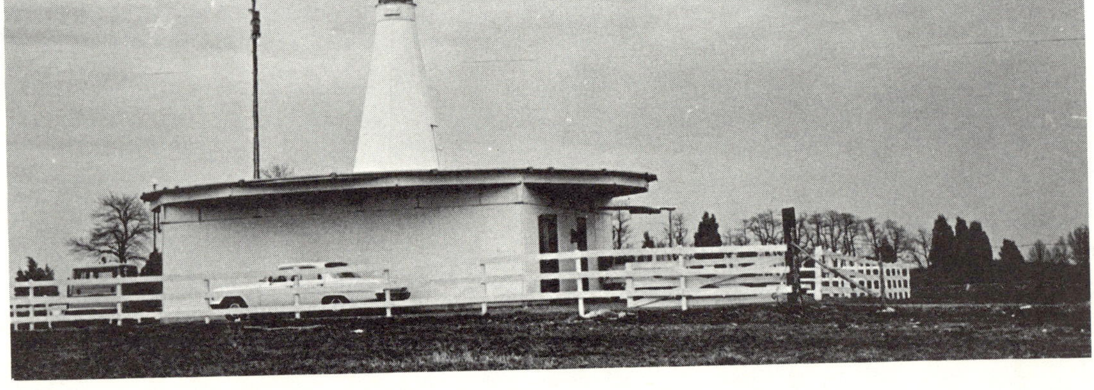

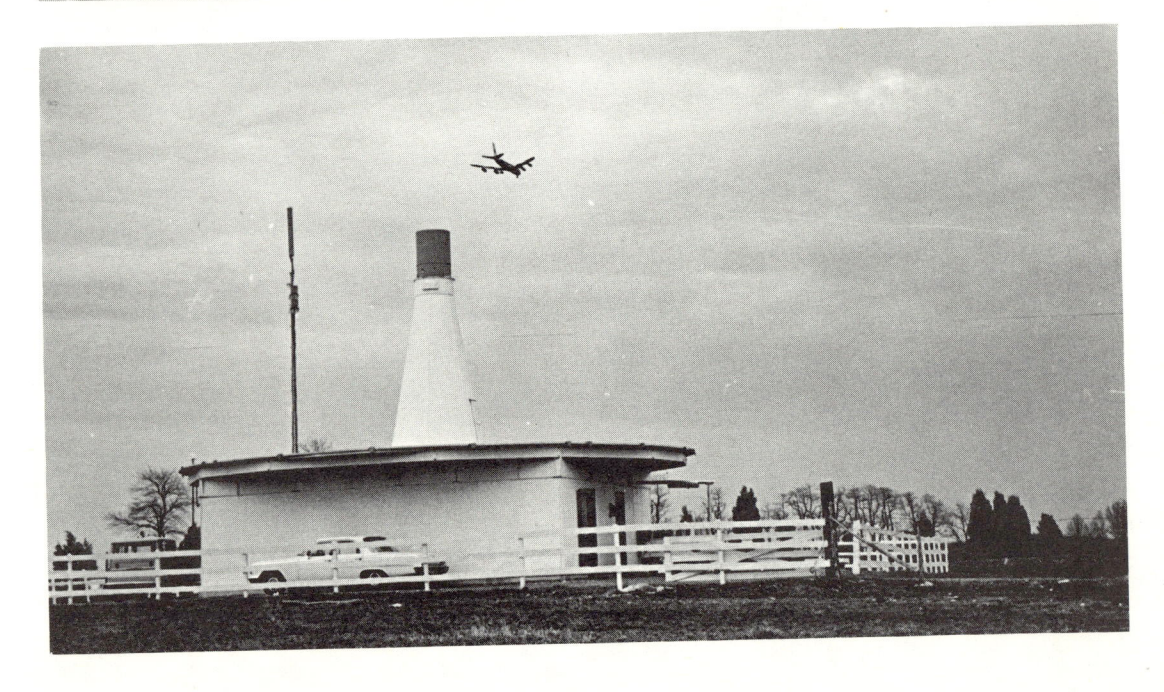

INTRODUCTION TO INSTRUMENT FLYING 1

When the airport conversation drifts around to instrument flying, the VFR pilot generally finds many conflicting ideas and opinions. The old, experienced instrument pilot talks about "needle-ball-airspeed." The ex-military pilot says "attitude instrument flying" is the real thing; while some of the airplane owners advocate the "180 degree turn method" for extricating themselves out of trouble.

Don't let all these terms or procedures confuse you. Keep this basic fact in mind: the airplane does not distinguish between "VFR" or "IFR" conditions. The same aerodynamic principles of stability and control apply whether the airplane is in or out of the clouds.

The big difference between VFR and IFR is not the control of the airplane but the REFERENCES and CUES used by the pilot to control it. His reference merely shifts from outside the cockpit to the inside. The same flight principles, control methods, and navigation procedures apply when "on instruments" as when flying in clear weather. The end result to you, the pilot, is the same VFR or IFR; that is, you must be able to control the airplane's ATTITUDE with relation to the earth and NAVIGATE it from one point to another. In addition however, control of TRAFFIC is another requirement of an IFR flight.

Thus instrument flying can be categorized into three elements:

- ATTITUDE CONTROL which consists of straight and level, turning, climbing and descending flight with reference to instruments only.
- NAVIGATION consists of flying from point to point using radio (and radar) signals only, without benefit of visual reference to ground check points.
- TRAFFIC CONTROL is necessary to prevent collision between aircraft when the "see-and-be-seen" principle cannot be used.

The effects of attempting to fly instruments without proper training are generally known. It has been shown that non-instrument trained pilots experienced complete dis-orientation from 20 seconds to 3 minutes after losing visual reference to the ground. The amount of VFR flight time was no criterion. ALL pilots lost complete control of their airplane whether they had 50 hours or 5000 hours of flight time.

The sense of sight is supported by other senses that help a pilot maintain orientation. Sometimes during instrument flying these supporting senses conflict with what is seen. Thus, without proper training, a normal human tends to follow his senses. This condition is generally called VERTIGO.

An instrument rating has many benefits for a pilot, whether he flies for business or pleasure. For one thing, an instrument rating has become somewhat of a "status symbol." Even more than a commercial certificate, an instrument rating immediately removes a pilot from "amateur" standing, even if he only has a private certificate.

Besides the obvious advantage of being able to fly in definitely instrument weather, an instrument rating provides additional confidence and safety in marginal weather flying. How often have you seen strictly VFR conditions in large city areas like Los Angeles or New York? It is almost always marginal VFR.

The most important advantage of an instrument rating is the one most pilots aren't really aware of. After completing instrument training you will find yourself a far better pilot regardless of your flight time. Whether it's VFR or IFR you will be able to obtain better performance from your airplane. Your flying will show the precision of the professional pilot. Flight planning will be methodical and quickly accomplished. Your navigation will be precise; the omni needle will look like it's "glued" on center. Weather will be less of a mystery; you may never be its master, but you will not be its slave.

Whether you ever actually fly IFR or not, after you obtain an instrument rating your day-to-day flying will reflect your increased confidence and safety.

2 FLIGHT INSTRUMENTS AND SYSTEMS

When flying without visual reference to the ground, the pilot must determine the attitude and performance of his airplane entirely with reference to his instruments. Therefore, a basic understanding of the flight instruments is necessary in order to fly "instruments" especially regarding their limitations, settings, and/or procedures to follow in case of malfunction of one or more of them.

In accordance with the Federal Aviation Regulations (FAR) the following basic flight instruments are required for instrument flight.

- Airspeed indicator
- Sensitive altimeter adjustable for barometric pressure
- Magnetic direction indicator
- Gyroscopic rate-of-turn indicator
- Bank indicator (usually combined with rate-of-turn indicator and called "turn and bank")
- Gyroscopic bank and pitch indicator (artificial horizon)
- Gyroscopic direction indicator (directional gyro or equivalent)
- Clock with sweep second hand

Figure 1 shows these required instruments as installed in light general aviation airplanes.

It should be noted that a vertical speed (rate of climb) indicator is NOT a requirement; however most instrument flight qualified aircraft have such an instrument installed. In addition to the required flight instruments, other instruments and equipment are required by FAR as discussed in the Appendix.

The flight instruments can be classified into two categories:

- PRESSURE INSTRUMENTS
  - Airspeed indicator
  - Altimeter
  - Vertical speed (rate-of-climb) indicator
- GYROSCOPIC (GYRO) INSTRUMENTS
  - Rate-of-turn indicator
  - Bank and pitch indicator (artificial horizon)
  - Direction indicator (directional gyro or equivalent)

The magnetic compass and clock, of course, are based on different principles of operation than differential pressure and gyroscopic. Complex instruments combining pressure, magnetic, gyro and radio together with electronic circuitry such as Flight Director Systems, Zero Reader, Automatic Flight Control Equip-

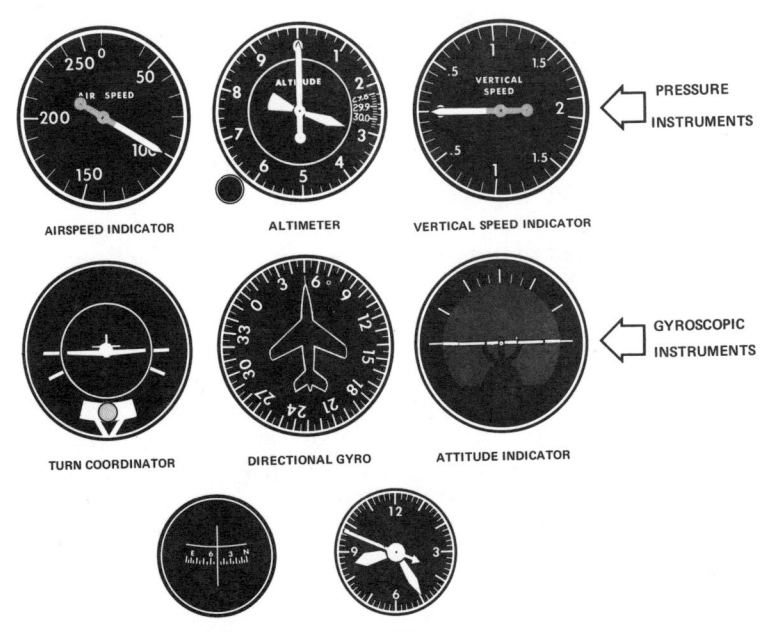

Fig.1 Flight instruments usually installed in airplanes. The vertical speed indicator is NOT required for instrument flight according to the FAR.

ment, etc., will not be discussed inasmuch as this equipment is not normally installed in General Aviation airplanes.

PRESSURE INSTRUMENTS

Each of the three pressure instruments, airspeed indicator, altimeter, and vertical speed indicator operates in response to pressures through the pitot-static system. A simplified pitot-static system is shown in Figure 2.

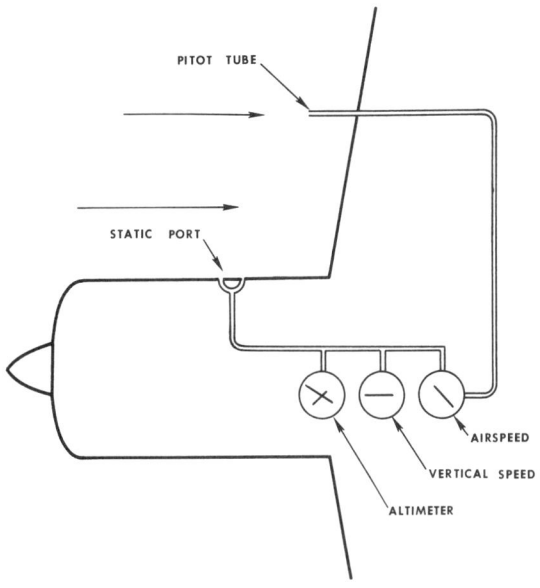

Fig. 2 Pitot-static system.

Essentially, the static port senses atmospheric pressure of "static" air or air that is not moving whereas the pitot tube senses the impact or "ram" pressure of the moving air. Figure 2 shows that the static port is at right angles to the air stream while the pitot tube opening is directly into the air stream. Since the entire airplane moves through the air, it is sometimes difficult to obtain a true static pressure source that is not somewhat affected by ram pressures. It is important therefore that the static ports be inspected for dirt or deformation which could apply a ram or suction to the static system or restrict the opening. Erroneous readings of the highly important flight instruments could result. Pitot tube installations on most instrument airplanes include a heater to prevent plugging from icing conditions.

AIRSPEED INDICATOR

The airspeed indicator is a relatively simple pressure instrument which measures the difference (differential) between the impact or "ram" pressure as sensed by the pitot tube and the static pressure as sensed by the static port.

For practical purposes, the student instrument pilot flying light aircraft will use:
- INDICATED AIRSPEED which is the value read directly on the face of the standard airspeed indicator. It is the pilot's immediate reference in flight.
- TRUE AIRSPEED is indicated airspeed corrected for air density error. True airspeed must be used for navigation. Corrections for true airspeed are discussed in Chapter 12, Flight Planning.

ALTIMETER

The altimeter measures atmospheric pressure as sensed through the static pressure port of the pitot-static system. The altimeter is based on the principle of the aneroid barometer as discussed in Chapter 9, Weather for the Instrument Pilot.

Inasmuch as the altimeter is a pressure measuring device, it is based on a standard air density variation with altitude which, in essence, never exists. For practical purposes, however, the altimeter reading is affected by:
- Pressure variations from standard
- Temperature variations from standard

In order to compensate for pressure variations an altimeter setting system has been provided for changes in barometric pressure.

Each weather reporting station takes an hourly measurement of atmospheric pressure and, according to the surveyed elevation of the station, corrects the value obtained to sea level pressure. The resulting altimeter setting is continually provided to pilots by Air Traffic Control (ATC). IT IS EMPHASIZED THAT PILOTS SHOULD CONTINUALLY CHECK AND ADJUST THEIR ALTIMETER SETTING DURING AN INSTRUMENT FLIGHT AND INSTRUMENT APPROACH. Proper altitude separation between airplanes, terrain clearance, radio reception and instrument approach procedures are all based on each pilot maintaining the proper altimeter setting.

Most altimeters have some error in the altimeter setting system which the pilot must check and compensate for. In other words, if the altimeter setting received from the tower is set in the barometric pressure window, the altimeter may not read the exact field elevation. If this error is greater than 75 feet, the altimeter should not be used for flight and should be repaired.

Altimeter readings are also affected to a lesser extent by non-standard temperature. A good rule to memorize is this:

- IF THE AIR IS *COLDER* THAN STANDARD, THE AIRPLANE IS *LOWER* THAN THE ALTIMETER INDICATES.

Most aeronautical computers provide for altimeter corrections due to temperature. However, altimeter corrections are normally NOT made for non-standard temperature. Since instrument flight in controlled airspace is accomplished at assigned indicated altitudes, aircraft separation is maintained because all aircraft using the same altimeter setting are equally affected by non-standard conditions at various levels. If, however, a pilot on an instrument flight believes a hazardous condition exists due to extremely cold conditions, for example, a temperature correction can be made. When such a correction is made, ATC should be notified to assure adequate altitude separation between airplanes.

In reading the altimeter the smallest hands should be read first, then the next larger.

VERTICAL SPEED INDICATOR

This instrument is commonly called a "rate-of-climb" indicator even though it reads rate-of-descent also. A vertical speed indicator is NOT required by FAR for instrument flight; however, most airplanes are equipped with this instrument.

The vertical speed indicator is contained within a sealed case, connected to the static pressure line through a calibrated leak. The rate of air leakage is a function of the airplane's rate of climb or descent.

Sudden or abrupt changes in aircraft altitude result in erroneous vertical speed indications. As discussed in the next chapter, vertical speed readings are only reliable during a STEADY climb or descent.

GYROSCOPIC INSTRUMENTS

The gyroscopic instruments are the rate-of-turn indicator (commonly known as "turn and bank" since a ball bank is included), bank and pitch (attitude indicator or artificial horizon), and direction indicator

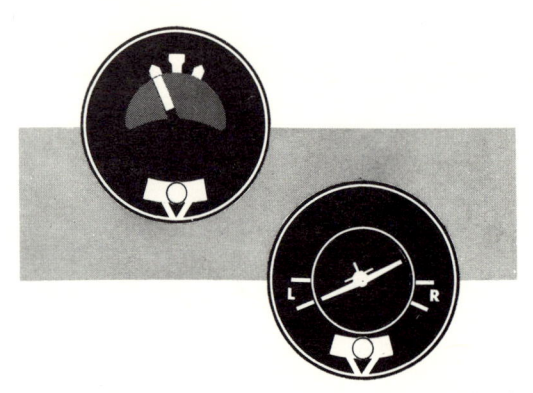

Fig. 3 Older airplanes may have "Turn-and-bank" indicator installed as shown on the left. Newer airplanes usually include a "Turn Coordinator". A "standard rate" (3 degrees per second) coordinated turn is shown.

(directional gyro). Without getting into technical details, it is sufficient for the pilot to know that they operate on the principle of the gyroscope which is "rigid in space." Therefore, in essence, the gyro axes remain fixed in space while the airplane rotates around them. Suitable linkages and dials present the proper information to the pilot at the instrument face.

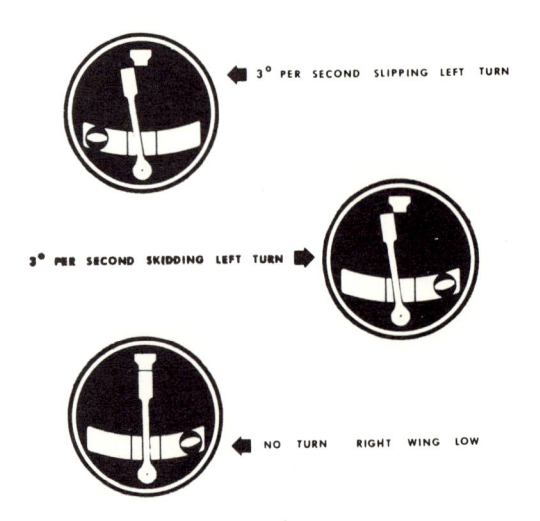

Fig. 3A Turn and bank indications.

Since a gyroscope depends on a relatively heavy "flywheel" rotating at high speeds, a power source is required. Some instruments use pneumatic pressures obtained from an engine driven vacuum pump or a venturri, to drive the gyro like a turbine. Electric motors are also used in some designs to provide gyro rotation.

Some older type attitude indicators and directional gyros can "tumble" the gyro when bank angles of approximately 100° and pitch angles of approximately 60° are

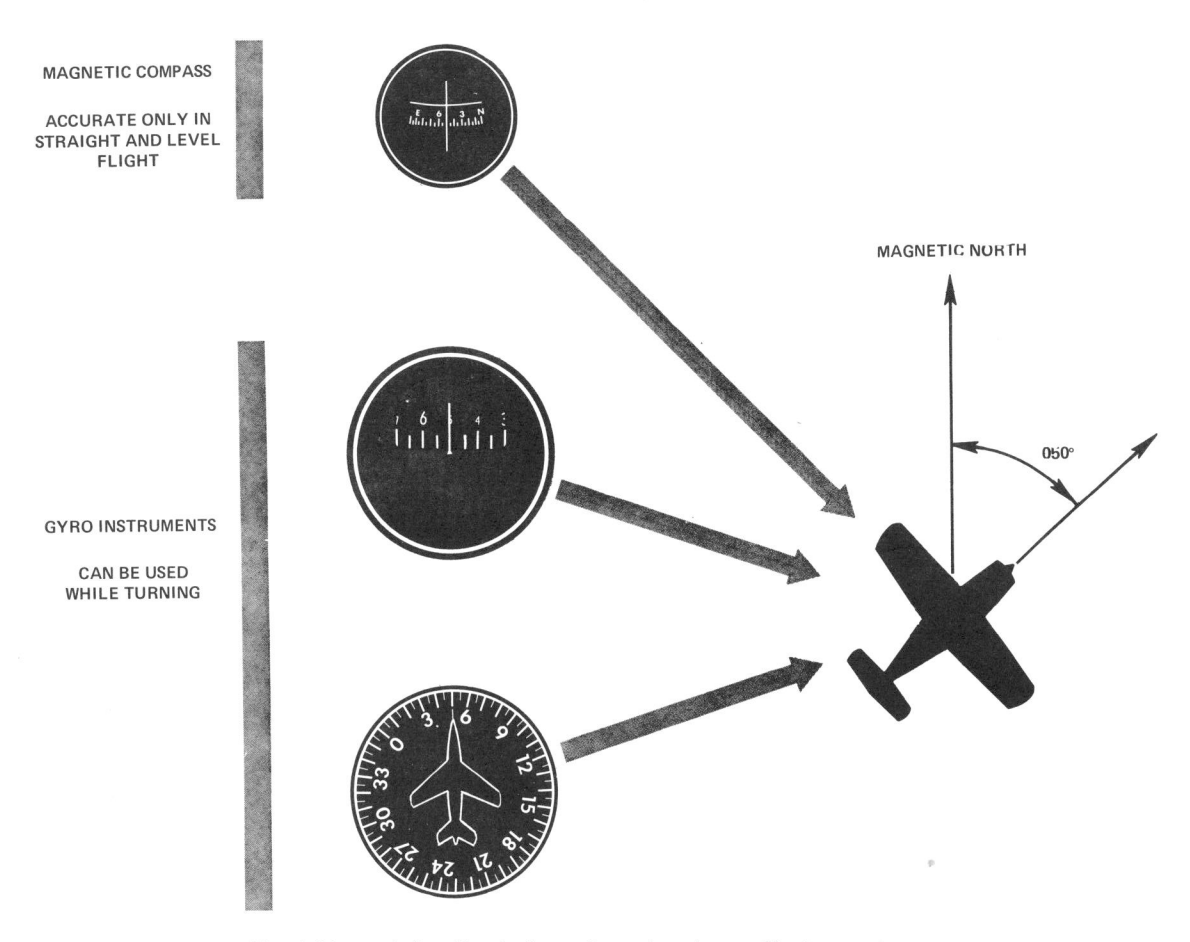

Fig. 4 Magnetic heading is shown by various types of instruments.

exceeded. These instruments provide caging mechanisms for use during violent flight maneuvers. Since the limits of light plane gyros are well beyond the attitude restriction on "normal category" aircraft, tumbling of the instruments does not normally occur during instrument flight.

The gyroscopic heading indicator (directional gyro) must be set to the magnetic compass. This instrument should be checked at least every 15 minutes during flight and reset to the correct heading. An error of no more than 3 degrees in 15 minutes is acceptable for normal operations. Gyroscopic direction indicators of various types are sometimes installed in different airplanes as shown by the two gyro indicators in Figure 4. The upper gyro instrument shown in this figure, or horizontal card type is the most common directional gyro installed in older airplanes. Newer airplanes are usually equipped with the middle or vertical card indicator. Both of these must be set with the magnetic compass while in straight and level flight.

The artificial horizon and directional gyro need no further explanation. The turn-and-bank indicator, however, deserves some discussion regarding interpretation of its indications. "Needle and ball" and "turn and slip indicator" are other commonly used terms for this instrument inasmuch as it is actually a combination of a gyroscopic rate of turn indicator and a gravity, or centrifugal force influenced, ball-in-glass-tube.

The turn and bank indicator shows both "quantity" and "quality" of the turn. Rate of turn (also direction of the turn) is shown by deflection of the needle while the position of the ball shows whether it is a "high quality" or coordinated turn. Figure 3A shows indications of slipping and skidding turns. Further discussion regarding the turn and bank indicator is included in the next chapter on flying basic instruments.

MAGNETIC COMPASS

The simple magnetic compass has been the basic heading (heading is the direction the nose is pointing) and direction indicator for centuries of navigation. Due to various errors such as magnetic dip, northerly turning error and acceleration error, the magnetic compass can only be used as a heading reference during stabilized straight and level flight.

NORTHERLY TURNING ERROR

This error is most apparent on headings of north and south. When making a turn from a heading of north, the compass briefly gives an indication of a turn in the opposite direction. When making a turn from south, it gives an indication of a turn in the correct direction but at a much faster rate than is actually occurring.

ACCELERATION ERROR

Because of the pendulous-type mounting, when accelerating on an east or west heading, the error appears as a turn indication toward north. When decelerating on either of these headings, the compass indicates a turn towards south. The word "ANDS" (Acceleration - North/Deceleration - South) may help you to remember the acceleration error.

Another error called DEVIATION is of vital importance to the pilot. The compass needles are affected not only by the earth's magnetic fields, but also by magnetic fields generated when aircraft electrical equipment is operated and by metal components of the aircraft. These magnetic disturbances within the aircraft, called deviation deflect the compass needles from magnetic north.

To reduce this deviation, each compass is checked and compensated periodically. The errors remaining after "swinging" the compass are recorded on a compass correction card mounted near the compass. It is emphasized that a properly compensated compass is an absolute necessity for instrument flight. A compass ten or twenty degrees off is not only hazardous but frustrating to the low time instrument or student instrument pilot.

COMPLEX INSTRUMENTS

See Appendix for a brief discussion of more complex flight instruments usually installed in high performance single-engine and twin-engine airplanes.

SUMMARY

FAR requires certain flight instruments to be installed in all airplanes certified for instrument flight. In addition to a magnetic direction indicator and clock with sweep second hand, the following flight instruments are necessary:
- PRESSURE INSTRUMENTS
  - Airspeed indicator
  - Sensitive altimeter adjustable for barometric pressure.
- GYROSCOPIC INSTRUMENTS
  - Rate of turn indicator (usually combined with a bank indicator) and called "turn and bank."
  - Bank and pitch indicator (artificial horizon).
  - Direction indicator (directional gyro or equivalent).

The pressure instruments obtain their inputs from the pitot-static system which senses both "static" or non-moving air and "impact" or moving air.

It is important that all flight instruments and systems be in good operating condition and properly calibrated.

LEARNING INSTRUMENT FLYING 3

FULL PANEL FLYING

Any instrument flight, regardless of the aircraft used or the route flown, is made up of basic maneuvers. These maneuvers must be learned by reference to instruments to control your flight path. Through control of the aircraft's position with relation to the natural horizon, you learn the maneuvers common to both "visual" and instrument flight.

To control attitude, you refer either to the natural horizon or to combinations of basic instruments discussed in the previous chapter. By means of pitch, bank, and/or power control, you will learn how to control movements of the aircraft about its lateral, longitudinal, and vertical axes. To follow a predetermined flight path, you must develop the ability to hold attitude constant, to change attitude, and to know when and how much to change it.

The procedures and techniques discussed in the following paragraphs are not new or different. A step-by-step procedure and organized approach is established however, to accomplish either or both of the following objectives:

- After about ten hours of instruction, the VFR pilot can safely control his airplane without visual reference to the ground and do a reasonable job of VOR navigation.
- Provide the basis for progression to radio navigation and instrument approaches leading to an instrument rating.

Only the basic fundamental flight attitudes such as straight and level flight, climb, descent and the standard rate turn will be discussed. All other maneuvers are modifications or combinations of these basic flight attitudes.

Although many pilots are not conscious of it, the basic principles of aircraft control are:

- *Power* is used to determine the rate of climb or descent or maintain level flight.
- *Elevator control* (pitch) is used to control *airspeed*.
- A *turn* can only be accomplished in a *banked* attitude. Rudder is merely a yaw control and used only during entry and recovery.
- *Trim* should only be used to relieve control pressures after a flight condition is changed. Trim *should not* be

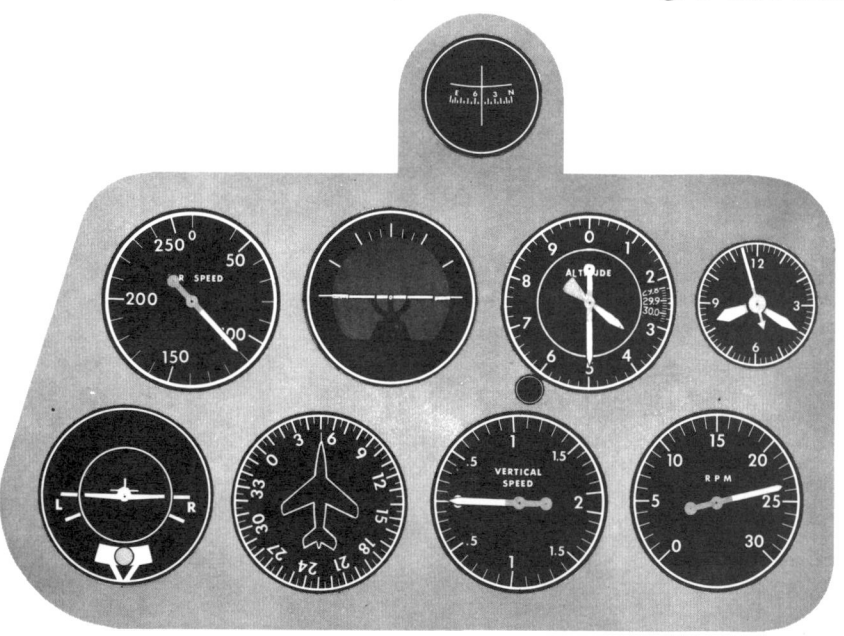

Fig. 5 During level flight, the wings of the little airplane on the artificial horizon should be exactly aligned with the horizon bar.

used to initiate a change in flight condition.

To begin with, a pilot should be familiar with the airspeeds and power settings required for level flight, climb and descent for his airplane. These values can be easily determined by trial during VFR flight in smooth air and should be recorded for use as a check list throughout the instrument training program. A typical set of performance figures for a four-place, 145-hp instrument training airplane using a fixed pitch propeller is:

Maneuver	Power (rpm)	Indicated Airspeed	Rate of Climb Rate of Descent
Level Flight	2350	110 mph	0
Normal Climb	2500	90 mph	500 fpm
Descent (No Flap)	1700	90 mph	500 fpm
Descent (20° Flap)	1600	80 mph	500 fpm

These figures were obtained at 3000 feet with pilot and instructor. In general, higher altitudes as well as higher gross weights will require higher power settings for the same airspeed. If the airplane is equipped with a constant speed propeller, manifold pressure, as controlled by the throttle, determines the power setting. With a little experimentation, a similar set of basic performance figures can be obtained for any airplane including a twin.

The procedures and techniques presented are equally applicable to either VFR or IFR flight. It is suggested that each condition described be first set up without using a hood but by reference to the instruments. The same conditions should then be practiced under the hood (with a qualified safety pilot or instructor).

Level Flight: By referring to the airspeed indicator, altimeter and vertical speed indicator, maintain the desired cruising airspeed at the recommended power setting. In our example airplane it is 110 mph indicated airspeed at 2350 rpm. After stabilized level flight is attained, trim out any control pressures. Now, carefully adjust the miniature airplane on the artificial horizon so that the wings of the little airplane are exactly aligned with the horizon bar. *Once this has been adjusted, do not change this setting.* Thus, there will never be any doubt regarding the pitch attitude of the airplane. If the wings of the miniature airplane are above the horizon bar, the airplane is in a nose high attitude. Conversely, if the wings of the miniature airplane are below the horizon bar, the airplane is in a nose low attitude. Figure 5 shows the instrument panel of our example airplane when set up for level flight.

Entering a climb from level flight: Unless otherwise required, all instrument climbs will be accomplished at a constant rate of 500 fpm. From the airspeed-power setting table, the predetermined values for a 500 fpm climb for our example are: airspeed 90 mph, power 2500 rpm. The step-by-step

Fig. 6 At climb power and airspeed the artificial horizon shows a slightly nose high attitude. At the proper airspeed-power setting, a rate of climb of exactly 500 fpm is obtained.

procedure is:
- With reference to the artificial horizon, raise the nose to climb attitude. Simultaneously add enough power to prevent excessive loss of rpm.
- When airspeed approaches climb airspeed (90 mph), positively add predetermined climb power (2500 rpm).
- Maintain climb airspeed with pitch (elevator) control. Re-adjust power slightly, as required, to maintain 500 fpm.
- Trim out elevator pressure after airspeed, rate-of-climb and power are stabilized.

As the climb is entered, you will notice a tendency for the airplane to turn to the left. Since the airplane is probably rigged (or trimmed with rudder trim, if available) for cruising conditions, the slower airspeed and higher power will produce a left turn tendency. During the climb, the turn needle is referred to for directional control. Generally, a little right rudder must be fed in to keep the turn needle centered. Wings are kept level by reference to the artificial horizon. After the climb is established and control pressures trimmed out, the instruments will look like Figure 6. In fact, after a little practice, you will be amazed at the appearance of the instruments. It will look like the needles are "glued" in place.

The object of a climb, of course, is to change from one altitude to a higher altitude. Normally, the level-off altitude is predetermined. A step-by-step procedure for level-off at a predetermined altitude is:
- Maintain climb attitude, airspeed, rate of climb and power setting until the altimeter reads 50 feet above your level-off altitude.
- As airspeed approaches cruising (110 mph in our example) reduce power to cruise setting.
- Maintain cruise airspeed with pitch control.
- Re-adjust power slightly to maintain zero vertical speed.
- Trim out control pressures.

During this transition period from climb to level flight you will notice a tendency for the airplane to turn to the right. Again, the turn needle should serve as the directional reference and determine your rate of relieving the right rudder pressure you held during the climb.

The 50 foot overshoot of your intended altitude is only a guide and should be determined by trial for different airplanes as well as by the individual pilot's rate of response. Experience indicates that a light airplane will lose approximately 25 to 50 feet during the level-off procedure and stabilize out at, or slightly above, the intended altitude.

As the airplane becomes larger and heavier the requirement for this 50 foot lag

Fig. 7 At the proper airspeed-power setting a rate of descent of exactly 500 fpm is obtained. Compare this with the instrument indications for a climb.

in beginning level-off generally becomes less. In fact, the inertia and momentum generated by a fast climbing military fighter may require a lead of several hundred feet in order to avoid excessive altitude overshoot.

Now for the all important descent to a predetermined altitude. Just as the climb, all descents will be conducted at 500 fpm. The step-by-step procedure for a descent from level cruising flight is:
- While maintaining level flight attitude with reference to the artificial horizon, unhesitatingly reduce power to descent power (1700 rpm in our example).
- When the airspeed approaches descent airspeed (90 mph), lower the nose slightly by reference to the artificial horizon to maintain this airspeed.
- Re-adjust power as required to provide exactly 500 fpm descent.
- Trim out control pressure.

Again refer to the turn needle to maintain directional control. However, during a descent the turning tendency may be very slight if apparent at all. Like the climb, a well executed descent will "glue" the needles to the dials and make your panel look like Figure 7.

Recovery from the descent to level flight at a predetermined altitude is accomplished like this:
- Maintain descent airspeed, rate of descent and power setting until the altimeter reads 50 feet above your level-off altitude.
- At 50 feet above level-off altitude, simultaneously raise the nose slightly to level flight attitude by reference to the artificial horizon and add cruise power or slightly more than cruise power.
- As airspeed builds up to cruise airspeed (110 mph), adjust power to maintain zero vertical speed.
- Trim out control pressures.

Some turning tendency will be noted depending on which builds up faster, power or airspeed. Rudder pressure should be used to keep the turn needle centered.

The 50 foot lead in beginning recovery is just a guide and will usually provide level flight a few feet above your intended level-off altitude. However, this value may vary with different airplanes as well as pilot techniques.

Almost without exception all turns under instrument conditions are *standard rate*. That is, the airplane turns at a constant rate of three degrees per second. Thus, a 45-degree turn will take 15 seconds, 180 degrees one minute, and 360 degrees two minutes. The turn needle part of the turn and bank indicator is a turning rate indicator.

You will see one of two types of turn indicators in most general aviation airplanes. The *sensitive* turn needle has two "dog houses," one on either side of the center, or straight flight index. A three degree per second, standard rate turn is accomplished when the needle is exactly aligned with the "dog house." The *non-sensitive* turn needle has no turn reference marks other than the center or straight flight index. A standard rate, three degree per second turn is accomplished by aligning the edge of the needle along the edge of the mark. Figure 8 shows how a standard rate turn looks with both types of turn and bank indicators. It is easier to fly with a non-sensitive needle in rough air.

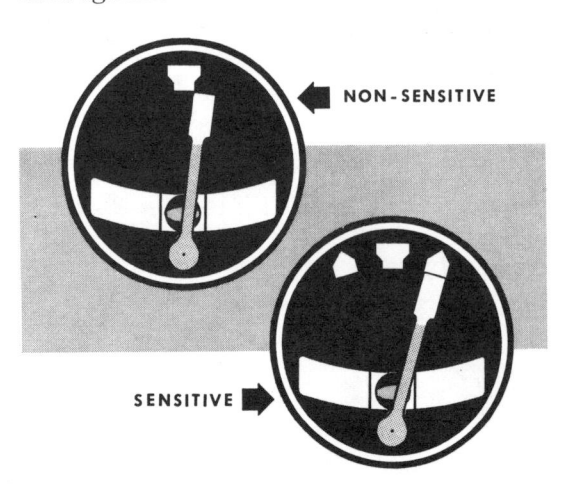

Fig. 8 You will find two types of turn and bank indicators installed in light airplanes. Needle deflections for a standard rate turn are shown for both sensitive and nonsensitive indicators.

A standard rate turn in a Cessna 172 or an Aero Commander will be accomplished in the same time and the turn needles will look identical. The difference, however, will be the angle bank used to accomplish the turn. At 110 mph (true airspeed) an angle of bank of 15 degrees will provide a standard rate turn, while at 200 mph an angle of bank of 27 degrees is required. At 400 mph an angle of bank of 45 degrees would be necessary for a three degree per second turn. Therefore, high speed aircraft have a four minute turn needle to

Fig. 9 Note the indications of both the turn needle and artificial horizon in a level flight, standard rate left turn.

avoid excessive bank angles. A jet airliner, for example, turns at 1½ degrees per second, requiring four minutes to complete a 360 degree turn.

With reference to the turn needle, ball-bank and artificial horizon, you can easily determine the angle of bank required for a standard rate turn in your airplane. As a guide, use the following table:

True Airspeed	Angle of Bank
110 mph	15 degrees
125	18
150	20
175	23
200	27

Prior to starting turns on instruments, don't forget this basic fact: Slowly roll into a turn using both rudder and aileron. After the turn is established, *relieve rudder pressure*. Again, on recovery, apply both aileron and rudder pressure. Thus, rudder is used only on entry and recovery. This fact applies to both visual and instrument flight.

The step-by-step procedure for accomplishing a standard rate, level flight turn to a predetermined heading is:

- Slowly and simultaneously apply both rudder and aileron pressure to enter the turn.
- With reference to the artificial hori-

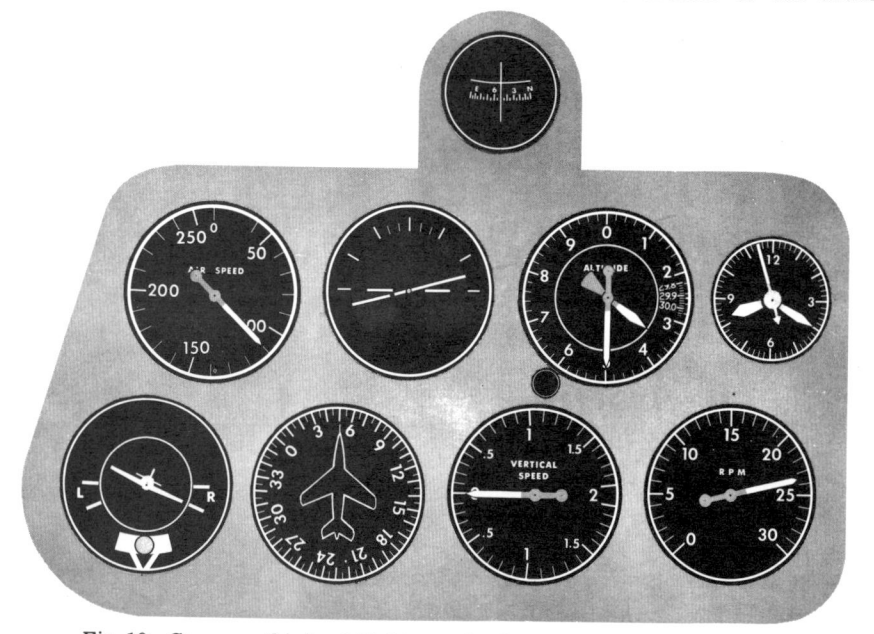

Fig. 10 Compare this level flight, standard rate right turn with Figure 9.

zon, stop the bank at the proper angle as indicated by the wings on the miniature airplane or the bank index on top of the artificial horizon.
- Relieve rudder pressure.
- Refer to the turn needle and make small corrections to the bank angle as required, to maintain a standard rate turn.
- When the heading indicator (directional gyro) is 5 to 10 degrees from your predetermined heading, begin the rollout with reference to the artificial horizon.
- As the wings become level, stop the rollout and maintain straight flight. The 5 to 10 degree lead is a guide only and should be determined by the individual pilot.

A guide for deciding the lead for rollout is to begin recovery the same number of degrees ahead of your predetermined heading as one-half your bank angle. Thus, for our example airplane which requires a 15 degree bank, a lead of 7 to 8 degrees generally works out pretty good.

An artificial horizon with the small "dot" in the center of the miniature airplane is a real help in maintaining altitude while turning.

A standard rate, level flight left turn is shown in Figure 9 while a standard rate right turn is shown in Figure 10. After a little practice, you will be able to "glue" the needles on and the airplane will turn as if it were "in a groove."

The instrument pilot should develop a scanning procedure so that his gaze continually covers or "cross-checks" all instruments. Attention should never be riveted to one instrument for any length of time. During certain maneuvers, however, some instruments become primary, requiring additional attention. As proficiency is improved, you will notice that you can carefully observe the primary instrument and still be able to adequately cross-check the other instruments in the panel.

In summary, remember the following:
- "Keep your eyes moving," don't spend too much time looking at one instrument.
- "Don't horse the airplane around." A gentle touch and slow control movements works wonders.
- "Do one thing at a time." Turn first and then descend, or climb first and then turn. Combine maneuvers only after gaining proficiency.
- "Plan ahead." Always decide ahead of time the altitude you want to reach or the direction of a turn and your recovery heading.

In the next section, we will discuss instrument flight using the emergency panel or "needle-ball-airspeed," timed turns, calibrating the turn needle, steep turns and recovery from unusual attitudes. Now get a good instructor and start in on "full panel" using the step-by-step method.

PARTIAL PANEL FLYING AND ADVANCED MANEUVERS

"Why fly needle-ball-airspeed; all airplanes I've ever seen have a full panel including gyros?" This question is posed by most student instrument pilots. There are two good reasons for a pilot to do a passable job of instrument flying without the help of the artificial horizon and directional gyro. First, these two gyro instruments are rather complex; they *can* fail. Therefore, because of this, the second reason for flying partial panel exists — the FAA requires it in order to obtain an instrument rating.

"Needle-ball-airspeed" is sometimes called "partial panel" or "emergency panel," depending on the vintage literature you happen to be reading. For our discussion however, "partial panel" seems to be the most appropriate. Although not recommended, *all* instrument flying including radio navigation and approaches can be done using partial panel. In fact, it was not too many years ago that installation of the artificial horizon and directional gyro finally became a requirement for airplanes certified by the FAA for instrument flight.

A few years ago, partial panel was taught to student instrument pilots before going to full panel. Present thinking however, is based on obtaining a reasonable degree of proficiency on full panel and then proceeding to partial panel. This procedure, from visual to full panel to partial panel, generally provides the easiest transition for most pilots. Thus, no new control procedures must be learned. The same piloting principles apply throughout. The only differences are that the pilot's references and cues become fewer and fewer.

Whether or not you have mastered full panel, as described previously, this discussion of partial panel flying is complete by itself.

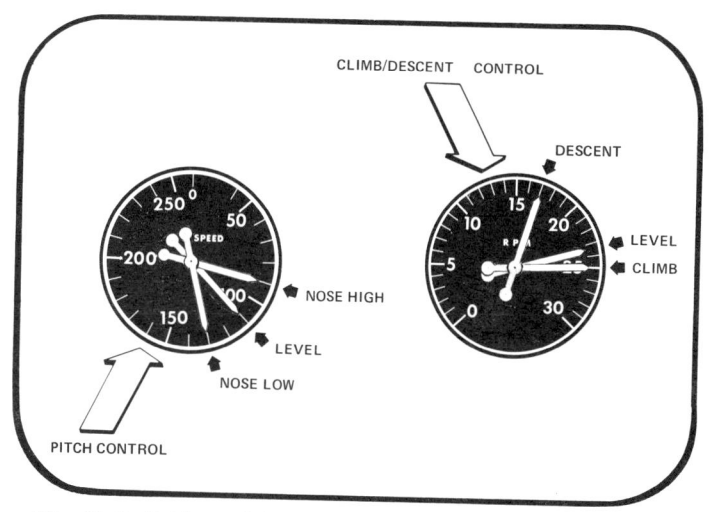

Fig. 11 When flying "Needle-Ball-Airspeed," use the airspeed indicator for pitch control, and use the tachometer (with a fixed-pitch propeller) for control of climb, descent, or level flight.

Prior to getting involved in specific maneuvers, we will again emphasize a few basic principles. First, you should make up a basic airspeed-power setting table for your airplane. An example is shown here for a typical light aircraft using a fixed-pitch propeller. This is the same as previously described under "full panel."

Maneuver	Power (rpm)	Indicated Airspeed	Rate of Climb Rate of Desc
Level Flight	2350	110 Mph	0 fpm
Normal Climb	2500	90 mph	500 fpm
Descent (No Flap)	1700	90 mph	500 fpm
Descent (20° Flap)	1600	80 mph	500 fpm

Also, remember that:
- *Pitch* (elevator) controls airspeed. Airspeed in turn, shows the attitude of the nose of the airplane.
- *Power* decides your airplane's rate of climb, descent, or level flight condition.
- *Trim* should be used to relieve control pressure after a flight condition has been changed. Trim should *not* be used to initiate a change to another flight condition. Figure 11, using our example airplane, shows the first two basic principles.

To this could be added:
- Bank attitude (as controlled by aileron pressure) determines the airplane's rate of turn. The *turn needle* is an indication of *bank attitude*. Rudder is merely a trim control used only during turn entry and recovery. The ball portion of the turn and bank indicator is used for proper coordination.

With these basic principles in mind, partial panel will be relatively easy, especially so if you have already flown a few hours using full panel. For partial panel practice, failure of the artificial horizon and directional gyro is simulated by either caging these instruments or using a card with masking tape to cover them. Covering them with a card is preferable inasmuch as lengthy operation of these instruments in the caged condition promotes excessive wear.

Now we will proceed with our partial panel work, using a step-by-step approach similar to that used during full panel flight. We will start with level flight.

Level flight: Applying the basic airspeed-power settings, maintain airspeed at 110 mph by means of pitch (elevator) control with power at 2350 rpm. At this power setting, a lower airspeed indicates a nose-high attitude with a corresponding gain in altitude. Conversely, an airspeed higher than our normal cruise indicates a nose-low attitude with a loss in altitude shown by the altimeter.

During partial panel flying, the turn needle is used for heading control. By coordinated rudder-aileron pressures, the turn needle is maintained in the center. An occasional glance at the magnetic compass is made to determine whether the aircraft has drifted off its heading. Figure 12 shows partial panel level flight.

After a little practice at partial panel level flight, you are ready to enter a climb to a predetermined altitude.

Entering a climb from level flight: The step-by-step procedure using partial panel is:
- With reference to the airspeed indicator, apply elevator backpressure to reduce airspeed to 90 mph.

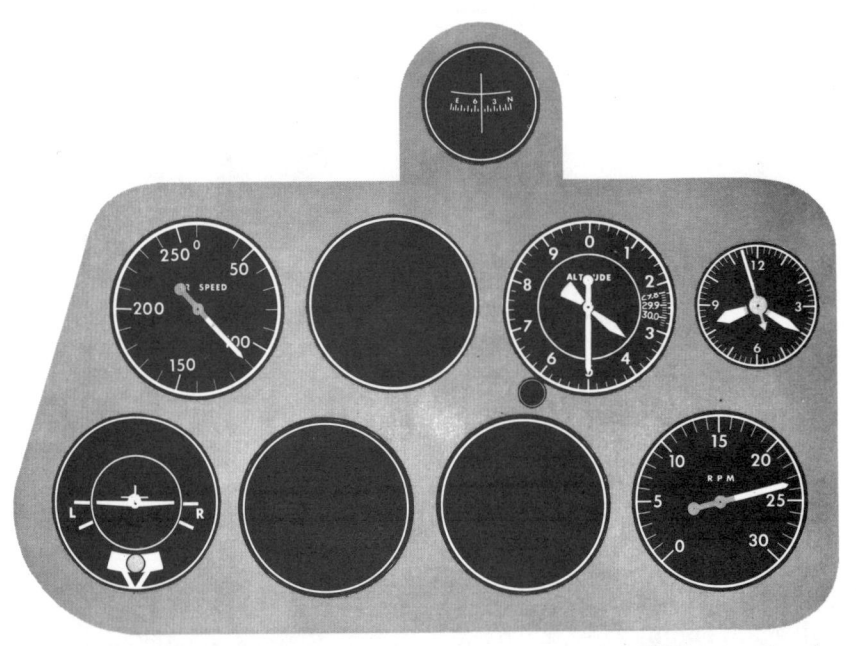

Fig. 12 At the proper power setting, the airplane will maintain level flight at cruise airspeed.

- When airspeed approaches 90 mph, positively add predetermined climb power (2500 rpm).
- Maintain climb airspeed with pitch (elevator) control. Make minor power adjustments to maintain 2500 rpm.
- Trim out elevator pressure after airspeed is stabilized.

As the climb is entered, you will notice a tendency for the airplane to turn to the left. Since the airplane is probably rigged (or trimmed with rudder trim, if available) for cruising conditions, the slower airspeed and higher power will produce a left-turn tendency. During the climb, the turn needle is referred to for directional control. Generally, a little right rudder must be fed in to keep the turn needle and ball centered. After the climb is established and control pressures trimmed out, the instruments will look like Figure 13 with all needles "glued" in place.

The partial panel level-off procedure is:
- Maintain climb airspeed and power

Fig. 13 Application of climb power, together with climb attitude as shown by the airspeed indicator will provide a 500 fpm rate of climb.

setting until the altimeter reads 50 feet *above* your level-off altitude.
- At 50 feet above level-off altitude, slowly lower nose to level flight attitude *with reference to the airspeed indicator.*
- As airspeed approaches cruising (110 mph in our example) reduce power to cruise setting (2350 rpm).
- Maintain cruise airspeed with pitch control.
- Readjust power slightly to maintain cruise power.
- Trim out control pressures.

During this transition period from climb to level flight, you will notice a tendency for the airplane to turn to the *right*. Again, the turn needle should serve as the directional reference and determine your rate of relieving the right rudder pressure you held during the climb.

The step-by-step procedure for a descent from level cruising flight is:
- While maintaining level flight attitude with reference to the airspeed indicator, unhesitatingly reduce power to descent power (1700 rpm in our example).
- When the airspeed approaches descent airspeed (90 mph), lower the nose slightly by reference to the airspeed indicator to maintain this airspeed.
- Readjust power as required to provide 1700 rpm.
- Trim out control pressure.

Again refer to the turn needle to maintain directional control. However, during a descent the turning tendency may be very slight if apparent at all. Like the climb, a well-executed descent will "glue" the needles to the dials and make your panel look like Figure 14.

Recovery from the descent to level flight at a predetermined altitude is effected like this:
- Maintain descent airspeed and power setting until the altimeter reads 50 feet *above* your level-off altitude.
- At 50 feet above level-off altitude, simultaneously raise the nose slightly to level flight attitude by reference to the airspeed indicator, and add cruise power or slightly more than cruise power.
- As airspeed builds up to cruise airspeed (110 mph), adjust power to maintain cruise rpm (2350).
- Trim out control pressures.

Some turning tendency will be noted, depending on which builds up faster, power or airspeed. Rudder pressure should be used to keep the turn needle centered.

During turns, the compass cannot be used as a heading indicator. Therefore, turns on partial panel must rely on the clock combined with the turn and bank indicator. One needle-width deflection (using a properly calibrated turn and bank indicator) will result in a 3-degree-per-second rate of turn. Thus, a 360-degree turn will take two minutes. Partial panel turns are

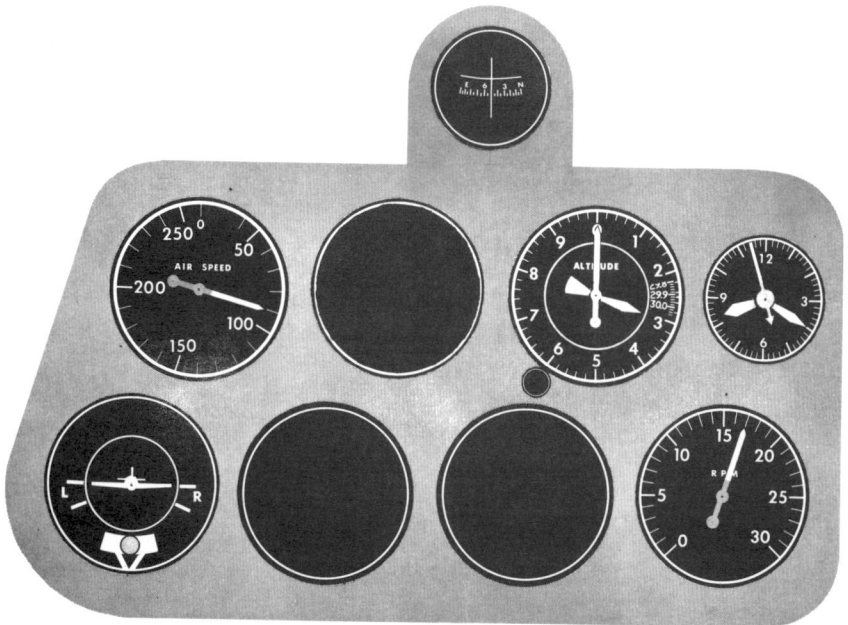

Fig. 14 Compare this with Figure 13. Airspeed is the same for a climb; however, power is different. It is POWER that determines whether the airplane is in a climb, descent, or in level flight.

Fig. 15 At cruise power and airspeed, a level-flight, standard-rate turn of 3 degrees per second is shown by the turn indicator. At the needle displacement shown, a 360-degree turn will take two minutes.

flown by using coordinated rudder and aileron pressures, using the turn needle for *bank* control with reference to the ball for coordination. The same principles apply that are used with full panel — or VFR for that matter, except fewer references are available.

The step-by-step procedure for accomplishing a partial panel, 360-degree standard-rate turn to a predetermined heading is:

- Watch the second hand of the clock. When it is at a good reference point (such as straight up on 12), begin your roll into the turn smoothly, using coordinated rudder and aileron pressures.
- With reference to the turn needle, stop the bank angle to maintain one needle width.
- Relieve rudder pressure.
- Refer to the turn needle and make small corrections to the bank angle as required to maintain a one-needle-width deflection (see Figure 15).
- When the second hand of the clock is exactly on your reference point (12 for example) for the second time (two minutes, elapsed time), begin your roll-out.
- As the turn needle centers, stop the roll-out and maintain straight flight.
- When the airplane is stabilized in straight and level flight, refer to the compass.

A properly executed 360-degree turn will result in a final heading within a few degrees of your entry heading.

Turns to any heading can be made by determining the number of seconds required at 3 degrees per second standard rate. A good rule of thumb is to *begin roll-in* at a good reference point on the clock and *begin roll-out* the required number of seconds later. This generally works out better than leading or lagging the clock.

An instrument pilot must recognize, and be able to recover from, an unusual attitude. An unusual attitude is any attitude of the aircraft not required for normal instrument flight. It may result from any one factor or a combination of several factors such as turbulence, vertigo, instrument failure, confusion of the pilot, or carelessness in cross-checking the instruments. Recovery from unusual attitude is effected using partial panel, or airspeed indicator, altimeter, turn needle, and power setting. The step-by-step procedure for recovering from unusual attitudes is:

- Using airspeed indicator and altimeter, determine whether the nose of the airplane is above or below the horizon.
- Nose-low unusual attitude: If the nose of the aircraft is below the horizon and the airspeed is high, to recover:
  - Reduce power.
  - Level wings by centering turn needle.

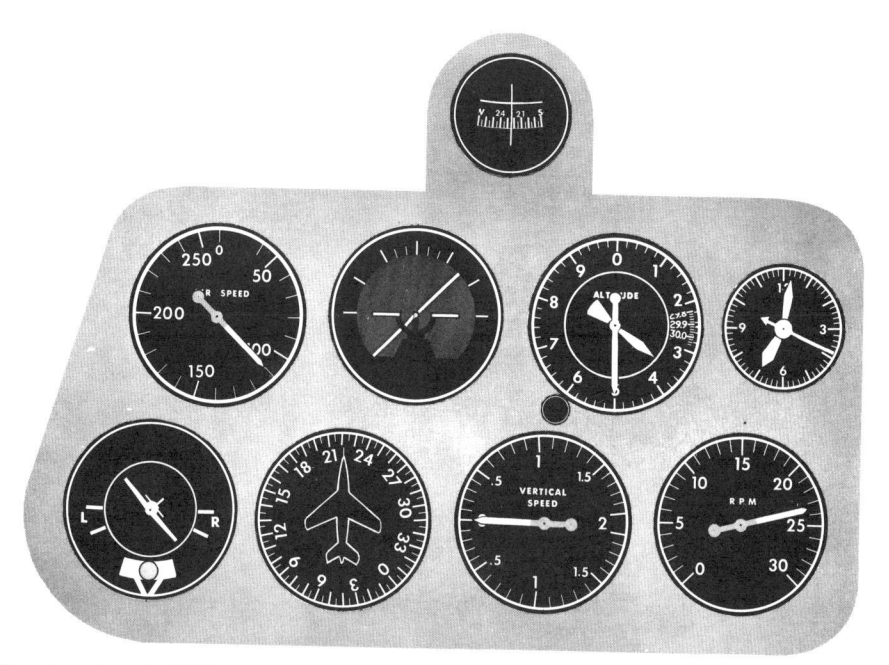

Fig. 16 The steep turn is NOT a normal instrument flight maneuver. It is required for the flight test, however. A 45-degree bank is shown by the artificial horizon.

- Correct pitch attitude to level flight.
- Nose-high unusual attitude. If the nose of the aircraft is above the horizon and the airspeed is low, to recover:
  - Add power immediately.
  - Apply elevator pressure to lower the nose.
  - Correct bank to wing-level attitude.

Change all components of control almost simultaneously with only a slight lead of one over the other; however, this should be in the sequence mentioned above.

You will notice that a good understanding of your airplane's airspeed-power setting requirements will allow you to recognize an unusual attitude quickly. Practice unusual attitude recovery only with an instructor. He will place the airplane in an unusual attitude, and you will be required to recover, using the above methods.

Although instrument flying is based entirely on the standard-rate turn, the student instrument pilot is required to accomplish 360-degree turns at a 45-degree angle of bank. This maneuver has no useful purpose in normal instrument flying. However, it is a good test of the pilot's skill. Successful execution of a 360-degree, 45-degree banked turn demonstrates the pilot's "feel" of the airplane. This maneuver is usually flown full panel and not timed. The procedure is:

- From level flight cruising speed, slowly roll into a turn, using coordinated controls.
- Using the artificial horizon, stop the bank at 45 degrees.
- Apply back pressure as required to hold the "dot" on the horizon bar of the artificial horizon (see Figure 16).
- Check altimeter for altitude control.
- Begin recovery at 22 to 23 degrees prior to your recovery heading.
- Relieve back pressure to avoid ballooning to a higher altitude on recovery.

Requirements are that altitude be maintained within plus or minus 100 feet. After a little practice, the airplane will act as if it were "in a groove." A useful guide is to begin recovery approximately the same number of degrees ahead of your predetermined heading as one-half your bank angle. Thus, a 45-degree bank would require a lead of 22 to 23 degrees.

Needless to say, an instrument pilot must recognize, and be able to recover from, a stall. Stalls are entered using full panel and need no special procedures on instruments. Recoveries should be initiated at the first positive indication of a stall. Recovery to straight and level flight should be executed with coordinated control usage and the least loss of altitude consistent with safety.

Instrument flight in turbulence is considerably simplified by following this simple procedure:

- Using the artificial horizon as the primary instrument, maintain level flight *attitude* with reference to it. Do not allow the wings of the little airplane to

Fig. 16A An instrument scan pattern based on the AI as the master instrument. The broad arrows indicate a constant scan path.

be displaced appreciably above or below the horizon bar.
- Maintain cruise power setting. Ignore minor deviations from cruise power. Do not chase the airspeed, vertical speed indicator, or altimeter. Do not attempt to correct minor deviations.

By following these simple rules (try them VFR also) you will be amazed at the smoother ride. Also, your altitude will generally average out to a constant value. The secret here is to keep the nose level by means of the artificial horizon. It is usually the nose up or down attitude resulting from chasing airspeed or altitude that provides the rough ride and excessive variations in both airspeed and altitude.

The instrument pilot should develop a scanning procedure so that his gaze continually covers or "cross-checks" all instruments. Attention should never be riveted to one instrument for any length of time. During certain maneuvers, however, some instruments become primary, requiring additional attention. As proficiency is improved, you will notice that you can carefully observe the primary instrument and still be adequately able to cross-check the other instruments in the panel.

SUMMARY — BASIC INSTRUMENTS

In summary, remember the following:
- "Keep your eyes moving." Don't spend too much time looking at one instrument.
- "Don't horse the airplane around." A gentle touch and slow control movements works wonders.
- "Do one thing at a time." Turn first and then descend, or climb first and then turn. Combine maneuvers only after gaining proficiency.
- "Plan ahead." Always decide ahead of time the altitude you want to reach or the direction of a turn and your recovery heading.

Now get a good instructor and start in on "full panel," using the step-by-step method, and then proceed through "partial panel."

The degree of proficiency expected of the student instrument pilot on basic instruments is summarized below:

Maneuver	Tolerances	
	Partial Panel	Full Panel
Straight and Level	±10° R or L ±100 feet ±10 mph	
Climb-Descent	±10 seconds of estimate	
Standard-Rate Turns	±20° for each 360° of turn. ±10 mph airspeed	
360° Steep Turns, 45° Bank		±100 feet
Recovery From Unusual Attitudes	Smooth-coordinated, within airspeed limits	
Stalls		±20° heading
Radio Navigation and Orientation		Within 100 feet of assigned altitude

4 RADIO AND NAVIGATIONAL AIDS

During instrument conditions, the pilot must navigate his airplane without visual reference to the ground. This is done by following signals or courses transmitted by ground based radio equipment supplemented by radar. This chapter describes the radio and radar facilities and equipment commonly used in instrument flying. Inasmuch as this equipment is highly complex electronically, explanations of the basic principles are provided and emphasis is placed on their proper and efficient use by the pilot.

FREQUENCIES

All radio equipment transmits and receives signals on a certain frequency or frequency range. The receiver must be tuned to the frequency of the transmitter in order to receive the radiated signal. Frequencies are measured in cycles per second, but even the lowest radio frequencies are at least in thousands of cycles per second, called "Kilocycles" (kc) and higher frequencies are measured in millions of cycles per second, called "megacycles" (mc). Thus, a megacycle is 1000 kilocycles. For example, 3023.5 kilocycles is the same as 3.0235 megacycles. Latest radio publications have replaced the term 'cycle' by HERTZ. Thus kilocycle (kc) is now Kilo Hertz (KHz) and megacycle (mc) is now Mega Hertz (MHz).

For convenience, radio frequencies have been classified into a spectrum ranging from Very Low to Super High. Those common to the spectrum assigned for civil aeronautical use are "L/MF" (Low and Medium Frequency) and "VHF" (Very High Frequency).

All radio transmitting frequencies, both ground based and airborne, are assigned and controlled by the Federal Communications Commission (FCC). Civil aeronautical radio has been assigned certain groups of frequencies along with other users of radio equipment such as commercial broadcast, television, amateur, military, industrial, etc.

Aeronautical radio is used both for navigation and communication. Some ground transmitting stations are used only for communication, some only for navigational purposes, and others transmit both communication and navigation signals.

During the late 1920's, 1930's and 1940's the basic aeronautical radio aid was the L/MF, four course radio range. These ground stations transmitted a series of signals which formed four "beams" for directional guidance. The airborne set consisted of a simple, tunable receiver. This frequency range of 190 to 410 Kilo Hertz was also used for ground-to-air voice communications. All air-to-ground communications was on one frequency, 3105 Kilo Hertz (later changed to 3023.5 KHz).

Although some of the L/MF radio range stations are still in use, practically all present day enroute navigation is based on the VHF (Very High Frequency) ommirange station. Two-way communications is now carried out almost entirely on VHF. The table below summarizes the radio frequencies and facilities of interest to the instrument pilot.

FREQUENCY UTILIZATION

AIR NAVIGATION AIDS

- 108.1-111.9 MHz: ILS localizer with simultaneous radio-telephone channel operating on odd-tenth decimal frequencies (108.1, 108.3, etc.)
- 108.2-111.8 MHz: VOR's operating on even-tenth decimal frequencies (108.2, 108.4, etc.)
- 112.0-117.9 MHz: Airway track guidance. (VOR's)

COMMUNICATIONS

- 118.0-135.95 MHz Air Traffic Control. Within this range, certain specific frequencies, mostly in the 121.0 MHz through 124.0 MHz range, are assigned

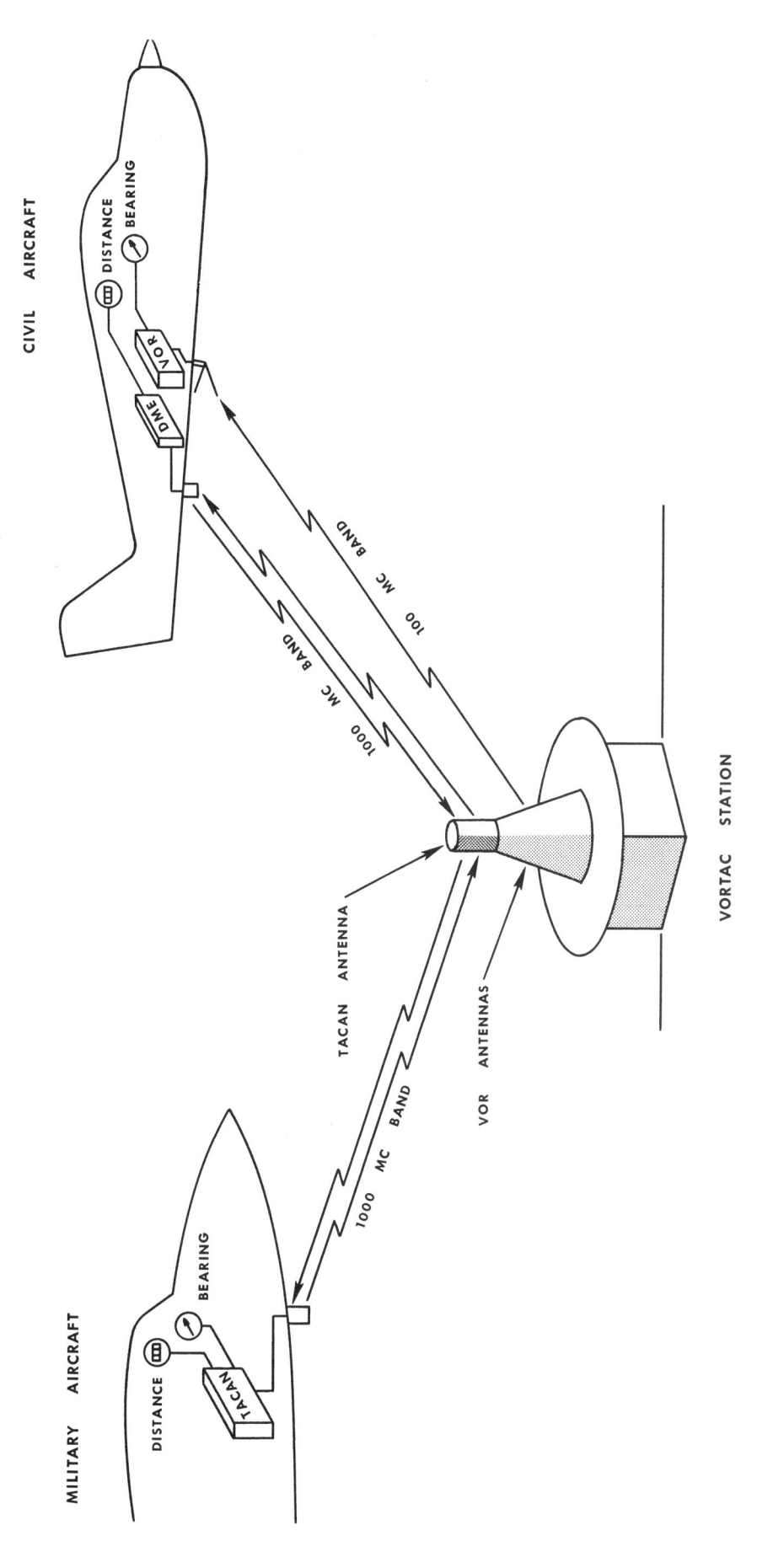

Fig. 17 A VORTAC station provides bearing and distance information to Civil VOR/DME equipped aircraft and military TACAN equipped aircraft.

for emergency (121.5 MHz), ground control, control towers, unicom and special requirements. The remaining frequencies are all used for Air Traffic Control purposes. Check the latest charts and the Airman's Information Manual (AIM) for all frequencies.

The L/MF frequencies generally have a greater reception distance at lower altitudes than VHF. L/MF signals travel both in ground waves and sky waves. The sky waves are bounced back to earth by the ionosphere. Depending on transmitter power, L/MF signals can be received for hundreds of miles. VHF, on the other hand, have no usable surface wave and their sky waves are little effected by the ionosphere. Thus, VHF reception is based on "line of sight". At lower altitudes, reception can be blocked by the curvature of the earth and obstructions. Normal reception distances are shown in the following table:

Altitude above Station	Maximum Reception Distance
1000 ft.	40 N.M.
3000	70
5000	85
10000	120

VOR, VORTAC AND DME

The Very High Frequency Omni-directional Range (VOR), commonly known as "omni", is the primary navigational aid used in instrument flying. The complete VHF or "Victor" airway system is based on VOR (or VORTAC) stations.

The omnirange operates within the 108-118 MHz band. The equipment is VHF, thus, it is subject to line-of-sight restrictions as discussed in the preceeding paragraphs.

A VORTAC station combines both VOR and TACAN, as shown in figure 17. To the civil pilot, a VOR and VORTAC are basically the same. He obtains bearing information in the 108-118 MHz range from either station. If he has DME (Distance Measuring Equipment), this is obtained from the TACAN portion of the station. TACAN provides both bearing and distance information primarily to the military pilot on VHF (960-1215 MHz). The airborne TACAN equipment however is set up so that the pilot selects a specific "channel" rather than the frequency. Thus, a military pilot using Kansas City VORTAC for example, would obtain both bearing and distance from channel 73, whereas a civil pilot would obtain the same information by setting up 112.6 in his equipment. Inasmuch as both stations provide bearing information to the pilot in the 108-118 MHz range, all further reference to these stations will be confined to VOR or VOR/VORTAC.

The omnirange produces an infinite number of courses which may be visualized as radiating from the center like spokes from the hub of a wheel. For all practical purposes however, the station can be considered to transmit 360 courses. The VOR receiving equipment in the airplane can select any one of these courses, enabling the pilot to fly TO or FROM a VOR station or determine his position.

The courses transmitted by the VOR are identified by their MAGNETIC BEARING OUTBOUND from the station. These courses are called RADIALS. In Figure 18, the pilot is flying OUTBOUND from the station on the 090° radial. In figure 19, he is flying INBOUND on the 090° radial even though his heading is 270°.

Although the receiving equipment pro-

Fig. 18 Flying outbound on a VOR radial.

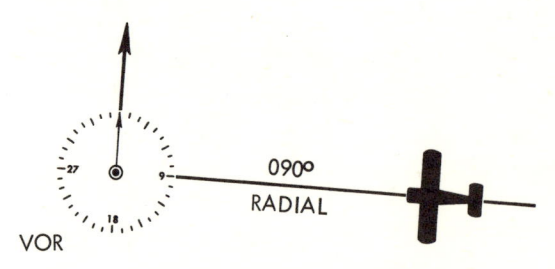

Fig. 19 Flying inbound on a VOR radial.

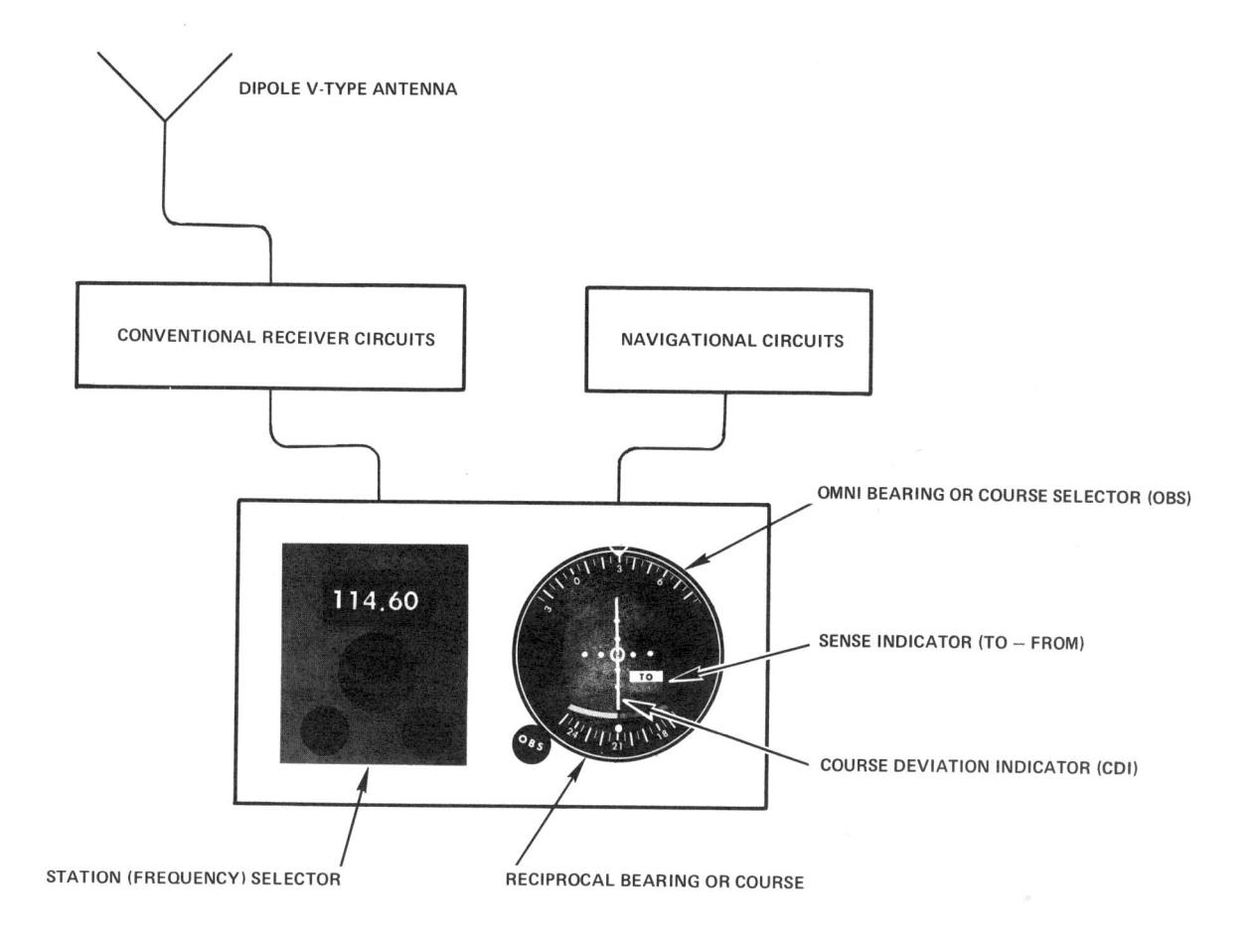

Fig. 20 Although many VOR sets look different, all consist of these basic components.

duced by various manufacturers may differ in appearance and arrangement, they all consist essentially of the components shown in Figure 20.

The station selector is used to tune the set to the published frequency of the desired station. Some older or lower cost receivers use a tunable station selector while others utilize crystal control. When the station is properly tuned in and within reception range, a continuous aural signal is received in the headset or speaker. This 1020 Hertz, keyed tone provides the station identification in morse code. Some stations also have a recorded voice identification as well as the code signal. Most of the VOR stations can also transmit voice over the VOR frequency usually from the Flight Service Station (FSS) which controls the particular VOR. In some of the larger terminal areas, tower, approach control and departure control can also transmit communications over the VOR frequency. During voice transmission, the station identification is interrupted.

After the station is tuned in, the bearing or course selector (OBS) is used to set in the desired course to or from the station. In some equipment the bearing selector, Course Deviation Indicator (CDI) and TO-FROM indicator are combined in one instrument as shown in Figure 21.

The accuracy of course alignment of the VOR ground equipment is generally plus or minus 1°. On some VOR's minor course roughness may be observed evidenced by course needle (CDI) or brief flag alarm (or TO-FROM) activity. At a few stations, usually in mountainous terrain, the pilot may occasionally observe a brief CDI oscillation, similar to the indication of "approaching station". Pilots flying over unfamiliar routes are cautioned to be on the alert for these vagaries, and in partic-

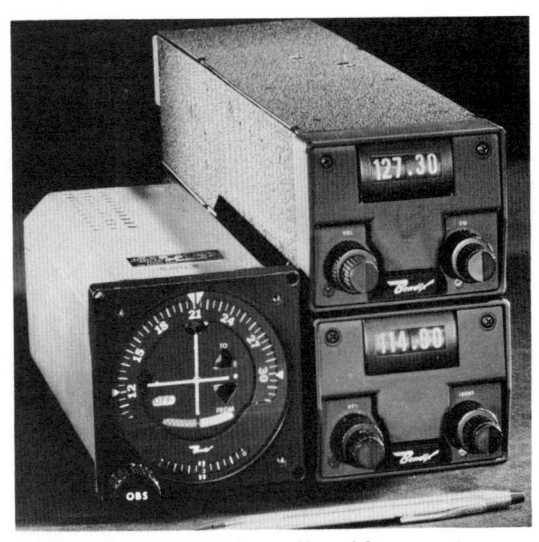

Fig. 21 A typical VOR radio with separate communications transceiver. The indicator contains a glide slope needle in addition to the course deviation indicator (CDI).

ular to use the TO-FROM indicator to determine positive station passage.

The terms VOR and VORTAC are general terms covering the VHF omni-directional bearing type of facilities without regard to the fact that the power, frequency protected area, equipment configuration and operational requirements may vary between the facilities at different locations. The table below lists the intended operational service volume or volumes of the various categories of VOR's and VORTAC's.

Class	Normally Anticipated Altitude Service	Normally Anticipated Interference-Free Distance Service
H	Up to 45,000 MSL	149.75 smi (130 nmi)
	Above 45,000-MSL	115.2 smi (100 nmi)
L	Up to 18,000-MSL	46.06 smi (40 nmi)
T	Up to 12,000-MSL	28.79 smi (25 nmi)

H = High   L = Low   T = Terminal

Note: An H facility is capable of providing L and T service volume and an L facility additionally provides T service volume.

VOR RECEIVER CHECK

Part 91.25 of the Federal Aviation Regulations provides for certain VOR equipment checks prior to flight under instrument flight rules. To comply with this requirement and to ensure satisfactory operation of the airborne system, the FAA has provided pilots with the following means of checking VOR receiver accuracy: (1) VOR test facility (VOT), (2) certified airborne checkpoints, and (3) certified checkpoints on the airport surface.

The VOT test facility is installed at major airports to provide an accuracy check of a VOR receiver while the aircraft is on the ground. The frequency of the VOT is included with the airport information of Part 3, "Operational Data and Notices to Airmen" section of the Airman's Information Manual (AIM).

The radiated test signal, available anywhere on the airport, is used by tuning the receiver to the published frequency of the test facility. With the CDI centered, the omni bearing selector (OBS) should read 0° with the TO-FROM indication reading FROM or the OBS should read 180° with a TO reading. Two means of identification are used with the VOT radiated test signal. In some cases a continuous series of dots is used while in others a continuous 1020 Hertz tone will identify the test signal.

Airborne and ground checkpoints consist of certified radials that should be received at specific points on the airport surface, or over specific landmarks while airborne in the immediate vicinity of the airport.

Should an error in excess of ± 4° be indicated through use of the ground check, or ± 6° using the airborne check, IFR flight shall not be attempted without first correcting the source of the error.

It is emphasized that the above checks can be made by a pilot; however, adjustments to the equipment can only be made by a qualified radio technician. Also, no correction other than the "correction card" figures (if any) supplied by the manufacturer should be applied in making these VOR receiver checks.

DISTANCE MEASURING EQUIPMENT (DME)

As shown in Figure 17, distance information is available to civil aircraft from the TACAN portion of a VORTAC station provided the aircraft is equipped with Distance Measuring Equipment (DME). A VORTAC station is depicted on En Route Low Altitude charts by the symbol (✪). A VOR station as symbolized by (○), does not provide distance information. The combination of bearing and distance from a geographical location (VORTAC station) completely defines an airplane's position.

Operating on the line-of-sight principle, DME furnishes distance information with a high degree of reliability. Reliable signals may be received at distances up to 199 NM at line-of-sight altitude with an accuracy of better than ¼ mile or 2% of the distance, whichever is greater. Distance information received from DME is SLANT

RANGE distance and not actual horizontal distance. In other words, if the aircraft is at an altitude of 6076 feet above the station, the airborne DME indicator will read 1 nautical mile (NM).

DME operates on frequencies in the UHF spectrum between 962 MHz and 1213 MHz. However, specific DME frequencies are paired with specific VOR frequencies so that the pilot obtains both bearing and distance information by setting the same number in both the VOR and DME equipment.

RADIO BEACON

A low or medium frequency radio beacon or "homer" transmits non-directional signals whereby the pilot of an aircraft equipped with Automatic Direction Finding (ADF) equipment can determine his bearing and "home" to the station. These facilities normally operate in the frequency band of 200 to 415 KHz and transmit a continuous carrier with 1020 Hertz modulation keyed to provide identification except during voice transmission.

The operational purpose for which the facility is installed generally determines the power output and the name classification. The facilities are classified as follows:

COMPASS LOCATORS: Power output less than 25 watts (15 miles)

MH FACILITY: Power output less than 50 watts (25 miles)

H FACILITY: Power output greater than 50 watts but less than 2000 watts (50 miles)

HH FACILITY: Power output greater than 2000 watts (75 miles)

When a LF nondirectional homing beacon, sometimes called "NDB" or "Rbn," is used in conjunction with the Instrument Landing System markers, it is called a Compass Locator.

All radio beacons except compass locators transmit a continuous three-letter identification in code except during voice transmissions. Compass locators transmit a continuous two-letter code as explained later under "Instrument Landing System." Voice transmissions are normally made on radio beacons unless the letter "W" (without voice) is included in the class designator.

Radio beacons are subject to disturbances that result in ADF needle deviations, signal fades and interference from distant stations during night operations. Pilots are cautioned to be on the alert for these vagaries. Typical ADF equipment is shown in Figure 22.

MARKER BEACON

Marker beacons serve to identify a particular location in space along an airway or on the approach to an instrument runway. This is done by means of a 75 MHz transmitter which transmits a directional signal to be received by aircraft flying overhead. These markers were generally used in conjunction with the now obsolete Low Frequency Radio ranges and are called fan markers (FM) and station location markers (Z-markers). Present day use of markers is in conjunction with the instrument landing system (ILS). ILS marker beacon information is included under "Instrument Landing System."

Figure 23 shows a 3-lite marker beacon. The white light indicates passage over a fan marker or Z-marker. The amber light indicates passage over the ILS middle marker and the purple light signals the ILS outer marker. Passage over markers is also indicated by a keyed aural tone. The ILS outer marker is identified by a series of dashes while the middle marker is identified by alternate dots and dashes. No voice transmissions are available through the marker beacons.

Fig. 22 Cockpit components of a typical ADF receiver.

Fig. 23 A three light marker beacon receiver.

INSTRUMENT LANDING SYSTEM (ILS)

The instrument landing system is designed to provide an approach path for exact alignment and descent of an aircraft on final approach to a runway. The ILS is generally illustrated in figure 55.

The ground equipment consists of two highly directional transmitting systems and, along the approach, two (or more) marker beacons. The directional transmitters are known as the localizer and glidepath transmitters. The system may be divided functionally into three parts:

LOCALIZER - course information
GLIDE PATH - descent information
MARKER BEACONS - range information
COMPASS LOCATORS and APPROACH LIGHT LANES supplement the three major components.

The localizer transmitter, located at the far end of the runway, transmits signals which enable the pilot to steer the required course to the runway. The transmitter, operating on one of twenty channels within the range of 108.1 MHz and 111.9 MHz, emits two signal patterns which overlap along a line formed by an elongation of the runway.

For purposes of reference, the signal area to the right of the approaching aircraft is called the Blue area and the area to the left of the approaching aircraft is called the Yellow area. The approach course of the localizer is called the front course. The course along the centerline of the runway in the opposite direction is called the back course. The localizer transmitter has a range of approximately 40 miles at an altitude of 5000 feet. Voice transmissions from Approach Control and Tower are available through the localizer frequency. Identification consists of three-letter signals preceeded by an I transmitted on the localizer frequency (I-XYZ).

The UHF glide path transmitter is located between 750 and 1250 feet from the approach end of the runway and offset 400 to 600 feet from the runway centerline. It transmits a glide path beam 1.4° wide.

Glide path signals are radiated principally in the direction of the final approach and although some radiation is in the reverse direction it is not usable. Although the glide slope signals are UHF in the 300 MHz range, the proper glide slope frequency is automatically set up in most airborne receiving equipment when the localizer frequency is tuned in.

The glide path projection angle is normally adjusted to 2.5 to 3 degrees above horizontal so that it intersects the middle marker at about 200 feet and the outer marker at about 1400 feet above the runway elevation.

In addition to the desired glide path, false course, reversal in sensing, will occur at vertical angles considerably greater than the usable path. These signals as well as glide slope indications when making back course localizer approaches, should be disregarded.

Ordinarily, two 75 MHz marker beacons, the outer and middle, are installed as major components of the ILS. However, there are exceptions at some locations.

The outer marker (OM) is approximately 4 to 7 miles from the approach end of the runway and on or close to the extended center line of the runway. Its signal is keyed to two dashes per second and flashes the purple light on the airborne 3-light marker beacon receiver.

The middle marker is located 3500 feet plus or minus 250 feet from the runway along the extended centerline. It transmits a series of alternate dots and dashes and flashes the amber light on the airborne 3-lite marker beacon receiver.

Compass locator transmitters or L/MF radio beacons are usually situated at the outer marker site and occasionally at the middle marker also. The transmitters have a power output of 25 watts, a range of 15 miles, and operate between 200 and 415 KHz. The basic function of the compass locator is to provide a means of transition from an airway fix to the outer marker, using airborne ADF equipment.

Compass locators transmit two-letter identification groups. The locator at the outer marker (LOM) transmits the first two letters of the localizer identification group and the locator at the mid-marker (LMM) (if installed) transmits the last two letters of the localizer identification group. At some locations voice transmissions from Approach Control and Tower are provided on the compass locator frequency.

RADAR

Use of radar provides ATC with a method of "seeing" aircraft without special airborne equipment. In effect, radar sends out a radio signal which is reflected off an aircraft. The reflected signal returns to the transmitting station. Although the signals travel at 186,000 miles per second (speed of light) the round trip is electronically timed by means of a cathode ray tube or "scope". If the aircraft is equipped with a transponder, the reflected signal is re-enforced and positively identified, providing the ground controller with a brighter "blip".

The radar antenna system can be made to move through an arc so that it can "look" at targets in a certain area. Or it can be made to rotate through 360°.

Three basic ground based radar systems are in use by ATC facilities:

- Airport Surveillance Radar (ASR) with a maximum usable range of 50 miles. Azimuth (direction) only information is available. Altitude information cannot be obtained.
- Precision Approach Radar (PAR) is available at many airports which can provide altitude and azimuth information for conducting precision instrument approaches.
- Air Route Surveillance Radar (ARSR) is long range radar used by the ARTC ("center") for control and separation of airway traffic.

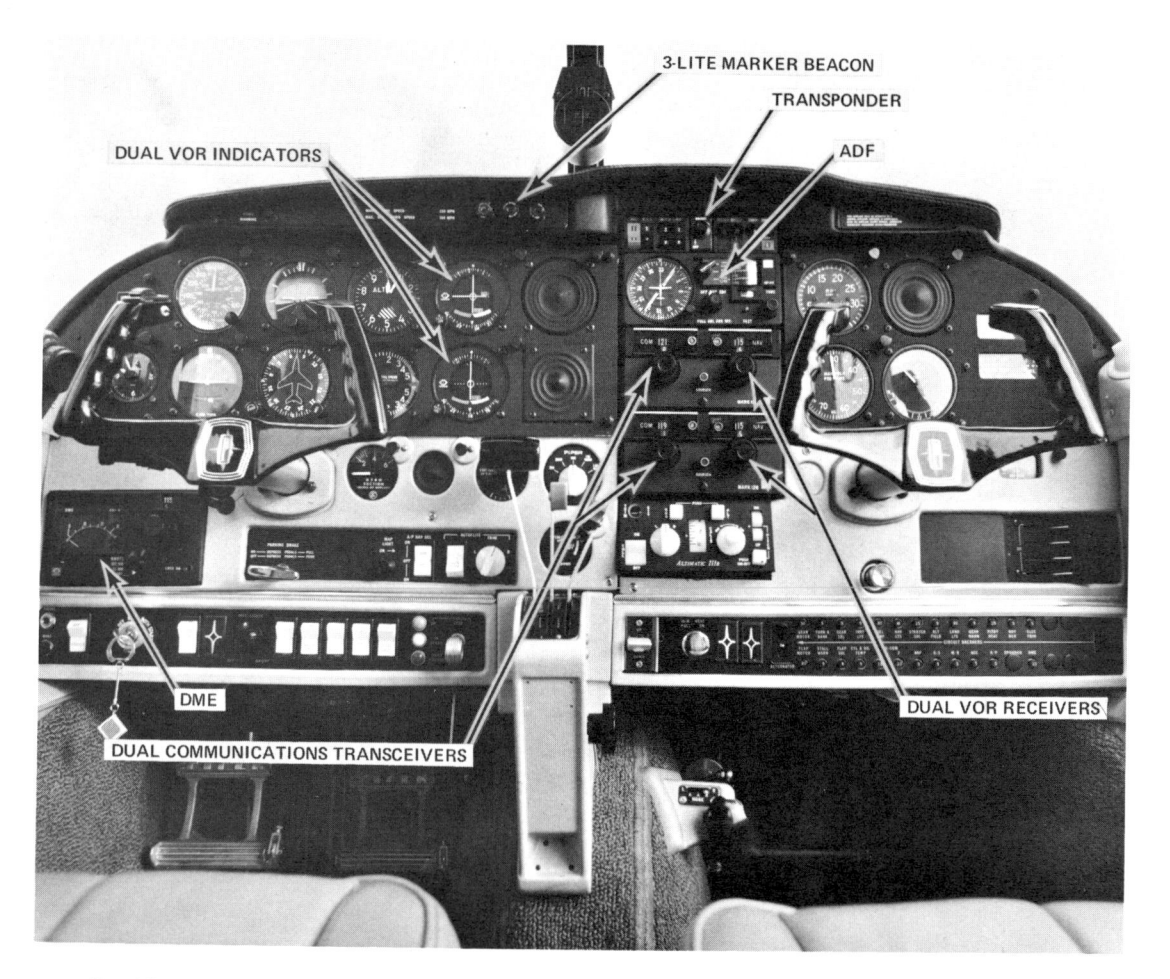

Fig. 23A Radio equipment installed in a single-engine retractable gear airplane (Piper Comanche).

SUMMARY

In summary, the following table shows the radio and radar facilities, equipment and function available to the instrument pilot.

Ground Facility and Frequency Range	Associated Airborne Equipment	Function
VOR/VORTAC 108.0 thru 111.8 even tenths 112.0 thru 117.9 MHz	VOR Receiver	Bearing information also voice ground to air.
DME 920 thru 1020 MHz	DME Receiver. Frequencies paired to appropriate VORTAC frequency.	Distance from VORTAC
TACAN (Military) 920 thru 1020 MHz	TACAN Receiver. Pilot selected "channels" paired with VOR frequency when combined with VOR in VORTAC.	Bearing and distance.
VHF Communications 118.0 thru 135.95 MHz 360 channels	VHF Receiver	Two way communications between aircraft and ground stations.
ILS Localizer 108.1 thru 111.9 MHz Odd tenths	VOR Receiver. Most VOR receivers automatically switch to ILS mode when odd tenths 111.9 and below are set in.	Flight path guidance to instrument runway.
ILS Glide Slope 329.3 thru 335.0 MHz	Glide slope receiver and cross pointer indicator. Frequency is paired to appropriate localizer frequency.	Glide path guidance to instrument runway.
Marker Beacon 75 MHz	Marker Beacon Receiver. 3-lite and/or aural tone.	Position identification.
Radio Beacon (Homer) (RBN)(NDB) or Compass Locator when associated with ILS, 190 thru 415 KHz.	Automatic Direction Finder (ADF) Receiver.	**Bearing information.**
Commercial Broadcast Stations. (Not for use in Instrument Flight) 550 thru 1750 KHz.	ADF Receiver.	Bearing information.
Radar	None except two-way radio for communications.	Position information; also altitude information on Precision Approach Radar (PAR).
Radar	Transponder	Amplify radar signal and provide positive identification to ground controller.

FLIGHT PROCEDURES USING RADIO 5

USING VOR

The instrument pilot must have a thorough understanding of VOR flight procedures. As simple as VOR is, under stress of instrument conditions and the complexities of many local areas, serious errors can result due to a misunderstanding of some of the basic VOR principles.

When tuned to a station and within range of it, the Course Deviation Indicator (CDI) can be centered by use of the OBS (Omni Bearing Selector) on any one of two bearings or courses, each 180 degrees apart. For example, the pilot in Figure 24 is southeast of the station on the 120 degree radial.

Regardless of the heading of the aircraft, it is on the 120 degree radial, therefore the CDI can be centered with a bearing FROM the station of 120 degrees. Also, the CDI can be centered with a bearing TO the station of 300 degrees. The TO or FROM indication does not necessarily mean that the aircraft is flying to or from the station but that the COURSE (or bearing) selected is TO or FROM the station. Thus, in Figure 24, if the pilot wished to fly to the station, he would turn his aircraft to a heading which agrees with the TO bearing in his OBS or 300 degrees. Likewise, if he wished to fly away from the station on a course of 120 degrees, the pilot would turn his aircraft to a heading which agrees with the FROM bearing in his OBS or 120 degress.

The pilot in Figure 25 can fly to the station with any one of two bearings set up in his OBS.

It is obvious that a heading of 060 degrees (assuming no wind) will take the aircraft to the station. However, the pilot could have selected either the 060 degree TO bearing or the 240 degree FROM bearing and obtain a centered CDI needle. In example A, the aircraft HEADING (as determined from the compass or heading indicator) agrees with the OBS; both indicate 060 degrees. Thus, if a cross wind drifts the airplane off course, the pilot corrects the heading by turning the aircraft TOWARDS the needle. In Example B the HEADING and OBS disagree by 180 degrees, therefore, the pilot would have to correct AWAY from the needle to maintain his course in a cross wind. This is undesirable and SHOULD NOT BE USED. The following basic rule should be memorized:

"In flying to or from a station, the heading of the aircraft should always agree with the OBS (except for wind corrections). Then, corrections in heading are made TOWARDS the needle." See Figure 26.

The pilot in Figure 27, is west of the station on the 270 degree radial and wishes to fly to the station and then after passing it, fly outbound on the 090 degree radial.

In position A, the pilot is tracking inbound on the 270 degree radial. His OBS is correctly set on 090 degrees with CDI needle centered. Since his airplane is also headed 090 degrees (except for wind correction), if the airplane drifts off course, the

Fig. 24 Two different OBS values can center the CDI while on a VOR radial.

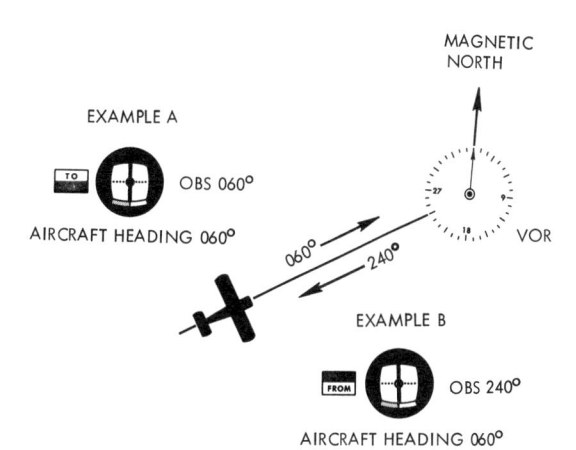

Fig. 25 In order to fly to the station, example A should be used. Example B should NOT be used.

Fig. 26 In order to provide proper sensing, the OBS should agree (except for wind correction angle) with the heading instruments.

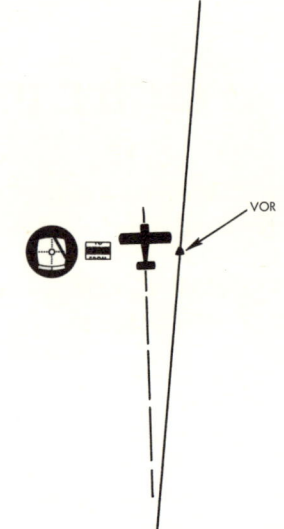

Fig. 28 The TO-FROM indicator will move more slowly if the aircraft does not pass directly over the station.

pilot makes heading corrections towards the needle.

Upon passing the station, the TO goes to FROM, positively indicating station passage. The aircraft is now flying outbound on the 090 degree radial (position B of Figure 27). However, no change in OBS or heading is required, since both the OBS and heading still agree. Also, since they agree (except for wind correction angle), off course corrections are still made by turning towards the needle.

As indicated in the preceeding section, station passage is indicated by the TO changing to FROM as the aircraft flies over the station. In Figure 28, if the pilot flies directly over the station, the TO-FROM indicator will flip over sharply.

If, however, the airplane passes some distance from the station, as in position A of Figure 28, the TO will go to FROM, more slowly. Generally, the farther the airplane is from the station, the slower the TO-FROM indicator will move. However, even in position A of Figure 28, positive station passage is indicated when the TO-FROM indicator is exactly one-half way between TO and FROM. This can be readily determined on most VOR receivers.

TRACKING

Tracking is the technique of maintaining a pre-determined course to or from the VOR. Under no wind conditions, once the CDI needle is centered, theoretically the aircraft will follow the course set in the OBS if the heading of the aircraft agrees

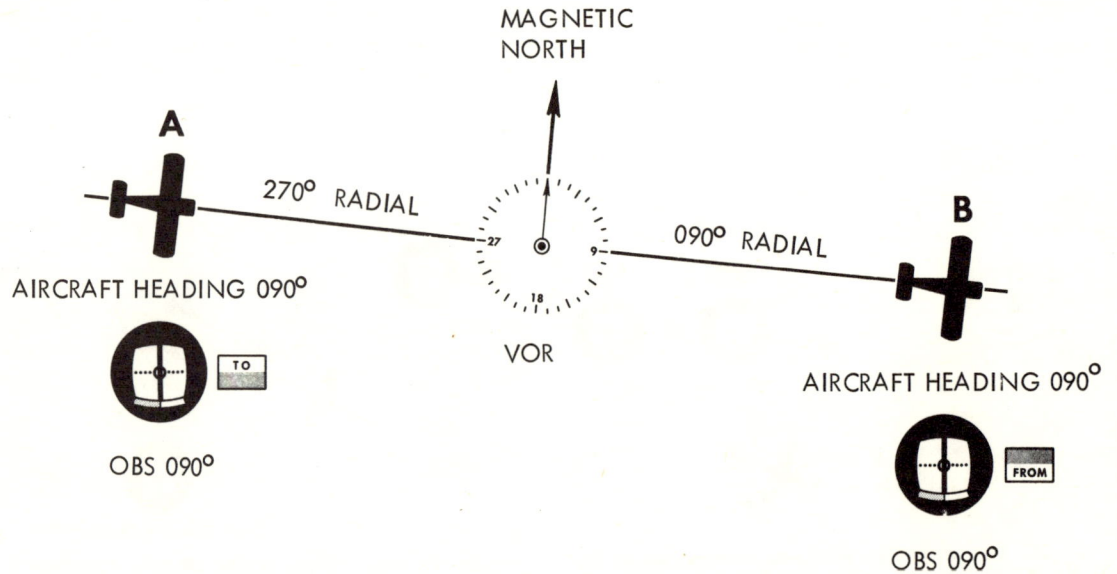

Fig. 27 Flying VOR radials to and from a station.

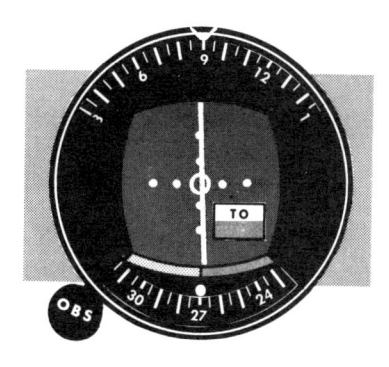

Fig. 29 Does the CDI look centered to you? Well, it isn't. It's off one needle width and time for a slight right turn of 5 or 10 degrees at the most.

with that set in the OBS. Practically however, besides wind effects, there are usually minor errors in the aircraft compass, gyro heading indicator, and the VOR equipment. All of these are usually corrected using the "trial and error" method.

To keep the needle centered and fly directly over the station, follow this procedure:

- Start with the heading of the airplane (using compass and directional gyro) EXACTLY the same as your omni bearing. If your OBS says 050 degrees, hold the heading of the airplane to 050, not 045 or 055.
- As soon as the needle moves, make a small heading correction such as 5 degrees or 10 degrees at the most, toward the needle. How much off center should the needle be in order to make a heading correction? That's easy, no more than ONE NEEDLE WIDTH. That's right, less than 1/32 of an inch (see Figure 29).
- Now fly your new heading EXACTLY for a few minutes.
- If the needle moves again (which it probably will), put in another 5 to 10 degrees correction toward the needle.
- Continue nibbling at it until you pass the station. Never let the needle get away from you any more than one needle width.

At first, all of these continuous small corrections will take a lot of concentration. However, after a few hours experience, you will find that it takes less and less conscious effort to keep that needle centered. The secret here comes in two parts:

- Fly exact headings, don't let your heading wander.
- Continuously make small heading corrections as required. Never let the needle get away.

If the needle does get away more than one needle width, like 1/16 or 1/8 inch, then larger corrections, possibly up to 20 or 30 degrees, are justified. A point to remember, however, is that there is normally no reason for your heading and omni bearing to differ more than about 10 degrees if the needle is approximately centered. For example, at a true airspeed of 150 knots, a wind correction angle of 10 degrees is required to keep on track in a 25 knot cross wind. Higher winds, of course, and lower airspeed will require somewhat greater wind correction angles. Also, it takes a direct cross wind equal to one-half your true airspeed to require a 30 degree wind correction angle. Thus at a true airspeed of 100 knots, a 50 knot direct cross wind would require a 30 degree wind correction angle.

INTERCEPTING BEARINGS

In following a Victor airway, departing from an airport to proceed direct to a VOR, thence to the airway, and during an instrument approach, a new VOR course must be intercepted after passing the station. This can be most easily accomplished by following a definite, methodical procedure.

In Figure 30, consider that you have received an IFR departure clearance to proceed direct to the XYZ VOR after take-off, before proceeding on course (your route is northbound along an airway).

In order to avoid trying to do too many things at once (a common error for the instrument flight student), it is best to avoid working the VOR (especially a tunable set) while in turning flight, while setting up a climb and possibly communicating with the tower.

After take-off, turn the aircraft to the general direction of the VOR. Then center the CDI and make a heading correction as indicated by the OBS. Track to the VOR. Now follow this step-by-step procedure:

- After passing the station, turn to a heading parallel to your new course. This should be a standard rate turn. Note time over station but do not report yet.
- While flying straight and parallel, set up your new omni bearing. Also, take care of any communications. (For example, report the time you crossed the station, even though it may have been 30 to 60 seconds ago).

- Turn 30 to 45 degrees towards your new course to intercept it.
- When needle centers, begin normal tracking.

ENROUTE PROCEDURES

Once you are established on the airway, proceeding from station to station towards your destination is relatively simple.

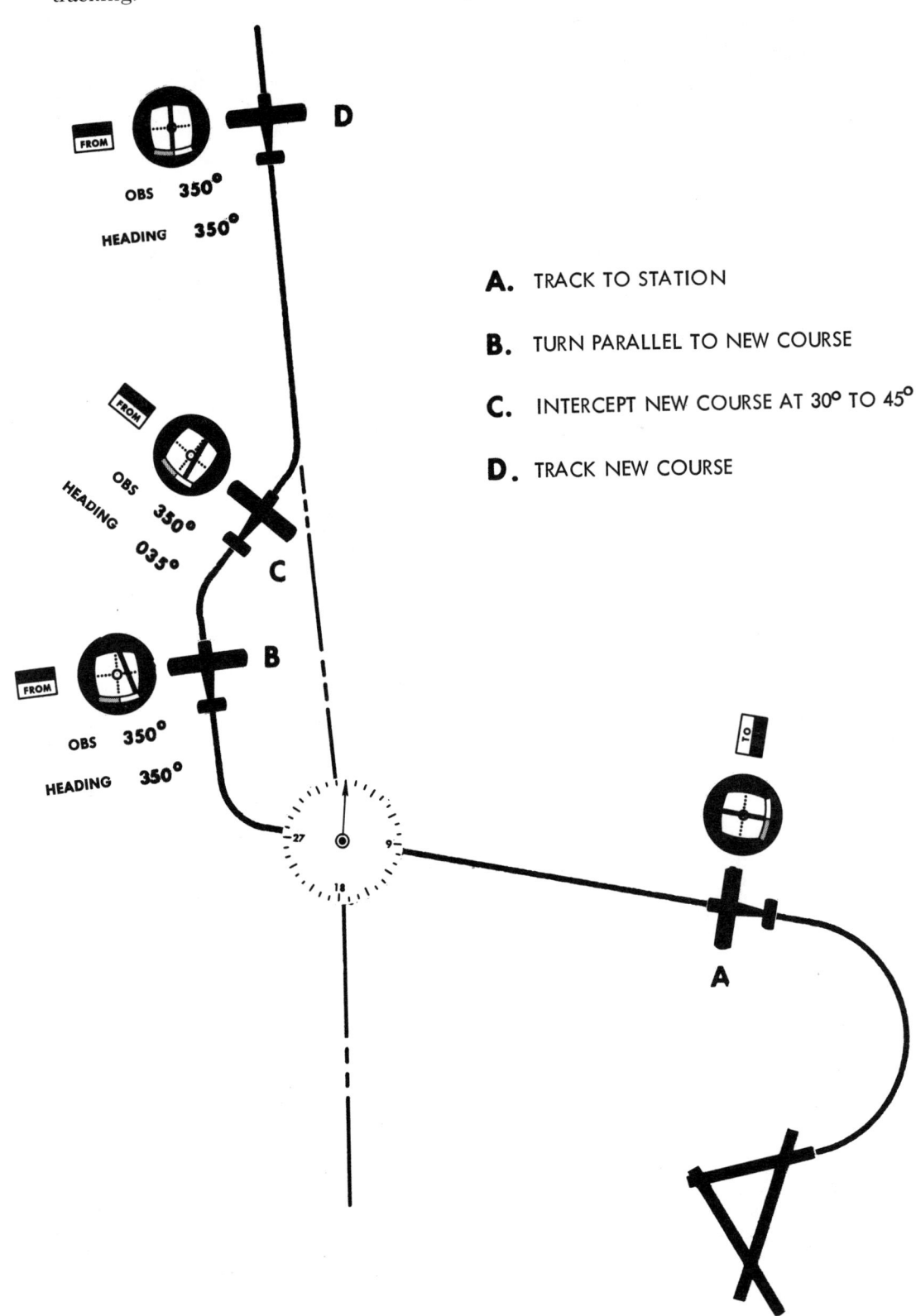

A. TRACK TO STATION

B. TURN PARALLEL TO NEW COURSE

C. INTERCEPT NEW COURSE AT 30° TO 45°

D. TRACK NEW COURSE

Fig. 30 Intercepting a new VOR bearing after passing the station.

The normal procedure is to fly outbound from the first VOR and approximately halfway, tune in the station ahead. When changing stations the needle will remain centered and the FROM will go to TO (due to small errors, the needle may indicate a slight off-course reading when changing stations).

The TO bearing is tracked until the station is passed. After passing the station, the bearing of the next airway leg is set in using the interception procedure explained previously, if required.

Normally, the next station is tuned in approximately at the halfway point. In some cases, the VOR changeover points are indicated on the Low Altitude Enroute Charts (Radio Facility).

DETERMINING INTERSECTIONS

VOR intersections form an important part of the airway traffic control system. Intersections are used as reporting and holding points along airways as well as in major terminal areas. An intersection is a point, indicated by a triangle (△ or ▲) on Radio Facility Charts, determinded by two intersecting radials from two different stations within reception distance.

Obviously, the easiest way to determine an intersection is with two VOR sets. For example, in Figure 31, the pilot would have one set tuned to station XYZ and follow normal tracking procedures. His second VOR would be tuned to station ABC and he would have the 350 degree bearing set in the number two OBS prior to reaching the intersection. When both needles are centered, he is at the intersection.

Many airplanes have only one VOR installed, however, and even if two VOR receivers are available, an instrument pilot must be able to determine an intersection and fly a holding pattern, using only one VOR set. This could occur during a real or simulated emergency whereby one VOR is inoperative. The applicant for an instrument rating must usually demonstrate a holding pattern using only one VOR receiver.

The secret of flying an intersection with one VOR set is to be able to visualize the complete setup. The pilot must postively know his position relative to the intersection. By observing the position of the CDI needle when tuned to the station determining the cross-bearing, the pilot must immediately recognize whether he has not reached the intersection yet, or has passed it. A serious air line collision has occurred during instrument conditions, whereby a pilot, with one of the dual VOR's inoperative, overshot an intersection.

Flying intersections requires practice, however, the procedure outlined below can be considered an excellent guide.

The pilot in Figure 31 is tracking towards station XYZ and must make a position report over Delta intersection. Since he has only one VOR set in the airplane, he must use it primarily for tracking towards station XYZ and occasionally tune it to station ABC

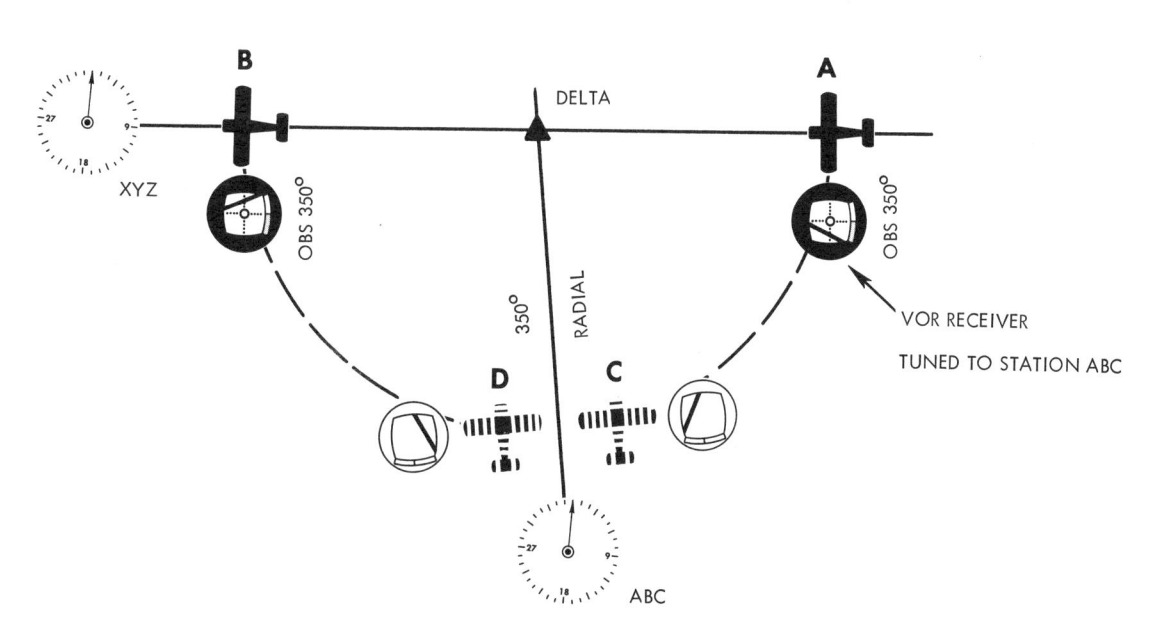

Fig. 31 Determining the aircraft's position relative to an intersection with one VOR set.

in order to check his position. Which side of center will the needle point if he hasn't reached the intersection yet? If he has already passed it, how will it indicate?

In position A, the pilot has not yet reached Delta intersection. If his VOR is tuned to station ABC and the 350 degree bearing set in the OBS the needle will lie to the LEFT of center. This can be determined by the pilot visualizing that he is tracking the 350 degree radial from station ABC. Thus if his needle were to the left it would indicate that his desired course was to his left as in position C. Now transposing himself back to his present position (A), the pilot would now know that he should be on the same side of the 350 degree radial that he was when he was imaginatively tracking it. Therefore his correct conclusion is that he has not yet reached the intersection.

Now, consider the pilot to be in position B. Using the same logic he can again visualize that he is tracking the 350 degree radial of station ABC. With the needle pointing to the RIGHT of center, the desired radial would be to the right of the airplane as shown in position D. Mentally transposing himself back to position B, since his needle is to the right, he has already passed the intersection.

It is important to note that it is ALWAYS the FROM bearing that is used to determine the cross bearing for an intersection. Either the TO or FROM bearing, as required, is used to fly the other leg of the intersection. Before wasting valuable flight time, it is suggested that the student fly intersections "on paper." Using Enroute Low Altitude Charts, he can visualize the CDI indicates by sketching the airplane at various locations relative to the intersection and visualizing the position of the needle.

PROCEDURE TURNS

A procedure turn is a PLANNED maneuver for reversing the direction of the airplane on the same VOR radial (procedure turns however, are used with all types of radio equipment besides VOR). The most common application of the procedure turn is during an instrument approach and letdown. It also may be used to enter a holding pattern when holding is required in a direction opposite to the one the airplane is flying. The applications of the procedure turn will be discussed later.

In Figure 32, the pilot in position A is tracking outbound from the fix on the 075 degree radial and wishes to reverse his direction of flight and track inbound to the fix.

If he is on an instrument approach, he will probably be close to the station and possibly in a descent. Therefore he must execute a procedure turn which will get him sufficiently away from the station and allow sufficient time to establish a good inbound track prior to reaching the station as well as descend to the required altitude.

After passing the fix, the pilot should track outbound from one to three minutes depending on wind and airspeed. In any

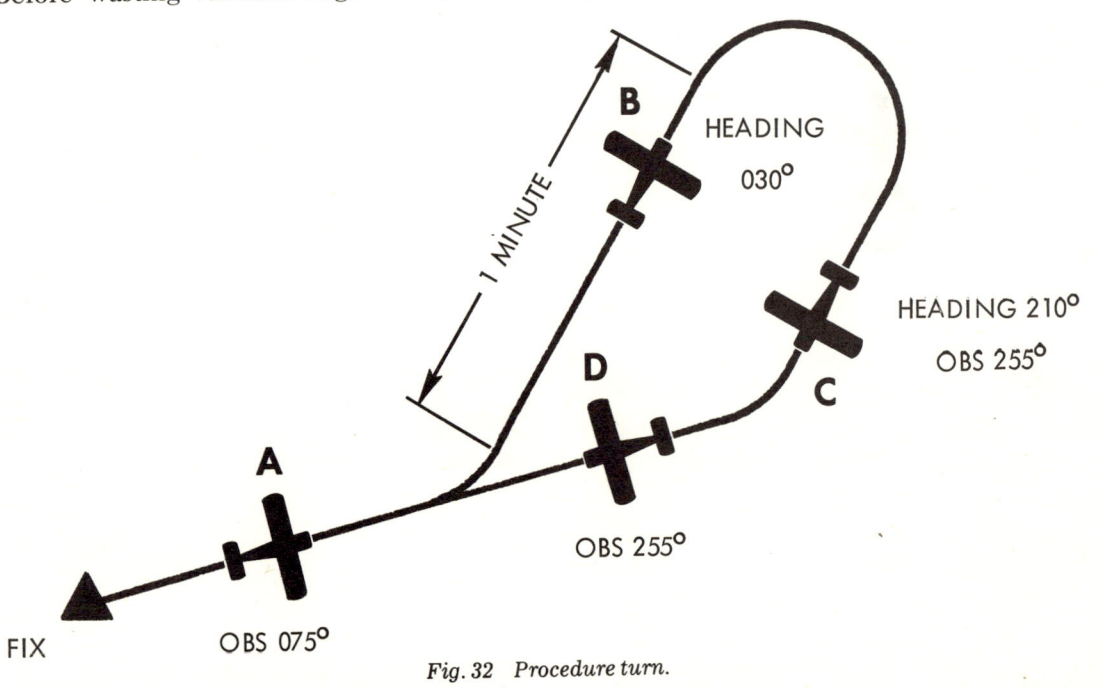

Fig. 32 Procedure turn.

case the entire maneuver should normally be completed within 10 NM of the fix. In position A of Figure 32, the pilot's OBS indicates 075 FROM, needle centered. The HEADING of the airplane, however, will be a few degrees more or less than 075 depending on wind correction angle required.

After the desired time from the fix, the pilot will turn LEFT (a non-standard procedure turn may require a right turn). The turn is made to a HEADING of 45 degrees from the outbound COURSE. In the example shown, the aircraft heading (position B) will be 030 degrees after completion of the turn. Normally, no wind correction is used during this leg of the procedure turn. After completing the turn, the 030 degree heading should be held for approximately one minute. The VOR CDI is used only as a reference to estimate the progress along this leg.

During the 030 degree leg, while in straight flight, is a good time to change the OBS to the reciprocal of the outbound bearing. In the example shown in Figure 32, the inbound bearing will be 075° + 180 or 255°.

After flying for one minute, a standard rate, right turn is begun to a HEADING of 030° + 180° or 210°. Upon completion of this turn (position C) the airplane will intercept the inbound course at a 45 degree angle. Here, the CDI needle must be closely observed in order to judge the time to begin the turn inbound. This 210 degree leg is normally flown with no drift correction. Also, it is not timed. The time required to intercept the inbound course will be a function of the distance from the station as well as the wind effects.

In position D of Figure 32, the pilot is established on the inbound course to the station and uses normal tracking procedures.

HOLDING

Since airplanes cannot be stopped in flight, some means of delaying or maintaining a certain position of an airplane must be available to Air Traffic Control. The "holding pattern" provides this tool to ATC. The standard right turn holding pattern when at altitudes at or below 14,000 MSL is shown in Figure 33. This "race track" pattern consists of two standard rate 180° turns (1 minute each) and two 1 minute straight flight legs, for a total pattern time of 4 minutes.

- When holding at or below 14,000 feet MSL, the initial outbound leg should be flown for one minute. Timing for subsequent outbound legs should be adjusted as necessary to achieve proper inbound timing.
- Begin outbound timing from abeam the holding fix. When abeam position cannot be determined, begin timing at completion of fix end turn.
- Maximum allowable airspeed for propellor driven aircraft is 175K IAS. Holding airspeed for a particular airplane should be as low as practically possible, consistent with safety, in order to conserve fuel. Speed should be reduced to holding airspeed at least three minutes prior to reaching fix.

Holding can be accomplished using any one of the following as a radio "fix".

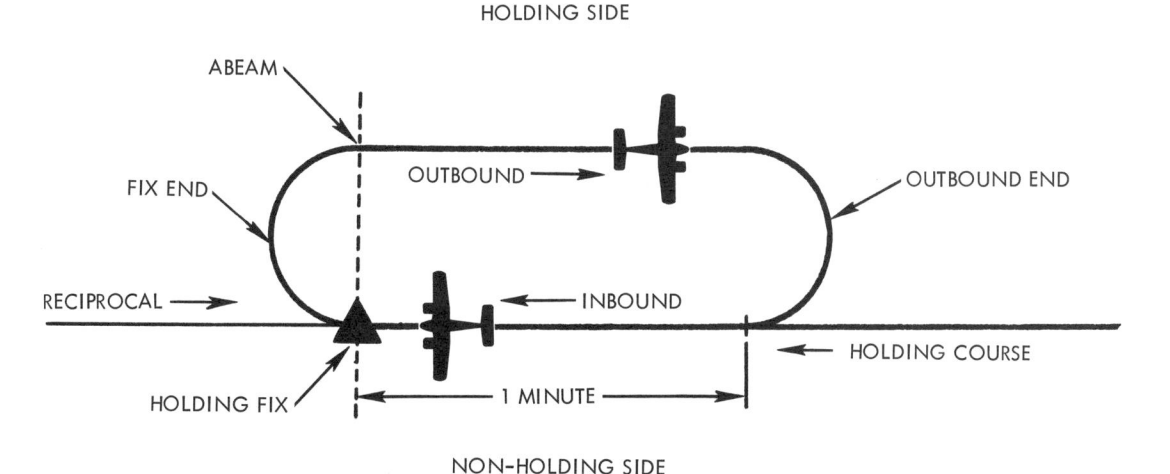

Fig. 33 A standard holding pattern. A non-standard holding pattern would consist of left turns.

- VOR/VORTAC
- Radio Beacon
- VOR/VORTAC Intersection
- ILS Outer Marker and/or Compass Locator
- DME Leg Length

At present, the majority of holding patterns utilize a VOR/VORTAC or a VOR/VORTAC intersection as a fix.

GENERAL HOLDING PATTERN INFORMATION

When holding at a VOR station pilots should use the first definite indication that the aircraft has arrived over the VOR in determining when to commence the turn to the outbound heading. This will be at the time at which the first complete reversal of the "to-from" indicator is accomplished.

The direction to hold with relation to the holding fix will always be specified by using Magnetic directions and referring to eight general points of the compass (North, Northeast, East, Southeast, South, Southwest, West, and Northwest).

Pilots are always expected to hold in a standard right hand pattern unless specifically advised otherwise by ATC. Due to the location of facilities in congested areas, or proximity to other routes, etc., nonstandard patterns may be utilized. When it is necessary that a nonstandard pattern be flown, the ATC clearance will specify "left turns".

ATC clearance requiring that an aircraft be held at a holding point will include the following information:
- To hold in a Standard Pattern:
  (a) The Direction to hold from Holding Point; DME Leg Length when appropriate.
  (b) On (specified) Radial, Course, Magnetic Bearing, or (Airway number).
  (c) Time to Expect Further Clearance, or Time to Expect Approach Clearance.
- To hold in a Nonstandard Pattern: Same as (a), (b) and (c) above and in addition, (d) specification of Left Turns.

HOLDING AT A VOR

This discussion will consider the aircraft already established on the holding course, preceeding inbound to the station. Methods of entry into the holding pattern when on a course other than the holding course, will be discussed later.

In Figure 35, the pilot of the airplane in position A is tracking to the station on the 055 degree radial. His OBS has 235 degrees TO set in and he has determined that a wind from his left requires a HEADING of 225 degrees in order to keep his CDI

"HOLD EAST" OF BLANK INTERSECTION

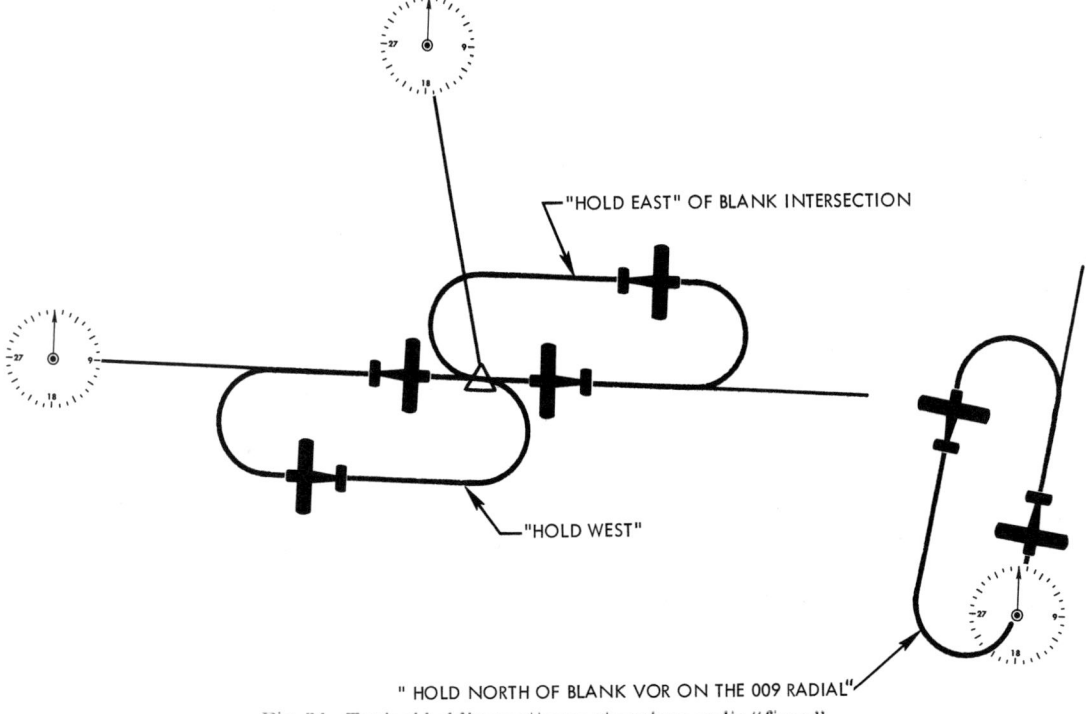

"HOLD WEST"

" HOLD NORTH OF BLANK VOR ON THE 009 RADIAL"

Fig. 34 Typical holding patterns at various radio "fixes."

needle centered. The pilot has received instructions from ATC to hold at ABC VOR, Northeast of the VOR on the 055 degree radial. At least three minutes prior to reaching the VOR the pilot should slow the airplane to the predetermined holding airspeed.

Upon reaching the VOR and the TO has positively gone to FROM, a standard rate one minute right turn is executed. DURING THE ENTIRE HOLDING PATTERN, THE VOR OBS IS LEFT ON 235 DEGREES OR THE INBOUND BEARING. Near the end of the first turn, the TO-FROM indicator is observed. With no head or tail wind, the TO-FROM indicator will be exactly one-half way (a red area on some indicators) between FROM and TO. This indicates that the airplane is exactly abeam the station.

Again assuming no head or tail wind component, the outbound leg is flown for one minute. During this leg a 10 degree drift correction into the wind or a HEADING of 065 degree (position B in Figure 35) is used since a 10 degree correction was required on the inbound leg. If in doubt as to the wind, it is best to hold no correction angle. On the outbound leg, the CDI is closely observed in order to determine whether the outbound leg is maintained at a sufficient distance from the inbound course. If the needle begins to drift toward center, a wind from the left is drifting the airplane back into the inbound course which will make the turn on the outbound end and inbound tracking much more difficult.

At the end of the outbound leg, a standard rate, one minute turn should bring the airplane back on the inbound course with needle centered. With no head or tail wind component, the pattern should be completed in FOUR minutes.

An uncompensated head or tail wind component can cause major errors in a holding pattern and can drift the airplane either too far from or too close to the station on the first inbound leg. If the pilot is too far from the station an excessive amount of time is consumed, while being too close to the station can cause complete disorientation.

Effects of an uncompensated head wind (relative to the inbound leg) is shown in Figure 36.

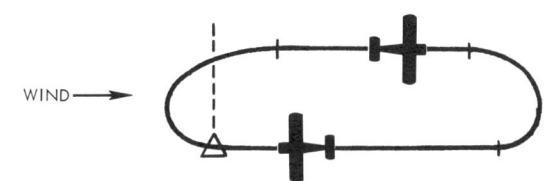

Fig. 36   Effects of head wind on inbound leg.

Thus a head wind on the inbound leg results in a holding pattern that may require up to 50 percent more time to complete if the outbound leg is flown for one minute, possibly causing a delay in receiving approach clearance.

If the pilot knows that a head wind exists, the outbound or down wind leg should be shortened so that the inbound leg is accomplished in one minute.

If the pilot does not know whether a head wind exists, close observation of the TO-FROM indicator during the fix end turn will indicate this. If the FROM goes to TO, before completing the one-minute turn, a head wind of considerable magnitude exists and the outbound leg should be shortened accordingly.

Effects of an uncompensated tail wind on the first inbound leg is shown in Figure 37.

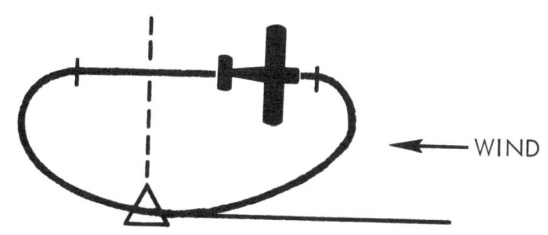

Fig. 37   Effect of tail wind on inbound leg.

Thus a tail wind on the inbound component can result in the airplane being directly over the station, or in extreme cases, past it, after completion of the outbound end turn.

The procedure to be used in the event of a tail wind on the inbound leg is shown in Figure 38.

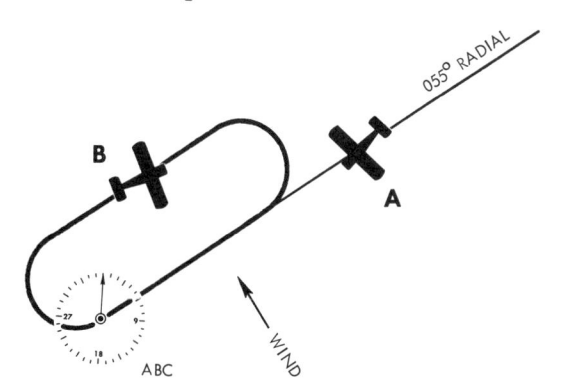

Fig. 35   Holding at a VOR.

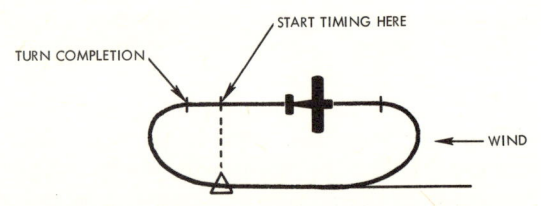

Fig 38 Correcting for tail wind on inbound leg.

As indicated in Figure 38, after completion of the fix end turn, the airplane is flown on the outbound heading until the airplane is directly abeam the station. This is determined by the TO-FROM indicator being exactly one-half way between FROM and TO. At this time, leg timing should begin.

EFFECTS OF A CROSS WIND

An uncompensated cross wind from the left when flying the outbound leg will result in the airplane drifting back into the inbound course as shown in Figure 39.

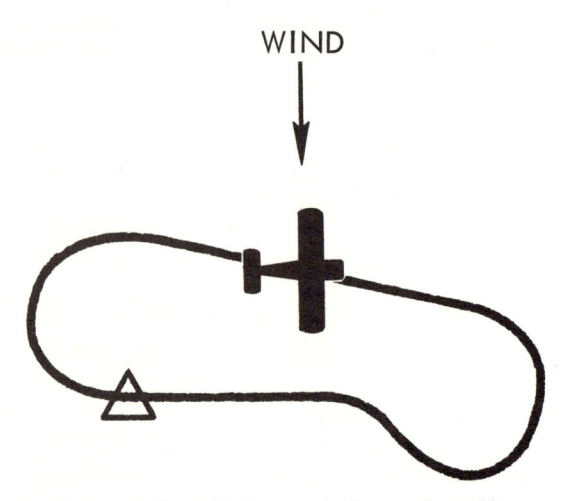

Fig. 39 Effect of left crosswind on outbound leg.

This provides difficulty in properly intercepting the inbound course. Another undesirable effect is the tendency for the pilot to excessively tighten up the fix end turn in order to avoid overshooting the inbound course.

With a little experience, the pilot can monitor his progress along the outbound leg by observing the CDI needle. Throughout the outbound leg, the needle should lie off center to the LEFT. If the pilot observes a tendency for the needle to swing towards center, a heading correction to the left should be made.

If, however, the airplane is too close to the inbound course so that a standard rate turn will cause overshooting, the pilot MUST NOT EXCEED AN ANGLE OF BANK OF 30 DEGREES. Some tightening of the outbound end turn is acceptable providing a 30 degree angle of bank is not exceeded. It is best to overshoot the inbound course, as shown in Figure 39 and then re-intercept it.

An uncompensated cross wind from the RIGHT on the outbound leg will have the effect shown in Figure 40.

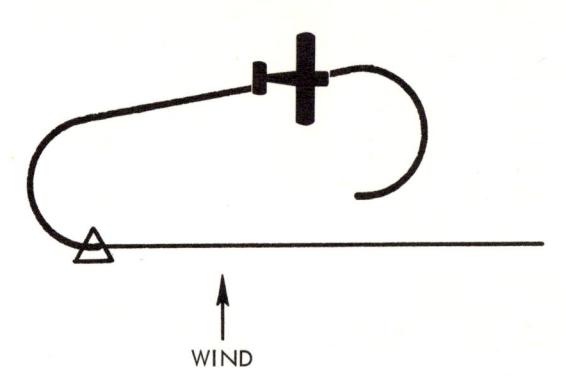

Fig. 40 Effect of right crosswind on outbound leg.

In this case, the CDI needle is still far from center after completion of the outbound end turn which can cause considerable confusion to the student instrument pilot.

If the effects of a right cross wind on the outbound leg are not known, close observation of the CDI needle during the outbound end turn will indicate the relative magnitude of the wind. The procedure to be used is shown in Figure 41.

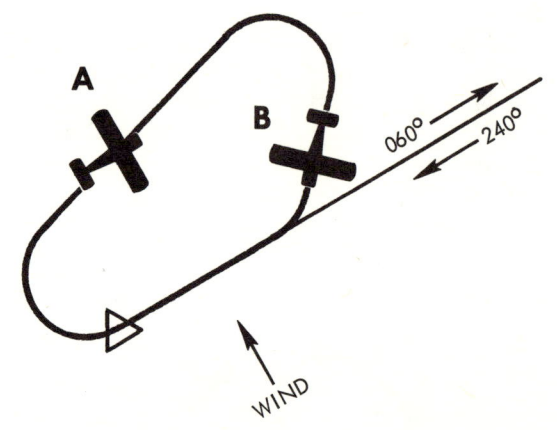

Fig. 41 Compensating for wind drift on outbound leg.

During the outbound end turn, the pilot observes his CDI needle. Normally, the no-wind outbound heading will be 060 degrees in position A of Figure 41. As the outbound end turn proceeds the pilot notices that at the 195 degree point, which is 45 degrees from the inbound course, the CDI still indicates full scale deflection. The pilot then recovers from the turn and holds the 195 degree heading (position B) until the needle shows that he is getting close to the inbound course whereupon a turn to the inbound heading is made. Subsequent holding patterns should be flown using a drift correction angle on the outbound leg.

In summary, the following general rules can be considered to apply regarding procedures for wind effects during holding:

- All turns should be standard rate with no turn modifications made to compensate for wind (except as noted below).
- The outbound end turn may exceed standard rate to avoid excessive inbound course overshoot; however, the angle of bank should not exceed 30 degrees.
- If a head wind exists on the inbound leg, timing of the outbound leg should be shortened.
- If a tail wind exists on the inbound leg, timing of the outbound leg should begin when abeam the station rather than after completion of fix end turn.
- If the direction of a cross wind on the outbound leg is unknown, it is best not to make any correction rather than guess the wrong way.
- An uncompensated cross wind which tends to blow the aircraft further away from the inbound course can be detected by observing the CDI needle during the outbound end turn. If the needle still shows a large deflection with only 45 degree turn remaining, this heading should be maintained so as to intercept the inbound course at 45 degrees.
- Throughout the holding pattern, the OBS should remain on the bearing of the inbound course.

HOLDING AT AN INTERSECTION

Holding at an intersection with only one VOR receiver is basically a combination of procedures described previously (Determining Intersections and Holding at a VOR). It is, however, more difficult to correct for head or tail winds, since there is no way to determine exactly when the aircraft is directly abeam the fix after completion of the fix end turn. Since intersection holding is usually accomplished along a course that the aircraft has been flying for a considerable length of time, the magnitude of the head or tail wind component should be determined prior to arrival at the intersection. Thus corrections as described previously can be made.

HOLDING PATTERN ENTRIES

In a majority of cases, the airplane will be approaching the holding fix already established on the inbound course. Entry into the holding pattern merely requires beginning of the fix end turn after passing the fix. Many times, however, holding is required on a course other than the course the airplane is flying. Thus, prior to reaching the fix, the pilot must plan a course of action to establish the airplane in the holding pattern.

Holding pattern entry procedures, as recommended by the FAA, are described in Figure 45. Although these procedures will considerably shorten the time required to enter a holding pattern, they are considered too difficult for the beginning instrument student. These procedures are considered one of the "short cuts" the instrument pilot can practice after obtaining some experience. However, an actual IFR flight under actual IFR conditions should use the FAA entry procedures.

A practically fool-proof method for entering a holding pattern which must be made on a course other than the one the airplane is flying is a combination of procedures described previously, "Intercepting Bearings" and "Procedure Turns." Various examples will be used to illustrate the use of these procedures.

EXAMPLE 1 — In this case, the pilot is approaching a fix in a direction opposite the holding course. At position A, in Figure 42 the pilot receives instructions from ATC to "hold east of Delta intersection on V18N (or the 064 degree radial of JAN VOR)."

In this example, the pilot must reverse course so that he approaches the fix from position B since he was instructed to "hold east." This is most easily accomplished by the Procedure Turn described previously. It is good practice to fly approximately 30 seconds beyond the fix before beginning the procedure turn, to assure the pilot of completing the procedure turn some distance east of the station. After completion of the procedure turn, holding is accomplished as previously described.

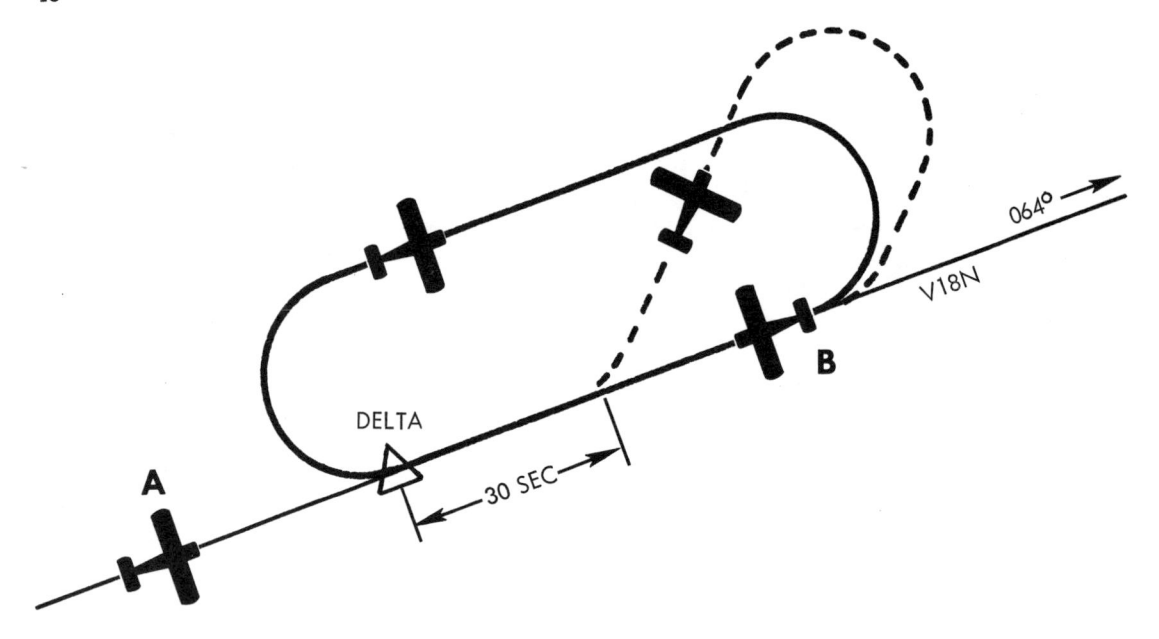

Fig. 42 Holding pattern entry when approaching fix in a direction opposite to the holding course.

EXAMPLE 2 — While flying toward JAN VOR along V18 (position A Figure 43), the pilot receives instructions to "hold north of the JAN VOR on the 009 radial."

"hold north of the JAN VOR on the 322 degree radial."

Fig. 43 Holding pattern entry when approaching fix from non-holding side.

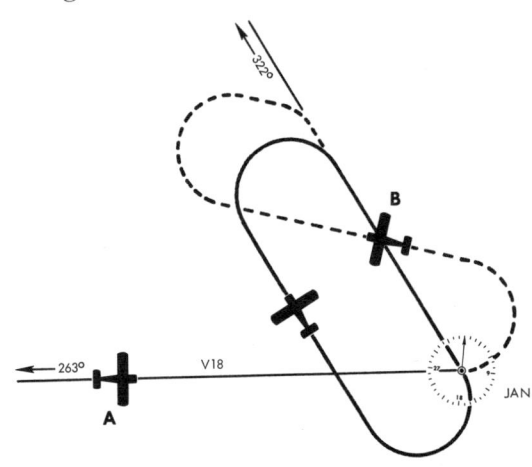

Fig. 44 Holding pattern entry when approaching fix from holding side.

After passing the fix, the pilot turns left to a procedure turn heading (322° - 045° or 277°). By setting 322° in his OBS soon after station passage, crossing of the 322° radial will be indicated by centering of the CDI at Position B. Thereafter, a standard procedure turn is flown and holding accomplished as previously described.

In this example, the pilot merely continues straight flight for 20 seconds beyond the fix and turns right to the outbound heading. The entry flight path is shown in dotted lines on Figure 43. Once the pilot is established inbound, normal holding procedures are used.

EXAMPLE 3 — While flying along V18 toward JAN VOR (position A in Figure 44) the pilot receives instructions to

After practice using these procedures, the student instrument pilot is ready for the FAA recommended entry procedures. Inspection of Figure 45 will show that the FAA entry procedures are merely "short cuts" based on the more deliberate and methodical procedures shown in Figures

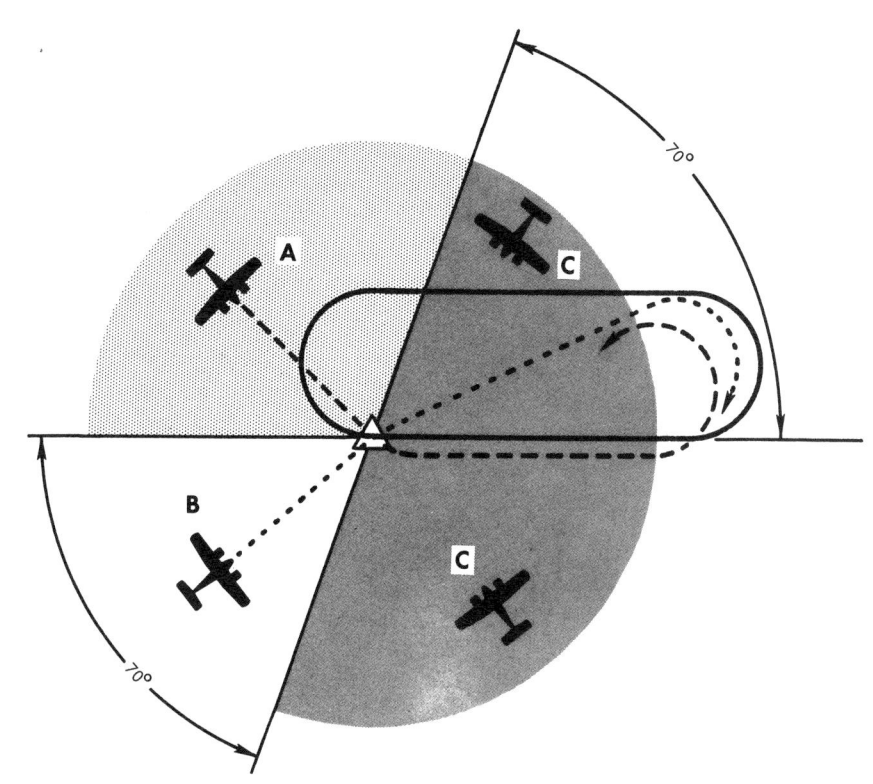

Fig. 45 FAA approved holding pattern entry procedures.

42 through 44. Also, the FAA procedures consume less airspace, which is significant with high performance aircraft but of little consequence at 100 knots.

VOR TIME-DISTANCE CHECK

If an airplane is equipped with only one VOR set and triangulation from other stations is not possible, time or distance from a VOR can be obtained by using a time-distance check procedure as described below. Although this procedure has limited practical use during instrument flying, it may be required for orientation during an instrument flight test.

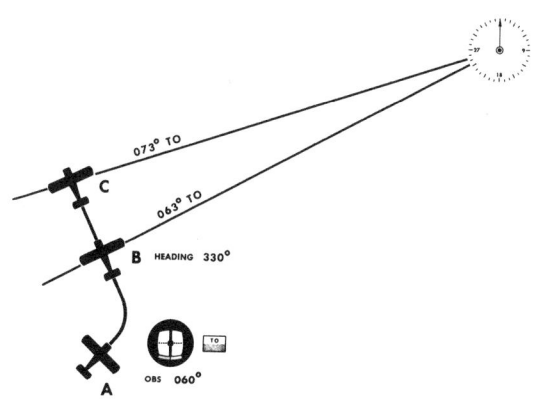

Fig. 46 VOR time-distance check.

For a time distance check, turn the airplane 90 degrees to the inbound bearing of the station. Time to the station, under no wind conditions, is:

Minutes to the station =

$$\frac{\text{seconds}}{\text{degree bearing change}}$$

or

$$\frac{60 \times \text{minutes}}{\text{degree bearing change}}$$

Unless you are far from the station, use a 10° bearing change; thus, if it requires 2 minutes, 20 seconds, to accomplish a 10° bearing change, your time to the station is (2x60) + 20 = 140 seconds ÷ 10 or 14 minutes.

The step-by-step procedure is: (refer to Figure 46 for an example).
- Rotate the OBS until the CDI is centered on a TO bearing (position A in Figure 46).
- Turn the aircraft either left or right (preferably the closest direction) to a heading 90° from the bearing on the OBS. In Figure 46, at position A, the CDI is centered on 060 TO. 060 minus 090 (since 060 is less than 090, add 360 to 030 = 420, then subtract 090) is 330 degrees.
- At the completion of the turn (to a heading of 330 degrees in Figure

46) rotate the OBS to recenter the CDI needle and START TIMING, as at position B. Although you may not be flying exactly perpendicular to the selected bearing, it will not materially affect the solution to the problem.

NOTE: After completing the turn, if you have to rotate the OBS more than 10 degrees to recenter the CDI, you are within two minutes of the station if you used a standard rate turn.

- Continue to fly straight ahead and when the CDI begins to move from the center turn the OBS 10 degrees (if you decided to use a 10 degree change) in the direction necessary to place the CDI on the opposite side of the center of the dial.
- When the CDI needle again centers itself, stop the timing (position C).
- Apply the formula above to determine time to station. For the example, it took 2 minutes 20 seconds to fly from B to C; thus, time to station is 2 x 60 + 20 = 140 seconds divided by 10, or 14 minutes.

This method is affected by wind and accuracy of timing; however, it is sufficiently accurate for most orientation purposes.

ADF PROCEDURES

The use of ADF in instrument flying is primarily for use in, or transition to, instrument approaches. It is rarely used for enroute navigation except for an occasional intersection determination. The most important role of the ADF is in negotiating the transition from the enroute airway fix (VOR/VORTAC or intersection) to the outer compass locator at the ILS outer marker. This uses the "homing" function of the ADF only. It also supplements the marker beacon in identifying the outer marker during an ILS approach. This transition distance from an airway fix to the ILS outer compass locator (LOM) is usually relatively short, rarely exceeding 15 miles.

Many small airports (many without a control tower) have only an ADF approach for use during instrument conditions. This is due to the relatively low cost of a ground based radio beacon station as compared to a VOR or ILS. Consequently efficient use of an ADF considerably improves the versatility of an instrument equipped airplane.

Without getting into technical details, it is sufficient for the pilot to know the following basic principles regarding use of the ADF.

- The frequency range is 190 to 1750 kilocycles. The frequency range of 190 to 440 kilocycles is assigned to aeronautical radio beacons utilized in instrument flying. Frequencies above 550 kilocycles are for predominantly VFR flying using commercial broadcast stations.
- Zero on the ADF indicator is always the nose of the airplane.
- The indicator or needle on the dial always points to the station to which the ADF is tuned, regardless of the airplane's heading. (Heading is the direction the nose of the airplane is pointing.)
- The number on the dial the needle points to is the angular direction of the station clockwise from the nose of the airplane. This is defined as RELATIVE BEARING. See Figure 47.

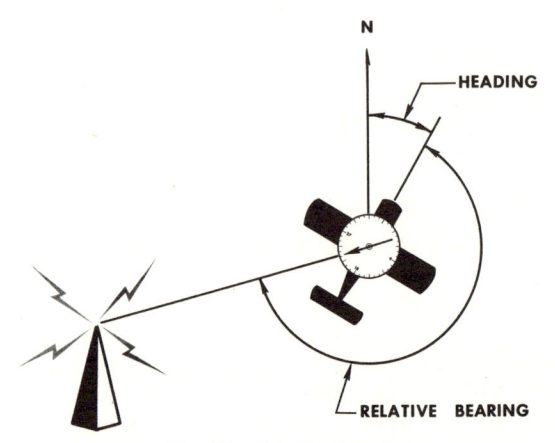

Fig. 47 Relative bearing.

The most common use of ADF is "HOMING" to a radio beacon (or commercial broadcast station, if VFR). During homing, the pilot merely turns the airplane until the ADF pointer is on zero. Thus the nose of the airplane is pointing directly to the station. For short distances like transitioning from an airway fix to the ILS outer compass locator, and most VFR requirements, homing provides a satisfactory flight path. However, for negotiating larger distances and for IFR flying TRACKING is required. The differences in flight paths between homing and tracking are shown in Figure 48.

During homing operation any number of

courses can get the airplane to the station. Conversely, there are any number of courses away from the station. Thus homing from the station by maintaining 180° on the ADF indicator cannot be accomplished. In other words, you can home to a station but not from the station.

Tracking to a station is less useful than tracking away from it; however it is easier so we will discuss this procedure first.

TRACKING INBOUND OR TO A STATION compensates for wind drift and requires flying a number other than zero on the ADF indicator (assuming a cross wind exists). Tracking uses a trial and error procedure as described below and illustrated in Figure 49.

- Upon tuning to and identifying the station, the pilot turns the aircraft until the ADF needle points to zero. The aircraft heading indicator (compass and/or directional gyro) will show 055° which is the course to the station in position A of the example shown in Figure 49.

The heading of 055° is maintained for

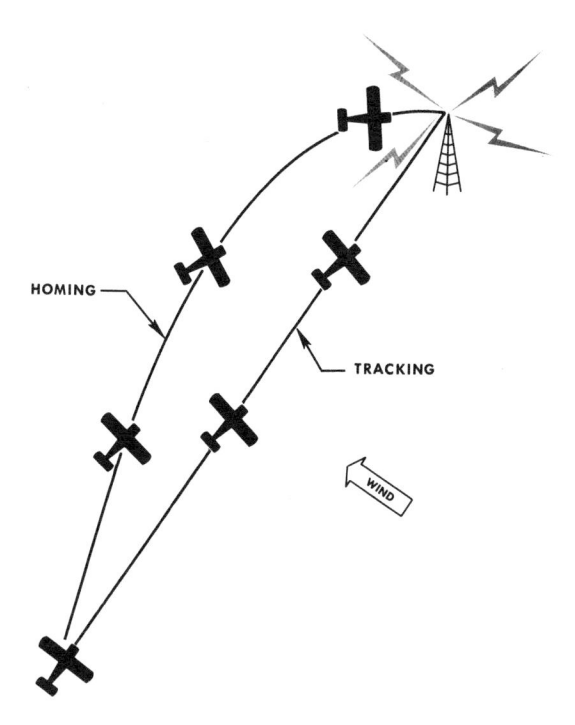

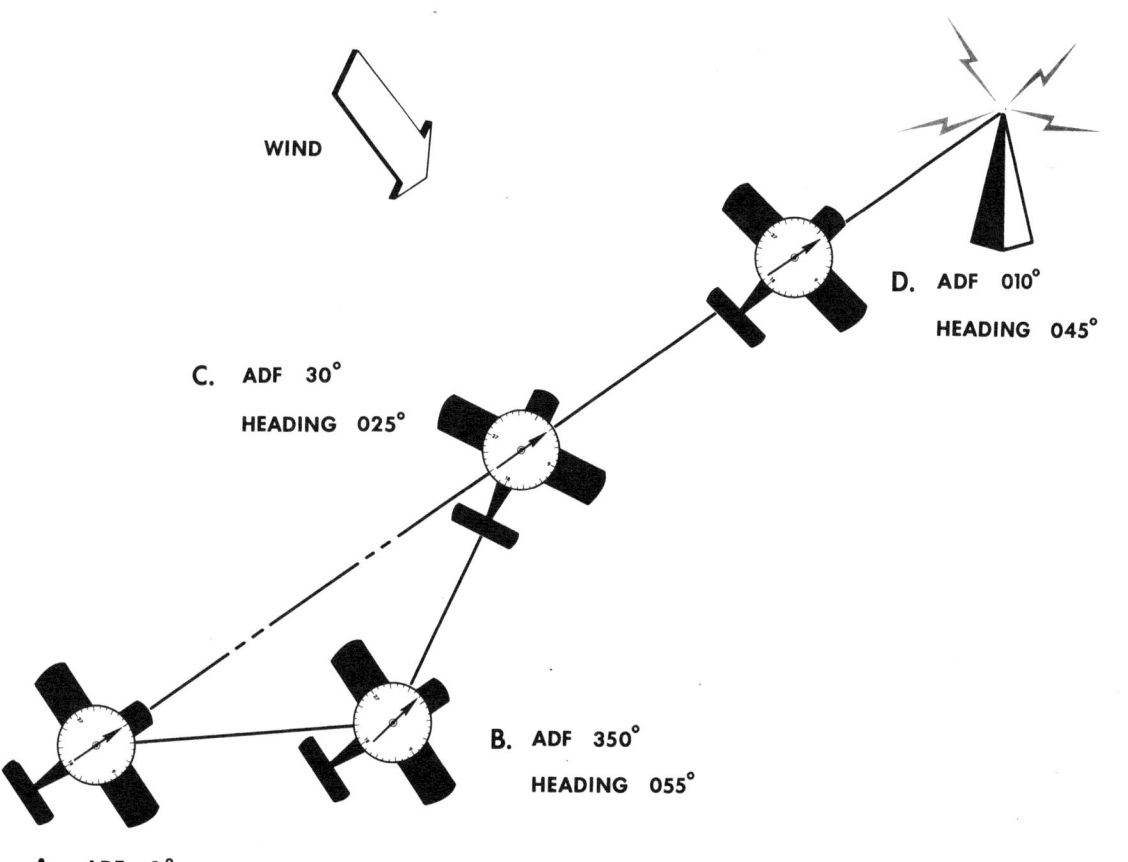

Fig. 48 ADF homing.

Fig. 49 Tracking inbound.

some time. If a cross wind exists, the ADF needle will swing off of zero. When the needle is 10° off of zero (350° in position B of Figure 49) due to a cross wind from the left, the pilot turns the airplane to the left 30° or to a heading of 025° to get back on course.

- When the ADF needle reaches 30° to the right of zero or 030° (in our example) the airplane is back on course or the intended track. It should be remembered that the ADF needle reads the amount of the interception angle when the airplane is back on course. If the first turn from position B (Figure 49) had been 45° to a heading of 010° instead of 30° shown in the example, the ADF needle would have indicated 45° to the right of zero or 045° when the airplane was back on course.
- As soon as the airplane is back on course (position C of Figure 49) the airplane must be turned to the right but not quite to zero on the ADF dial. In our example, the pilot estimated a wind correction angle of 10°, therefore the pilot maintains a heading of 045° (the original 055° heading minus a 10° wind correction angle). Thus the ADF needle points to 010° in position D of Figure 49.
- If this combination, a heading of 045° and an ADF indication of 010° maintains the ADF needle on 010° then the 10° wind correction angle was exactly correct. If the ADF needle again moves off of 010° while maintaining a heading of 045°, then the complete process must be repeated to find a heading whereby the ADF needle will stand still.

TRACKING OUTBOUND OR AWAY FROM A STATION is much more useful than tracking to a station. The same basic principles apply however, except that 180 is used as the ADF reference instead of zero. In the example shown in Figure 50, the pilot's intended track is a course of 055° from the station to which his ADF is tuned.

- After passing the station a heading of 055° is maintained with the ADF needle on 180° (position A of Figure 50). With no wind, this combination will provide a track equivalent to the intended course.
- The heading of 055° is maintained until the ADF needle is 10° off of 180. At position B of Figure 50, a right cross wind has drifted the airplane to the left of the course and the ADF needle points to 170°. The pilot turns the airplane 30° to the right or to a heading of 085° to get back on course.
- When the ADF needle reaches 30° to the right of 180 or 150°, the airplane is back on course as in position C of Figure 50. As in tracking to the station, the ADF pointer will read the interception angle to the left or right

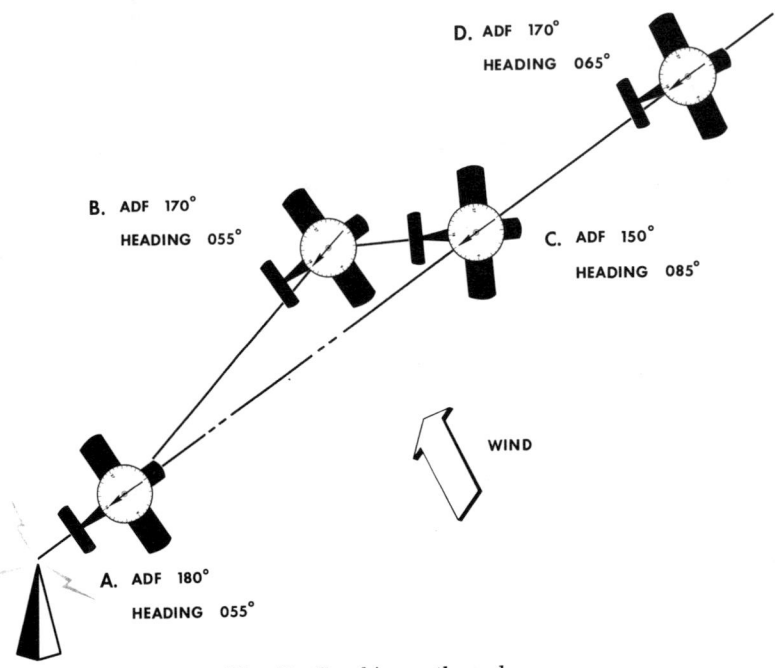

Fig. 50 Tracking outbound.

of 180, depending on the direction of the cross wind.

- As soon as the airplane is back on course (position C of Figure 50) the airplane must be turned to the left but not quite to 180 on the ADF dial. In our example, a 10° wind correction was estimated, therefore the pilot maintains a heading of 065° (the original 055° heading plus a 10° wind correction angle). Thus the ADF needle points to 170° as in position D of Figure 50.
- As in tracking to the station, if the 065° heading succeeds in keeping the ADF on 170 then the 10° wind correction angle will make the airplane's track coincide with the intended course, otherwise the procedure must be repeated.

INTERCEPTING A COURSE FROM A STATION is necessary to accomplish an ADF approach. In the example shown in Figure 51, the outbound course from the station is 080°.

- In position A the pilot has departed the airway fix and is proceeding directly to the radio beacon using either homing or tracking procedures.
- After passing the station, the pilot follows the same rule normally used in intercepting a VOR radial (see Figure 30), i.e., turn parallel to the intended course or to a heading of 080° as shown in position B of Figure 51. The ADF will point to some value to the right of 180 however, the exact number will change and is not important.
- In order to intercept the outbound course, the pilot turns the airplane to the right to a heading of 125 (the original heading of 080° plus a 45° interception angle).
- At C in Figure 51, the airplane is back on course since the ADF reads the interception angle of 45° or the needle points to 180 minus 45 or 135°. The airplane is turned to the left to track away from the station as in position D of Figure 51.

The remainder of the ADF approach is accomplished by tracking inbound, tracking outbound and interception procedures as previously described. Study the ADF approach procedure chart shown in Figure 58 and see how to apply these procedures. Also note the use of an intersection using a VOR radial to obtain lower landing minimums.

Use of ADF in obtaining a fix while flying a VOR airway is almost as good as dual VOR or DME. Determination of position along a VOR radial by means of ADF is a relatively simple procedure; however, some arithmetic is required. In performing the calculations as explained below, don't be afraid to admit that you can't do it mentally. Write it all down in some sort of organized procedure. For example, carry along a clipboard with a few clean sheets of paper for just such a purpose.

DETERMINING AN ADF FIX. There are a number of methods for obtaining a magnetic bearing to or from a station using ADF to establish a fix. Three procedures are discussed.

Method 1

This is the simplest and most foolproof method, but not necessarily the most desirable. In Figure 52, the airplane's heading of

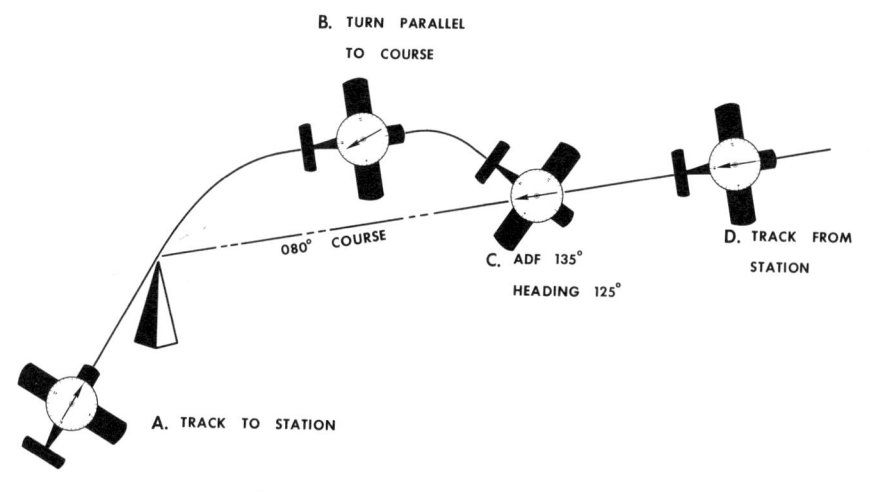

Fig. 51 Intercepting ADF bearing.

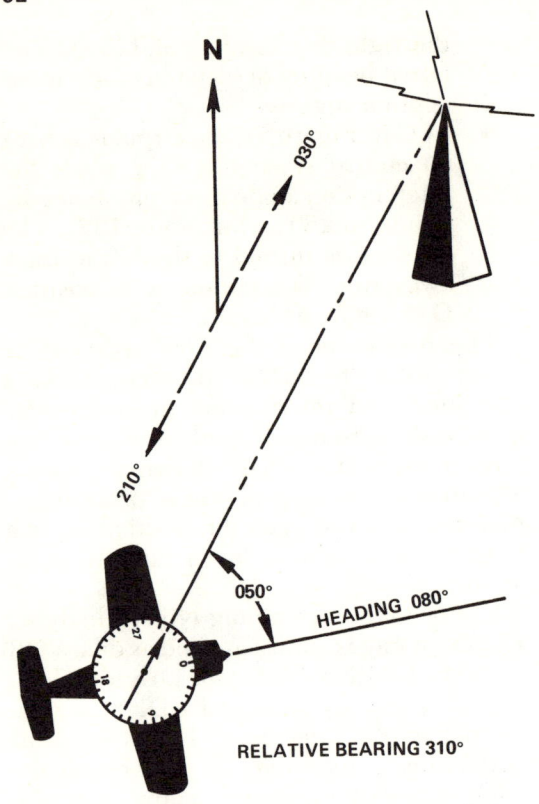

Fig. 52 Determining the airplane's position relative to a station using ADF with a fixed azimuth dial usually requires some calculations.

080 degrees is required to maintain a course. A cross bearing on a station to the left of the course is desired to establish a position. The most straight-forward method is:
- Turn the airplane to the left until the ADF pointer is on zero. The airplane is now heading directly for the station.
- When flight conditions are stablilized, read the magnetic bearing TO the station on the heading indicator (D. G.) or compass. In Figure 52, this is 030 degrees. Add or subtract 180 degrees to obtain the magnetic bearing FROM the station, 210 degrees in Figure 105 example.
- After obtaining the bearing, turn right (in our example) and resume course.
- Draw a line of position on the chart, from the radio station's transmitting tower using a protractor. The intersection of this line of position and the airplane's course, pinpoints its position. To plot a line of position on a sectional chart subtract Westerly variation from the magnetic bearing FROM the station or add Easterly variation to obtain a true bearing.

Method 2

By using this method, the airplane remains on course but you make the turn mentally. Again using Figure 52 whereby the airplane is on a heading of 080 degrees, a cross bearing on a station to the left of the course is desired. The step-by-step procedure is:
- Maintain heading required to maintain course (080 degrees in figure 52). Note reading of ADF pointer (310) degrees in our example).
- Count off the number of degrees that you would have to turn to place "zero" under the tip of the ADF pointer (360 - 310 = 050 degrees in our example).
- The airplane's heading is 080 degrees, therefore a left turn of 050 degrees would be required to zero the ADF pointer. Instead of actually turning, subtract 050 from 080 which results in a magnetic bearing of 030 degrees TO the station.
- In order to plot a line of position on a sectional chart add (or subtract) 180 to obtain the magnetic bearing FROM the station and then add Easterly or subtract Westerly variation to obtain a true bearing.

Method 3

This is probably the most satisfactory except that it requires memorization of a simple formula:

Magnetic Heading of Aircraft + Relative bearing to station = Magnetic Bearing to station

or

MH + RB = MB

In other words, just ADD the readings on the airplane's heading indicator (D. G. and/or compass) and the ADF dial. That's really pretty simple. Using Figure 52 as an example:

Magnetic Heading of Aircraft	= 080 degrees
Relative Bearing	= 310
	390
(When over 360 subtract 360)	360
Magnetic Heading TO station	= 030 degrees

Again, add (or subtract) 180 degrees to obtain magnetic bearing FROM station and add Easterly or subtract Westerly variation to obtain a true bearing FROM the station to plot a line of position on a sectional chart.

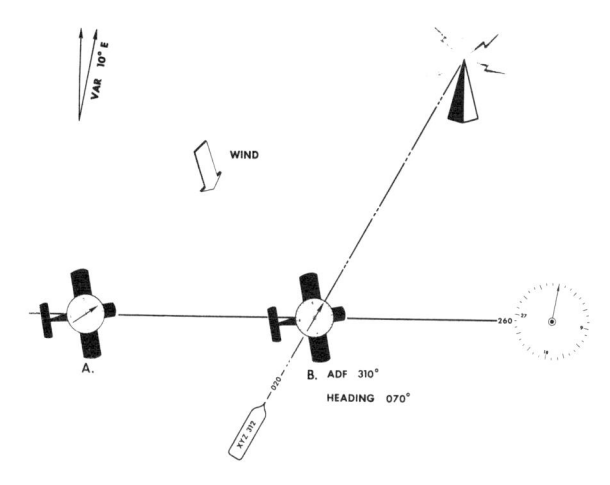

Fig. 53 Establishing pre-determined ADF bearing.

DETERMINING AN ADF INTERSECTION is a rare case but occasionally encountered during IFR flights.

- In position A, Figure 53, the pilot is flying a VOR airway using VOR as primary navigation. ATC has requested a position report at the intersection determined by a 020 bearing to radio beacon XYZ on a frequency of 312 KHz. A heading of 070 degrees is required to maintain the VOR course of 080 degrees TO the VOR.
- Prior to reaching the intersection, the pilot must determine where the ADF needle will point when the aircraft has arrived at the intersection. In other words, he must compute the RELATIVE BEARING of the station from the aircraft. In our example, the pilot knows that the station is to his left. By a combination of reasoning and calculation, he also determines that the ADF needle will point to a number of degrees to the left of zero equivalent to his airplane's heading of 070° minus the ADF bearing of 020° or 50 degrees to the left of zero. Since zero is also 360 degrees, 360 minus 50 is 310 degrees.
- At position B in Figure 53, the airplane is at the intersection when the ADF points to 310 degrees.

USE OF ADF WITH ROTATABLE AZIMUTH DIAL

When homing with a rotatable dial ADF, it is best to rotate the dial so that zero is on top under the index. Zero then, is the nose of the airplane just like with the fixed dial ADF. By varying heading to keep zero under the arrow of the indicator pointer, the airplane will fly directly to the station. In other words, homing is accomplished exactly as discussed previously for the fixed azimuth dial ADF.

The advantage of the rotatable azimuth dial is that it simplifies determination of cross-bearings.

Using Figure 54 which is the same setup as discussed previously for establishing a cross-bearing with a fixed azimuth dial ADF, follow this procedure:

- Rotate the ADF azimuth dial to agree with the magnetic heading of the aircraft as obtained from the compass/directional gyro (080 degrees under the index in our example).
- Read the magnetic bearing TO the station under the ADF indicator pointer arrow (030 degrees in Figure 54). Remember, the pointer always points TO the station.
- Read the magnetic bearing FROM the station under the tail of the indicator pointer (210 degrees in our example).
- To plot the bearing on a sectional chart for obtaining a line of position, add

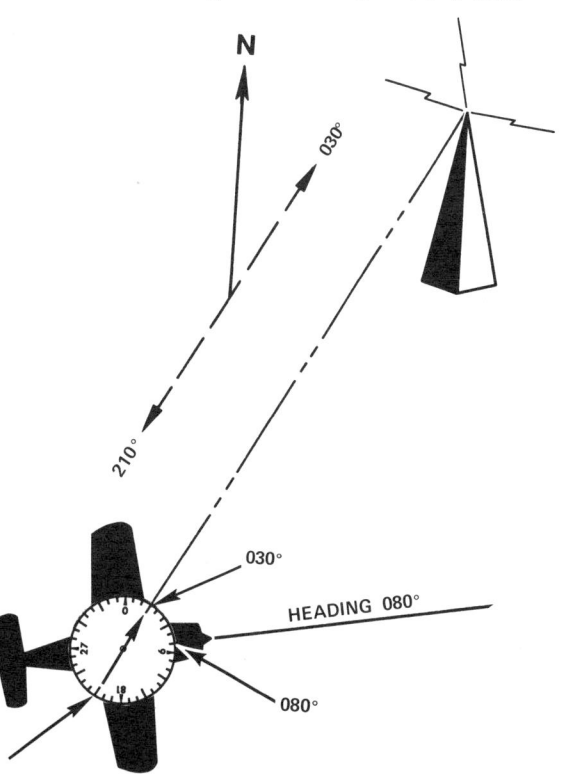

Fig. 54 Determining the airplane's position relative to a station using ADF with a rotatable azimuth dial. No calculations are necessary.

easterly variation or subtract westerly variation to obtain a true bearing.

In effect, the use of a rotatable azimuth dial is the same as method 1, as discussed previously. Instead of turning the airplane, you turn the azimuth dial.

SUMMARY, VOR/VORTAC FLIGHT PROCEDURES

- In flying to or from a station, the heading of the aircraft should always agree with the Omni Bearing Selector (OBS), except for wind corrections. Then, corrections are always made TOWARDS the Course Deviation Indicator (CDI).
- Station passage is indicated by "TO" going to "FROM."

VOR/VORTAC TRACKING

- "Tracking" a VOR/VORTAC course requires "trial and error" technique.
- If heading of aircraft agrees with OBS and CDI needle is centered, only small corrections in heading will be required.
- As soon as needle deviates slightly (like one needle width) turn aircraft towards needle 5 to 10 degrees.
- Keep making small corrections towards the needle as soon as it moves one needle width.
- Keep "hacking away" at heading corrections to keep needle centered. After considerable practice, you will find that the number of heading corrections required will be reduced.
- If needle is off center something like 1/4 inch and you are more than 5 miles from station, make 20 to 30 degree heading corrections to get back on course.

INTERCEPTING NEW VOR/VORTAC BEARINGS

Normally a course change is necessary after crossing a VOR/VORTAC. Always follow this procedure:
- After crossing station IMMEDIATELY turn aircraft to HEADING of new course.
- After this turn, aircraft is flying parallel to new course.
- While flying parallel, set in new course in OBS.
- Turn toward new course 20 to 45 degrees to intercept new course.
- After interception, begin normal tracking.

ENROUTE PROCEDURES

- Use normal tracking procedures by flying outbound from one VOR/VORTAC and inbound to the next station.
- After crossing station, follow procedure for "INTERCEPTING NEW VOR/VORTAC BEARINGS" to acquire the next leg of your flight.

DETERMINING INTERSECTIONS

- An intersection is determined by two crossing radials from two different VOR/VORTAC stations.
- Using one VOR set, a course to or from one of the stations must be accurately tracked with occasional check on progress by tuning to frequency of other station determining intersection.
- To determine whether intersection has not been reached — or whether it has been passed — requires a visualization of the complete setup.

PROCEDURE TURNS

- A procedure turn is a PLANNED maneuver to reverse course on a VOR radial (ADF bearing or ILS localizer).
- To accomplish a standard procedure turn:
  - Turn left to heading of 45° less than course the airplane is flying.
  - Fly this heading for one minute, then begin a 180° right turn.
  - Fly straight until intercepting inbound course.

HOLDING

- Holding is a procedure to delay an airplane to facilitate ATC procedures. The standard holding pattern consists of a "race track" pattern described by:
  - A 180° right turn about the holding fix.
  - A one minute straight leg.
  - Another 180° right turn.

- One minute straight leg back to the fix.
- Total time to complete one holding pattern is 4 minutes.
- Corrections for head, tail or cross winds must be made.

HOLDING PATTERN ENTRIES
- In most cases, the airplane will be approaching the holding fix already established on the inbound holding course, thereby requiring only a right turn after crossing the fix.
- If holding is required on a course other than the course the airplane is flying, planned procedures are necessary to establish the airplane in the holding patterns.

TIME-DISTANCE CHECK
- For a time distance check, turn the airplane 90 degrees to inbound bearing. Time to the station under no wind conditions is:

$$\text{Minutes to station} = \frac{\text{seconds}}{\text{degree bearing change}}$$

or

$$\frac{60 \times \text{minutes}}{\text{degree bearing change}}$$

To facilitate calculations, use a 10 degree bearing change.

ADF PROCEDURES
- The ADF needle always points to the station to which it is tuned.
- Zero on the dial is always the nose of the airplane.
- RELATIVE BEARING is the angular direction clockwise, of the station from the nose of the airplane.
- Homing is accomplished by flying headings to keep the needle on zero.
- Tracking requires a trial and error procedure to correct for drift.
- In order to accomplish an ADF instrument approach, tracking inbound and tracking outbound from a station must be accomplished with relative precision.
- Intercepting a new course after passing a station is accomplished similar to VOR procedures, that is, turn parallel to new course and then intercept it at a 30 to 45 degree angle.
- An ADF fix requires simple calculations based on the airplane's heading and relative bearing.

6 THE INSTRUMENT APPROACH

Contrary to popular belief, no instrument or "blind" landings are conducted in IFR weather. All landings are made with visual reference to the ground; the approach, however, is made "on instruments" using radio or radar facilities for controlled letdown and direction to the airport. Complete instrument approaches through touchdown and rollout have been made on an experimental basis. However, operational procedures still depend on a visual landing from an instrument approach.

Instrument approaches are set up by the FAA for hundreds of airports using various radio and radar facilities. These complete procedures for each individual airport are depicted on the Instrument Approach Procedure charts issued by the National Ocean Survey (NOS). Some airports like Lambert Field in St. Louis, for example, have twelve different approaches using various radio facilities and one using radar. Pratt Kansas Airport, however, has only one type of approach. Generally, one of more approach procedures are set up for each radio facility serving the airport. These facilities are VOR (omni), non-directional homing beacon (NDB) for use with airborne ADF, and the old standby, ILS (Instrument Landing System). In addition, PAR and ASR approaches, using radar, may be available.

Basic flight procedures are the same for all types of radio facility approaches as shown in Figure 55 and outlined below:
- After initial approach to the facility the pilot flies outbound on the approach course, descending as necessary to procedure turn altitude.
- A procedure turn at an altitude indicated on the charts is conducted within ten nautical miles from the facility, to reverse course. The inbound course is intercepted at a 45 degree angle. (Some procedures do not require a procedure turn.)
- When established on the inbound course, a descent is made to the altitude indicated on the chart as the crossing altitude on final approach. This is approximately 1000 to 1300 feet above runway elevation.
- After crossing the facility, descent to the minimum altitude is conducted. This is from 200 to 700 feet above the runway elevation depending on the type of facility and local conditions.
- Upon descent to minimum altitude the pilot should see the field when within ½ to 2 miles, again depending on facility and local conditions.
- Visual landing is conducted or, if the airport is not sighted, a "missed approach" is accomplished.

When holding over the final approach fix, and approach clearance is recieved, a procedure turn is NOT necessary. The approach is accomplished directly from the holding pattern (see Figure 57).

Each approach is assigned a minimum altitude to which descent is authorized and a minimum visibility value. If a visual landing cannot be conducted at these conditions, a different approach must be used, if available, or the pilot must proceed to an alternate airport. Conditions affecting the allowable minimums are:
- Type of radio facility
- Distance of facility from airport
- Alignment of approach course with runway
- Terrain and obstructions in approach path
- Size and speed of airplane in relation to runway length and wind conditions.

In general, approaches using VOR or ADF procedures can be used down to 500 feet authorized altitude and one mile visibility if the facility is sufficiently close to the field, the approach course is aligned within 30 degrees of the runway heading and no appreciable obstructions exist on the approach course, minimums of 400 and one are assigned.

The Instrument Landing System (ILS), however, has normal minimums down to 200 foot authorized altitude and ½ mile visibility with all components of the ground and airborne system, including glide slope, in operation. Without glide slope, these minimums normally go to 400-¾. ILS approaches to minimums lower than 200 feet are authorized under Category II operations. Category II requirements are presented in the Appendix and in Part 91 of the

APPROACH FACILITY
VOR
RADIO BEACON
or ILS OUTER MARKER

A. "INITIAL APPROACH" TO APPROACH FACILITY FROM AIRWAY FIX
   DESCEND TO MEA OR ASSIGNED ALTITUDE

B. AFTER CROSSING FACILITY DESCEND TO PROCEDURE TURN ALTITUDE

C. INTERCEPT FINAL APPROACH COURSE AT 45°

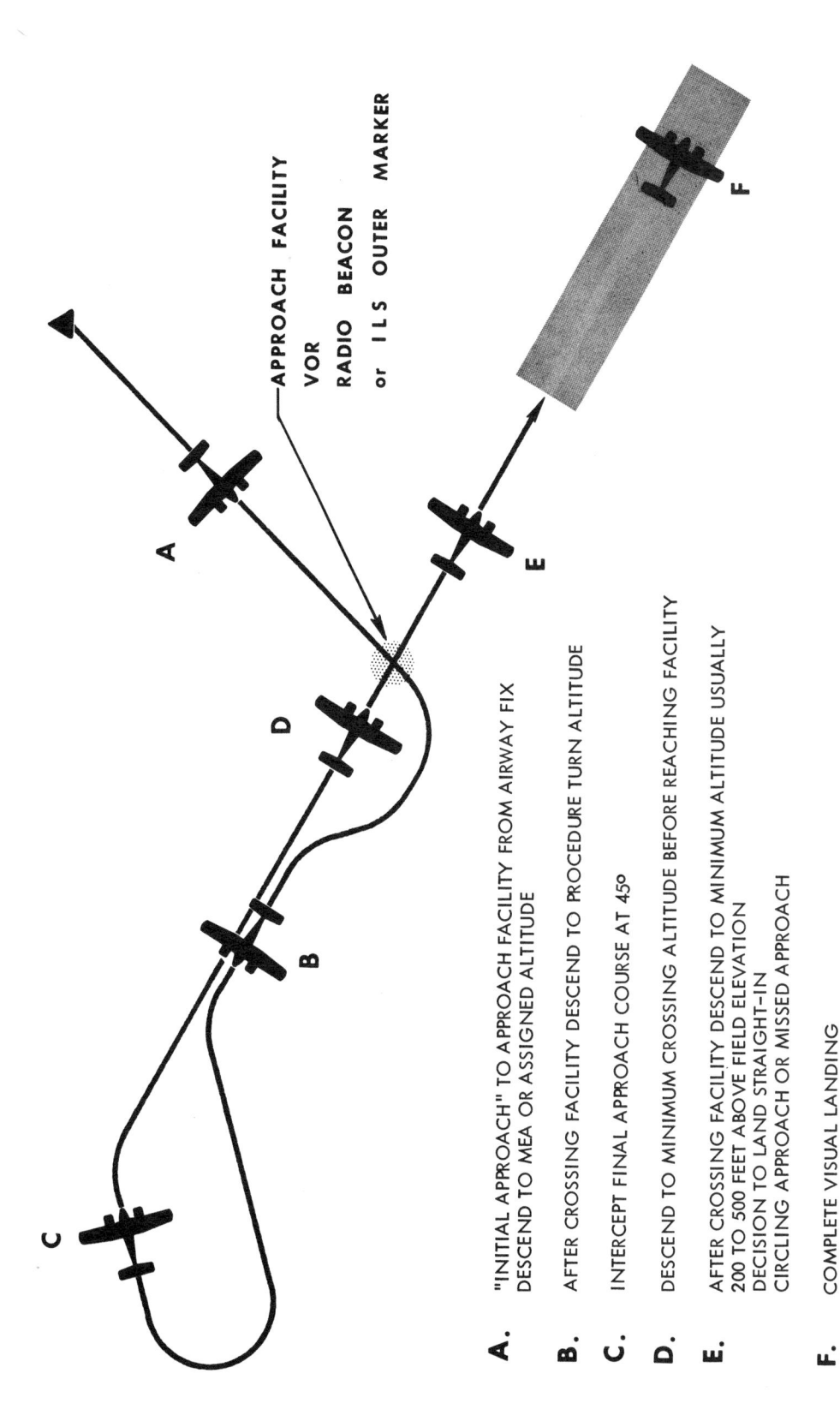

D. DESCEND TO MINIMUM CROSSING ALTITUDE BEFORE REACHING FACILITY

E. AFTER CROSSING FACILITY DESCEND TO MINIMUM ALTITUDE USUALLY
   200 TO 500 FEET ABOVE FIELD ELEVATION
   DECISION TO LAND STRAIGHT-IN
   CIRCLING APPROACH OR MISSED APPROACH

F. COMPLETE VISUAL LANDING

Fig. 55 All instrument approaches use the same basic flight procedures.

Federal Aviation Regulations and will not be discussed here.

It is obviously important for the pilot to plan his flight so that the weather at his destination is not below the published minimums considering the type of approach and his airplane and its equipment.

The ILS presents a considerably more precise course to the airport than either VOR or ADF. Among the many reasons for this is the fact that the ILS course becomes more accurate as the airport is approached whereas courses from the other facilities become less accurate, requiring more altitude and visibility for final maneuvering to the runway upon sighting the airport. In addition, the ILS course accuracy is approximately four times as sensitive as a VOR course. This is indicated to the pilot by the rate of deviation or displacement of the CDI needle. For example, a full scale needle deflection would indicate that the airplane was 10 degrees off course when using omni. A full scale deflection of the same indicator when using ILS, however, would occur when only 2½ degrees off course.

All instrument approaches are either "straight-in" or "circling". In general, a straight-in approach is where the course from the facility to the airport is aligned within 30 degrees of the runway heading. The ILS, however, is always installed so as to be exactly aligned with a given runway. A circling approach is necessary when the approach requires considerable maneuvering in order to land on a specific runway.

Conditions can occur where a circling approach is necessary from an ILS approach. For example, the tail wind or cross wind components down the instrument runway may preclude a landing on it. Minimums of 500-1 therefore apply (400-1 for some local conditions).

In conducting a circling approach from an ILS, the pilot conducts normal ILS procedures except that descent is limited to 500 feet (or the circling altitude specified on the approach chart) above airport elevation during final. Assuming conditions to be exactly 500 and 1 the pilot will see the airport when within 1 mile from it. He then circles to the active runway, keeping the airport in sight.

VOR and ADF are primarily enroute navigational aids. They are therefore generally not ideally located for approaches to airports. Also, their accuracy is not sufficient for landing minimums below 500 and 1 or precise alignment with a specific instrument runway. The Instrument Landing System (ILS) is therefore the primary approach facility. In fact, approaches using VOR or ADF at an airport that also has ILS are discouraged by Air Traffic Control (ATC). A VOR approach, for example, ties up the VOR as well as the airport for a considerable length of time. Since departing aircraft are usually cleared out of the terminal area to the VOR, traffic can come to a complete halt for periods of 10 to 20 minutes while an aircraft is conducting a VOR approach in a non-radar area.

As explained previously, two types of radar approaches are also available at some airports. Radar (ASR or PAR) approaches require only that the pilot follow instructions from the air traffic controller. Landing minimums for ASR approaches are usually 500 and 1 while minimums of 200 and ½ usually apply for the more precise PAR approaches.

The pilot must judge his rate of descent during an approach without electronic glide slope so as to reach the various prescribed altitudes ON OR BEFORE reaching certain locations and not to descend to any lower altitude until after crossing them. This will normally involve a step type descent. For example, after completing the procedure turn (see Figure 55) at procedure turn altitude, the pilot begins descent to the crossing altitude of the facility. Level flight is maintained at this altitude until the facility is crossed. After crossing the facility at the prescribed altitude, descent is again initiated to the allowable minimums as shown on the Instrument Approach Procedure charts.

An exception to the step type descent however, occurs when conducting an ILS approach using glide slope. When glide slope is utilized, the rate of descent is adjusted to maintain the glide slope needle centered. Use of ILS without glide slope however, requires the step type descent as described above. Without glide slope, higher minimums, usually 400 feet authorized altitude and ¾ mile visibility, apply.

The procedures as described above and shown in Figure 55 apply when Approach Control radar is not available. In most large metropolitan areas, Approach Control radar is used to vector the airplane to the final approach course, thereby eliminating the need for the procedure turn. Normally the airplane is vectored to intercept the

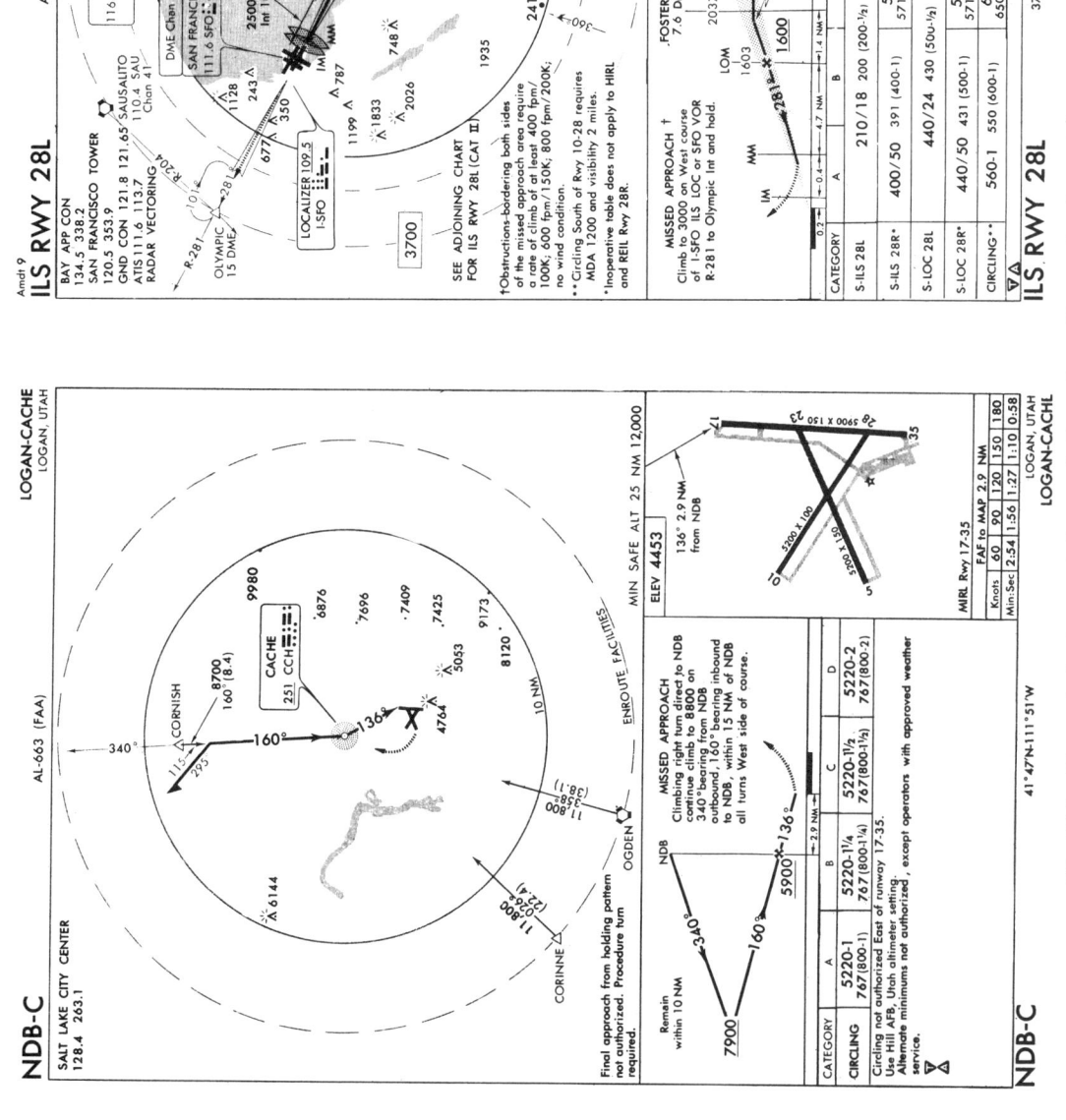

Fig. 55 A *Example Instrument Approach Procedure Charts showing minimum and maximum facilities.*

final approach course at a 45° angle approximately three miles from the approach facility (outer marker for an ILS approach). The approach is then completed using radio aids. Under some conditions, the approach may be monitored by approach control using Precision Approach Radar (PAR) and advisory information provided the pilot only when large deviations exist from flight path or glide slope.

FLYING THE ILS

The standard procedure for flying the ILS is similar to that shown in Figure 55, which is applicable to all types of instrument approaches. There are some basic points to remember however, in flying an ILS approach:

- The same CDI is used for flying ILS as is used for VOR.
- When an ILS frequency (every odd tenth from 108.1 through 111.9 mc) is tuned in, the OBS (omni-bearing selector) becomes inoperative and the TO-FROM indicator reads TO regardless of position of the aircraft relative to the localizer transmitter. A red TO-FROM flag indicates either ground or airborne equipment is inoperative.
- The CDI is four times as sensitive when flying ILS compared to VOR. Full scale CDI deflection is 2½° for ILS compared to 10° for VOR.
- In all cases THE NEEDLE ALWAYS POINTS TO THE COLOR THE AIRCRAFT IS IN (see Figure 56).
- When flying TOWARD the runway on the front course or AWAY from the runway on the back course correct TOWARD the needle (see Figure 56).
- When flying TOWARD the runway on the back course or AWAY from the runway on the front course, correct AWAY from the needle (see Figure 56).
- Glide slope is usable only on the front course.
- Spurious, unusable glide slope signals exist above the normal glide slope. Ignore these signals. No false glide slope signals exist below the normal glide path.

The ILS is always aligned with a specific runway. The localizer transmits a similar beam in both directions from the transmitter. However, proper adjustment of the front course is given precedence at the expense of the back course. In some installations however, the back course is usable for approaches and Instrument Approach Procedure charts are issued. In no case, however, is glide slope available on the back course. As previously discussed, use of the back course should proceed with caution regarding interpretation of the CDI indications. When flying towards the runway on the back course, corrections must be made AWAY FROM the CDI needle as shown in Figure 56. Marker beacons are usually not installed. Position along the flight path is therefore determined by means of a VOR radial intersection with the localizer or a radio beacon.

In flying the front course ILS, transition to the ILS outer marker is usually accomplished by tuning the ADF to the outer marker compass locater (LOM) (radio beacon). Thus, in position A of Figure 55, (if flying an ILS approach), the pilot has departed the airway fix and is homing to the LOM. This distance is usually not in excess of 15 miles.

Extreme caution should be used when flying the ILS glide path where the indicator shows the position of the aircraft to be under the glide path. The suggested limits are not to exceed three dot deviation up to the middle marker and to allow no "fly-up" condition from the middle marker to completion of landing.

INSTRUMENT APPROACH FROM HOLDING PATTERN

During IFR weather at high traffic density areas, many airplanes converge on the terminal area for an instrument approach at approximately the same time. Usually only one instrument runway is in use requiring a sequencing system so that each airplane can land, one at a time. Approach Control may have airplanes hold at outlying holding points, then route them to the final approach fix (usually the ILS outer marker) and "stack" them. "Stacking" is generally used only in a non-radar environment. However, a pilot should be familiar with the procedures involved.

Each airplane in the stack is issued holding instructions on the final approach course using the final approach fix and spaced at 1000 foot altitude intervals. As an airplane lands, each airplane descends 1000 feet while in the holding pattern. The

UNUSABLE "SPURIOUS" GLIDE PATH SIGNALS

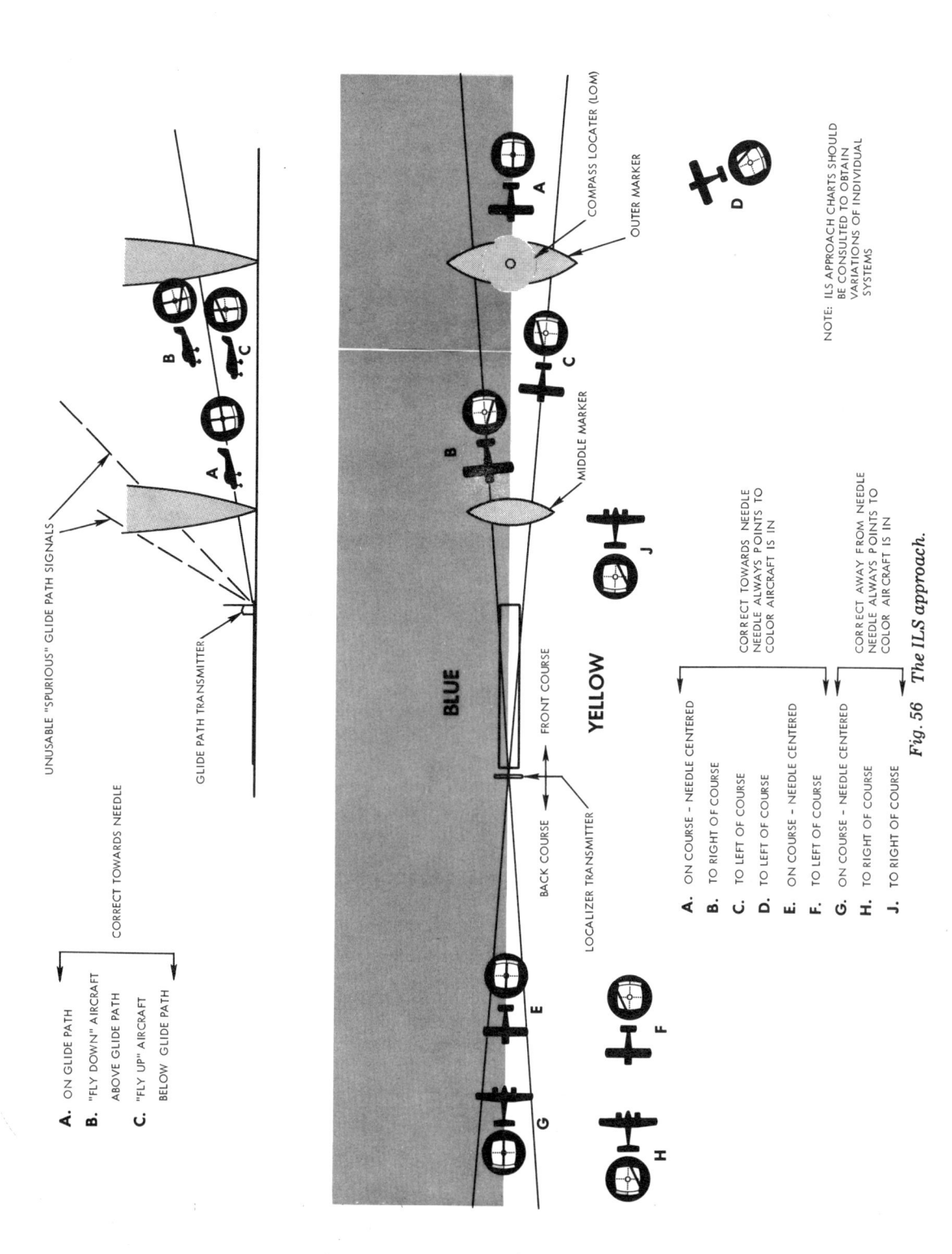

CORRECT TOWARDS NEEDLE

GLIDE PATH TRANSMITTER

A. ON GLIDE PATH
B. "FLY DOWN" AIRCRAFT ABOVE GLIDE PATH
C. "FLY UP" AIRCRAFT BELOW GLIDE PATH

COMPASS LOCATER (LOM)
OUTER MARKER
MIDDLE MARKER
BLUE
YELLOW
FRONT COURSE
BACK COURSE
LOCALIZER TRANSMITTER

CORRECT TOWARDS NEEDLE
NEEDLE ALWAYS POINTS TO
COLOR AIRCRAFT IS IN

CORRECT AWAY FROM NEEDLE
NEEDLE ALWAYS POINTS TO
COLOR AIRCRAFT IS IN

A. ON COURSE - NEEDLE CENTERED
B. TO RIGHT OF COURSE
C. TO LEFT OF COURSE
D. TO LEFT OF COURSE
E. ON COURSE - NEEDLE CENTERED
F. TO LEFT OF COURSE
G. ON COURSE - NEEDLE CENTERED
H. TO RIGHT OF COURSE
J. TO RIGHT OF COURSE

NOTE: ILS APPROACH CHARTS SHOULD BE CONSULTED TO OBTAIN VARIATIONS OF INDIVIDUAL SYSTEMS

Fig. 56 The ILS approach.

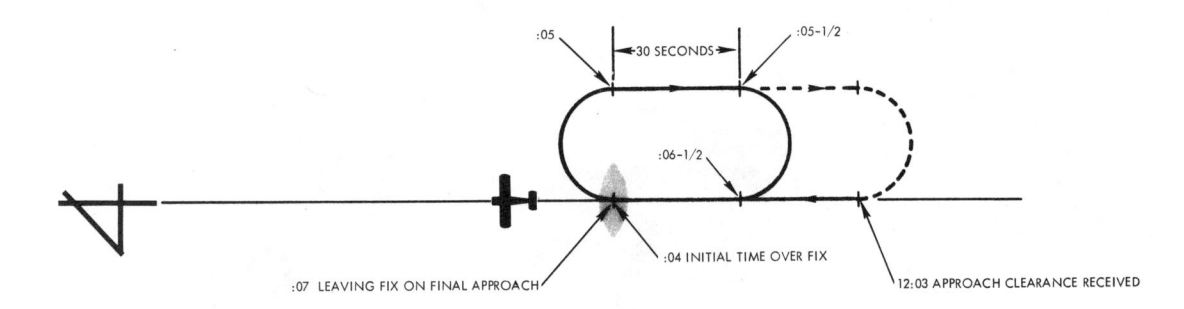

Fig. 57 Instrument approach from holding pattern.

lowest airplane is usually in a holding pattern 1000 feet above procedure turn altitude. Each pilot in an approach sequence will be given advance notice as to the time he should leave the holding point on approach to the airport. When a time to leave the holding point has been received, the pilot should adjust his flight path by modifying the holding pattern, to leave the fix as closely as possible to the designated time. It is emphasized that A PROCEDURE TURN IS NOT NECESSARY WHEN IN A HOLDING PATTERN ON THE APPROACH COURSE ABOUT THE FIX.

The procedure for modifying the holding pattern in order to leave the fix on final approach at a designated time, is shown by example:

The dotted line in Figure 57 indicates a one-minute holding pattern, thus a complete holding pattern requires four minutes of flying time. The solid line in Figure 57 indicates the flight path from the time the clearance was received.

At 12:03 local time, in the example shown, a pilot holding receives instructions to leave the fix inbound at 12:07. These instructions are received just as the pilot has completed turn at the outbound end of the holding pattern and is proceeding inbound towards the fix. Arriving back over the fix, the pilot notes that the time is 12:04 and that he has three minutes to lose in order to leave the fix at the assigned time. Since the time remaining is more than two minutes, the pilot plans to fly a race track pattern rather than a 360° (standard rate) turn which would use up two minutes. The turns at the end of the race track pattern will consume approximately two minutes. Three minutes to go, minus two minutes required for turns, leaves one minute for level flight. Since two portions of level flight will be required to get back to the fix inbound, the pilot halves the one minute remaining and plans to fly level for 30 seconds outbound before starting his turn back towards the fix on final approach. If the winds are negligible at flight altitude, this procedure would bring the pilot inbound across the fix precisely at the specified time of 12:07. However, if the pilot expected a headwind on final approach, he should shorten his 30-second outbound course somewhat. On the other hand, if the pilot knew he would encounter a tailwind on final approach, he should lengthen his calculated 30-second outbound heading somewhat.

Approach clearance will always be given to a pilot sufficiently in advance so that he can plan his holding pattern in order to leave the fix at the designated time. Inspection of the standard holding pattern will show that the pilot can arrive over the fix from anywhere in the holding pattern within a maximum of two minutes. With experience, a pilot should be able to plan his holding pattern to arrive over the fix within 20 seconds of the designated time.

USING THE INSTRUMENT APPROACH PROCEDURE CHARTS

As discussed previously, Instrument Approach Procedure Charts are issued for hundreds of airports which are approved for use of an instrument approach. These charts contain a wealth of information and instrument pilots must be thoroughly familiar with their use.

Civil Instrument Approach Procedures are established by the Federal Aviation Administration after careful analysis of obstructions, terrain features, and navigation facilities. Based on this information, the National Ocean Survey (of the National

Oceanic and Atmospheric Administration), and other charting agencies, publish instrument approach procedure charts as a service to the instrument pilot. The Federal Aviation Regulations require use of specified procedures by all pilots approaching for landing under Instrument Flight Rules. Appropriate maneuvers, which include altitudes, courses, and other limitations, are prescribed in these procedures. They have been established for safe letdown during instrument flight conditions as a result of many years of accumulated experience. It is important that all pilots thoroughly understand these procedures and their use.

There are two basic types of instrument approach procedures:
- PRECISION APPROACH PROCEDURE means a standard instrument approach in which an electronic glide slope is provided (ILS or PAR).
- NON-PRECISION APPROACH PROCEDURE means a standard instrument approach in which no electronic glide slope is provided (VOR, NDB or ADF, ASR, ILS back course, localizer (ILS without glideslope).

DEFINITIONS (Also contained in the Appendix)
- MDA — "Minimum descent altitude" means the lowest altitude exressed in feet above mean sea level, to which descent is authorized on final approach or during circling-to-land maneuvering in execution of a standard instrument approach WHERE NO ELECTRONIC GLIDE SLOPE IS PROVIDED.
- DH - "Decision Height" with respect to the operation of aircraft, means the height at which a decision must be made DURING AN ILS OR PAR INSTRUMENT APPROACH, to continue the approach or to execute a missed approach. This height is expressed in feet above mean sea level (MSL), and for Category II operation, the decision height is additionally expressed as a radio altimeter setting.
- HAA — "Height above airport" indicates the height of the MDA above the published airport elevation. THIS IS PUBLISHED IN CONJUNCTION WITH CIRCLING MINIMUMS
- HAT — "Height above touchdown" indicates the height of the DH or MDA above the highest runway elevation in the touchdown zone (first 3,000 feet of runway.). THIS IS PUBLISHED IN CONJUNCTION WITH STRAIGHT-IN MINIMUMS.
- No PT — means No Procedure Turn Required.

IFR LANDING MINIMUMS Ceiling minimums are not prescribed as a landing minimum. However, ceiling and visibility are shown parenthetically, e.g., (200-½) for use by certain military services and should be disregarded by civil users. Approaches are allowed down to the prescribed Minimum Descent Altitude (MDA) or Decision Height (DH) without regard to reported ceiling. THE PUBLISHED VISIBILITY IS THE LIMITING CONDITION FOR LANDING.

DESCENT BELOW MDA OR DH is not allowed unless:
- The aircraft is in a position from which a normal approach to the runway of intended landing can be made; and
- The approach threshold of that runway, or approach lights, or other markings identifiable with the approach end of that runway, are clearly visible to the pilot.
- If, upon arrival at the missed approach point, or at any time thereafter, any of the above requirements are not met, the pilot shall immediately execute the appropriate missed approach procedure.

DEPICTION OF MINIMUMS ON CHARTS. An example of the format is shown in Figure 58. The minimums for straight-in and circling appear directly under each aircraft category. When a minimum is omitted under a category, the minimum listed for the previous category also applies. In Figure 58, the S-ILS-27 minimum for Category B is the same as for Category A, i.e., 1352/24.

AIRCRAFT/APPROACH CATEGORIES. Aircraft are grouped according to approach speed and gross weight. On the chart format, minimums are specified for various aircraft speed/weight combinations. Speeds are based upon a value of 1.3 times the stalling speed of the aircraft in the landing configuration at maximum certified gross landing weight. Thus they are COMPUTED values. An aircraft can fit into only one category, that being the highest category in which it meets either speed or weight. For example, a 30,000 pound aircraft landing weight combined

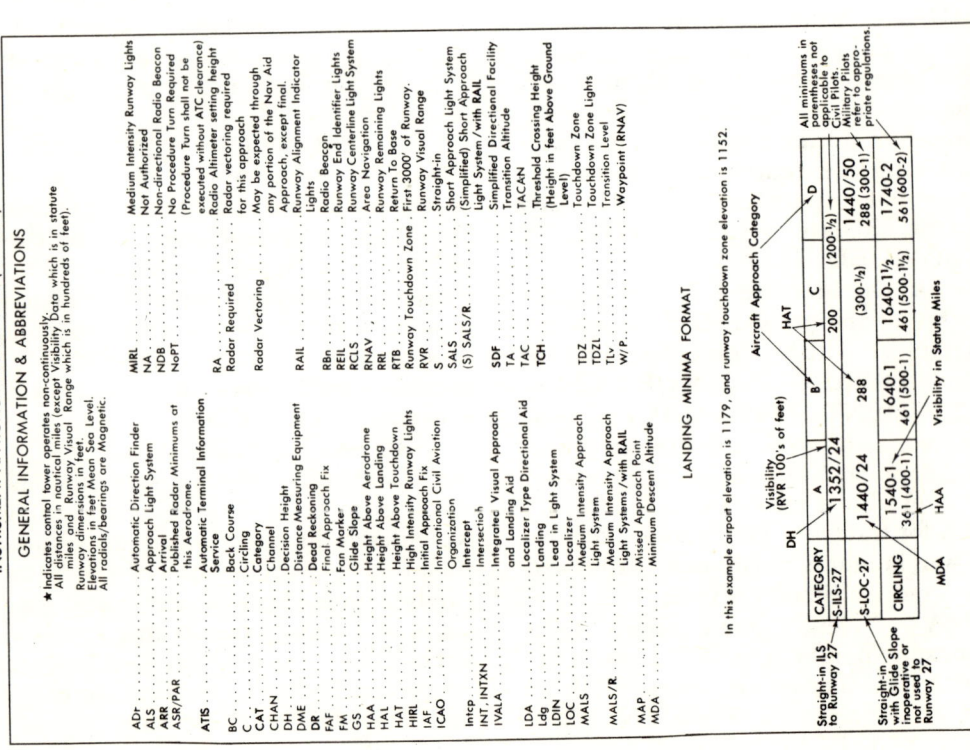

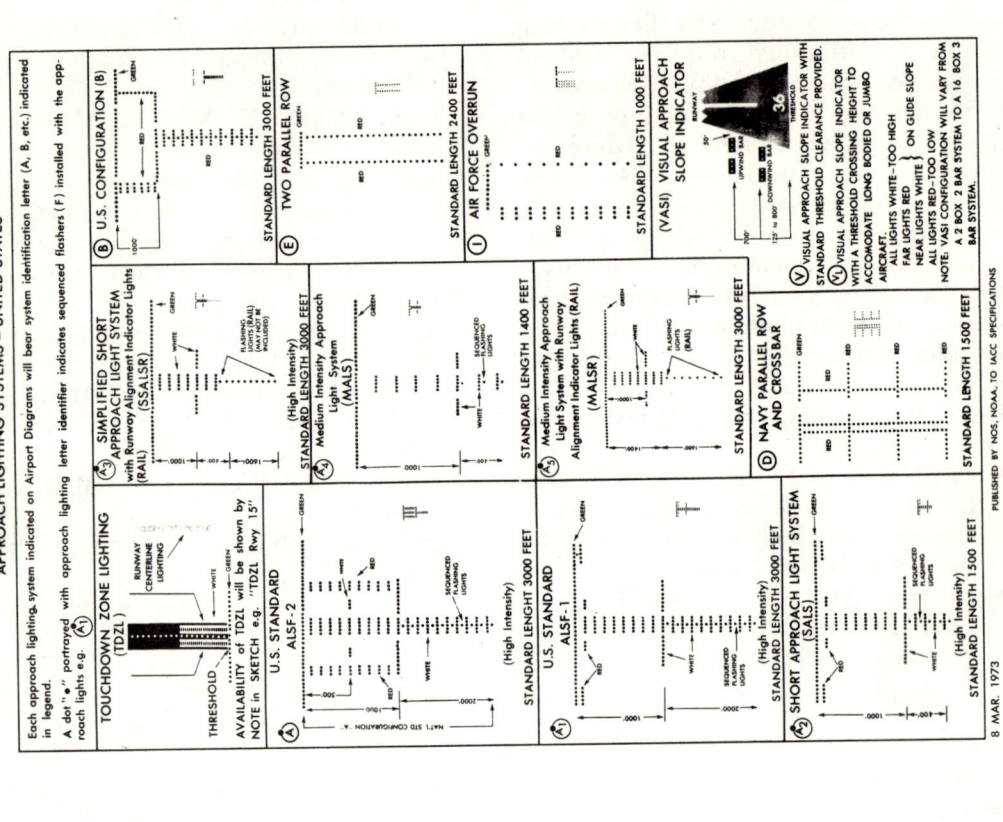

Fig. 58 *Legend, Instrument Approach Procedure Charts, general information and abbreviations, landing minima format, and approach lighting systems.*

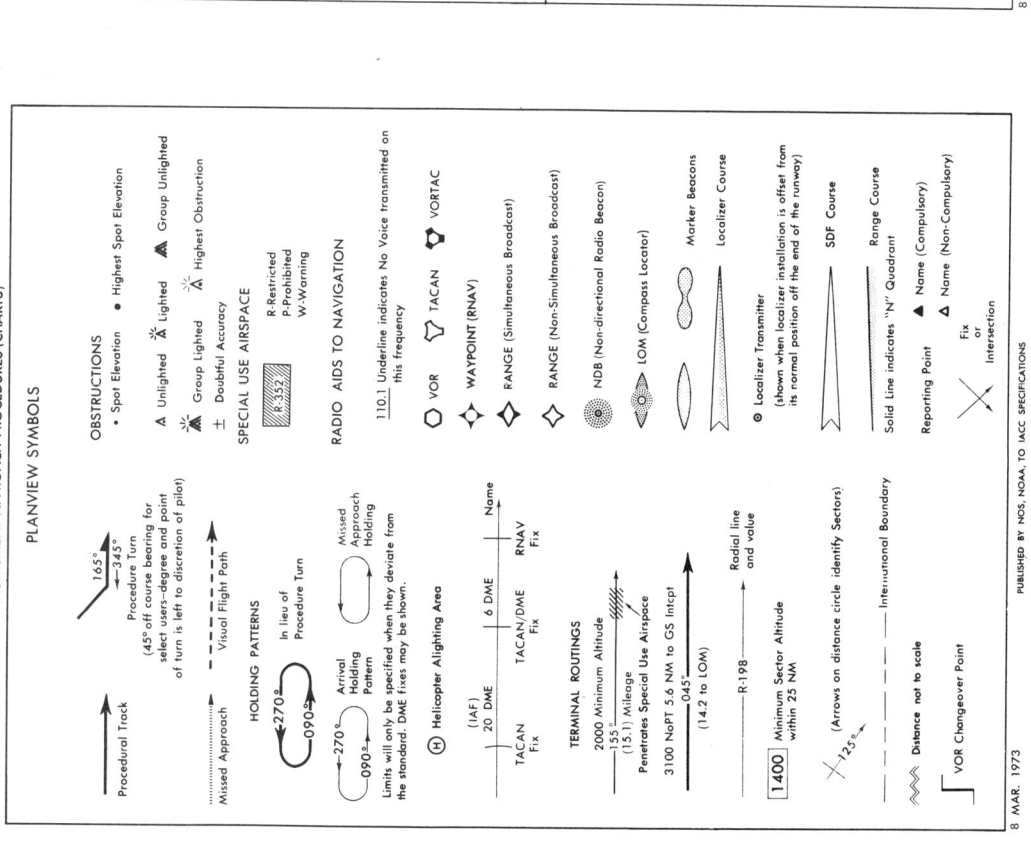

Fig. 59 *Legend, Instrument Approach Procedure Charts, plan view symbols, profile and aerodrome sketch.*

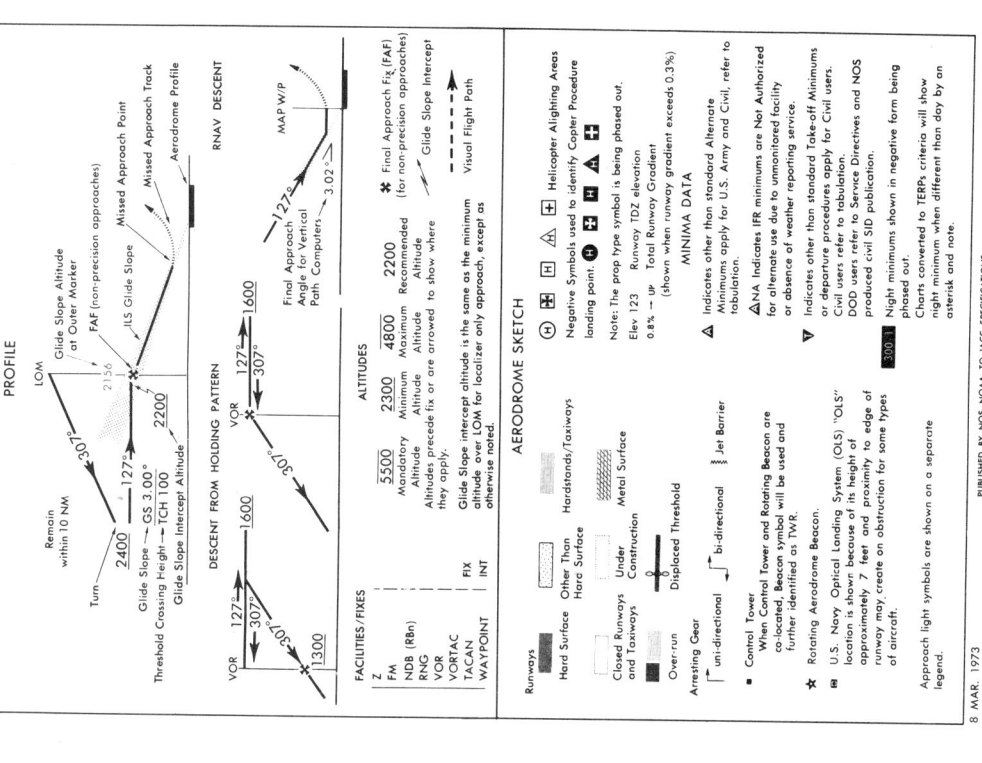

```
┌─────────────────────────────────────────────────────────────────────────┐
│             INSTRUMENT APPROACH PROCEDURES (CHARTS)                     │
│                      WESTERN UNITED STATES                              │
│           ▽ IFR TAKE-OFF MINIMUMS AND DEPARTURE PROCEDURES              │
│   FAR 91.116(c) prescribes take-off rules and establishes standard      │
│   take-off minimums as follows:                                         │
│   (1) Aircraft having two engines or less - one statute mile.           │
│   (2) Aircraft having more than two engines - one-half statute mile.    │
│   Aerodromes within this geographical area with IFR take-off minimums   │
│   other than standard are listed below alphabetically by aerodrome      │
│   name. Departure procedures and/or ceiling visibility minimums are     │
│   established to assist pilots conducting IFR flight in avoiding        │
│   obstructions during climb to the minimum enroute altitude.            │
│   Take-off minimums and departure procedures apply to all runways       │
│   unless otherwise specified.                                           │
├─────────────────────────────────────────────────────────────────────────┤
│ AERODROME NAME   TAKE-OFF MINIMUMS    AERODROME NAME   TAKE-OFF MINIMUMS│
├─────────────────────────────────────────────────────────────────────────┤
│                                                                         │
│  ARCATA ................. Rwy 1, 500-1   BERMUDA DUNES                  │
│  Arcata-Eureka, California  Rwy 13, 300-1  Bermuda Dunes, California    │
│                             Rwy 31, RVR/24  Rwy 29 turn right and cross │
│  Rwy 1, left turn within 1 NM.             airport SE bound. Climb      │
│  Rwy 13, right turn within 1 NM.           direct to TRM VORTAC         │
│  All aircraft climb on ACV R-178           continue climb on R-107      │
│  CW through R-291 to V27.                  within 10 NM to MCA for      │
│                                            direction of flight.         │
│                                                                         │
│  AURORA STATE                             BISBEE-DOUGLAS INTL           │
│   Aurora, Oregon                           Douglas, Arizona             │
│   Climb runway heading to 500 then         Climb to 5700 in holding     │
│   direct to UBG VORTAC before              pattern thence assigned      │
│   proceeding on course.                    route.                       │
└─────────────────────────────────────────────────────────────────────────┘
```

Fig. 60 Sample listing, IFR takeoff minimums and departure procedures for airports requiring other than standard minimums. (Standard minimums are: Aircraft having two engines or less—one statute mile. Aircraft having more than two engines—one-half statute mile).

with a computed approach speed of 130 knots would place the aircraft in Category C.

Aircraft/approach categories are as shown below:

APPROACH CATEGORY	SPEED/WEIGHT
A	50 - 90 knots, 30,000 lbs. or less
B	91 - 120 knots or 30,001 - 60,000 lbs.
C	121 - 140 knots or 60,001 - 150,000 lbs.
D	141 - 165 knots or over 150,000 lbs.
E	Speed over 165 knots, weight not considered.

IFR TAKEOFF MINIMUMS. Ceiling minimums are not prescribed for takeoff except for runways where a ceiling minimum is required to enable the pilot to see obstructions. Visibility minimums are:

- Aircraft having two engines or less - one statute mile.
- Aircraft having more than two engines one-half statute mile.

In cases where departure procedures or non-standard take-off minimums are prescribed, a symbol is shown on the chart indicating that the separate listing should be consulted. Figure 60 is an example of this listing.

ALTERNATE AIRPORT MINIMUMS specified for an instrument approach procedure require both ceiling and visibility minimums. FAR 91.83 established standard alternate minimums as follows:

- Precision approach procedure (ILS with glide slope or PAR): Ceiling 600 feet and visibility two statute miles.
- Non-precision approach procedure (NDB, VOR, LOC, VORTAC, VOR/DME or ASR), ceiling 800 feet and visibility two statute miles.

Airports that require alternate minimums other than standard or alternate minimums with restrictions are listed separately. These are denoted by a symbol (see Figures 63 and 63A) on the chart indicating that the separate listing (shown in Figure 61) should be consulted.

See FAR 91.83 for conditions whereby an alternate airport need NOT be listed in the IFR Flight Plan.

INOPERATIVE COMPONENTS OR VISUAL AIDS

When some components or aids of the system are inoperative or not utilized, generally higher minimums prevail. A separate table (Figure 62) is presented to aid in adjusting minimums when a ground component or visual aid is not utilized in the procedure.

INSTRUMENT APPROACH PROCEDURES (CHARTS)
WESTERN UNITED STATES
△ IFR ALTERNATE MINIMUMS
(Not applicable to USAF/USN)

Standard alternate minimums for nonprecision approaches are 800-2 (NDB, VOR, LOC, TACAN, LDA, VORTAC, VOR/DME or ASR); for precision approaches 600-2 (ILS or PAR). Aerodromes within this geographical area that require alternate minimums other than standard or alternate minimums with restrictions are listed below. NA- means IFR minimums are not authorized for alternate use due to unmonitored facility or absence of weather reporting service. U. S. Army pilots refer to Army Reg. 95-1 for additional application. Civil pilots see FAR 91.83. USAF/USN pilots refer to appropriate regulations.

AERODROME NAME	ALTERNATE MINIMUMS	AERODROME NAME	ALTERNATE MINIMUMS
ARCATA Arcata-Eureka, California	NDB-A, 1000-2	DERBY FIELD Lovelock, Nevada	VOR-A, 2000-2
BAKER MUNI Baker, Oregon *Category D, 1400-2	VOR-A, 1700-2 VOR/DME Rwy 12*	ELKO MUNI Elko, Nevada	VOR-A, 1800-2 VOR/DME-A 1200-2
BARSTOW-DAGGETT Daggett, California	VOR Rwy 21, 1400-2	EL MONTE El Monte, California *Categories C and D.	VOR-A, 1600-2*

Fig. 61 Sample listing, IFR alternate minimums for airports requiring other than standard minimums. - Standard minimums for non-precision approaches are 800-2 (NDB, VOR, LOC, TACAN, LDA, VORTAC, VOR/DME or ASR;) for precision approaches, 600-2 (ILS or PAR)].

INOPERATIVE COMPONENTS OR VISUAL AIDS TABLE   Civil pilots see FAR 91 117(c)

(1) ILS and PAR.

Inoperative Component or Aid	Increase DH	Increase Visibility	Approach Category
OM* MM*	50 feet	None	ABC
OM* MM*	50 feet	¼ mile	D
ALS	50 feet	¼ mile	ABCD
SALS, MALSR	50 feet	¼ mile	ABC

*Not applicable to PAR

(2) ILS with visibility minimum of 1,800 or 2,000 feet RVR.

Inoperative Component or Aid	Increase DH	Increase Visibility	Approach Category
OM MM	50 feet	To ½ mile	ABC
OM MM	50 feet	To ¾ mile	D
ALS	50 feet	To ¾ mile	ABCD
HIRL, TDZL, RCLS	None	To ½ mile	ABCD
RVR	None	To ½ mile	ABCD

(3) VOR, VOR/DME, LOC, LDA, and ASR.

Inoperative Visual Aid	Increase MDA	Increase Visibility	Approach Category
ALS, SALS, MALSR	None	½ mile	ABC
HIRL, MALS, REILS	None	¼ mile	ABC

(4) NDB (ADF) and RNG.

Inoperative Visual Aid	Increase MDA	Increase Visibility	Approach Category
ALS, MALSR	None	¼ mile	ABC

(5) LOC Approaches.

Inoperative Component or Aid	Increase MDA	Increase Visibility	Approach Category
ALS, MM	None	¼ mile	D

Fig. 62 Inoperative components or visual aids table. Landing minimums shown on Instrument Approach Procedure Charts are based on full operation of all components and visual aids. Higher minimums are required with inoperative components or visual aids.

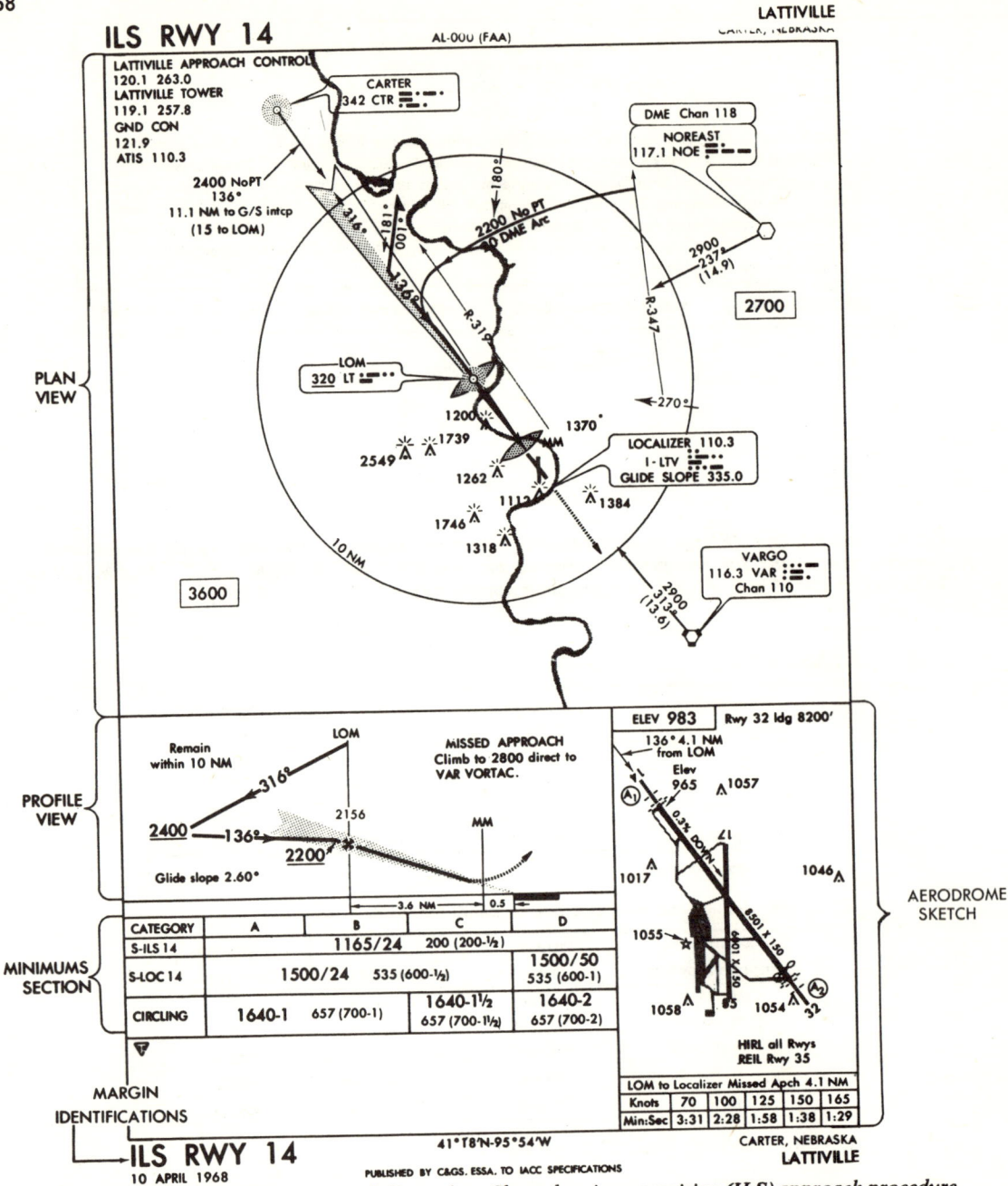

Fig. 63 Sample Instrument Approach Procedure Chart showing a precision (ILS) approach procedure. Explanations for the plan view, profile view, minimums, section and aerodrome sketch are shown in Figure 63A.

EXPLANATION OF THE INSTRUMENT APPROACH PROCEDURE CHARTS

To simplify the introduction to the charts, two typical Instrument Approach Procedure Charts are presented:

- Figure 63 shows a Precision Approach (electronic glide slope), an ILS approach to the airport at the fictitious city of Lattiville.
- Figure 64 shows a Non-Precision Approach (no electronic glide slope), a VOR approach to runway 12R at the fictitious city of Grenzell-West.

These same charts are then shown in their several segments (Figures 63A and 64A). At first glance, they may appear cluttered and complicated. Broken down into their various essential elements however, the charts will become less mysterious and present their information in a more simple manner than many other charts used routinely by pilots. Let's take portions of the charts and compare them individually with the legend sheets shown in Figures 58 and 59.

PRECISION APPROACH

Complete Explanation

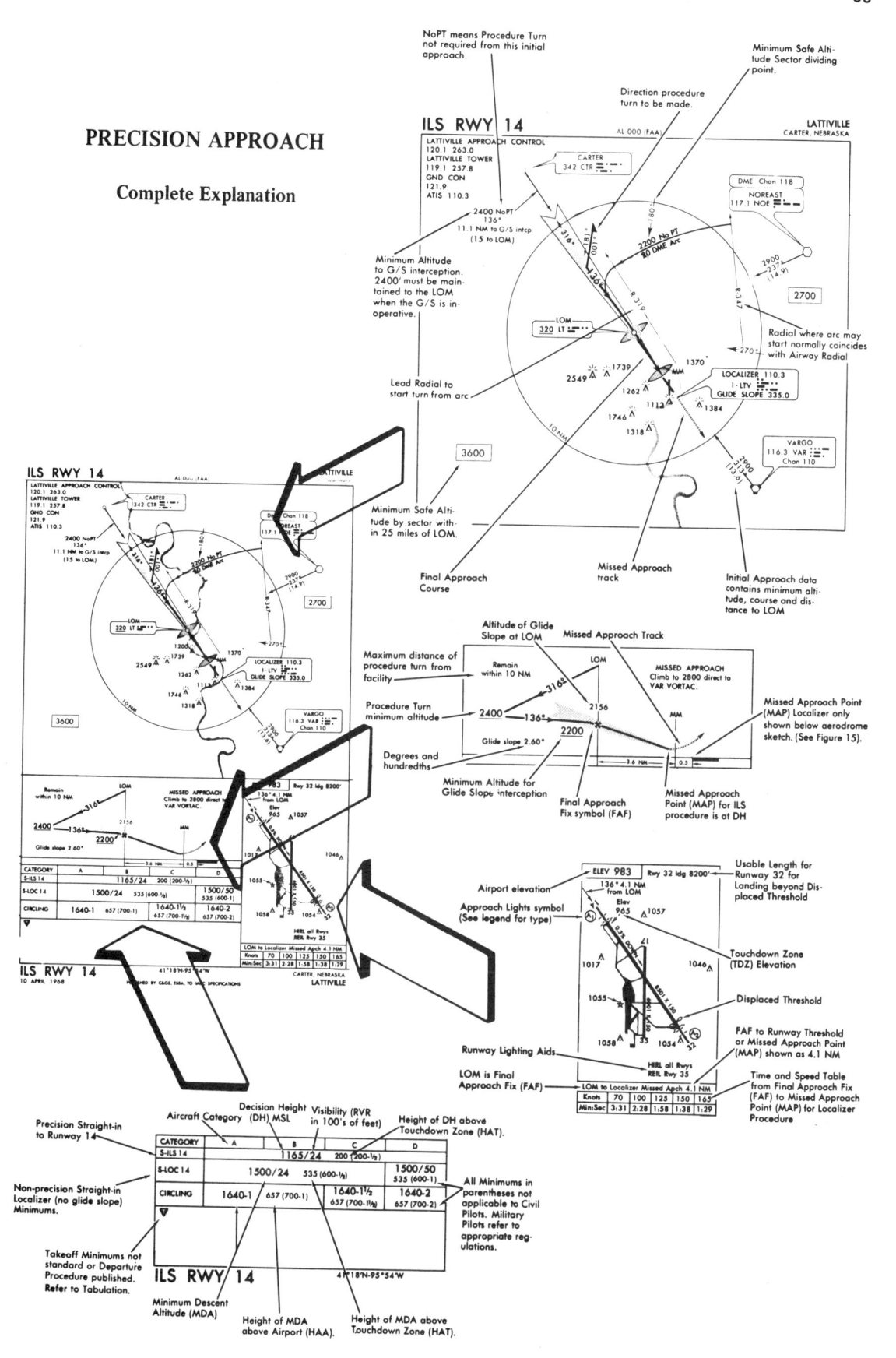

Fig. 63A Explanation of the precision approach procedure shown in Fig. 63.

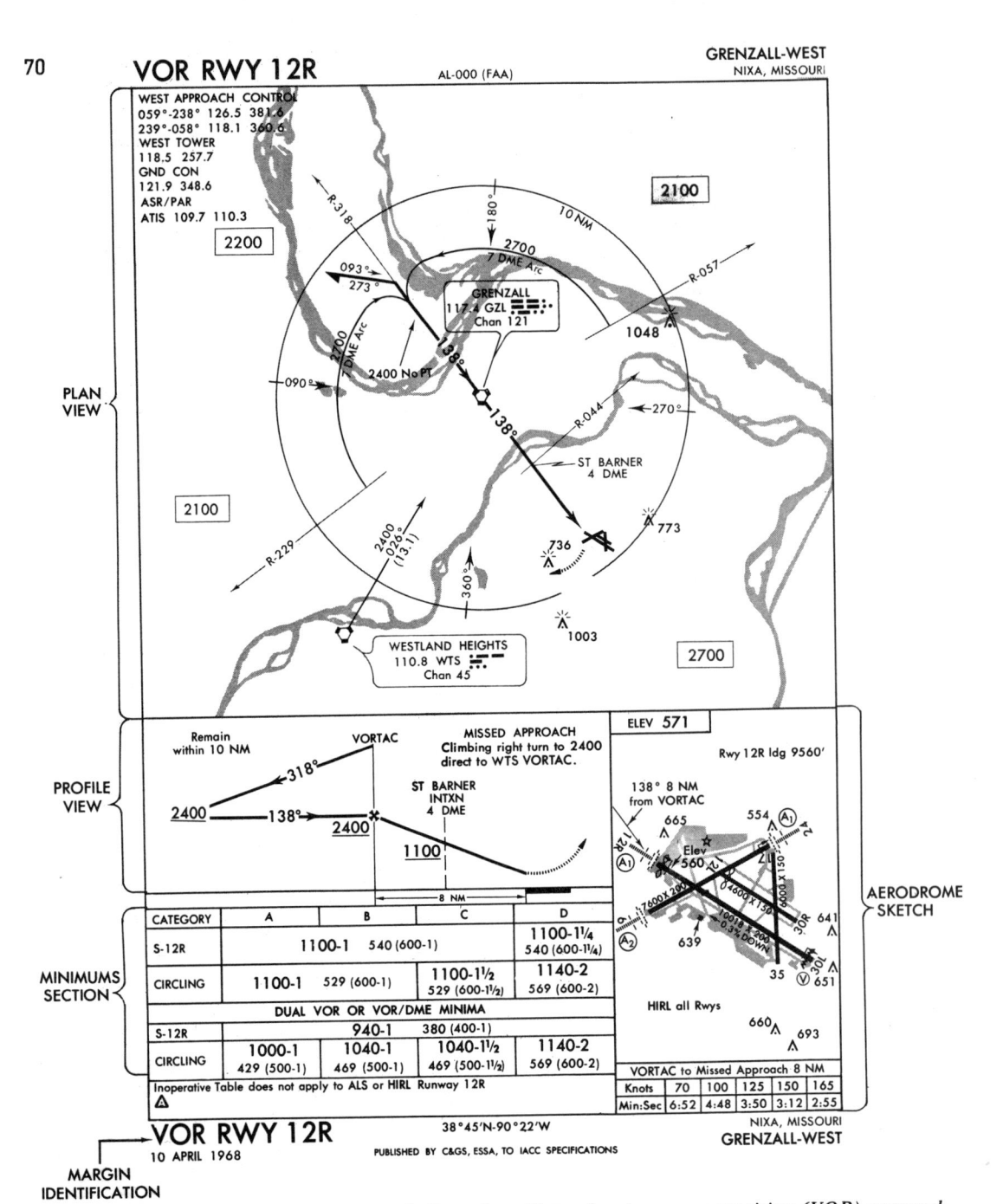

Fig. 64 Samplet Instrument Approach Procedure Chart showing a non-precision (VOR) approach procedure. Explanations for the plan view, profile view, minimums section and aerodrome sketch are shown in Fig. 64A.

MARGIN IDENTIFICATION indicates the type of chart (ILS, VOR, etc.), chart number, procedure number, airport name, its location and coordinates.

PLAN VIEW

Immediately under the top margin identification of the "Approach Plate" as the chart is commonly called, we find a plan (bird's eye) view of the prescribed approach itself (Figures 63 and 64). In addition to depiction of the aid to be used in the particular approach, other radio aids, communications frequencies, intersections, the airport itself, prominent obstructions, minimum safe altitudes, etc., are shown. The availability of radar is indicated below the communications information by the appropriate and applicable letters "ASR", "PAR", "ASR/PAR", or "RADAR VECTORING".

Figures 63A and 64A show the plan views with explanations, for precision and non-precision approaches respectively.

NON-PRECISION APPROACH

Complete Explanation

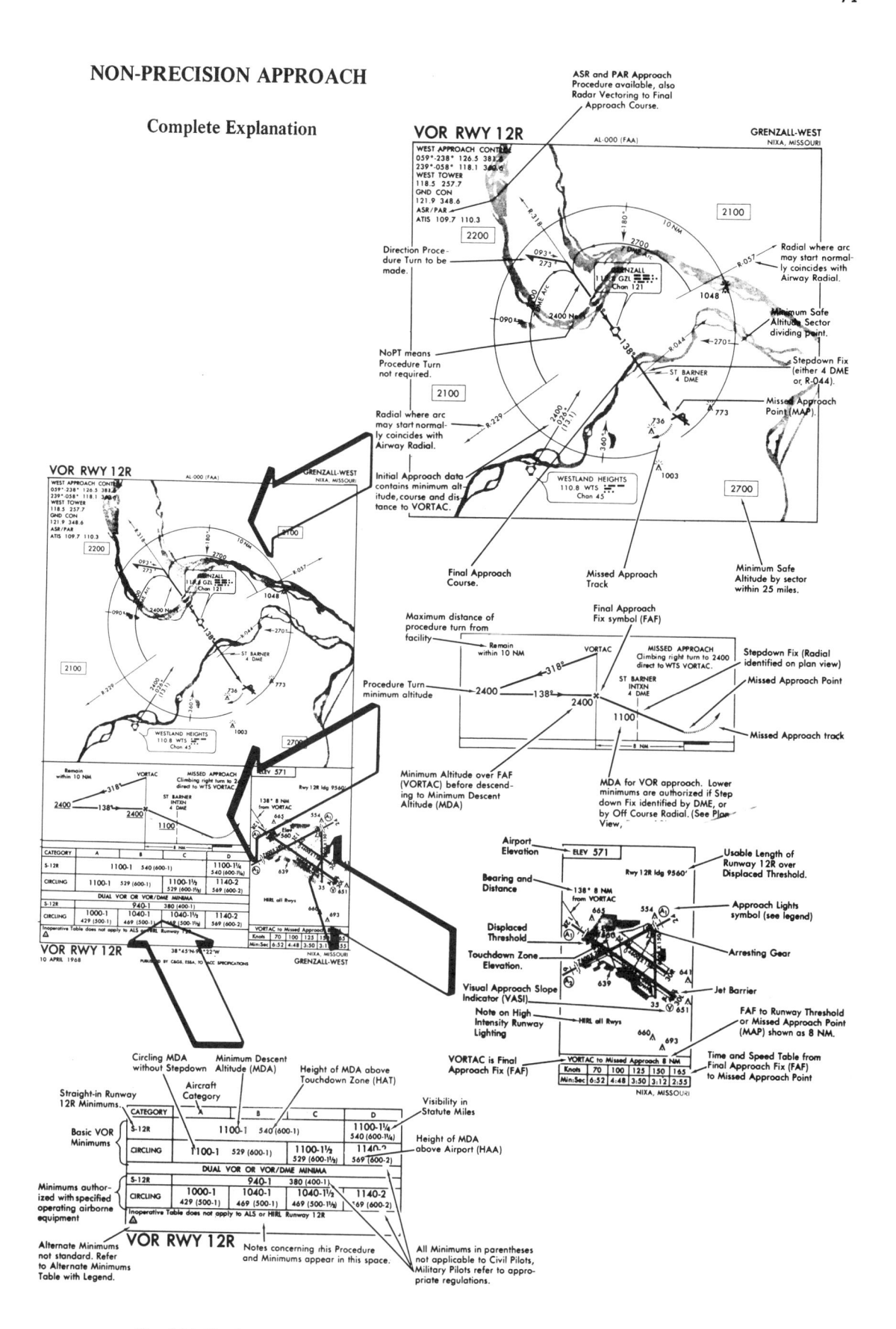

Fig. 64A Explanation of the non-precision approach procedure shown in Fig. 64.

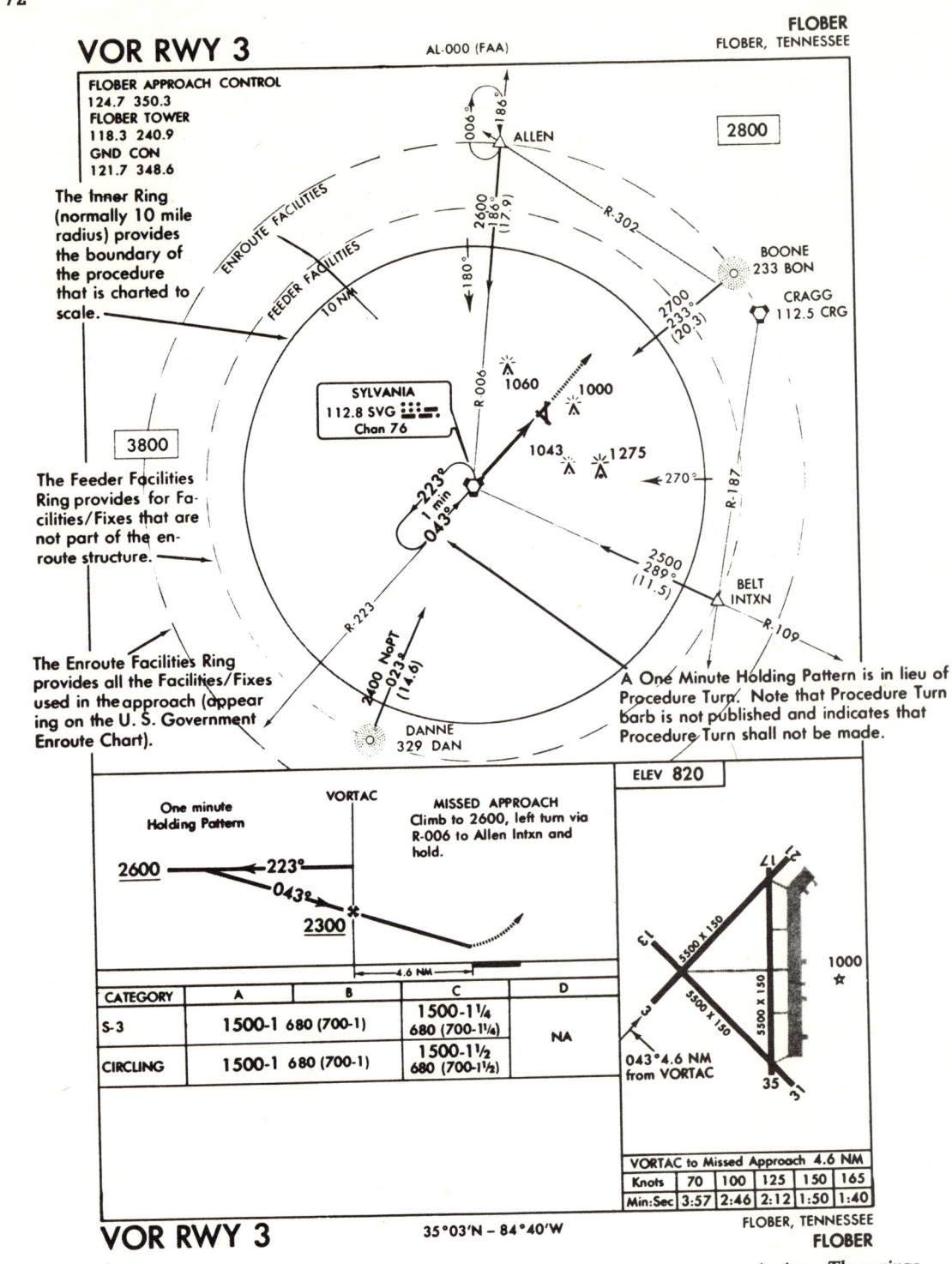

Fig. 65 Explanation of an Instrument Approach Procedure Chart showing concentric rings. These rings are used when it is necessary to chart facilities which lie beyond the chart area if the procedure was charted to scale.

CONCENTRIC RINGS

These rings are used when it is necessary to chart facilities which lie beyond the chart area if the procedure was charted to scale. The rings are normally centered on the Approach Facility. Figure 65 shows an explanation of a typical chart with concentric rings.

PROFILE OR SIDE VIEW

Directly under the plan view is a profile or side view of the approach, (Figures 63

MISSED APPROACH-EXAMPLES

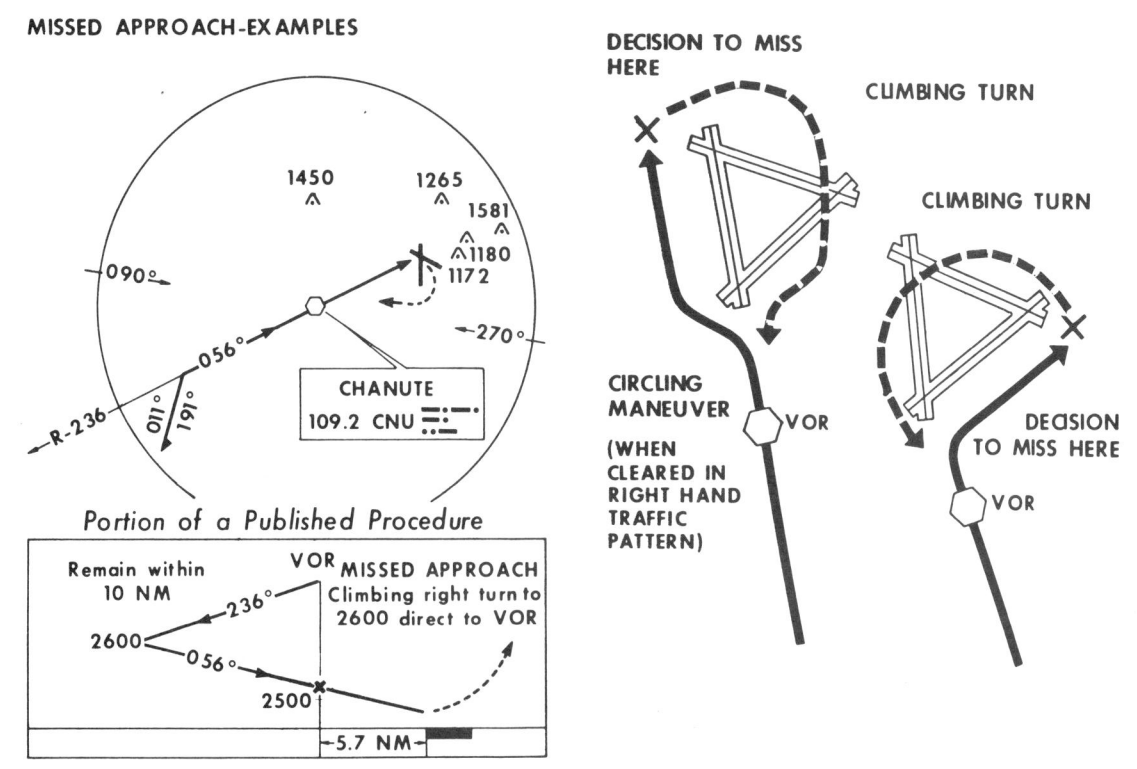

Fig. 66 Sample missed approach procedure from an Instrument Approach Procedure Chart and an example of its implementation.

and 64). We find this readily interpreted by referring to the symbol explanations on the legend sheets. Note that all altitudes prescribed here and anywhere else on the chart are above mean sea level (MSL). Figure 63A shows the profile view with explanations, for a precision approach (ILS) while Figure 64A presents the details of a nonprecision approach profile view.

MINIMUMS SECTION

Landing minimums have been previously discussed. Figures 58, 63A, and 64A show the minimums section together with explanations.

AIRPORT DATA

Airport information is conveniently shown as a plan view of the airport with data necessary for the instrument pilot. Figures 63A and 64A provide explanatory information.

MISSED APPROACH PROCEDURE

When a landing cannot be accomplished upon reaching the missed approach point defined on the approach procedure chart, the pilot must comply with the missed approach instructions for the procedure being used or with an alternate missed approach procedure specified by Air Traffic Control.

If visual reference is lost while circling to land from an instrument approach, the missed approach specified for that particular procedure must be followed (unless an alternate missed approach procedure is specified by Air Traffic Control). To become established on the prescribed missed approach course, the pilot should make an initial climbing turn toward the landing runway and continue the turn until he is established on the missed approach course. Inasmuch as the circling maneuver may be accomplished in more than one direction, different patterns will be required to become established on the prescribed missed approach course depending on the aircraft position at the time visual reference is lost. Adherence to the procedure, illustrated in Figure 66, will assure that an aircraft will remain within the circling and missed approach obstruction clearance areas.

At locations where ATC radar service is provided the pilot should disregard the published procedure and conform to radar vectors when provided by ATC.

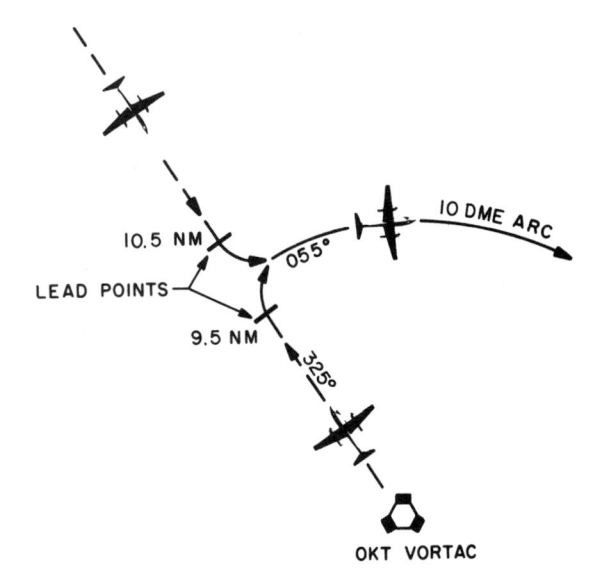

Fig. 67 Intercepting a DME arc. DME arcs are shown on the sample Instrument Approach Procedure Charts in Figures 63, 64, and 68.

FLYING DME ARCS

The FAA is publishing an increasing number of instrument approach procedures which incorporate DME arcs. The procedures and techniques given for intercepting and maintaining these arcs are applicable to any facility which provides DME information. Such a facility may or may not be collocated with the facility which provides final approach guidance.

Unless the pilot is highly proficient in the use of his airborne equipment and in performing a specific procedure, it is recommended that DME arcs be flown only when RMI equipment is available. (See Appendix for description of the RMI).

DME ARC INTERCEPTION. A DME arc interception of approximately 90° may be required when flying on a radial either inbound toward or outbound from a facility. Referring to Figure 67, follow these steps to intercept a 10 DME arc when outbound on a radial.

- Track outbound on the OKT 325° radial, frequently checking the DME mileage readout.
- For groundspeeds below 150 knots, a .5 NM lead is satisfactory.
- Upon reaching the lead point (9.5 NM) turn approximately 90° to the arc and set the OBS to 335°. The heading will be 055° in no-wind conditions.
- During the last part of the intercepting turn, monitor the DME closely. If it appears the arc is being undershot, roll out of the turn early. If the arc is being overshot, continue the turn past the originally-planned rollout point.

The procedure for intercepting an arc when inbound on a radial is basically the same, the leadpoint being 10.0 NM plus .5 NM or 10.5 NM.

MAINTAINING THE DME ARC. In flying the DME arc, it is important that the pilot keep a continuous mental picture of his position relative to the facility. Since the drift correction angle is constantly changing throughout the arc, wind orientation is important. In some cases, wind can be used in returning to the desired track. Arcs of large radii are easier to fly because of their "flat" curve. High groundspeeds require more pilot attention because of the higher rate of deviation and correction. Maintaining the arc is simplified by keeping slightly inside the curve. Thus, the arc is always turning toward the aircraft and interception may be accomplished by holding a straight course. If the aircraft is outside the curve, the arc is "turning away" and a greater correction is required.

With an RMI, in a no-wind condition, the pilot should theoretically be able to fly an exact circle around the facility by maintaining a relative bearing of 90° or 270°. In actual practice, a series of short legs are flown. To maintain the arc, proceed as follows:

- With the bearing pointer on the wing tip reference (90° or 270° position) and the aircraft at the desired DME range, maintain the heading and allow the bearing pointer to move 5° to 10° behind the wing tip. This will cause the range to increase slightly.
- Next, turn toward the facility to place the bearing pointer 5° to 10° ahead of the wing tip reference and maintain the heading until the pointer is again behind the wing tip. Continue this procedure to maintain the approximate arc.
- If a crosswind is blowing the aircraft away from the facility, establish the reference ahead of the wing tip. If a crosswind is blowing the aircraft toward the facility, establish the reference behind the wing tip.
- As a guide in making range corrections, change the relative bearing 10° to 20° for each ½ mile deviation from the desired arc. For example, under no-wind conditions, if the aircraft is ½ mile outside the arc and the bearing

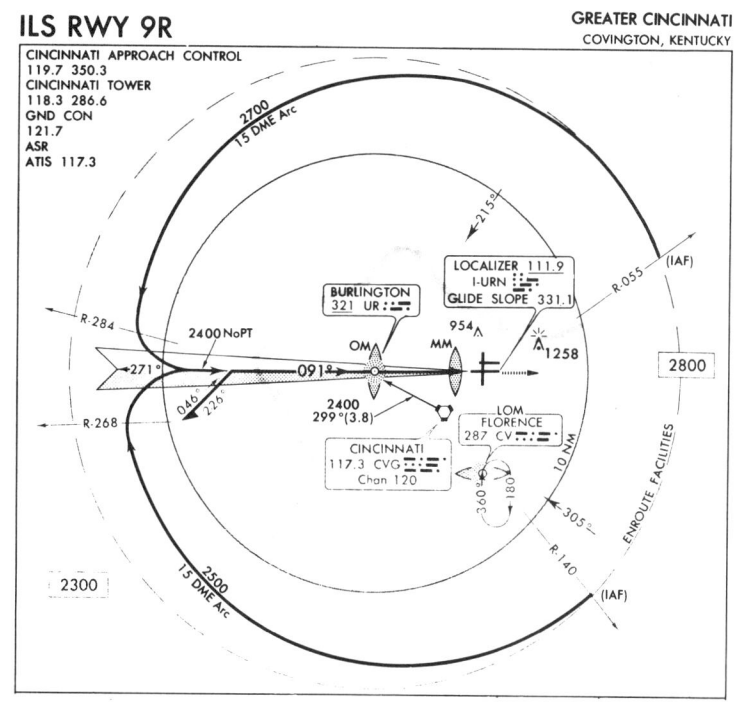

Fig. 68 Localizer interception from a DME arc.

pointer is on the wing tip reference, turn the aircraft 20° toward the facility to return to the arc.

Without an RMI, orientation is more difficult since the pilot does not have a direct azimuth reference. However, the procedure can be flown by using the OBS and CDI for azimuth information and the DME for arc distance.

Example (see Figure 67):
- If the rollout on the 055° heading places the aircraft on the arc, the DME will read 10.0 NM. If the CDI is centered (with the OBS set to 335°), the aircraft is crossing the 335° radial.
- If the CDI reads right of center and the DME reads 10.5 NM, the aircraft is outside (left) of the arc and approaching the 335° radial. Correct heading to the right and monitor the DME for closure with the arc.
- As the arc and the 335° radial are achieved, set the OBS ahead to 355° and correct heading 100° from the 335° radial (to a no-wind heading of 075°). Hold this heading until the 355° radial is crossed or the arc is intercepted. At this point, set the OBS ahead 20° and correct heading 100° from the radial the aircraft has intercepted. This techniqe will maintain a track slightly inside the desired arc (in no-wind conditions).

INTERCEPTING A RADIAL FROM A DME ARC. The lead will vary with arc radius and groundspeed. For the average general aviation aircraft flying arcs such as are depicted on most approach charts, at speeds of 150 knots or less, the lead will be under 5°. There is no essential difference between intercepting a radial from an arc and intercepting it from a straight course.
- With an RMI, the rate of bearing movement should be monitored closely while flying the arc. Set the course of the radial to be intercepted as soon as possible and determine the approximate lead radial. Upon reaching this point, start the intercepting turn.
- Without an RMI, the technique for radial interception is the same except for azimuth information, which is available only from the OBS and CDI.

INTERCEPTING A LOCALIZER FROM A DME ARC. The technique is similar to that described for intercepting a radial from an arc; however, lead radials are ALWAYS DEPICTED (Figure 68). At the lead radial, a pilot having a single VOR/LOCALIZER receiver should simultaneously begin his turn to the final approach course and set in the localizer frequency. With dual VOR/LOCALIZER receivers, one unit may be used to provide azimuth information and the other set to the localizer frequency.

FLYING THE INSTRUMENT APPROACH

An instrument approach is a series of precision maneuvers during which the pilot must be in complete command of his airplane. The previous sections discussed the flight procedures for all phases of radio navigation, including the instrument approach. The airspeeds, power settings, flap settings, and landing gear position should be pre-determined for all phases of the approach for the airplane you will be flying. The chart below shows the flight configuration for some representative airplanes. It is emphasized that this chart is merely a guide. Similar data should be determined for YOUR airplane. Refer to Figure 55 for the various phases of the approach.

It is recommended that the landing gear be extended (if flying a retractable) after completing procedure turn, on final approach and before reaching the final approach fix. An exception to this is an approach where the final approach facility is in excess of 5 miles from the airport. In this case, the landing gear can be extended after passing the final approach fix. For example, some VOR approaches are based on a VOR located 10 miles or more from the airport. Such an approach usually has weather minimums of 500 and 1 or greater and require a circling approach. Therefore, the gear can be extended in the pattern after visual contact with the airport.

SUMMARY

- Instrument approaches combine all procedures such as tracking, bearing interception, station passage, procedure turns, and holding together with precision letdown.

- Instrument approaches using VOR, ADF, and ILS follow the same basic flight procedures.

- Most VOR, ADF, and back course ILS approaches require weather minimums of 500 and 1 or better. A circling approach is usually required except for the back course ILS.

- An ILS approach at most airports can be used with weather minimums of 200 and ½. The ILS is always aligned with a runway for a "straight-in".

- Circling approaches are usually based on 500 and 1 weather minimums. Weather minimums for alternate airport instrument approaches are usually 800 and 1.

- Minimums as well as approach procedures can vary for individual airports due to many local conditions.

- In a radar environment, a procedure turn is not required.

- Radar vectoring is used to place the aircraft on the final approach course or on a heading allowing its interception at a 45 degree angle within approximately 3 miles from the final approach fix.

- When holding over the final approach fix, a procedure turn is not necessary when cleared for an approach.

- A pilot must be thoroughly familiar with the approach procedure charts.

- Flight data for all phases of an instrument approach such as procedure turn, holding, final approach, etc., should be pre-determined for an individual airplane. Airspeeds, power settings, flap position and when to let down the gear, should be set up.

Sample flight data for various airplanes during different phases of an instrument approach

	Aero Commander	Bonanza 35 (various models)	Beech 95 Travelaire	Cessna 310	Piper Apache	Piper Comanche 250
In Range Check	Normal Cruise	Normal Cruise	Normal Cruise	Normal Cruise	Normal Cruise	Normal Cruise
Initial Approach Decelerate at Level Flt. 500 fpm Descent	140 MPH 2500 RPM 19 in. M.P. 23 in. M.P. 17 in. M.P. 0° flap	120 MPH 2100 RPM 17 in. M.P. 19 in. M.P. 15 in. M.P. 0° flap	120 MPH 2400 RPM 16 in. M.P. 18 in. M.P. 14 in. M.P. 0° flap	120 MPH 2300 RPM 20 in. M.P. 22 in. M.P. 16 in. M.P. 15° flap	110 MPH 2100 RPM 23 in. M.P. 25 in. M.P. 21 in. M.P. 0° flap	120 MPH 2300 RPM 14 in. M.P. 16 in. M.P. 13 in. M.P. 0° flap
Procedure Turn Holding 500 fpm Descent	140 MPH 2500 RPM 23 in. M.P. 0° flap 17 in. M.P.	120 MPH 2100 RPM 19 in. M.P. 0° flap 15 in. M.P.	120 MPH 2400 RPM 18 in. M.P. 0° flap 14 in. M.P.	120 MPH 2300 RPM 22 in. M.P. 0° flap 16 in. M.P.	110 MPH 2100 RPM 25 in. M.P. 0° flap 21 in. M.P.	120 MPH 2300 RPM 16 in. M.P. 0° flap 13 in. M.P.
Final Approach Mixture Rich Level Gear Up Gear Dwn. 500 fpm Gear Up Descent Gear Dwn.	140 MPH 2500 RPM 23 in. M.P. 25 in. M.P. 0° flap 17 in. M.P. 21 in. M.P.	120 MPH 2100 RPM 19 in. M.P. 21 in. M.P. 0° flap 15 in. M.P. 17 in. M.P.	120 MPH 2400 RPM 18 in. M.P. 20 in. M.P. 0° flap 14 in. M.P. 16 in. M.P.	120 MPH 2300 RPM 22 in. M.P. 24 in. M.P. 15° flap 16 in. M.P. 18 in. M.P.	110 MPH 2100 RPM 25 in. M.P. 27 in. M.P. 0° flap 21 in. M.P. 23 in. M.P.	120 MPH 2300 RPM 16 in. M.P. 18 in. M.P. 0° flap 13 in. M.P. 15 in. M.P.
Final Letdown Gear Down 500 fpm Descent	120 MPH 2750 RPM 21 in. M.P. 15° flap	110 MPH 2400 RPM 12 in. M.P. 15° flap	110 MPH 2400 RPM 14 in. M.P. 15° flap	110 MPH 2300 RPM 16 in. M.P. 15° flap	105 MPH 2400 RPM 18 in. M.P. 20° flap	110 MPH 2300 RPM 14 in. M.P. 20° flap

"NOTE: All performance data shown are to be used as a guide only. Values will vary with altitude, gross weight, and individual airplane configuration. The applicable airplane flight manual should be consulted to set up approach procedures for a particular airplane and operating conditions."

7 AIRWAYS AND AIR TRAFFIC CONTROL (ATC)

Although the "aerial highways" or airways are used extensively during VFR conditions, the airway and associated traffic control system is designed for use during instrument weather. Under these conditions, the pilot must avoid collision with other aircraft, mountains, TV towers, and other obstructions. He must fly accurately to his airport of destination. Finally, the pilot must leave the relative safety of higher altitudes and descend with precision to a pinpoint of the earth's surface — the airport. All of this must be accomplished without being able to see either ground or sky and at speeds ranging from 90 to 600 or even more, miles per hour.

The airway and air traffic control system is used under both VFR and IFR conditions by general aviation, airlines, and the military. Thus, it is flexible enough to accommodate airplanes from a Cessna 150 to a Boeing 707 or B-52. The main purpose of this complex and versatile system is to provide air transportation with all weather capabilities. This is accomplished by providing:

- An "aerial highway" or airway system for navigating from one place to another as well as letdown and approaches to land, under both VFR and IFR conditions.
- An air traffic control system used dur- IFR conditions to provide separation between aircraft flying the airways and prevent collisions.

THE AIRWAYS SYSTEM

Two route systems have been established for air navigational purposes in the contiguous 48 states; the VOR System and the Jet Route System. The Jet Route System consists of jet routes established from 18,000 feet MSL and will not be extensively discussed in this publication.

The VOR airways are predicated solely on VOR/VORTAC navigation aids and are depicted on aeronautical charts by a "V" ("Victor") followed by the airway number, e.g. V12. These airways are numbered similar to U. S. highways. As in the highway numbering system, a segment of an airway which is common to two or more routes carries the numbers of all of the airways which coincide for that segment. When such is the case, a pilot in filing a flight plan needs to indicate only that airway number of the route which he is using. Alternate airways are identified by their location with respect to the associated main airway. "Victor 9 West" indicates an alternate airway associated with, and lying to the west of, Victor 9.

The VOR Airway System consists of airways designated from 1200 feet, above the surface (or in some instances higher) to, but not including, 18,000 feet MSL. These airways are depicted on Enroute Low Altitude Charts — U.S. Series L-1 through L-28.

Portions of Enroute Low Altitude Charts, together with a legend, are shown in the Appendix. These charts contain a wealth of information and should be thoroughly studied by the student instrument pilot.

AIR TRAFFIC CONTROL SYSTEM

During instrument weather conditions and/or aircraft on IFR flight plan, all air traffic using the airway system is controlled by one or more Air Route Traffic Control Centers, commonly referred to as "Center." The continental U.S. is divided into 22 areas, each controlled by a "Center" such as "Oakland Center" or "Los Angeles Center." Each center is in turn subdivided into "sectors." See Figure 69.

Headquarters for a center is a large building in the general vicinity of a large city. Each center is a massive radar and communications complex employing up to 200 controllers, not counting general administrative and maintenance personnel. Ground communications links (telephone and teletype) connect each center with other centers, civil airport control towers, military airports, and Flight Service Stations (FSS). In addition, each center has a series of radio communication frequencies assigned to each sector, for communication with IFR aircraft. Most of these frequencies are transmitted and received from a remote site, thus a pilot can be in continuous VHF radio communication with a center although he may be 300 miles from its geographical location.

Centers also are equipped with Air Route Surveillance Radar (ARSR). This long range radar is normally used for controlling enroute traffic in heavy traffic areas. The entire area controlled by a center is generally not under radar coverage.

DEPARTURE AND APPROACH CONTROL

"Center" controls all enroute traffic flying the airways. The transition of an aircraft after take-off to the airway system is handled by "Departure Control." Conversely, transition of an aircraft from the airway system to an approach facility as well as control of the approach itself, is handled by "Approach Control."

DEPARTURE CONTROL

While an airplane is taxiing prior to take-off, it is on "Ground Control." Just prior to take-off and during the take-off run "Tower" takes over, while approximately "over the fence," "Departure Control" is in charge. These are all on different communications frequencies.

Departure Control is normally located in the airport control tower. The job of Departure Control is to guide the aircraft from the airport to the enroute airway system. In a radar equipped area, this is accomplished by providing the pilot with heading information so he can intercept the appropriate airway. In a non-radar area a more or less elaborate departure clearance may be given such as "AFTER TAKE-OFF, TURN LEFT AND PROCEED DIRECT TO JACKSON VORTAC BEFORE PROCEEDING ON COURSE."

When the aircraft is established on the airway, the pilot is normally told to contact the center on a particular communications frequency.

APPROACH CONTROL

On the last leg of an enroute airway, usually approximately 10 minutes prior to arriving at a "fix" (a VOR/VORTAC or intersection) near the pilot's destination airport, "center" will tell the pilot to contact "approach control" on the appropriate frequency. Approach control is normally also located in the control tower. If radar is used, approach control is usually in a darkened room just below the tower. The purpose of approach control is to guide the aircraft to the approach facility (usually the ILS). In a radar area this is again accomplished by providing the pilot with heading information to place the aircraft on the final approach course of the particular approach procedure in use.

SUMMARY — AIRWAYS AND AIR TRAFFIC CONTROL (ATC)

INSTRUMENT FLIGHT REQUIRES:
- Airways for navigating without visual reference to the ground.
- An Air Traffic Control System to prevent collision between aircraft.

AIRWAY SYSTEM
- "VICTOR" airways based on VOR/VORTAC.
- Airway system (below 18,000 feet MSL) is depicted on Enroute Low Altitude Charts.
- "JET ROUTE SYSTEM" begins at 18,000 feet.

AIR TRAFFIC CONTROL SYSTEM
- "DEPARTURE CONTROL" guides IFR aircraft from airport to airway system.
- AIR ROUTE TRAFFIC CONTROL (ARTC) "CENTER" controls enroute traffic on airway system.
- "APPROACH CONTROL" guides aircraft from airway system to approach facility.

80

Fig. 69 A typical Air Route Traffic Control Center (ARTCC).

AIR TRAFFIC CONTROL (ATC) PROCEDURES 8

When weather conditions are below VFR minimums, all traffic within a control zone or control area must be controlled by ATC to prevent collisions. What is "ATC"? This is an abbreviation for the Air Traffic Control Service of the Federal Aviation Administration (FAA). Depending on the location of the aircraft, "ATC" can be any one of these facilities:
- Airport Control Tower
- Departure Control
- Flight Service Station (FSS)
- Air Route Traffic Control Center ("Center")
- Approach Control

ATC must know the location of all IFR aircraft at all times when within controlled airspace. Proper separation between aircraft must be maintained to assure safety. Separation is maintained in a number of ways or a combination of them:
- Altitude Separation
- Radar Separation
- If radar is not available, ATC effects separation by providing a minimum time interval between aircraft on the same course; and by assigning different flight paths.

During IFR flight the aircraft is in direct radio contact with ATC through the appropriate communications frequency, at all times. In fact, the pilot must maintain a "listening watch" throughout the flight in order to receive any message pertinent to his flight. During each flight, the pilot will be requested to change communications frequencies frequently. Thus, a full complement of transmitting and receiving frequencies in the aircraft, considerably facilitates IFR flight. If communications channels are limited, ATC can call an aircraft through most navigational aids such as VOR/VORTAC and ILS.

FLIGHT PLAN

Prior to departure from within, or prior to entering a control area or control zone, a pilot must submit a complete flight plan (and receive an air traffic clearance), if weather conditions are below VFR minimum. Instrument flight plans are submitted to the nearest Flight Service Station or airport traffic control tower either in person or by telephone (or by radio if no other means are available). Pilots should file IFR flight plans at least 30 minutes prior to estimated time of departure to preclude possible delay in receiving a departure clearance from ATC. When filing a flight plan for flight in an aircraft equipped with a radar beacon transponder and/or DME, this capability should be so stated. A sample flight plan is shown in Figure 99.

ATC CLEARANCE

A "clearance" is an authorization by ATC for the purpose of preventing collision between known aircraft, for an aircraft to proceed under specified traffic conditions within controlled air space. After filing the flight plan, the initial clearance is usually issued to the pilot by radio while on the ground at his departure airport, after engine runup. Normal procedure is shown by example:

Aircraft: (On ground control frequency 121.9 or 121.7 MHz.) "GROUND CONTROL THIS IS BEECHCRAFT ONE THREE ONE FIVE NINER ON WEST RAMP. READY TO TAXI, INSTRUMENT FLIGHT TO ST. LOUIS, OVER."

Ground Control: "BEECHCRAFT ONE THREE ONE FIVE NINER(RUNWAY ONE SIX, WIND ONE SEVEN ZERO DEGREES AT ONE FIVE, ALTIMETER THREE ZERO FOUR, TIME ONE FOUR TWO SIX GREENWICH. TAXI NORTH HOLD SHORT OF RUNWAY ONE SIX."

After completing the pre-flight check (or before, if conditions are such that a clearance can be accepted while taxiing), the clearance will be issued by Ground Control. (At busy locations, however, pilots may be instructed by the ground controller to "CONTACT CLEARANCE DELIVERY" on a frequency designated for this purpose.)

Example:

Ground Control: "BEECHCRAFT ONE THREE FIVE NINER CLEARED TO ST. LOUIS LAMBERT FIELD VIA VICTOR NINER MAINTAIN EIGHT THOUSAND. AFTER TAKEOFF PRO-

CEED DIRECT TO THE JACKSON VORTAC."
Aircraft: "BEECHCRAFT ONE THREE FIVE NINER CLEARED TO ST. LOUIS LAMBERT FIELD VIA VICTOR NINER, MAINTAIN EIGHT THOUSAND. AFTER TAKEOFF PROCEED DIRECT TO THE JACKSON VORTAC, OVER,"
Ground Control: "CLEARANCE CORRECT."

Unless a delay is experienced, Ground Control will advise the pilot to change to tower frequency for take-off clearance.

A clearance will generally be given to a pilot as filed, if possible; however, due to traffic conditions, different altitudes and/or different routing will be given by ATC. For many reasons (such as altitude too high for his airplane) a pilot may not wish to accept a clearance different than he filed. If so, ATC should be advised; however a time delay can be expected while a new clearance is being processed. A clearance usually consists of two parts:
- Enroute (altitude and routing)
- Departure instructions to establish the aircraft on the airway system and provide traffic separation in the local airport conjested traffic area.

In a radar area departure instructions (issued by Departure Control) require the pilot to maintain heading and altitudes as given by the controller. In a non-radar area, more or less elaborate departure instructions may be given.

During the flight, the initial clearance issued to the pilot prior to departure may be changed at any time by ATC to facilitate safe and orderly traffic flow.

STANDARD INSTRUMENT DEPARTURES (SIDS)

A standard Instrument Departure (SID) is an air traffic control coded departure routing which has been established at certain airports to simplify clearance delivery procedures.

Pilots of aircraft operating from locations where SID procedures are effective may expect ATC clearances containing a SID. Use of a SID requires pilot possession of at least the textual description of the approved effective SID. If the pilot does not possess a preprinted SID description or for any other reason does not wish to use a SID, he is expected to advise ATC. Notification may be accomplished by filing "NO SID" in the remarks section of the filed flight plan or by the less desirable method of verbally advising ATC.

All effective SIDs are published in textual and graphic form by the National Ocean Survey in East and West SID booklets.

HOLDING

As explained in Chapter 5, holding is a procedure available to ATC to delay an aircraft so that it does not proceed beyond a certain location. Holding consists of a "race track" pattern about a fix, usually a VOR/VORTAC or an intersection, however, holding can be accomplished over a radio beacon, L/MF range, or the ILS outer marker.

Detailed holding procedures are discussed in Chapter 5.

STANDARD TERMINAL ARRIVAL ROUTES (STARS)

A standard terminal arrival route (STAR) is an air traffic control coded instrument flight rules (IFR) arrival route established for application to arriving IFR aircraft destined for certain airports. Its purpose is to simplify clearance delivery procedures.

Pilots of IFR aircraft destined to locations for which STARs have been published may be issued a clearance containing a Star whenever ATC deems it appropriate.

Use of STARs requires pilot possession of at least the approval textual description. As with any ATC clearance or portion thereof, it is the responsibility of each pilot to accept or refuse an issued STAR. A pilot should notify ATC if he does not wish to use STAR by placing "NO STAR" in the remark section of the flight plan or by the less desirable method of verbally stating the same to ATC.

STARs are published in textual and graphic form by the National Ocean Survey in a bound booklet.

ROUTE OF FLIGHT

It is vitally important that the route of flight be accurately determined and described in the flight plan to permit accurate plotting and planning by ATC.

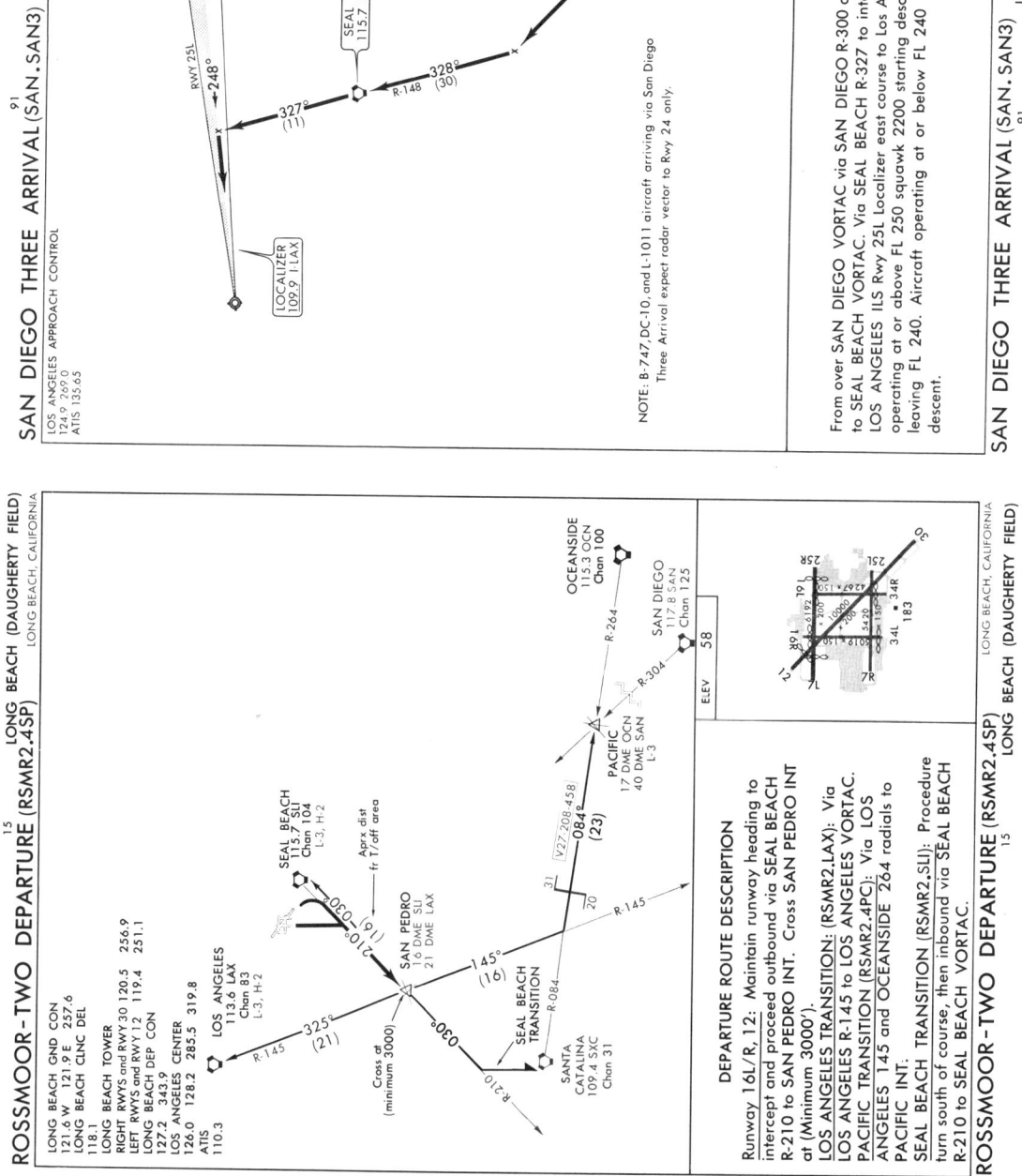

SAN DIEGO THREE ARRIVAL (SAN.SAN3)
LOS ANGELES INTERNATIONAL
LOS ANGELES, CALIFORNIA

LOS ANGELES APPROACH CONTROL
124.9 269.0
ATIS 135.65

NOTE: Chart not to scale

NOTE: B-747, DC-10, and L-1011 aircraft arriving via San Diego Three Arrival expect radar vector to Rwy 24 only.

From over SAN DIEGO VORTAC via SAN DIEGO R-300 and SEAL BEACH R-148 to SEAL BEACH VORTAC. Via SEAL BEACH R-327 to intercept and proceed via LOS ANGELES ILS Rwy 25L Localizer east course to Los Angeles Airport. Aircraft operating at or above FL 250 squawk 2200 starting descent, then squawk 1500 leaving FL 240. Aircraft operating at or below FL 240 squawk 1500 starting descent.

SAN DIEGO THREE ARRIVAL (SAN.SAN3)
LOS ANGELES, CALIFORNIA
LOS ANGELES INTERNATIONAL

Fig. 71 *A sample Standard Terminal Arrival Chart (STAR).*

ROSSMOOR-TWO DEPARTURE (RSMR2.4SP)
LONG BEACH (DAUGHERTY FIELD)
LONG BEACH, CALIFORNIA

LONG BEACH GND CON
121.6 W 121.9 E 257.6
LONG BEACH CLNC DEL
118.1
LONG BEACH TOWER
RIGHT RWYS and RWY 30 120.5 256.9
LEFT RWYS and RWY 12 119.4 251.1
LONG BEACH DEP CON
127.2 343.9
LOS ANGELES CENTER
126.0 128.2 285.5 319.8
ATIS
110.3

DEPARTURE ROUTE DESCRIPTION

Runway 16L/R, 12: Maintain runway heading to intercept and proceed outbound via SEAL BEACH R-210 to SAN PEDRO INT. Cross SAN PEDRO INT at (Minimum 3000').
LOS ANGELES TRANSITION: (RSMR2.LAX): Via LOS ANGELES R-145 to LOS ANGELES VORTAC.
PACIFIC TRANSITION (RSMR2.4PC): Via LOS ANGELES 145 and OCEANSIDE 264 radials to PACIFIC INT.
SEAL BEACH TRANSITION (RSMR2.SLI): Procedure turn south of course, then inbound via SEAL BEACH R-210 to SEAL BEACH VORTAC.

ROSSMOOR-TWO DEPARTURE (RSMR2.4SP)
LONG BEACH, CALIFORNIA
LONG BEACH (DAUGHERTY FIELD)

Fig. 70 *A sample Standard Instrument Departure Chart (SID).*

Example: 7000 MSPV97 V171 V8 MDW
Spelled out: Requesting 7000 feet from Minneapolis St. Paul International Victor 97, Victor 171, Victor 8 to Chicago Midway.

ALTITUDE REQUIREMENTS

Aircraft operating in accordance with IFR must be flown at not less than the minimum altitude established for that portion of the route over which the operation is conducted. These minimums are shown on the Enroute Low Altitude Charts such as:
  MEA, Minimum Enroute Altitude
  MOCA, Minimum Obstruction Clearance Altitude
  MRA, Minimum Reception Altitude
  MCA, Minimum Crossing Altitude

If no minimum has been established (such as for an off-airways flight between two VOR/VORTAC stations), flight must be conducted at not less than 1000 feet above the highest obstacle within a horizontal distance of five statute miles from the center of the course to be flown. However, in those areas designated as mountainous areas, a clearance of 2000 feet must be maintained.

Unless otherwise specified by ATC, aircraft which will change to a higher or lower altitude while enroute should normally begin climb or descent immediately after passing the fix beyond which the new enroute altitude will be used. An exception to this is where the aircraft is being flown at an enroute altitude below the minimum crossing altitude (MCA) established for the fix. In this case, climb should begin prior to reaching the fix so as to cross the fix at the established crossing altitude or at a higher altitude if specified in the ATC clearance.

ATC clearance will normally require the pilot to "MAINTAIN" a specified altitude. Thus, altitude changes cannot be made without further ATC clearance.

The term "CRUISE" may be used instead of "MAINTAIN" to signify to the pilot that descent from cruising altitude may be commenced at his discretion without further clearance from ATC. "CRUISE" is normally used only for relatively short flights in uncongested areas and is authorization for the flight to proceed to, and make an approach at, destination.

AIRCRAFT CLIMBING/DESCENDING

During any phase of flight, pilots are requested to adhere to the following procedures whenever cleared by ATC to descend or climb to an altitude.
- If an altitude change of 1000 feet or less is required, descend or climb at a rate of not more than 500 feet per minute; or
- If an altitude change of more than 1000 feet is required, descend or climb as rapidly as practicable to 1000 feet above or below the assigned altitude and then at a rate of not more than 500 feet per minute until assigned altitude is reached.

POSITION REPORTING

The safety and effectiveness of traffic control depends to a large extent on accurate position reporting. In order to provide the proper separation and expedite aircraft movements, ATC must be able to make accurate estimates of the progress of every aircraft operating on an IFR flight plan.

Pilots are required to maintain a continuous listening watch on the appropriate frequency and furnish position reports as indicated by symbols on the Enroute Charts. The designated reporting point is the solid triangle (▲). These are usually VOR/VORTAC stations but may be intersections of VOR/VORTAC radials and/or airways. The "on-request" reporting point is an open triangle (△). Reports over an "on-request" reporting point are only necessary when requested by ATC.

Position reports should include the following items:
- Identification
- Position   ⎫ "PTA" will help
- Time   ⎬ remember this
- Altitude   ⎭
- Type of flight plan (not required if IFR position reports made direct to ARTC Centers or approach control)
- ETA over next reporting point
- The name only of the next succeeding reporting point along the route of flight
- Pertinent remarks

Example:
An aircraft operating along Victor Airway 30 between Pittsburgh and Minneapolis

would make the following report when over Litchfield, Michigan:

"NOVEMBER NINER TWO ONE XRAY OVER LITCHFIELD FIVE SIX AT EIGHT THOUSAND INSTRUMENT FLIGHT PLAN ESTIMATING PULLMAN ONE FOUR ONE EIGHT MILWAUKEE."

A corrected estimate should be forwarded to ATC any time that it becomes apparent that an estimate as previously submitted is in error in excess of *three* minutes.

The following reports should be made to ATC or FSS facilities without request:
- The time and altitude reaching a holding fix or point to which cleared.
- When vacating any previously assigned altitude for a newly assigned altitude.
- When leaving any assigned holding fix or point.
- When leaving final approach fix inbound on final approach.
- When an approach has been missed. (Request clearance for specific action, i.e., to alternate airport, another approach, etc.)

Pilots encountering weather conditions which have not been forecast, or hazardous conditions which have been forecast, shall forward a report of such weather to ATC.

POSITION REPORTING IN A RADAR ENVIRONMENT

When informed by ATC that their aircraft is in "RADAR CONTACT," pilots will discontinue position reports over compulsory reporting points and monitor normal ATC communications frequencies. Pilots shall resume normal position reporting when ATC advises "RADAR CONTACT LOST" or "RADAR SERVICE TERMINATED."

DIRECT COMMUNICATIONS- CONTROLLERS/PILOTS

Air Traffic Control facilities are equipped with radio transmitters and receivers for direct communications with IFR traffic on certain VHF frequencies. These frequencies normally are published on appropriate enroute charts. Aircraft operating on IFR flight plans shall maintain a listening watch on one of the following frequencies unless otherwise advised by ATC.
- 122.1 transmit, receive on VOR frequency
- ARTC ("Center"), transmit and receive on discrete frequency as directed.

As explained previously, a pilot may be in direct contact with the ARTC Center. An ARTC Center is divided into sectors; each sector is handled by one controller or team of controllers and has its own sector discrete frequency. As an IFR flight progresses from one sector to another, the pilot is requested to change to the appropriate sector discrete frequency.

SUMMARY-AIR TRAFFIC CONTROL (ATC) PROCEDURES

WHAT IS "ATC?"
- Depending on location of aircraft, "ATC" can be:
  - Airport Control Tower
  - Departure Control
  - Flight Service Station (FSS)
  - ARTC "Center"
  - Approach Control

ATC MAINTAINS SEPARATION OF IFR TRAFFIC BY:
- Altitude Separation
- Radar Separation
- If radar not available, separation is provided by minimum time interval between aircraft or assigning different flight paths.

FLIGHT PLAN
- Prior to departure from within, or prior to entering a control area or control zone, a pilot must submit a complete flight plan (and receive an air traffic clearance) if weather is below VFR minimums.

ATC "CLEARANCE"
- "CLEARANCE" is authorization by ATC to proceed under specific conditions within controlled airspace.
- Issued for purpose of preventing collision between aircraft.
- Provides separation only between IFR flights.

ALTITUDE REQUIREMENTS
- Minimum altitudes specified on Enroute, Low Altitude Charts.

- Enroute altitude changes should normally begin after passing the fix beyond which new altitudes will be used, except:
  - Where minimum crossing altitude (MCA) is established for the fix.
- ATC clearance will normally require pilot to "MAINTAIN" specified altitude. ATC clearance must be obtained for altitude changes.
- "CRUISE" may be used instead of "MAINTAIN" for short flights. Pilot can begin descent without further ATC clearance.

AIRCRAFT CLIMBING/DESCENDING

- For altitude changes less than 1000 feet climb/descend at 500 feet per minute.
- For altitude changes greater than 1000 feet, climb/descend as rapidly as practicable to within 1000 feet of assigned altitude, then 500 feet per minute.

POSITION REPORTING

- Compulsory reporting points shown on Enroute Low Altitude Charts by symbol (▲)) These are normally VOR/VORTAC stations and intersections.
- Position report should include:
  - Identification
  - Position ⎫
  - Time   ⎬ "PTA"
  - Altitude ⎭
  - IFR Flight Plan (not required when in Direct Contact with Center)
  - ETA over next reporting point
  - Name only of next succeeding reporting point
- Corrected estimate should be forwarded to ATC when previous estimate is expected to be in error in excess of *three minutes*.
- Following reports should be made to ATC without request:
  - Time and altitude reaching a hold-fix to which cleared
  - Vacating previously assigned altitude for newly assigned altitude
  - Leaving assigned holding fix
  - Leaving approach fix inbound on final approach
  - When approach has been missed.

DIRECT COMMUNICATIONS-CONTROLLERS/PILOTS

- Pilots must maintain "listening watch on assigned frequencies

HOLDING

- Race track pattern about a fix used by ATC to delay aircraft

AVIATION WEATHER FOR THE INSTRUMENT PILOT 9

Although meteorology is a subject by itself, a minimum weather knowledge is required of a pilot. At least he must be able to read and interpret weather data available to him at the Weather Bureau and apply it to his flight consistent with his equipment and piloting capability.

No attempt will be made to present a complete study of aviation weather in this publication, however, a basic review will be presented with emphasis on use and interpretation of Weather Bureau data.

THE ATMOSPHERE

The earth is surrounded by a sea of air. Although extremely light, air has weight and is highly elastic and compressible. Because of its weight, the atmosphere exerts a certain pressure upon the surface of the earth amounting to about 15 pounds per square inch at sea level.

Air contains variable amounts of impurities such as dust, salt particles and soot. These particles are important because of their effect on visibility and especially because of the part they play in the condensation of water vapor. If the air were absolutely pure, there would be little condensation; these minute particles act as nuclei for condensation of water vapor.

The earth receives heat energy from the sun by radiation. During the day the earth absorbs heat and at night some of the heat is reflected back into space. During winter months, the hemisphere experiencing the winter season absorbs less heat than in summer due to shorter days and less direct sun rays. Also, the amount of heat absorbed during the daytime is based on the earth's surface characteristics. Surface characteristics also determine the degree of heat retention during the night. Cloud layers reduce the amount of heat reflected to space at night.

This wide variation in the earth's heating and cooling affects the sea of air surrounding it. The mass of air over a warm surface becomes heated, expands and rises. Colder air moves in to replace the rising air. This constant movement of air about the earth's surface, together with varying moisture content causes the phenomenon known as "weather."

Since basic weather is a function of temperature, pressure, and moisture content, these characteristics as applied to the "sea of air" will be reviewed.

TEMPERATURE

Although a more technical definition involves the velocity of molecules, it is sufficient to define temperature as the "degree of hotness or coldness" of a substance. The two different temperature scales that are unfortunately used in aviation weather are shown in Figure 72.

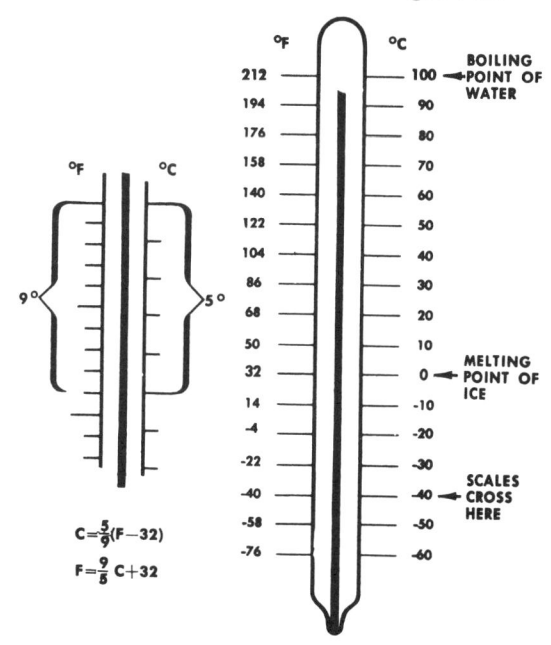

Fig. 72 Fahrenheit and Celsius temperature scales.

When you get in an airplane and take off you will notice an overall decrease in temperature as you gain altitude. This is due to the fact that the air nearest the earth is heated the most — it is closer to the radiator. The variation in temperature with altitude is called the LAPSE RATE.

Generally, the rate of temperature change with altitude indicates the STABILITY of the air. If the temperature decreases slowly with altitude the air is termed STABLE. If it decreases rapidly with altitude the air is considered UNSTABLE. The average rate of temperature decrease with altitude is 3½ degrees F. (2 degrees C.) for each 1000 feet. If the temperature increases with altitude an INVERSION exists. This in effect puts a "lid on the air pot" and prevents smoke, haze, etc., from rising. Thus, visibility is reduced in the SMOG. The basic cause of smog with its subsequent reduction of visibility in the Los Angeles basin is due to a temperature inversion.

ATMOSPHERIC PRESSURE AND ALTITUDE

Atmospheric pressure is the force exerted by the weight of the atmosphere on a unit area. Since air is not a solid object its weight is not easily measured by conventional means. In spite of this, it was discovered three centuries ago, that the atmosphere could be weighed by balancing it against a column of mercury. The device used for this became known as a BAROMETER meaning weight meter. A mercury barometer is shown in Figure 73. The barometer is used by weather stations for measuring air pressure. Since variations in pressure are important weather and aeronautical data (like altimeter setting, for example) accurate measurement of air pressure is made periodically and converted to sea level pressure for standardization. Thus, a pressure measurement taken in Denver at 5280 feet elevation can be compared with a reading taken in New York. The STANDARD SEA LEVEL PRESSURE IS 29.92 INCHES OF MERCURY.

Another type of atmospheric pressure measuring device is called the aneroid barometer shown in Figure 74. The essential feature of an aneroid barometer is a cell made of thin metal and corrugated to make it flexible. The air which is sealed in the cell expands it slightly as the pressure falls and compresses it when the pressure increases. A linkage system magnifies this movement to move a pointer across a dial. An aneroid barometer is usually calibrated with a mercury barometer. An aircraft altimeter is an aneroid barometer with the pressure units changed to altitude units.

Most weather information presents pressure data in terms of inches of mercury; however, weather map pressure is in MILLIBARS. Thus, standard air pressure of 1013.2 millibars is equivalent to 29.92 inches of mercury. Also 760 millimeters of mercury and 14.7 pounds per inch are pressure measurements of standard air.

Air pressure decreases rather uniformly with altitude. Up to 10,000 feet, the air pressure decreases approximately one inch of mercury for every 1000 feet.

Weather maps depict the variation in air pressure by means of ISOBARS. Each isobar is a line of constant pressure. The pattern of isobars determines the wind direction (it flows from a region of high pressure to a region of low pressure). Figure 75 shows high and low pressure areas and the subsequent circulation of air. When the isobars are close together, high winds result whereas a wide spacing indicates light winds.

Fig. 74 Aneroid barometer.

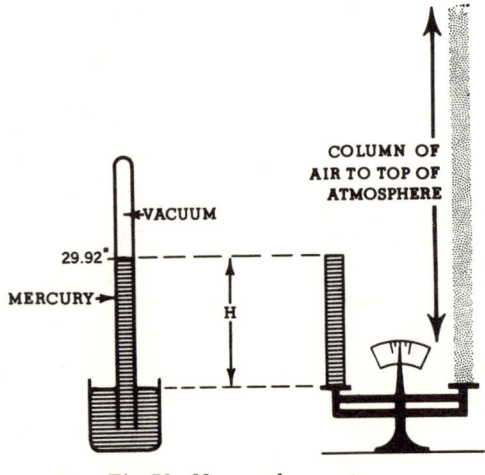

Fig. 73 Mercury barometer.

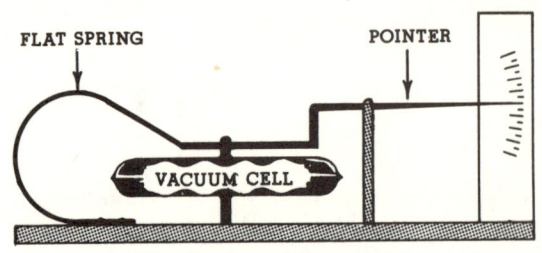

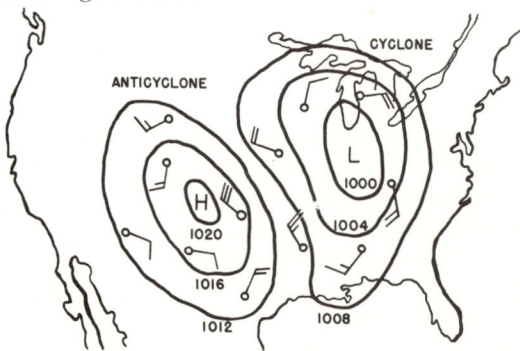

Fig. 75 High and low pressure areas as shown on surface weather chart.

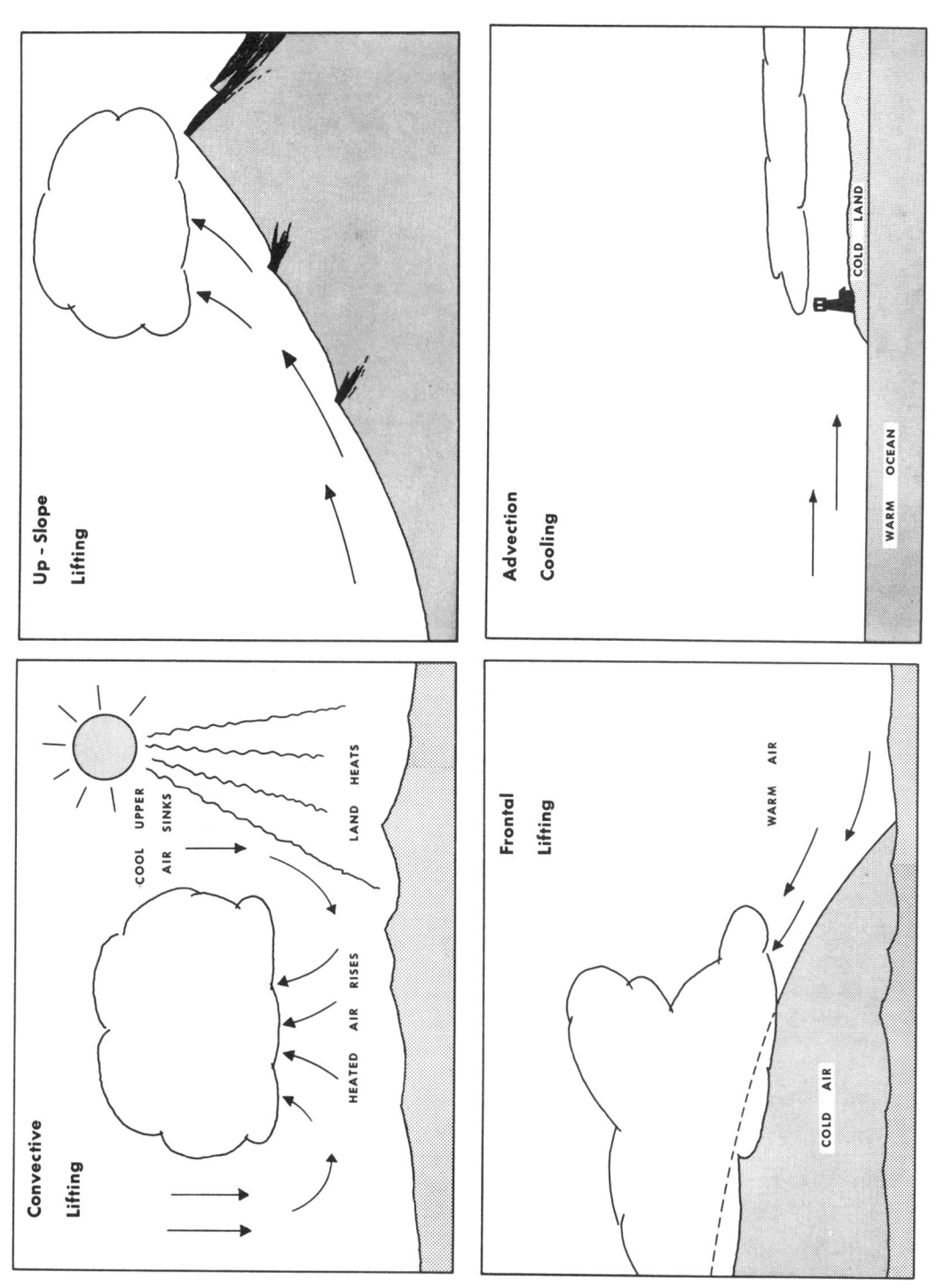

Figs. 76, 77, 78, and 79 Cloud formation by lifting and advection.

ATMOSPHERIC MOISTURE

Practically all weather that interferes with the operation of aircraft is directly associated with water in some form. Air ALWAYS contains some amount of moisture in the following forms:
- GAS
  - Water Vapor
- LIQUID
  - Minute Droplets in Clouds or Fog
  - Rain
- SOLID
  - Snow
  - Hail
  - Ice
  - Ice Crystals in Clouds or Fog

Depending on the temperature (and indirectly on pressure) moisture can change from VAPOR, which is invisible, to any of the other liquids or solids which are not invisible. All air masses contain some amount of moisture in the form of invisible water vapor. When this air is cooled to its DEW POINT the air becomes SATURATED, that is, it contains all the moisture it can hold. Further reduction in temperature causes the moisture to CONDENSE out, resulting in visible moisture like fog, clouds, or rain (hail, snow, or ice crystals, depending on temperature levels).

All weather reports contain both air temperature and dew point. WHEN THE TEMPERATURE APPROACHES THE DEW POINT WITHIN 3 OR 4 DEGREES, FOG CAN BE EXPECTED, ESPECIALLY IN THE EVENING ON THE SEA COAST. Or, when air is lifted by rising air currents on the side of mountains or along a weather front (see Figures 76, 77, and 78) its temperature decreases to the dew point, forming clouds. Warm, moist air moving over a cold surface (see Figure 79) also causes condensation forming fog or clouds.

SIGNPOSTS OF THE SKY

Practically all weather phenomena are associated either directly or indirectly with cloud formations of some kind. Therefore your ability to read these "signposts of the sky" will enable you to make pertinent flight decisions effecting both safety and comfort for you as well as your passengers.

Each individual cloud type can indicate the atmospheric processes in operation. During pre-flight planning as well as throughout the flight, the cloud formations can tell you whether to expect a smooth or rough flight, good or poor visibility, the type of icing if any, as well as possible hazardous weather to avoid.

Clouds are a suspension of water droplets and/or ice crystals in the air. All clouds are formed by a cooling process whereby moist air containing water vapor is cooled to below its dew point. Thus, the water vapor is changed to water droplets through condensation. Sometimes the water vapor is transformed directly into ice crystals without going through the liquid state. This process is called sublimation.

The most common processes by which air is cooled to form clouds are expansion and advection:
- Cooling by expansion is the result of lifting the air to a higher altitude where the pressure is lower. The lift is provided by rising currents formed by thermal or mechanical means. Thermal lifting is the result of surface heating which produces rising convection currents. Mechanical lifting results when moist air is forced to rise over mountains (upslope lifting) or over colder air masses during frontal conditions. See Figures 76, 77, and 78.
- Cooling by advection results when a warm, moist air mass is moved (advected) over a colder surface. This cooling process usually results in condensation in the form of fog or low clouds. See Figure 79.

All clouds fall into one of two broad categories — CUMULIFORM and STRATIFORM. Cumuliform clouds are formed by rising air currents in unstable air, usually the result of cooling by expansion. Stratiform clouds are formed by cooling air in stable layers such as advection cooling whereby warm moist air moves over a colder surface. However, stratiform clouds are sometimes also formed during warm front conditions whereby the air is lifted so slowly that clouds form in stable, stratiform layers.

Cumuliform clouds are cauliflower-like in appearance with appreciable vertical development and dome-shaped upper surfaces. They are characteristic of unstable air and are produced by rising air currents. Usually, cumuliform clouds are separate and distinct from each other. They also have flat bases and rarely cover the entire sky. Whereas, the clouds themselves give evidence of rising air currents, the space between them is characterized by descending air currents. Needless to say, cumuliform clouds provide turbulent flying conditions. The extent of vertical development is usually indicative of the intensity of the turbulence.

Precipitation from cumuliform clouds is usually of a showery nature. Thus, any time aviation weather reports and forecasts indicate rain showers or in more extreme cases, thundershowers, the pilot can expect cumuliform clouds with their associated turbulence.

Stratiform clouds occur in sheets or layers and often cover the entire sky. Although these cloud layers have some thickness, they do not have the vertical development of cumuliform clouds. Stratiform clouds are indicative of stable air not associated with the extreme vertical lifting of unstable air forming cumuliform clouds. Precipitation from stratiform clouds is generally in the form of light continuous rain, drizzle, or snow. While flying conditions are usually smooth, the extensive precipitation areas can produce low visibility and possibly IFR conditions even beneath the cloud bases.

The two categories of clouds, cumuliform and stratiform are again grouped into four families — high clouds, middle clouds, low clouds, and clouds with accentuated vertical development. These families are distinguished by both the form of the cloud and height of the cloud's base above the ground. They are classified as follows:

- High or "Cirro" clouds include Cirro-stratus and Cirro-cumulus. These clouds occur from 20,000 feet upwards.
- Middle or "Alto" clouds are Altostratus and Altocumulus which usually occur at 6000 to 20,000 feet.
- Low clouds with bases generally below 6000 feet are Stratus, Nimbostratus, and Stratocumulus.
- Vertical Development clouds can vary from bases at 500 feet to tops at 40,000 feet or higher. These are the Cumulus and Cumulonimbus clouds.

The term CEILING is used by meteorologists to indicate the amount of sky coverage and height of the bases of the clouds above the ground. Whenever "ceiling" is used by the Weather Bureau or Air Traffic Control, the pilot should know that considerable more than one-half of the sky is covered by clouds.

High clouds which usually occur from 20,000 to 40,000 feet are composed entirely of ice crystals.

The cirrus cloud is a delicate, white, feather-like cloud which often appears bright yellow or red because of the reflection of light from the setting or rising sun. Because of their thinness, cirrus clouds do not blur the outlines of the sun or moon, and on most occasions do not make an appreciable change of the appearance of the sky. Isolated cirrus clouds are usually indicative of good weather.

Cirro-stratus clouds are thin, whitish veils of clouds which give the sky a milky look. They can be distinguished from cirrus clouds by the halo phenomena which the light from the sun or moon usually produces in them.

The cirrocumulus clouds consist of patches of small rounded masses or white flakes arranged in groups or lines with ripples similar in appearance to wind-swept sand dunes.

The middle or "Alto" clouds usually occur at altitudes of 6000 to 20,000 feet in the middle latitudes encompassing the United States. They are found at altitudes near the lower limit of this range in the colder seasons, and at altitudes near the upper limit in the warmer seasons. Middle clouds are composed primarily of water droplets, although certain forms may consist of ice crystals.

Altostratus clouds appear as a veil of gray or bluish clouds which look fibrous or straited. The thinner forms of altostratus differ very little in appearance from the thicker forms of cirro-stratus. Altostratus clouds are associated with stable or smooth air layers in the atmosphere, and light rain or snow occasionally falls from these clouds. The outline of the sun shows dimly through the thinner altostratus clouds as through frosted glass.

Altocumulus clouds are a layer or series of patches of rather flattened, rounded cloud masses. They occur in a variety of forms, and in some cases may exist at several levels at the same time. In some instances they may be derived from decaying cumulus clouds.

One type of altocumulus cloud, with extensive vertical develoment, is charac-

Fig. 80   Typical summertime convective type cumulus cloud buildup.

Fig. 81 A Navy fighter flies in smooth air "on top" of cumuliform clouds. Cumulus clouds are off the right wingtip with stratocumulus off the left wing tip.

teristic of unstable air at the level of formation. Altostratus and altocumulus clouds freqeuntly merge in layers where the stability of the air is changing.

The bases of the low clouds are general-ly below 6000 feet. Stratus are low, uniform, sheet-like clouds resembling fog, but not resting on the ground. They usually give the sky a hazy appearance. The base of stratus clouds is usually ragged, therefore, the ceiling is sometimes reported as "indefinite" by the Weather Bureau.

Layers of stratus clouds may be quite extensive and frequently cover thousands of square miles. These clouds are usually quite thin, varying in thickness from a few hundred feet to several thousand feet. They normally form in stable air associated with a temperature inversion. An inversion exists when air at higher altitudes is warmer than air at lower altitudes.

Stratus clouds are frequently accompanied by layers of fog, haze, or smoke between their bases and the ground. These obstructions to visibility merge into the cloud, therefore, the determination of a ceiling is difficult. Precipitation from stratus clouds is usually in the form of light snow or drizzle.

Nimbostratus clouds form in a low, shapeless, thick layer of dark gray color. Since nimbus" means "rain cloud," nimbostratus clouds are always accompanied by continuous rain or snow of variable in-intensity.

Nimbostratus clouds usually begin as altostratus or altocumulus clouds whose bases lower as the clouds thicken. Because of its thickness, sometimes in excess of 15,000 feet, the nimbostratus is sometimes classified as a cloud of vertical development. Although they are called stratus type, usually associated with smooth flying, the air is sometimes very turbulent in and around these clouds. There is generally a progressive development of low ragged fractocumulus or altocumulus clouds under the nimbostratus. These clouds are isolated at first but gradually fuse into a solid, continuous layer.

Stratocumulus clouds form a low layer of clouds composed of patches of rounded masses or rolls. Like the stratus, the stratocumulus cloud differs from the stratus in that the stratocumulus normally consists of numerous rounded cloudlets of patchy appearance. The base of the stratocumulus is usually higher and rougher than the stratus. Stratocumulus frequently change into stratus, and stratus into stratocumulus. The latter condition usually occurs due to heating from below causing vertical currents to form the cumuli type cloud.

Clouds of vertical development cannot be classified according to height since they may extend through all of the levels assigned to the low, middle and high cloud groups. Their bases vary from 500 to 10,000 feet or higher while their tops can vary from 1500 to 50,000 feet. Some types are associated primarily with good weather and others with stormy weather, however they all occur in relatively unstable air and are frequently accompanied by strong vertical currents and extreme turbulence.

The cumulus cloud is a dense cloud with vertical development. Its base is flat and uniform in height above the earth and its top is domed or cauliflowered in shape. Cumulus clouds appear white when they reflect the sunlight toward the observer but when viewed from directly beneath the clouds or when they are between the observer and the sun, they may appear dark with bright edges. Cumulus clouds tend to develop during the waning of the day and mark the top of the vertical rising air currents, where the dew point temperature has been reached. Over land, cumulus clouds form during the day and tend to dissipate during the cooling of the night unless they progress to the cumulonimbus stage. This day and night variation does not occur over water due to the relatively constant temperature of large bodies of water.

In mid-latitudes, cumulus clouds are not composed of ice crystals in their tops. Ice crystals in the tops of cumulus clouds would indicate that they had passed into the cumulonimbus stage discussed below.

Cumulonimbus are towering cumulus cloud masses which extend to great heights because of the intense vertical development of air currents. The upper portions resemble mountains or towers capped with a fibrous texture. The caps of these clouds often spread out in an anvil shape. The cumulonimbus is the thickest and most active of all clouds. Cumulonimbus clouds form as a result of the continuous upward development of cumulus clouds, and occur only in unstable air. The violent vertical currents constantly change the outline of the clouds.

The chief distinguishing characteristic of the cumulonimbus from the cumulus is the veil of ice crystal clouds which surrounds the upper part of the cumulonimbus. In the middle latitudes, the ice crystals seem to be necessary for the production of moderate or heavy precipitation. Thunderstorms, squalls, turbulence, and hail are characteristics of cumulonimbus clouds.

In general, we see that CUMULIFORM

	CUMULIFORM	STRATIFORM
Size of Water Droplet	Large	Small
Stability of Air	Unstable	Stable
Flying Conditions	Rough (turbulent)	Smooth
Precipitation	Showery	Continuous (of uniform intensity)
Surface Visibility	Good, except in precipitation and blowing snow or dust	Visually Poor
Aircraft Icing	Predominately Clear	Rime

Relationship of the two predominant cloud formations to flying weather.

CLOUDS indicate turbulent air and are associated with showery precipitation and possible thunderstorm activity. The large water droplets in cumuliform clouds are favorable for the rapid formation of clear ice on aircraft if the temperature is close to freezing. Visibility is generally good under cumuliform clouds except during precipitation.

STRATIFORM CLOUDS usually indicate relatively smooth flying conditions. Continuous precipitation, covering extensive areas, may be associated with stratiform clouds. Visibility is usually very poor beneath low stratiform clouds which can easily deteriorate into IFR conditions. Also, in stratiform clouds, rime icing is predominant with the proper temperature.

Clouds, such as altostratus and stratocumulus, which possess the characteristics of both forms, usually produce weather which is less intense than that of cumuliform clouds.

To the pilot who is continually aware of cloud formations, they are indeed "signposts of the sky."

THUNDERSTORMS

The most common thunderstorms are so-called "air mass" thunderstorms and those associated with frontal activity. The air mass thunderstorm is relatively local and is the result of convective lifting of warm moist air as shown in Figure 76. Frontal thunderstorms result from warm moist air being lifted over the cold air "wedge" of a front as illustrated in Figure 78.

Another type of thunderstorm encountered in mountainous country is due to upslope lifting as shown in Figure 77.

All thunderstorms could be defined as the ultimate manifestation of the growth of a cumulus cloud.

Thunderstorms are of particular concern to pilots because many of the most severe atmospheric hazards are found within them. They are almost always accompanied by strong gusts of wind and severe turbulence. Heavy rain showers usually occur and hail is not uncommon.

Obviously, thunderstorms should be avoided if possible. When forced to fly through them, even heavy aircraft must adhere to established safety precautions and procedures. But with about 44,000 thunderstorms occuring daily over the world, almost every pilot can expect to encounter one occasionally.

The basic requirements for formation of a thunderstorm are the same as for any other cumulus type cloud:
- Unstable air
- Some type of lifting action
- High moisture content of the air

Since the basic requirements are the same, one may ask why only fair weather cumulus clouds are present on one sultry, summer afternoon, and thunderstorms are in abundance the next. The difference lies in the degree in which the casual factors are present.

Individual air mass or local convective type thunderstorms vary in diameter generally from 5 to 10 miles. Frontal and "squall line" thunderstorms however can become an impenetrable wall extending for hundreds of miles.

The life cycle of a thunderstorm cell consists of three distinct phases:
- The cumulus stage
- The mature stage
- The dissipating or anvil stage

CUMULUS STAGE

Although most cumulus clouds do not become thunderstorms, the initial stage of a thunderstorm is always a cumulus cloud. The chief distinguishing feature of this cumulus or building stage is an updraft, which prevails throughout the entire cell. As an updraft continues through the vertical extent of the cell, water droplets coalesce, and raindrops are formed.

MATURE STAGE

The beginning of surface rain and adjacent updrafts and downdrafts initiates the mature stage. By this time, the average cell has attained a height of 25,000 feet or more. As the raindrops begin to fall, the frictional drag between the raindrops and the surrounding air causes the air to begin a downward motion. Being unstable, this air becomes colder than its surroundings and its rate of downward motion is accelerated. This is a downdraft. The downdraft reaches maximum speed in a short time after the rain starts its initial fall. Maximum downdrafts occur at all levels within the storm.

The mature cell generally extends far above 25,000 feet and in the lower levels consists of sharp updrafts and downdrafts adjacent to each other. Large water droplets are encountered suspended in the updrafts and descending with the downdrafts as rain.

DISSIPATING OR ANVIL STAGE

Throughout the life span of the mature cell, more and more air aloft is being dragged down by the falling raindrops. Consequently, the downdraft spreads out to take the place of the dissipating updrafts. As this process progresses, the entire lower portion of the cell becomes an area of downdraft. Since this is an unbalanced situation, and since the descending motion in the downdraft effects a drying process, the entire structure now begins to dissipate. The high winds aloft have now carried the upper section of the cloud into the familiar anvil form, indicating that gradual dissipation is overtaking the storm cell.

WEATHER WITHIN THE STORM

The pilot, upon entering any thunderstorm, can expect to encounter considerable quantities of liquid moisture. Statistics show that, although heavy rain was generally reported at all levels of a mature storm, specific flight altitudes seem to present the greatest frequency of heavy rain. In all observations the greatest incidence of heavy rain occurred in the middle and lower levels of the storms. The 10,000- to 11,000-ft. level showed the greatest frequency and the 5,000- to 6,000-ft. level showed the next greatest frequency of heavy rainfall. Altitudes above the freezing level showed a sharp decline in the frequency of rain of any intensity.

Statistics show that hail was encountered at a maximum of 10 percent of the traverses at any given altitude. When it was observed, its duration was very short. The total occurrence was found to be at a maximum at the middle levels for all intensities of hail.

The maximum frequency of moderate and heavy snow occurs at the 20,000- and 21,000-ft. levels.

There is a certain definite correlation between turbulence and precipitation. Previously it was believed that precipitation would have a dampening effect on turbulence. This has been found to be nearly 100 percent in error. It is clearly evident that the intensity of associated turbulence, in most cases, varies directly with the intensity of precipitation.

According to pilot reports, lightning strokes occurred in less than 2 percent of all penetrations. In general, damage was minor, being limited to small punctures in the aircraft skin. Conditions most favorable for lightning strokes exist in frozen precipitation at temperatures near the freezing point.

Since icing presents an obvious flight hazard, it is well to analyze data relating to this problem. At the 20,000-ft. level, ice was encountered on more than 50 percent of all traverses. The majority of this ice was classified as rime.

FLYING THUNDERSTORM WEATHER

The best rule for flying through a thunderstorm in light aircraft is . . . DON'T.

When flying through a thunderstorm area, a thorough weather check and evaluation should be made. A visit to the weather bureau and evaluation of weather radar data provides location and intensity information. Weather radar is especially effective in thunderstorm detection because hail, if any, and the large drops of water give the strongest return signals (bright areas on the scope). Smaller droplets result in dimmer areas on the scope. A direct relationship exists between icing and turbulence and the strength of radar echoes.

The following features, gleaned through interpretation of weather radar scopes, should be of particular interest to pilots:
- A thunderstorm with radar echoes indicated to above 35,000 feet often contains extreme turbulence and hail.
- Hazardous weather associated with scattered echoes usually can be circumnavigated. But if the lines or areas are reported as broken or solid and of moderate or strong intensity, hazardous weather can be avoided only if the aircraft is radar equipped.
- Severe clear air turbulence and hail may be experienced between thunderstorms if the separation between echoes is less than 30 miles.

Pilots, particularly those flying light aircraft, should avoid all thunderstorms. However when conducted properly, penetration can be accomplished safely. The following procedures are well to remember when entering a thunderstorm:
- Establish a penetration altitude. Avoid altitudes from the freezing level upward. If freezing level was not obtained prior to takeoff, request it from the traffic controller or Flight Service Station. The "softest" altitude is usually between 4000 and 6000 feet.
- Reduce airspeed to manufacturer's recommended maneuvering speed or airspeed for turbulent air penetration. This reduces structural stress on the aircraft.
- Change power settings to establish the reduced airspeed before entering the storm.
- Keep constant power settings in the storm.
- FLY ATTITUDE using the gyro instruments as discussed in Chapter 3, Learning Instrument Flying. Avoid unnecessary maneuvering. Don't chase pressure instruments.
- Pick a heading that will take you through the storm in minimum time and hold it.

ICING

The same basic rule for flying through thunderstorms applies to flying light aircraft through icing conditions . . . . . DON'T.

A thorough weather evaluation will usually provide information regarding icing areas and altitudes. The Area Forecast provided by the weather bureau is the basic source of icing data for flight planning purposes.

The most important hazards associated with icing are:
- Loss of power due to propeller, carburetor, and carburetor airscoop icing.
- Loss of lift and controllability and increase in drag due to icing of the wing and other structural members.

Most modern light airplanes can cope with powerplant icing; however, structural and propeller ice prevention or removal requires special equipment usually not available for these airplanes.

Aircraft in flight are susceptible to structural icing when the free air temperature is 0° C. or colder, and there is either supercooled visible liquid moisture or an abundance of sublimation nuclei combined with high humidity. The most severe icing occurs with temperatures between 0 degrees C. and −10 degrees C. However, icing can occur as high as 4 degrees C.

Caution must be exercised in determining the free air temperature from the aircraft thermometer unless the pilot is reasonably sure of its accuracy or amount of error.

ICE ACCRETION RATE

The accretion (accumulation) rate of structural ice may vary from less than one-half inch per hour to as high as 1 inch per minute for brief periods of 2 or 3 minutes. The factors influencing the rate of ice formation are:
- Amount of liquid water. Ice forms more rapidly in thick clouds than in thin ones.
- Drop size. Small water droplets tend to follow the airstream as it is de-

flected by the airfoil. Larger drops tend to resist this deflection and collect more easily and rapidly on the surface.
- Airspeed. The rate of ice formation increases as airspeed increases up to about 400 knots.
- Size and shape of airfoil. Ice forming on an aircraft is more likely to take the shape of the airfoil if it is thin, smooth, and highly streamlined than if it is blunt-nosed and/or rough. Once a coating of ice has already accumulated on the airfoil, it presents a larger collecting surface and accelerates further ice accretion.

TYPES OF STRUCTURAL ICING

The physical characteristics of ice which accumulates on exposed surfaces of the aircraft depend on the accretion rate. The types of ice are:
- Clear (glaze)
- Rime

Clear ice is transparent with a glassy surface identical to the glaze which forms on trees and other objects during a freezing rain. It is smooth and streamlined when deposited from large droplets without solid precipitation. But if mixed with snow or sleet it is rough, irregular, and whitish. The deposit then becomes very blunt-nosed.

Conditions most favorable for clear ice formation are high water content, large droplet size, temperature only slightly below freezing, high airspeed, and thin airfoils. Encountered most frequently in cumuliform clouds, clear ice also accumulates rapidly on aircraft flying in freezing rain or drizzle.

Rime ice is a milky, opaque, and granular deposit with a rough surface. Rime ice is formed by the instantaneous freezing of small supercooled water droplets upon contact with exposed aircraft surfaces. This instant freezing traps a large amount of air, giving the ice its opaqueness and making it very brittle. Rime ice usually forms on leading edges and protrudes forward into the airstream as a sharp nose. It has little tendency to spread over and take the shape of the airfoil.

Fast freezing rime ice most likely occurs between temperatures of −10 degrees C. and −20 degrees C. However, rime ice can accumulate when the temperature is anywhere between 0 degrees C. and −40 degrees C. Most frequently encountered in stratiform clouds, it is also common in cumuliform clouds at temperatures below −10 degrees C.

You can see examples of clear and rime ice in your refrigerator. The ice cubes are clear ice while the ice which accumulates on the freezer compartment is rime ice. The conditions forming refrigerator ice are similar to those discussed above. The clear ice cubes are obviously of a high water content and large droplet size. The rime ice accumulation on the freezer compartment occurs by instant freezing of the moisture contained in the room air which comes in contact with the cold surfaces when the door is opened. Thus it is opaque, whitish, brittle, and contains a large amount of entrapped air.

FRONTS AND FRONTAL WEATHER

When two different air masses are brought together, a discontinuity called a "front" is formed between them. This transition zone, normally many miles in width, is shown on the weather map as a line. Fronts are especially important to pilots be-

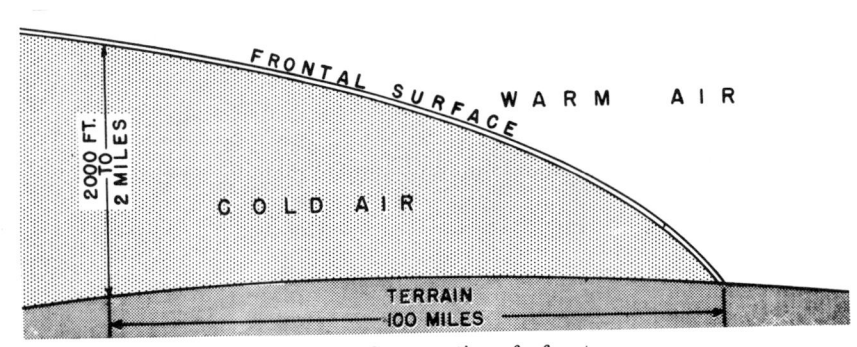

Fig. 82 Cross section of a front.

cause many weather hazards to aviation may accompany them.

A cold air mass, being heavier, will always tend to underrun a warm air mass. The front slopes upward over the cold air mass; thus, cold air is below and warm air is forced up over it. See Figure 82.

If the cold air is replacing the warm air, it is called a "cold front." It brings cold weather as it passes. The moving front which occurs when warm air advances is called a "warm front." It brings warm weather as it passes. Figure 83 shows a cold front as depicted on a weather map. The triangles on the frontal line indicate the direction of movement. Figure 84 shows a warm front as presented on a weather map. Again, the semi-circles are on the side of the frontal line indicating the direction of movement. Note the change in direction of the isobars at the front and the approximately 90 degree wind shift. Weather data for stations on either side of the frontal line will also show a noticeable difference in temperature.

If the front has essentially stopped moving it is called a "stationary front" and is shown on the weather map by a line with both triangles and semi circles on both sides of the line. See Figure 85.

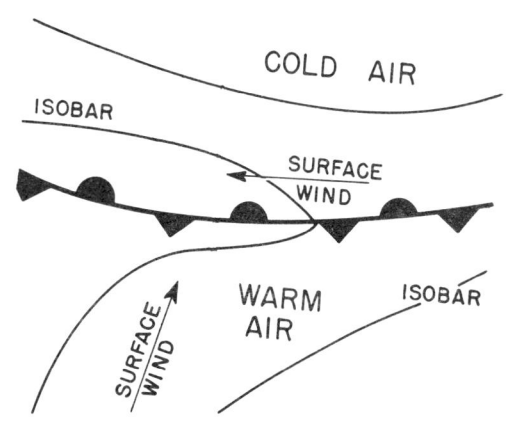

Fig. 85 Stationary front as shown on a surface weather chart.

Cold fronts move predominantly toward the southeast pivoting about a "Low." Warm fronts move predominantly toward the north, also pivoting about a "Low." If both fronts pivot about the same Low (see Figure 86) the cold front may catch up with the warm front at or near the Low used as the common pivot, since the cold front is faster than the warm front. When this condition occurs, a mass of warm air is forced upward above the surfaces of both the cold and warm fronts. This is called an OCCLUDED front and shown in Figure 86. The occluded front is depicted on the weather chart by means of both triangles and semi circles on the same side of the front line.

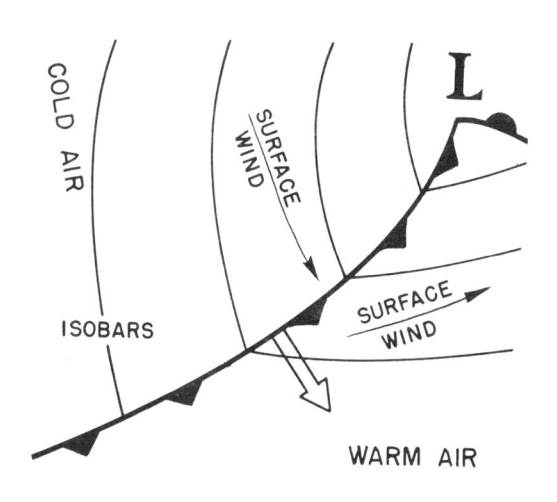

Fig. 83 Cold front as shown on a surface weather chart.

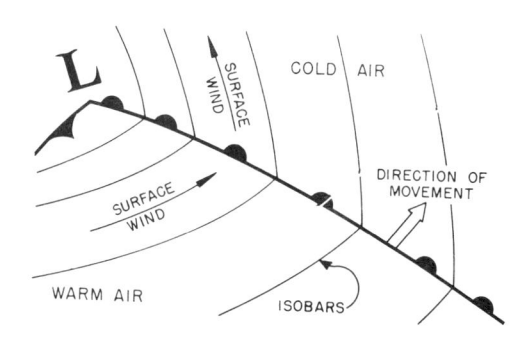

Fig. 84 Warm front as shown on a surface weather chart.

As discussed in the preceding section on clouds and as shown in Figures 76, 77 and 78, moisture condensation is the result of lifting of warm moist air. It is characteristic of all fronts that the cold air slides under the warm air like a wedge causing it to be lifted. Thus, a frontal zone is usually accompanied by extensive cloud formations, precipitation, and thunderstorms if the lifting occurs rapidly. Cold fronts usually are characterized by more severe frontal weather than warm fronts. This is due to the steeper cold front slope causing more rapid lifting of the warm air. Due to the warm front's less steep slope, it may cover more area and contain stratus type clouds with accompanying steady precipitation.

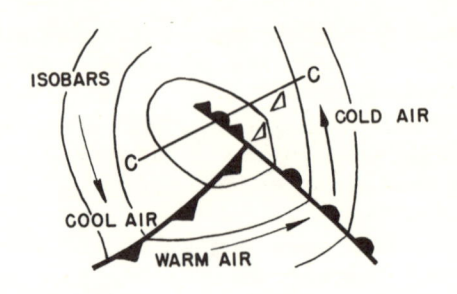

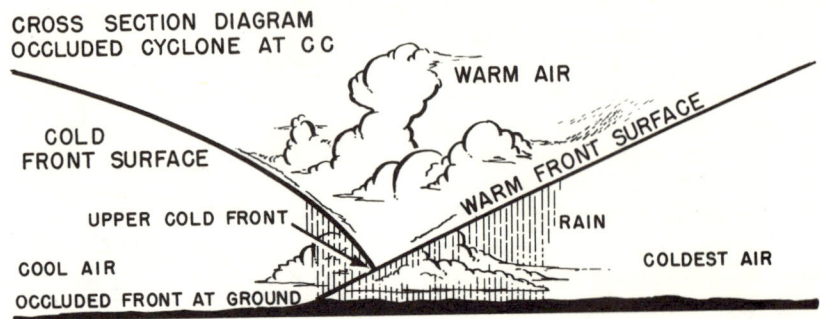

Fig. 86 An occluded front.

CHARACTERISTICS OF A COLD FRONT

The characteristics of a cold front are:
- *Wind Shift Across the Front.* There are winds from a southerly direction ahead of the front and winds from a northerly direction behind the front. See Figure 83.
- *Temperature Drop Across the Front.* There is warm air ahead of the front and cold air behind the front.
- *Cloud Formations.* The degree of instability and the moisture content of the warm air which is being lifted determines the intensity and types of clouds. At times there will be no clouds associated with the front because of the dryness of the lifted air. Cloud formations can occur in both stable and unstable uplifted air.

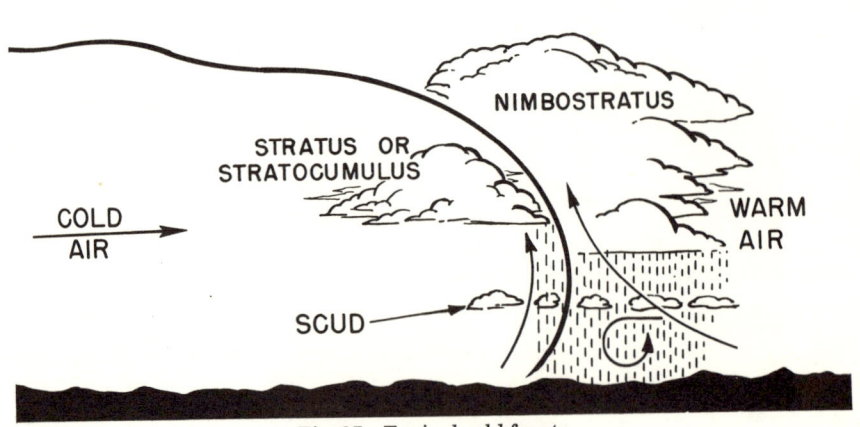

Fig. 87 Typical cold front.

Fig. 88 Typical warm front.

- *Direction of Movement.* Cold fronts move predominantly toward the southeast in the middle latitudes (30 degrees N. to 60 degrees N.)
- *Velocity of Movement.* Slow moving cold fronts move at 10 to 15 knots and fast moving cold fronts move at 25 knots and above. The average speed of cold fronts is approximately 20 knots. Cold fronts move faster than warm fronts.
- *Width of Weather Band.* The width of the weather band depends on the abruptness or shallowness of the frontal slope and the stability of the upgliding air. A relatively steep cold front may have a weather band of 50 miles in width whereas a shallow cold front may have a weather band of 200 to 500 miles in width.

CHARACTERISTICS OF A WARM FRONT

The characteristics of a warm front are:
- *Wind Shift Across the Front.* The winds are from an easterly direction ahead of the front and from a southerly direction behind the front. See Figure 84.
- *Temperature Drop Across the Front.* There is cold air next to the earth's surface ahead of the front with warm overlaying air aloft. Warm air will be next to the earth's surface and aloft behind the front.
- *Cloud Formations.* The degree of instability and the moisture content of the upgliding air determines the intensity and types of clouds. Inadequate moisture in the warm air would lead to a cloudless situation. Stratus type cloud formations are more likely to occur in a warm front than a cold front.
- *Direction of Movement and Velocity.* Warm fronts move predominantly toward the north at a speed of 5 to 30 knots. The average speed of a warm front is 10 knots.
- *Width of Weather Band.* The area affected by an active warm front may be very large; sometimes it is 600 miles or more across.

10 AVAILABLE WEATHER DATA

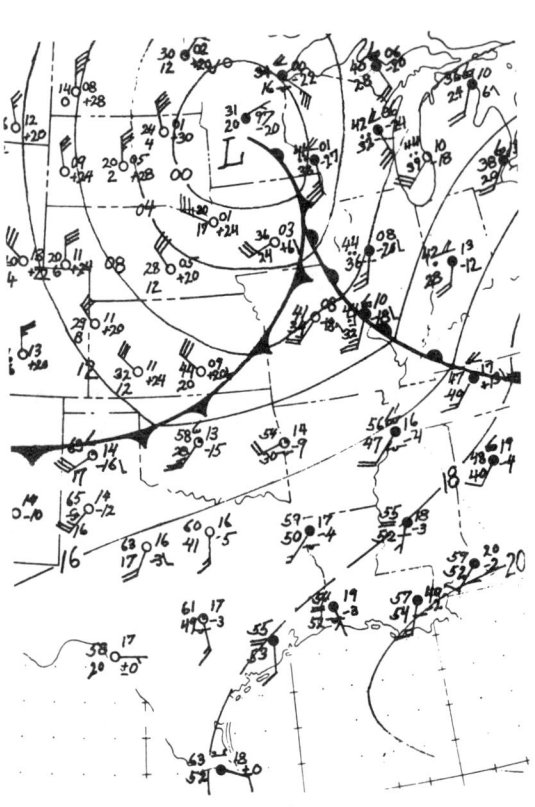

Fig. 89 Section of a surface weather map as transmitted on facsimile.

Aviation weather is made available to the pilot in the following formats:
- Weather maps (or charts)
- Aviation weather reports (hourly and special reports)
- Weather forecasts ((Terminal (FT) and Area (FA))
- Winds aloft forecasts (FD)
- In-flight weather advisories (SIGMETS and AIRMETS)
- Pilot reports (PIREPS)

WEATHER MAPS (OR CHARTS)

The National Weather Service prepares a multitude of weather charts, some of them specifically for aviation. You can easily learn to interpret and use a few of them in determining weather significant to your proposed flights. This discussion emphasizes those weather charts which are *most* useful to the pilot. Omission of certain other weather charts is not intended to imply that they have no usefulness. The following paragraphs cover those charts displayed in a typical Weather Service Office and in some Flight Service Stations.

SURFACE WEATHER CHART

The surface weather data which are observed and recorded almost simultaneously by weather stations throughout the world are collected and plotted on surface weather charts. In addition to plotted data, the surface weather chart provides an analysis of pressure patterns at mean sea level and the surface locations of fronts. Figure 89 is an example of a facsimile surface chart distributed from NMC.

The pilot should concentrate on pressure patterns and fronts more than on plotted data on the surface chart. More up-to-date weather data are available through the Aviation Weather Reports. The observational data on surface charts is included primarily for weathermen. Since it is about 2 hours old by the time the chart reaches the field office, it may be more misleading than helpful for pilots.

Surface weather charts for an area including the 48 contiguous States are distributed every 3 hours beginning at 0000 GMT. Surface charts of the entire northern hemisphere are prepared every 12 hours. Comparison of the current surface weather chart with earlier ones gives the pilot a first approximation of how weather systems are progressing. However, it is not safe to assume that they will continue to progress in the same fashion, and the pilot is not briefed (self-briefed or otherwise) until he is thoroughly familiar with weather conditions forecast for his route and planned destination. (If the forecast weather for his planned destination is poor, he should have an alternate destination.) Chapter 11 discusses the content of briefings more completely.

WEATHER DEPICTION CHART

The weather depiction chart (Figure 206) portrays graphically areas of low ceiling and restricted visibility, areas of marginal ceilings, and areas of good ceilings and vis-

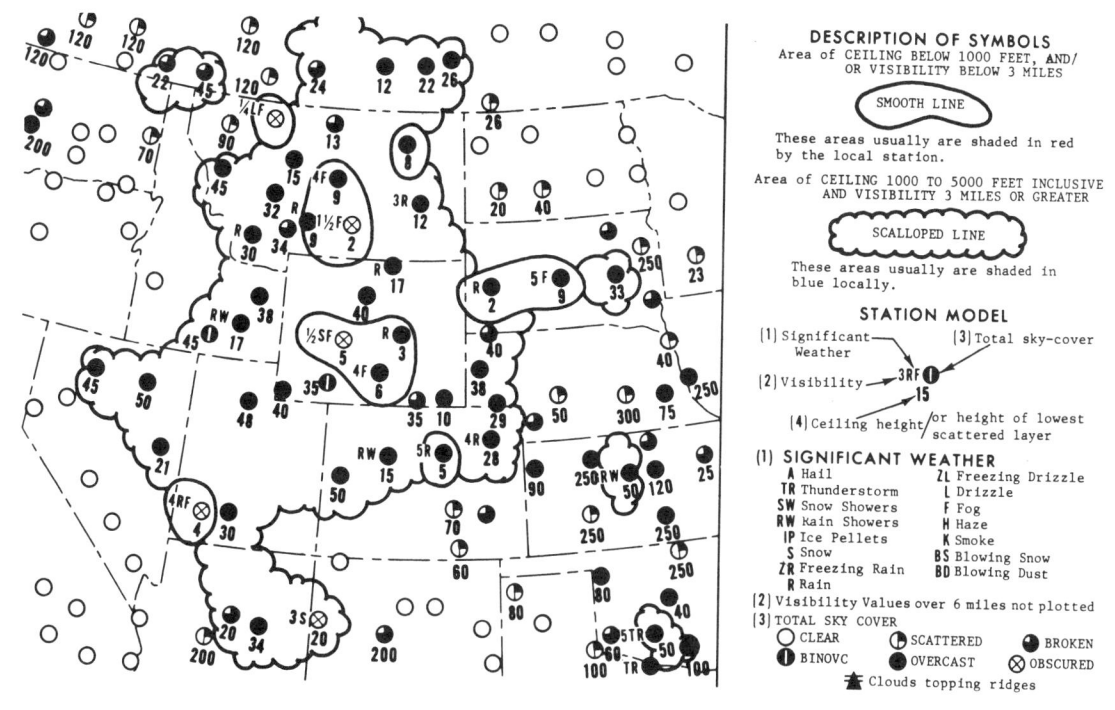

Fig. 90 A weather depiction chart.

ibilities. The chart provides at a glance, basic information on areas of cloud cover, heights of cloud bases, visibility conditions and visibility values. It's like looking down from space to "see" the areas where VFR, marginal VFR and IFR weather conditions prevail.

Weather depiction charts are issued 8 times daily, at approximately 3-hour intervals. Each chart is marked with the hour of collection (GMT) of the weather data from which the chart was made. It is important to remember that the chart may not depict the *present* situation; each chart is approximately 1 1/3 hours old when it is distributed and will be approximately 4 1/3 hours old before it is replaced.

RADAR SUMMARY CHART

Weather radar generally observes precipitation only; it does not ordinarily detect small water droplets such as are found in fog and nonprecipitating clouds. The larger the drops, the more intense is the radar return. Thus one would expect a stronger return from thunderstorms and hail than from precipitation, and this is what happens. The radar summary chart shows areas of significant precipitation and accentuates areas of heavy precipitation associated with showers and thunderstorms. It *will not* depict areas of low ceilings and restricted visibilities. The radar summary chart deals primarily with weather of a potentially hazardous nature, and for this reason it is important in a pilot weather briefing. Anything shown on this chart along or near a pilot's route of flight must be taken into account and considered carefully.

Complete radar summary charts are transmitted via facsimile, at 3-hour intervals. However, sections of the chart may be sent at 1-hour intervals when strong or significant radar echoes are observed. The analysis east of the Rocky Mountains is based on radar observations taken at over 90 weather radar locations. In western regions, the analysis is based on observations taken by Weather Service Radar Meteorologists using the FAA's Air Traffic Control Radars. The charts show actual areas of radar echoes which are produced by a concentration of liquid or frozen water drops. Those echoes represent the interior regions of moisture-laden clouds, and the greater the concentration and size of the drops (as in cumulonimbus clouds), the stronger the echoes.

Unlike the weather depiction chart, which shows areas of low *cloud cover* and *cloud bases,* the radar summary chart shows precipitation areas and the approximate heights of *echo tops.* The radar summary chart also distinguishes between gentle precipitation and the more hazardous showers and thunderstorms. Together, these two charts provide a three-dimensional picture of clouds and precipita-

GENERAL

Two methods of data depiction appear on these charts. East of the Rockies radar reports are plotted and grouped in certain configurations. West of the Rockies, actual echo patterns from ARTC radar sites are shown. Most of the symbols used are common to both sections of the map.

SURFACE WEATHER ASSOCIATED WITH ECHOES

T	Thunderstorm	IP	Ice Pellets
R	Rain	L	Drizzle
RW	Rain Showers	ZR	Freezing Rain
S	Snow	ZL	Freezing Drizzle
SW	Snow Showers	A	Hail

PRECIPITATION INTENSITY

-- Very Light + Heavy
- Light ++ Very Heavy
No Sign Moderate U Unknown

Intensity of echoes is given in terms of the estimated precipitation intensity. No intensity is ascribed to drizzle, hail, sleet or snow. Echoes located farther than a specified range, usually 125 nautical miles, are given an intensity of unknown or "U".

INTENSITY TREND

+ Increasing NEW New Development
− Decreasing

Intensity trend follows the precipitation intensity and is preceded by a slash mark. The absence of a symbol means that there has been no change in the intensity.

STATUS OF EQUIPMENT

NE No echoes
NA Observation not available
OM Equipment out for maintenance
CP Moderate to strong echoes reported only
STC Reduced detection capability within 30 miles of radar
MAG Radar on reduced power
Last three items from ARTC reports only

SAMPLE RADAR SUMMARY CHART
WW NR 555 Valid Til 0200Z

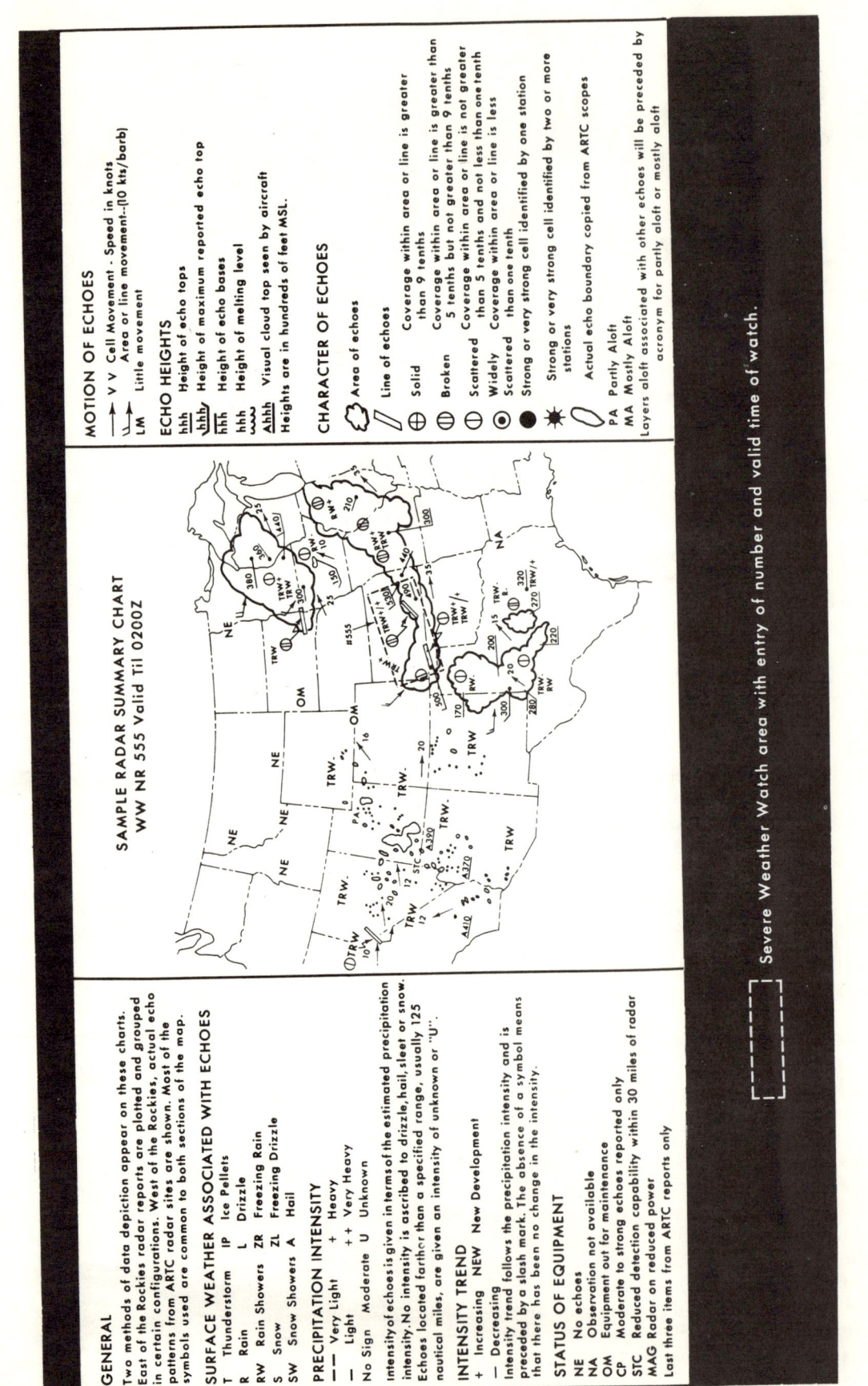

MOTION OF ECHOES

→ V V Cell Movement - Speed in knots
⇢   Area or line movement—(10 kts/barb)
LM   Little movement

ECHO HEIGHTS

hhh   Height of echo tops
h̄h̄h̄   Height of maximum reported echo top
ḥḥḥ   Height of echo bases
hhh   Height of melting level
Ahhh Visual cloud top seen by aircraft
Heights are in hundreds of feet MSL.

CHARACTER OF ECHOES

⌒ Area of echoes
/   Line of echoes
⊕ Solid   Coverage within area or line is greater than 9 tenths
⊖ Broken   Coverage within area or line is greater than 5 tenths but not greater than 9 tenths
⊘ Scattered Coverage within area or line is not greater than 5 tenths and not less than one tenth
⊙ Widely   Coverage within area or line is less Scattered than one tenth
● Strong or very strong cell identified by one station
✳ Strong or very strong cell identified by two or more stations
⬭ Actual echo boundary copied from ARTC scopes

PA Partly Aloft
MA Mostly Aloft
Layers aloft associated with other echoes will be preceded by acronym for partly aloft or mostly aloft

⬚ Severe Weather Watch area with entry of number and valid time of watch.

Fig. 91 Sample radar summary chart.

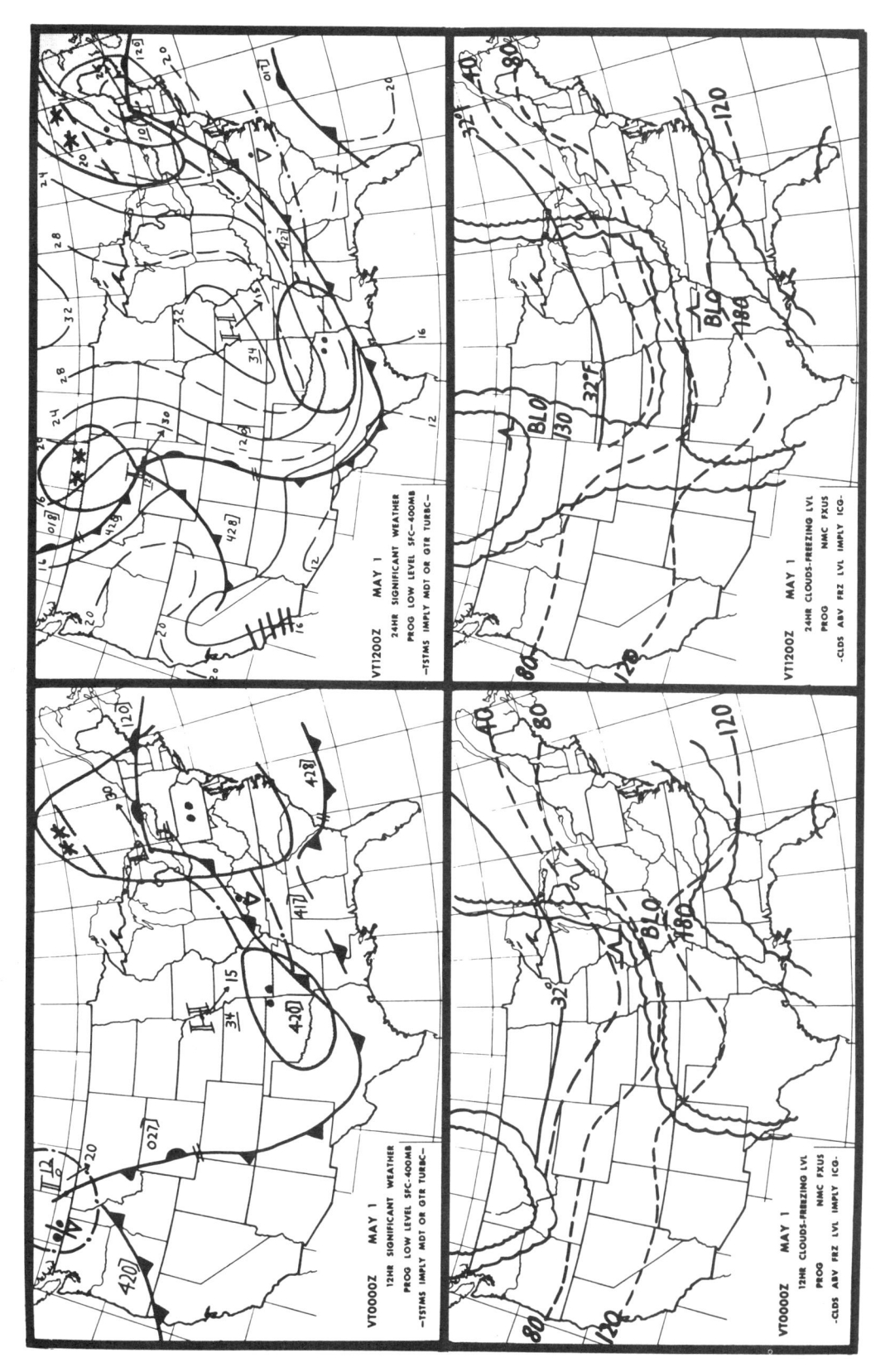

Fig. 92 Twelve and 24-hour surface and significant weather prognostic charts. Facsimile transmission is a four-panel chart.

Fig. 93 Symbols used on surface and significant weather prognostic charts. These are used on the charts shown in Fig. 92.

tion.

Figure 91 is a sample radar summary chart which shows the different presentations east of the Rocky Mountains and over the western part of the United States. This chart shows considerable shower and thunderstorm activity. By referring to the legend and explanations on the chart, you should be able to interpret and understand every feature of the chart.

LOW LEVEL PROGNOSTIC CHARTS (VISUAL WEATHER FORECASTS)

The low level prognostic charts, as the name implies, show a *prediction* of low level (below 25,000 ft.) weather conditions. These charts are issued as 4 panels:
- 2 panels show the 12-hour and 24-hour forecast of clouds and freezing levels, and:
- 2 panels show the 12-hour and 24-hour forecast of significant weather conditions.

These charts are issued 4 times daily: 0000 Z, 0600 Z, 1200 Z, and 1800 Z. The valid time (in actual time at which the charted situation is expected to exist) is indicated on each chart. Due to the time required for chart preparation (approximately 3 hours), the valid time of the 12-hour chart is about 9 hours from the time of issuance. You will have at least 3 hours of valid forecast time remaining from the previous chart when you receive the latest one.

A complete set of PROG charts is reproduced in Figure 92. The legend for these charts is shown in Figure 93.

Remember that the low level prognostic charts represent a *forecast* of weather conditions which are expected to — but *do not always* — develop. The pilot weather briefer on duty will help you examine current and pertinent weather details by referring to surface weather reports, terminal forecasts, area forecasts, radar information, AIRMETS, SIGMETS and PIREPS. After making a decision to fly into an area of marginal weather, *always* plan an alternate course of action in case the weather goes "sour".

AVIATION WEATHER REPORTS

Changes in weather frequently are so rapid that conditions at the time of flight are likely to be quite different from those shown on weather maps issued several hours previously. The very latest information is available in reports distributed by teletypewriter.

Aviation weather reports are sometimes called "hourly surface reports", "sequence reports", or "teletype reports". These are reports of "present weather" (about 15 minutes to 1¼ hours old), from over 600 terminal airports in the United States. Aviation weather reports *are not* forecasts but merely reports on weather conditions existing at the time of observation. These reports usually arrive at the local Weather Service Offices or Flight Service Stations approximately 5 minutes after the hour. They are normally issued every hour, however, special observations are distributed when the weather changes significantly between scheduled observations.

A series of 3 aviation weather reports, each one hour apart, is shown below:

SCHEDULED HOURLY AVIATION WEATHER REPORTS

0700C   1300 Z

```
LBB  6⊙⊕7  129/54/46/2508/997
ABI  E8⊕⊕15  133/59/52/3404/997
MWL  S  E5⊕1TRWF  128/64/63/3212G18/993/TB06
OVHD MOVG EWD LTGIC ALQDS
```

```
        LOCATION              SPECIAL           SKY AND          VISIBILITY      SEA-LEVEL    TEMPERATURE                    ALTIMETER
        IDENTIFIERS           REPORT            CEILING          WEATHER AND     PRESSURE     AND DEW POINT    WIND          SETTING
                                                                 OBSTRUCTION
                                                                 TO VISION

         MKC   S   15①M25⊕   4R-K   132   /58/56   /1807   /993/
```

SKY AND CEILING

Sky cover symbols are in ascending order. Figures preceding symbols are heights in hundreds of feet above station.

Sky cover Symbols are:

○ = Clear: Less than 0.1 sky cover.
① = Scattered: 0.1 to less than 0.6 sky cover.
⓪ = Broken: 0.6 to 0.9 sky cover.
⊕ = Overcast: More than 0.9 sky cover.
– = Thin (When prefixed to the above symbols.)
-X = Partial Obscuration: 0.1 to less than 1.0 sky hidden by precipitation or obstruction to vision (bases at surface).
X = Obscuration: 1.0 sky hidden by precipitation or obstruction to vision (bases at surface).

Letter preceding height of layer identifies ceiling layer and indicates how ceiling height was obtained. Thus:

A Aircraft
B Balloon (Pilot or ceiling)
D Estimated height of cirriform clouds on basis of persistency
E Estimated heights of noncirriform clouds
M Measured
R Radiosonde Balloon or Radar
W Indefinite
U Height of cirriform ceiling layer unknown

/ Height of cirriform non-ceiling layer unknown
'V' immediately following numerical value indicates a varying ceiling

+ S indicates that report contains important change

VISIBILITY

Reported in Statute Miles and Fractions (V = Variable)

WEATHER SYMBOLS

A = Hail	L = Drizzle	SP = Snow Pellets
AP = Small Hail	R = Rain	SW = Snow Showers
E = Sleet	RW = Rain Showers	T = Thunderstorm
EW = Sleet Showers	S = Snow	ZL = Freezing Drizzle
IC = Ice Crystals	SG = Snow Grains	ZR = Freezing Rain

INTENSITIES are indicated thus:

-- Very Light — Light (no sign) Moderate + Heavy

OBSTRUCTION TO VISION SYMBOLS

D = Dust	H = Haze	BD = Blowing Dust
F = Fog	IF = Ice Fog	BN = Blowing Sand
GF = Ground Fog	K = Smoke	BS = Blowing Snow

WIND

Direction in tens of degrees from true north, speed in knots 0000 indicates calm
G indicates gusty Peak speed of gusts follows G or Q when squall is reported
The contraction WSHFT followed by local time group in remarks indicates wind-shift and time of occurrence
EXAMPLES 3627 360 Degrees, 27 Knots,
          0127 010 Degrees, 27 Knots,
          1027 100 Degrees, 27 Knots,
          3627G40 360 Degrees, 27 Knots Peak speed in gusts 40 Knots

ALTIMETER SETTING

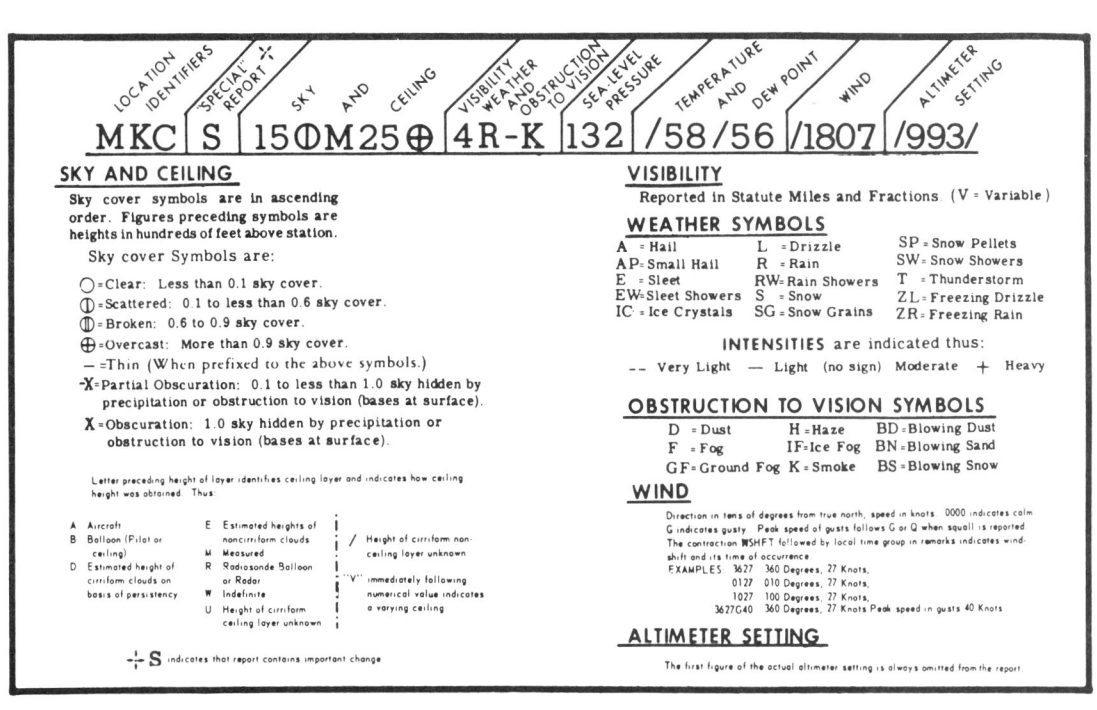

The first figure of the actual altimeter setting is always omitted from the report.

Fig. 94 A key for reading and interpreting scheduled hourly aviation weather reports.

```
FTW M13⓪35①10  127/70/68/1212G18/991/①V⊕
GSW M11⊕7  127/71/66/1315G24/993/RB27 RE43
030 (CIRCUIT 8030)
SPS 80①/-⊕15+  132/81/61/1922G27
```

0800C

```
029 SA291814OO
LBB 015+  132/57/42/2708/998/FEW CU SE
ABI E90①15  133/61/50/2908/997/CLDS DRK SE
MWL M25①/①10  129/65/59/3012G18/995/TSTM SE
FTW M20⓪50①10  128/72/65/2210G16/993/RB34
RE50 TSTM E MOVG SE CLDS DRK SW WSHFT 0740(
GSW M20⊕7TRW-  127/70/68/1620G26/993/LN
TSTMS SW-NE MOVG E
SPS /①15+  135/80/55/1715G20/998
```

1300C

```
029 SA291819OO
LBB 025  134/61/40/2710/999
ABI 015+  134/64/46/2810/999
MWL E90⓪15  133/66/50/3508G12/998
FTW E10⓪①15  131/68/52/2906/997
GSW 012  130/69/50/3110G15/996
030
SPS 020  135/78/50/1810/998
```

Using the key for reading and interpreting aviation weather reports and forecasts shown in Figure 94, the 1300 Z report for LBB (Lubbock, Texas) is decoded below:

LBB	Station Identifier
	Lubbock, Texas
60①	Sky condition
	Scattered clouds at 6,000 ft.
7	Visibility
	Visibility 7 miles
129	Sea level pressure
	1012.9 millibars
54	Temperature
	54 degrees F.
46	Dew point temperature
	46 degrees F.
2508	Wind direction and speed
	From 250 degrees, 8 knots
997	Altimeter setting
	29.97 inches of mercury

Now for the Remarks following "altimeter setting" in the Aviation weather reports. Frequently, remarks are added at the end of the report to cover unusual aspects of the weather, and often contain information which is as important as that found in the main body. The Remarks section is generally ignored by pilots who believe that the abbreviated information is difficult to interpret and meaningful only to meteorologists or air traffic control personnel. Admittedly, the coded NOTAMS (for example, — TUL 3/47 XX 4/8 UR) also found in this section, are of particular significance to weather and traffic personnel and require special knowledge to decode. The weather remarks of importance to pilots, however, utilize standard weather symbols (○, ⊕, RW, T, K, H, etc.) and simple abbreviations or contractions of words. The few special code words used occasionally can be easily memorized. The contractions are formed by omitting vowels and other letters in a way that the meaning of the information remains obvious. For example, WND DRCTN VRBL T

OVHD MOVG E should be read as WIND DIRECTION VARIABLE THUNDERSTORM OVERHEAD MOVING EAST.

The symbols and contractions introduced here include only those which are most frequently used and most significant to pilots. Your ability to interpret abbreviated remarks will improve with practice. A partial list of standard remarks is provided in the following paragraph. Samples of typical reports, followed by translations of the Remarks section, are presented below for familiarization purposes. Note how, in these samples, the weather situation reported in the main body, takes on a different perspective when the remarks are considered in the overall weather picture. In the first report, the surface visibility of 20 miles looks good, but in reading further, we find the visibility at flight altitudes is reported to be restricted by smoke and haze.

TRANSLATION OF REMARKS

1. towering cumulus clouds (TCU) southwest (SW), smoke (K), and haze (H) aloft (ALF).
2. heavy (HVY) cumulonimbus clouds (CB) and blowing dust (BD) in all quadrants (ALQDS).
3. mountain tops (MTN TOPS) obscured (OBSCD) west (W), rain showers (RW) of unknown intensity (U) north (N).
4. rain began (RB) 32 mins. after preceding hour, ended (E) 45 mins. after preceding hour, thunderstorm (T) east (E), pressure falling rapidly (PRESFR).
5. line (LN) cumulonimbus clouds (CB) southwest through north (SW-N), occasional (OCNL) lightning (LTG) cloud-to-ground (CG) northwest (NW), cumulonimbus mamma clouds (CM) north (N).

The abbreviated remarks listed here serve only as an introduction to the manner in which weather conditions are often described in weather reports and forecasts. An expanded list of standard abbreviations and contractions is found in the Appendix.

ACSL W — altocumulus standing lenticular clouds west.
BINOVC — breaks in the overcast.
CIG RGD — ceiling is ragged.
CU E — cumulus clouds east.
(CB — cumulonimbus) (CM — cumulonimbus mamma).
CFP cold front passage. (FROPA — frontal passage).
D5 — dust obscuring 5/10 of the sky.
FQT THDR NW — frequent thunder northwest.
KH ALF — smoke and haze aloft.
HIR CLDS VSB — higher clouds visible.
ICGIC — icing in clouds.
LN TSTMS E — line of thunderstorms east.
LTGIC — lightning in clouds. (CG — cloud-to-ground) (CC — cloud-to-cloud).
MTN RDGS OBSCD — mountain ridges obscured.
PRESFR — pressure falling rapidly. (RR — rising rapidly).
RADAT 75125 — (Radiosonde data) relative humidity 75% at lowest freezing level 12,500 feet.
RWU E — rain showers of unknown intensity east.
RB32 — rain began 32 mins. after preceding hour. (E — ended).
TCU ALQDS — towering cumulus in all quadrants.
SQLN NW — squall line northwest.
VIRGA — precipitation falling but not reaching the ground.
⊕ 65 — top of overcast is 6,500 feet.

TERMINAL FORECASTS (FT)

Valid for 24 hours, these forecasts (see Figure 95) are prepared for specific terminals with high aviation activity. Prepared every 6 hours, they are transmitted by teletypewriter to replace prior issuances. The basic forecast is for 18 hours. The last 6 hours are less specific. Weather conditions are stated as "VFR", "IFR", or "MVFR" (marginal VFR).

CONTENT

Each terminal forecast includes heights

SAMPLES OF COMPLETE REPORTS

1. DEN /⊕20 174/57/36/1103/015 TCU SW KH ALF.
2. ALS E500⊕12040 155/54/30/2117/015 HVY CB BD ALQDS.
3. ABQ E700⊕12040 111/68/55/1311/010 MTN TOPS OBSCD W RWU N.
4. LIT 45⊕E100⊕10 133/70/33/2409/977 RB32E45 T E PRESFR.
5. ACT 30⊕U015 078/85/64/1815/985 LN CB SW-N OCNL LTGCG NW CN N.

109

Station Designator	Date	Time (Greenwich)	Ceiling Designator	Cloud Amount	Weather	Wind
XYZ	06	1045	C34	⊕	3RW-FK	1815

Cloud Height (under C34); Visibility, Obstruction to Vision (under 3RW-FK)

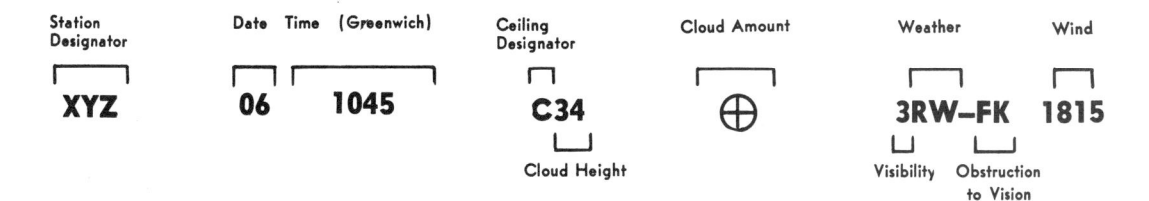

```
     FT INTMD EAST 182247
     FMN 182323 C70①2515. 03Z C40①OCNL C20⊕RW-SW-. 17Z MVFR..
     OGD 182323 C15①OCNL 2SW-. 03Z C15⊕3SW- OCNL C10X1S-F.
     17Z MVFR BCMG VFR.
     DEN 182323 140①C250①. 09Z 80①C140① 1912 ①V①. 17Z MVFR..
```

Fig. 95 The Terminal Forecast.

and amounts of sky cover, ceiling identifier "C" when appropriate, visiblity, weather, and/or obstruction to vision, surface wind, and, as necessary, remarks. Terminal forecasts do not include specific information concerning cloud tops or hazards such as icing and turbulence. This information is included in area forecasts.

TIME USED

The filing time and valid time are shown in Greenwich mean time. Time changes in the body of the forecast are also in Greenwich mean time. The weather conditions stated immediately following the terminal identifier are expected to occur at the beginning of the valid time.

SYMBOLS AND NOTATIONS

Symbols and notations used in terminal forecasts are the same as those used in Aviation Weather Reports, and appear in the same order.

CEILING IDENTIFIER

The forecast ceiling is identified by the "C" immediately preceding the height figures for the layer representing the ceiling.

CLOUD HEIGHTS AND SKY COVER

The heights of cloud bases or vertical visibility into a total surface-based obscuration are indicated by the standard symbols ○, ①, ⓪, ⊕, -①, -⓪, -⊕, -X, and X. Sky cover includes all cloud layers up to and including the ceiling layer (if any) and any layers significant to flight operations above a broken layer; for example, 8① C17① 50⊕. Adjacent broken or overcast layers with bases above 5,000 feet are considered as one layer when the tops of the lower layer are less than 3,000 feet from the base of the upper layer. Thus, if the forecaster expected conditions of C60① 80⊕, he would code this condition C60⊕.

VISIBILITY

A forecast of prevailing visibility appears only if it is expected to be 8 statute miles or less. Weather and/or obstructions to vision follow the visibility value when the visibility is forecast to be 6 statute miles or less, as in the examples: 6K, 3R.

SURFACE WIND

Surface wind is shown by using two numbers to indicate the direction (to 36 points of the compass and with reference to true North) from which the wind is expected to blow, followed by the speed in knots. If the wind speed is forecast to be less than 10 knots, the entire wind group is omitted. If gusty wind conditions are expected, this is indicated by the letter "G" following the speed, i.e., 2425G which menas "wind two four zero degrees, 25 knots and gusty". Peak gusts are shown following the "G" when gusts are expected to equal 35 knots; i.e., 2425G35 means "wind two four zero degrees, 25 knots, peak gusts 35 knots".

EXPECTED CHANGES IN WEATHER CONDITIONS

Significant changes in weather conditions are included if they are expected. A figure group in Greenwich mean time preceding the forecast changes shows the time that changes are expected to occur. The absence of indicated forecast changes implies generally uniform conditions throughout the 24-hour period of forecast validity. A gradual transition from one condition to another is indicated by modifying remarks.

READING THE FORECAST

Following are several examples of parts of terminal forecasts as they would appear on teletypewriter. The interpretation of each is given following the example. Notice that omission of an element can imply a forecasted condition just as though it were explicitly stated.

EXAMPLES INTERPRETATION

30①C50①

Three thousand scattered, ceiling five thousand broken, (visibility greater than 8 miles, wind less than 10 knots).

C3X1/2R-F

Ceiling three hundred, sky obscured, visibility one-half (mile), light rain and fog, (wind less than 10 knots).

◯

Clear, (visibility greater than 8 miles, wind less than 10 knots).

50①100−① C250⊕ 3615G

Five thousand scattered, one zero thousand thin broken, ceiling two five thousand overcast, (visibility greater than 8 miles), wind three six zero degrees, one five knots and gusty (when gusts are expected to equal or exceed 35 knots, the gust speed will be entered following the letter "G", i.e., 3615G40).

GROUPING OF FORECASTS

Several terminal forecasts may appear under one heading with each forecast beginning on a separate line. When the same conditions are forecast for one terminal as for another, this may be indicated by using "DO", meaning ditto, as shown in the following example:

BUR 182323 C15① 3215.　　1730P◯
LAX 182323 DO BUR

AMENDED TERMINAL FORECASTS

Amended terminal forecasts are issued principally when it is advisable for safety and efficiency of aircraft operations, including flight planning, dispatches, operational control and in-flight assistance to aircraft.

PLAIN LANGUAGE INTERPRETATION

Figure 95 shows a series of 24-hour terminal forecasts and a key for reading and interpreting them. In the terminal forecast shown in Figure 95 the heading is:

FT INTMD EAST 182247

FT indicates that the forecast will be a terminal forecast. INTMD is the general area location (intermountain). EAST is the direction from the forecasting office. 182247 indicates the date (18th of the month) and the time (2247) in Greenwich mean time that the forecast was transmitted to the receiving office.

The terminal forecast for Denver, Colo. and its plain language interpretation is:

DEN　182323　140①　C250①.　09Z　80① C140① 1912 ①V①. 17Z MVFR..

The station identifier for Denver is DEN. The forecast is for the 18th of the month and is for 24 hours from 2300 Greenwich mean time to 2300 GMT the next day. At 2300 GMT on the 18th; Scattered clouds at 14,000 feet, with a ceiling of 25,000 broken clouds. After 09Z scattered clouds at 8,000 feet and a ceiling of 14,000 broken, is predicted. Wind from 190 degrees at 12 knots. The scattered clouds will be variable to broken. After 1700 GMT, weather is expected to be marginal VFR.

AREA FORECASTS

Area forecasts are issued and/or amended every 6 hours by several forecast offices covering the 50 states. Each area comprises several states or portions of states. The forecast includes expected weather for an 18-hour period in detail and a brief outlook for an additional 12 hours. It describes areas of clouds and significant weather, ceilings, height of cloud bases and tops, surface visibilities and the movements of major weather disturbances such as thunderstorms and squall lines. It also gives heights of the freezing level and zones of expected icing.

Area forecasts have the following format:
- Heading
- Synopsis of expected weather in the forecast area
- Significant cloud and weather in detail for an 18-hour period followed by a brief 12-hour outlook
- Icing

Area forecasts are rather hard to read at first, but after a while you will get the hang of it. Their text is a combination of symbols used in hourly aviation weather reports and extreme abbreviations and contractions as listed in the Appendix.

A sample area forecast is shown with its plain language interpretation below.

SLC FA 021240
13Z SUN-072 MON
OTLK 07Z-19Z MON

MONT IDA NEV UTAH ARIZ

HGTS ASL UNLESS NOTED

SYNS...CDFNT VCNTY VEL-GCN-PHX LN AT 13Z MOVG TO NR FMN-DUG BY 19Z AND EWD THRU N MEX THRFTR. ASSOCD UPR TROF WILL MOVE TO ERN MONT S TO ERN UTAH BDR BFR 07Z.

SIGCLDS AND WX..

SERN IDA ERN NEV UTAH NRN ARIZ
MTNS RTHR GENLY OBSCD ABV 70-80 BY CLDS AND OCNL SNW EXCP E OF FNT UTAH AND NRN ARIZ CLD LYR MOSTLY 120-140 BKN. TOPS LYRS MSTLY 160-180. LCL CIGS AND VSBYS AOB 1 THSD AND 3 MIS IN OCNL SNW. BY 19Z IPVG 80 80-1000 WITH ONLY ISOLD SW–. FTHR IPVMT AFTN AND EVE. OTLK... GENLY VFR

WRN NEV AND SRN ARIZ
NO SIGCLD OR WX. OTLK...VFR

SWRN IDA
CHC FEW SW– WITH ASSOCD CLDNS 80-100 BKN BCMG MSTLY SCT BY 01Z. OTLK...VFR

NRN IDA AND MONT
MSTLY 80-1100 TOPS TO 160 WITH WDLY SCT SW– EXCP NRN IDA AND WRN MONT OCNLY 70 BKN WITH MTNS OCNLY OBSCD. SOME LO ST AND FOG NWRN PTN MONT E OF DVD GENLY DSIPTG BY 19Z. ALG E SLPS DVD IN MONT WLY SFC WNDS GUSTY TO 30 KTS AFTN. AFT 01Z SW– OVR AREA BCMG ISOLD. OTLK...VFR EXCP OCNL MVFR MTNS

ICG. GENLY LGT ICGIC SLD CLD AREAS EXCP CHC MDT SERN IDA UTAH NRN ARIZ TIL CLDS DCR. FRZLVL SFC TO 50 EXCP 80-100 E OF FNT THEN LWRG TO SFC TO 80.

HEADING. Salt Lake City (SLC) office issued the area forecast (FA) on the 2nd of the month at 1240 GMT. It is valid for an 18-hour period from 1300 Z (GMT) to 0700 Z Mon. A 12-hour outlook is presented for the time period of 0700 Z to 1900 Z Mon. for Montana, Idaho, Nevada, Utah, and Arizona. All heights are above sea level (ASL) unless noted.

SYNOPSIS. Cold front vicinity Vernal (Utah) — Grand Canyon — Phoenix line at 1300 Z moving to near Farmington — Douglas (N.M.) by 1900 Z and eastward through New Mexico thereafter. Associated upper trough will move to eastern Montana south to eastern Utah border before 0700 Z.

SIGNIFICANT CLOUDS AND WEATHER for southern Idaho, eastern Nevada, Utah, and northern Arizona: Mountains rather generally obscured above 7,000-8,000 by clouds and occasional snow except east of front. Utah and northern Arizona, cloud layer mostly 12,000-14,000 broken. Tops of layers mostly 16,000-18,000. Local ceilings and visibilities about 1,000 and 3 miles in occasional snow. By 1900 Z improving to 8,000-10,000 broken with only isolated light snow showers. Further improvement afternoon and evening. Outlook — VFR.

For western Nevada and southern Arizona. No significant clouds or weather. Outlook — VFR.

For southwestern Idaho. Chance of few light snow showers with associated cloudiness of 8,000-10,000 broken becoming mostly scattered by 0100 Z. Outlook — VFR.

For northern Idaho and Montana. Mostly 8,000-10,000 broken, tops to 16,000 with widely scattered light snow showers except western Idaho and western Montana occasionally 7,000 broken with mountains occasionally obscured. Some low stratus and fog northern portion Montana east of divide generally dissipating by 1900 Z. Along east slopes of divide in Montana, westerly surface winds gusty to 30 knots in the afternoon. After 0100 Z light snow showers over area becoming isolated. Outlook — VFR except occasional marginal VFR over mountains.

ICING. Generally light icing in clouds in solid cloud areas except chance of moderate icing in southern Idaho, Utah, northern Arizona until clouds decrease. Freezing level from the surface to 5,000 except 8,000-10,000 east of front then lowering to surface to 8,000.

WINDS ALOFT FORECASTS

Charted winds aloft observations are available at most briefing outlets equipped with facsimile. However, these reports are several hours old when received and do not necessarily represent wind that will be encountered during subsequent flights.

The pilot is most interested in the *winds- and temperatures-aloft forecast* which forecasts the winds and temperatures at selected altitudes and is issued every 6 hours. Depending upon station elevation, wind direction and speed are normally forecast for mean sea level (MSL) altitudes of 3,000 ft., 6,000 ft., 9,000 ft., and 12,000 ft., and for pressure altitudes of 18,000 ft., 24,000 ft., 30,000 ft., 34,000 ft., and 39,000 ft. (Pressure altitude is the altitude shown on a pressure altimeter set at the standard altimeter setting of 29.92 inches.) Because of terrain effect, no forecasts will be made for levels less than 1,500 ft. above station elevation. For example, if station elevation is more than 1,500 ft. (mean sea level), no forecast will be given for the 3,000-foot level. If station elevation is more than 4,500 ft., no forecast will be given for the 6,000-foot level, and so on.

Temperatures are forecast for all wind forecast levels except the 3,000-foot level or the lowest level when this level is less than 2,500 ft. above station elevation. The 3,000-foot level will not have a forecast temperature at any time. If the first forecast wind level for a given station is 6,000 ft. but the station elevation is greater than 3,500 ft., then there will be no forecast temperature for the 6,000-foot level because the first reported wind level is less than 2,500 ft. above the station elevation.

Wind direction is forecast in *true* direction from which it is blowing and speed is forecast in knots (nautical miles per hour).

Temperature is forecast in degrees Celsius (Centigrade). Temperatures are preceded by a plus (+) or minus (-) sign up through the 24,000-foot level, depending upon whether the temperature is above or below 0°C. Above this forecast level, the minus (-) sign is omitted.

Weather briefing stations equipped with facsimile will display charted FDs, and some stations not so equipped may plot the charts locally.

INTERPRETATION OF WINDS AND TEMPERATURES-ALOFT FORECASTS

In the first line "FD WBC 190545," "FD" indicates a winds-aloft forecast. "WBC" indicates that the winds-aloft forecast is prepared at the National Meteorological Center through the use of digital computers. (Since all winds-aloft forecasts are now prepared by computers in the National Meteorological Center, the coding WBC will appear on all FD reports.) In "190545" the first two digits (19) mean the nineteenth day of the month. "0545" indicates the time (24-hour clock) of the report in Greenwich Mean Time (Z). The second line, "BASED ON 190000Z DATA," indicates that the forecase is based on data collected at midnight, Greenwich Mean Time, on the nineteenth day of the month.

The third line "VALID 191200Z FOR USE 0600-1500Z" means that the forecast data is valid at 6 a.m. CST, and the forecast is to be used by pilots between 0600Z and 1500Z or midnight to 9:00 a.m. (CST).

In the fourth line of the report "FT 3000, 6000 ...," "FT" represents feet and "3000, 6000, etc." represent the altitudes at which winds and temperatures are forecast. The temperature is never forecast for the 3,000-foot level. The wind forecast for each station at 3,000 feet MSL appears in the column below "3000"; the wind and temperature (if applicable) at 6,000 ft. MSL appear in the column below "6000 FT" and so on.

The first reporting station is Dallas, Texas, (DAL). The group of figures "1625"

EXAMPLES OF WINDS-ALOFT FORECASTS (To 24,000 ft.)

```
FD WBC 190545
BASED ON 190000Z DATA
VALID 191200Z FOR USE 0600-1500Z. TEMPS NEG ABV 24000
FT      3000    6000     9000     12000    18000    24000
DAL     1625    1827+10  2133+06  2339-02  2345-12  2357-23
ABI             1826+08  2033+05  2242-03  2349-14  2359-24
ABQ                      2227+08  2235-01  2352-13  2363-25
HOU     9900    9900+14  2310+08  2415+01  2427-10  2442-21
```

appear in the "3000" column opposite DAL. The first pair of digits of this group when multiplied by 10 represents the true wind direction (the same result is obtained by adding a zero to these two digits). The second pair of digits represents the wind speed in knots. Applying these rules on the group of figures, the wind direction at 3,000 ft. above sea level (MSL) at Dallas, Texas, is forecast to be from 160° (true) and the wind speed is forecast to be 25 knots. The figure group "1827+10" is in the column headed by "6000 FT" for Dallas. Applying the rules to this grouping, the wind direction at 6,000 ft. above sea level at Dallas is forecast to be from 180° (true), wind speed is forecast to be 27 knots, and the temperature is forecast to be +10°C. The temperature at 18,000 ft. at Dallas is forecast to be -12°C.

The first reported level for Abilene, Texas (ABI), is 6,000 ft. The elevation at this location is more than 1,500 ft. and less than 4,500 ft., so the first forecast wind level would be 6,000 ft. Note that temperature forecasts are not included with the 3,000-foot level.

When the wind speed reaches 100 knots or more, a special rule must be applied to the four-digit grouping to find wind direction and speed. Since most pilots will not normally fly at altitudes where such wind speeds will be encountered, the rule will not be covered in this text. The group of figures "9900" indicates a light and variable wind. Note that a light and variable wind is forecast for the Houston area at 3,000 and 6,000 ft.

INTERPOLATION FOR INTERMEDIATE WINDS AND TEMPERATURES

To obtain the wind direction and speed at an altitude intermediate to those given in the winds-aloft forecast, you must interpolate. For example, the forecast wind direction, wind speed, and temperature at 7,500 ft. at Dallas are 195° (true) 30 knots, and 8°C. We find these values by first finding the value of the wind direction and speed and temperature forecast at 6,000 and 9,000 ft.

Level	Wind Direction	Wind Speed	Temperature
6,000	180°	27	+10
7,500	?	?	?
9,000	210°	33	+06

Since 7,500 ft. is halfway between 6,000 ft. and 9,000 ft., we assume that the wind direction and wind speed are halfway between the respective values at 6,000 ft. and 9,000 ft. 195° is halfway between 180° and 210° and 30 knots is halfway between 27 and 33 knots.

IN-FLIGHT WEATHER ADVISORIES

When weather is not adequately covered by the latest forecasts, the National Weather Service issues short-term forecasts of potentially hazardous weather by means of unscheduled IN-FLIGHT WEATHER ADVISORIES. These warning forecasts are in two categories — SIGMETs and AIRMETs.

SIGMET (WS) A SIGMET identifies weather phenomena of particular significance to the safety of transport category and other aircraft. This advisory covers tornadoes, lines of thunderstorms (squall lines), embedded thunderstorms, hail of three-quarters inch or more, severe and extreme turbulence, severe icing, and widespread duststorms or sandstorms lowering visibilities to less than 2 miles.

AIRMET (WA) An AIRMET identifies weather phenomena less severe than those covered by a SIGMET but still important to light aircraft safety. This advisory covers moderate icing; moderate turbulence; extensive areas of visibilities less than 2 miles and/or ceilings less than 1,000 ft., including mountain ridges and passes; and winds of 40 knots or more within 2,000 ft., including mountain ridges and passes; and winds of 40 knots or more within 2,000 ft. of the surface.

Each FSS broadcasts any advisory which affects an area within 150 nautical miles of the station or within 150 nautical miles of a remote facility controlled by the station. They broadcast the advisory for the first hour after issuance; during the remainder of its valid period, they broadcast only the advisory number and state that it is current. An AIRMET is broadcast at 15 and 45 minutes past the hour; and a SIGMET, on the hour and at 15, 30, 45 minutes past the hour. Advisory broadcasts at 15 minutes past the hour are part of the scheduled broadcast.

During preflight briefing, the FSS or National Weather Service briefer will advise you of any SIGMET or AIRMET for an area and valid time that may affect your proposed flight. In flight you will receive these advisories during radio contacts with FSS stations.

EXAMPLE OF A SIGMET

SAT WS 081830
081830-082300
SIGMET CHARLIE 1. OVR SRN TEX WITHIN AN AREA BNDD BY SAN ANTONIO-PALACIOS-40 S OF CORPUS CHRISTI-COTULLA SCTD TO LCLY NMRS SHWRS AND TSTMS FQTLY IN BRKN LNS WITH TOPS TO 450. CONDS CONTG BYD 23Z.

PLAIN LANGUGE INTERPRETATION

"WS" indicates an in-flight advisory (SIGMET); SAT (San Antonio, Texas, the originating station); "08" the eighth day of the month, and 1830 GMT (12:30 p.m. CST) the time at which the advisory was made and it is valid from 12:30 p.m. to 5 p.m. on the eighth day of the month.

SIGMET Charlie 1 Over Southern Texas, within an area bounded by the four points of San Antonio, Palacios, 40 miles south of Corpus Christi and Cotulla, there will be scattered to locally numerous showers and thunderstorms frequently in broken lines with tops to 45,000 ft. Conditions will continue beyond 5 p.m.

EXAMPLES OF AIRMETS

ELP WA 081710
081710-082200
AIRMET ALPHA 1. IN SRN ARIZ SRN NM AND EXTRM SWRN TEX MDT TURBC OCNLY SVR FOR LGT ACFT BLO 130 MSL AFT 1800.

SAT WA 081605
081605-081800
AIRMET BRAVO 1. OVR SWRN TEX 50 MI EITHER SIDE OF A LN FM 40 E OF EAGLE PASS TO 30 NNE OF FORT STOCKTON CIGS FQTLY BLO 1 THSD WITH VSBYS OCNL LESS THAN 2 MI IN PCPN AND FOG. HIR TRNN AND HILLS OCNL OBSCD. CONDS CONTG TIL 18Z.

PLAIN LANGUAGE INTERPRETATION

AIRMET ALPHA 1 is valid on the eighth day of the month from 1710 Greenwich Mean Time (10:10 a.m., Mountain Standard Time) to 2200 GMT (3 p.m. MST). In southern Arizona, Southern New Mexico, and extreme southwestern Texas, moderate turbulence will occur and occasionally become severe for light aircraft below 13,000 ft. mean sea level after 11 a.m. MST.

AIRMET BRAVO 1 is valid on the eighth day of the month from 1605 GMT (10:05 a.m. CST) to 1800 GMT (12 noon CST). Over southwestern Texas, 50 miles to either side of a line from 40 miles east of Eagle Pass to 30 miles north-northeast of Fort Stockton, ceilings frequently will be below 1,000 ft. with visibilities occasionally less than 2 miles in precipitation and fog. Higher terrain and hills occasionally will be obscured. Conditions will continue until 12 noon.

PILOT REPORTS (PIREPS)

Surface weather reports spot sample the weather and frequently weather between reporting stations will differ from that shown by the spot reports. Also, the surface observer cannot observe cloud tops, cloud conditions above an overcast, turbulence, or icing. Pilot reports are the only source of these observations, and a pilot must rely heavily on these reports when available. It behooves all pilots to report weather in flight to aid his fellow flyers. Some pilot-reported information is included in the remarks section of the hourly Aviation Weather report and some in individual pilot reports. Periodically, pilot reports are summarized into a single report called the pilot report summary.

EXAMPLES OF PILOT WEATHER REPORT SUMMARY

SAT UB 081835Z
GDP SMOOTH 85 PA28
20 NNE CRP-3 NNE ALI 25   SCTD RW
24 NNE CRP LN TSTMS NW-SE CIG 3 HND VSBY 1/4
JCT-SAT 40   60
30E SAT RW MDT TURBC
INK ALMOST SLD   BECOMES THEN
25 W MAF TOPS 50
   INK TO ELP

PLAIN LANGUAGE INTERPRETATION

This pilot report summary (UB) was filed from San Antonio, Texas, (SAT) on the 8th day of the month (08) at 1835 GMT (12:35 CST).

Guadalupe Pass (GDP) was smooth at 8,500 ft. MSL reported by a PA28 (Piper Cherokee).

Twenty miles north-northeast of Corpus Christi to a point 3 miles north-northeast of Alice, a broken layer of clouds with bases at 2,500 MSL, and rainshowers.

Twenty-four miles north-northeast of Corpus Christi, a line of thunderstorms extends northwest-southeast, with ceilings of 300 ft. and visibility ¼ mile.

From Junction to San Antonio, an overcast layer of clouds with bases at 4,000 ft. MSL and tops at 6,000 ft. MSL.

Thirty miles east of San Antonio, rainshowers with moderate turbulence.

Over Wink, there is an almost solid overcast with tops at 5,000 ft. MSL becoming clear 25 miles west of Midland.

Clear from Wink to El Paso.

SUMMARY, AVAILABLE WEATHER DATA

Aviation weather is made available to the pilot in the following format:

- Weather maps (or charts)
  - Surface weather chart
  - Weather depiction chart
  - Radar summary chart
  - Low-level prognostic charts
- Aviation weather reports (hourly or sequence reports)
- Weather forecasts
  - Terminal forecast (FT)
  - Area forecast (FA)
- Winds aloft forecast
- In-flight weather advisories
  - SIGMETS
  - AIRMETS
- Pilot reports (PIREPS)

The instrument pilot must be able to read and interpret all available weather data and evaluate it with respect to his flight.

11 WEATHER BRIEFING

Fig. 96 Pilot briefing center at a Weather Service Office airport station.

PREFLIGHT

What should the pilot do to prepare himself for a cross-country flight? Among other important things, a weather briefing is necessary — in fact it is a Federal Aviation Regulation. As a reminder, we quote FAR, Part 91, in part:

"Each pilot in command shall, before beginning a flight, familiarize himself with all available information concerning that flight. This information must include, *for a flight under IFR or a flight not in the vicinity of an airport, available weather reports and forecasts,* fuel requirements, alternatives available if the planned flight cannot be completed . . .".

Careful preflight planning including a weather briefing, is extremely important. With adequate planning the pilot can complete his flight with greater confidence, ease and safety. Without it, he may become a statistic — figures show *inadequate preflight planning* is a significant cause of fatal accidents.

There are many important steps in preflight planning, however we will concentrate on weather briefing. You may wish to check the weather before you continue with other aspects of flight planning to see, first of all, if the flight is feasible and, if it is, which route is best. You should visit the local National Weather Service airport station or the nearest FAA Flight Service Station, if available. A personal visit is best because you will have access to the latest weather maps and charts, area forecasts, terminal forecasts, SIGMETS and AIRMETS, hourly sequence reports, PIREPS, and winds-aloft forecasts, and you will have a weather briefer to interpret the weather for you.

If a visit is impractical, telephone calls are welcomed. Some National Weather Service stations have "restricted" (unlisted) telephone numbers on which *only* aviation weather information is given. These numbers, along with other National Weather Service and FSS numbers, are listed in the Airman's Information Manual, part 2. When telephoning for aviation weather information, identify yourself as a pilot; state your intended route, destination, intended time of takeoff, approximate time en route; and advise if you intend to fly only VFR.

HOW TO GET A BRIEFING

- Personal visit — Visit the nearest National Weather Service airport station or FAA Flight Service Station.
- By telephone — Call the nearest National Weather Service airport station or FAA Flight Service Station, or call PATWAS (Pilot Automatic Telephone Answering Service). The telephone numbers of these facilities may be found in the Airman's Information Manual.
- By radio — Tune to any L/MF (Low/Medium Frequency) "H" Radio Beacon for continuous transcribed weather broadcasts (TWEBS). Tune to any NAVAID with voice broadcast at 15 minutes after each hour for scheduled weather broadcasts. Call the nearest FAA Flight Service Station radio facility.

PERSONAL VISIT TO NWS OFFICE OR FSS

By far the best procedure is a personal visit to the nearest National Weather Service airport station or FAA Flight Service Station. Available aviation weather reports, forecasts and weather charts are displayed at these locations. Pilots should feel free to help themselves to this information or to ask the assistance of the duty employee.

Flight Service Specialists are qualified and certificated by the NOAA/NWS as Pilot Weather Briefers. They are not authorized to make original forecasts but are authorized to translate and interpret available forecasts and reports directly into terms of the weather conditions which you can expect along your flight route and at destination.

They also will assist you in selecting an alternate course of action in the event adverse weather is encountered.

To make the preflight visit to the NWS or FSS productive and efficient, a systematic procedure should be followed:

- FIRST — Look at the weather charts to provide you with an overall weather "picture." Locations of frontal activity and IFR weather areas can be seen at a glance.
- SECOND — Look at the latest hourly sequence reports for stations along your route. Writing them down helps to retain the information.
- THIRD — Evaluate the terminal forecasts at your destination as well as stations along your route. Also, write these down for emphasis as well as future use. Are forecast conditions consistent with your flying ability and your airplane?
- FOURTH — Study the area forecasts for weather, cloud conditions, cloud tops and icing.
- FIFTH — Write down wind aloft forecasts for use in flight planning.
- SIXTH — Check pilot reports, radar reports, SIGMETS and AIRMETS. You can also add a seventh step: Talk to the weather man on duty. Save step seven to the last. Don't take the easy way out and do this as step one.

TELEPHONE BRIEFING

The following information for the briefer is considered essential:
- Your name, type of pilot certificate held, e.g., student, private, commercial, and whether instrument rated.
- Type of aircraft and aircraft number.
- Point of departure and destination.
- Proposed route and flight altitude.
- Estimated time of departure and arrival plus time needed to reach alternate if required.
- Whether you wish to go IFR or VFR.

Pilots should provide this information promptly, in a brief and well-organized manner.

A preflight weather briefing will be incomplete unless it includes:
- Weather synopsis (position of lows, fronts, ridges, etc.)
- Current weather conditions.
- Alternate routes (if necessary).
- Hazardous weather.
- Forecast winds aloft.

Fig. 97 Pre-flight service for pilot briefing is available at all Flight Service Stations (FSSs).

All of these items are on the weather briefer's checklist.

(PATWAS) Pilot's Automatic Telephone Weather Answering Service offers transcribed weather forecasts by telephone for a 250-mile radius of service in most large U.S. cities. As previously stated, the telephone numbers of these facilities may be found in the Airman's Information Manual. At the conclusion of a PATWAS recording, you may get additional information by holding the phone and waiting for the weather briefer to answer.

BRIEFING BY RADIO

Continuous transcribed weather broadcasts (TWEB) on L/MF radio facilities provide recorded aeronautical and meteorological information for an area of 250 miles radius of the broadcast outlet. The context of the transcribed broadcast is: A description of the synoptic weather situation, warnings (if applicable), a forecast of aviation weather including winds aloft, pilot reports, and radar reports (if available) and not more than 20 current surface weather reports. These items are repeated making the service continuous. Material is updated as new reports and revised forecasts are issued. In most areas FAA uses non-directional (NDB) radio beacons in the 200-400 kHz range for these weather braodcasts while in a few areas automatic broadcasts are made combining L/MF and VHF outlets. There are now over 100 TWEB outlets in the 48 conterminous states including the VOR's.

IN-FLIGHT WEATHER DATA

Weather service reports, forecasts, and advisories are broadcast over radio communication facilities of the Federal Aviation Administration (FAA).

Aviation weather broadcasts are perhaps best described under the categories of "scheduled broadcasts" and "continuous broadcasts" (TWEB described previously). They differ in that some are transmitted over low/medium frequencies (L/MF) ranging from 200 to 400 kiloHertz (kHz) and others are broadcast on the very high frequencies (VHF) of 108 to 118 megaHertz (mHz).

Scheduled aviation broadcasts are made once each hour at 15 minutes past the hour. Included is the latest available local weather report, plus not more than 12 weather reports from airways and off-airways locations selected to serve the needs of the local users. As available, scheduled broadcasts include: warnings of potentially hazardous weather such as thunderstorms, turbulence, icing, and fog; pilot reports; and radar weather reports. Most scheduled aviation weather broadcasts are transmitted on the VHF channels but a few are found on the L/MF channels.

EN ROUTE FLIGHT ADVISORY SERVICE

En Route Flight Advisory Service is a service specifically designed to provide the pilot with timely weather information pertinent to his type of flight intended, route of flight and altitude. It will be available throughout the conterminous U.S. along prominent and heavily traveled flyways at a service criterion of 5000' above ground level at 80 miles from an En Route Flight Advisory Service communications outlet. En Route Flight Advisory Service will be provided from selected FAA FSSs controlling one or more remote communications outlets covering a large geographical area. All communications will be conducted on the designated frequency, 122.0 MHz using the radio call *(name of station)* **FLIGHT WATCH**. Routine weather information plus current reports on the location of thunderstorms and other hazardous weather as observed and reported by pilots or observed on weather radar may be obtained from the nearest flight watch facility.

To contact a flight watch facility on 122.0 MHz use the name of the controlling FSS and the words FLIGHT WATCH or, if the controlling FSS is unknown, simply call "FLIGHT WATCH' and give the aircraft position in relation to the nearest VOR.
Example:
OAKLAND FLIGHT WATCH, PIPER TWO SEVEN
SIX THREE PAPA etc.
FLIGHT WATCH, PIPER TWO SEVEN SIX
THREE PAPA, OVER RED BLUFF VOR, OVER

PILOT WEATHER REPORTS (PIREPS)

Whenever 5,000 ft. or lower ceilings, 5-mile or lower visibilities, or thunderstorms and related phenomena are reported or forecast, FAA stations are required to solicit and collect PIREPS which describe conditions aloft. Pilots are urged to cooperate and volunteer reports of cloud tops, upper cloud layers, thunderstorms, ice, turbulence, strong winds and other signficant flight condition information. PIREPS should be given directly to FAA stations on normal en route frequencies.

SUMMARY

1. The National Weather Service (NWS) maintains a comprehensive surface and upper air weather observing program and a nationwide aviation weather forecasting and pilot briefing service.

2. Weather observations are made each hour or more often at over 600 locations in the United States. These observations may be used to determine the present weather conditions for flight planning purposes.

3. Every six hours the Weather Service Forecast Offices (WSFO) prepare detailed flying weather forecasts for 12-hour periods for about 427 air terminals in the United States including Alaska and Hawaii. In addition, 24-hour terminal forecasts are provided for about 139 major airports throughout the country. Every six hours a detailed 12-hour area forecast is prepared for each of the 14 areas into which the conterminous United States has been divided for forecasting purposes. Area forecasts are also issued for Alaska and Hawaii. Winds aloft forecasts are provided for about 120 locations in the United States and Alaska for flight operational purposes. All of the above flying weather forecasts are given wide distribution via teletypewriter circuits.

4. Available aviation weather reports and forecasts are displayed at each Weather Service Office and FAA Flight Service Station. Pilots should feel free to help themselves to this information or to ask the assistance of the duty employee.

5. When telephoning for information, use the following procedures:

a. Identify yourself as a pilot and give aircraft identification if known. (Many persons calling Weather Service Offices want information for purposes other than flying.)

b. State your intended route, destination, proposed departure time, and estimated time en route.

c. Advise if prepared to fly IFR.

6. Flight Service Specialists are qualified and certificated by the NOAA/NWS as Pilot Weather Briefers. They are not authorized to make original forecasts but are authorized to translate and interpret available forecasts and reports directly into terms of the weather conditions which you can expect along your flight route and at destination. They also will assist you in selecting an alternate course of action in the event adverse weather is encountered. It is not necessary to be thoroughly familiar with the standard phraseologies and procedures for air/ground communications. A brief call stating your message in your own words will receive immediate attention. If a complete weather briefing is desired, advise the FSS accordingly. The FSS only provides that weather information which is specifically requested.

7. Combined station/tower (CS/T) personnel are not certificated pilot weather briefers; however, they can assist you by providing factual data from weather reports and forecasts.

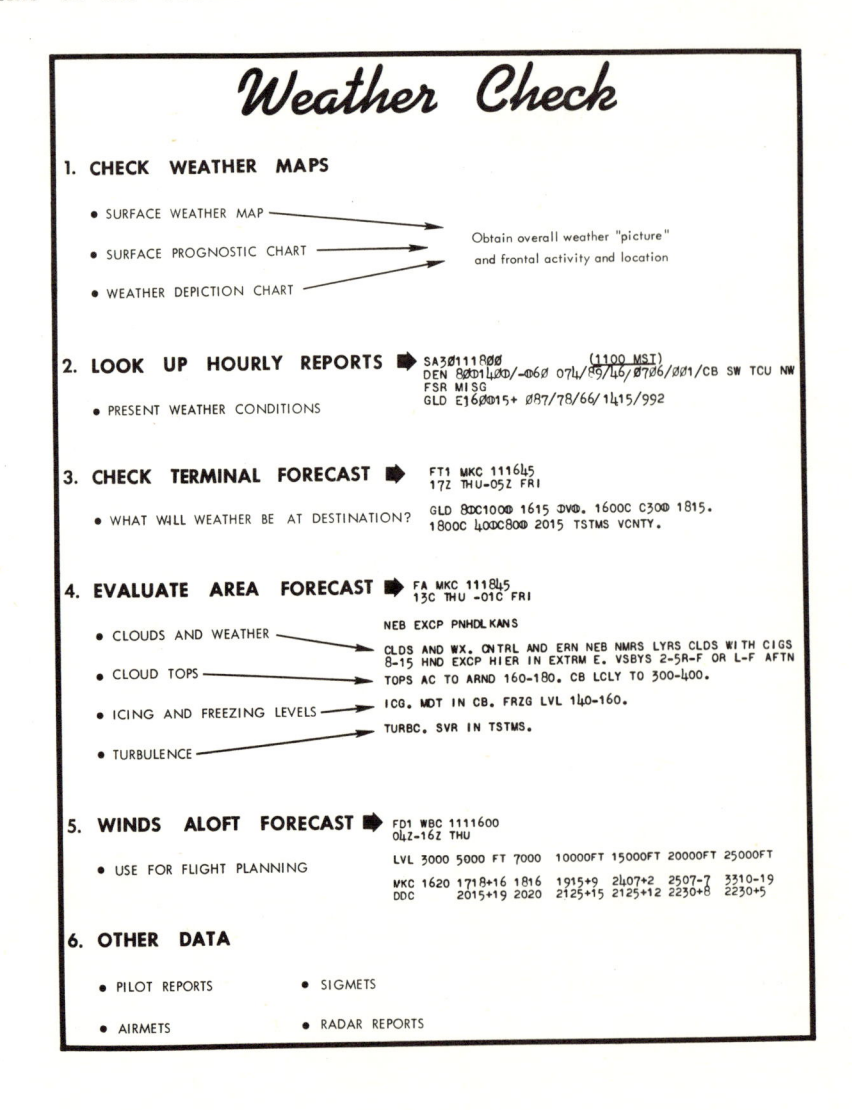

Weather Check

1. **CHECK WEATHER MAPS**
   - SURFACE WEATHER MAP
   - SURFACE PROGNOSTIC CHART
   - WEATHER DEPICTION CHART

   → Obtain overall weather "picture" and frontal activity and location

2. **LOOK UP HOURLY REPORTS** →
   ```
   SA301111800                (1100 MST)
   DEN 80⊕140⊕/-060 074/89/46/0706/001/CB SW TCU NW
   FSR MISG
   GLD E160015+ 087/78/66/1415/992
   ```
   - PRESENT WEATHER CONDITIONS

3. **CHECK TERMINAL FORECAST** →
   ```
   FT1 MKC 111645
   17Z THU-05Z FRI
   GLD 8⊕C100⊕ 1615 ⊕V⊕. 1600C C30⊕ 1815.
   1800C 40⊕C80⊕ 2015 TSTMS VCNTY.
   ```
   - WHAT WILL WEATHER BE AT DESTINATION?

4. **EVALUATE AREA FORECAST** →
   ```
   FA MKC 111845
   13C THU -01C FRI

   NEB EXCP PNHDL KANS
   CLDS AND WX. CNTRL AND ERN NEB NMRS LYRS CLDS WITH CIGS
   8-15 HND EXCP HIER IN EXTRM E. VSBYS 2-5R-F OR L-F AFTN
   TOPS AC TO ARND 160-180. CB LCLY TO 300-400.
   ICG. MDT IN CB. FRZG LVL 140-160.
   TURBC. SVR IN TSTMS.
   ```
   - CLOUDS AND WEATHER
   - CLOUD TOPS
   - ICING AND FREEZING LEVELS
   - TURBULENCE

5. **WINDS ALOFT FORECAST** →
   ```
   FD1 WBC 1111600
   04Z-16Z THU

   LVL  3000 5000 FT 7000  10000FT 15000FT 20000FT 25000FT
   MKC  1620 1718+16 1816  1915+9  2407+2  2507-7  3310-19
   DDC       2015+19 2020  2125+15 2125+12 2230+8  2230+5
   ```
   - USE FOR FLIGHT PLANNING

6. **OTHER DATA**
   - PILOT REPORTS
   - AIRMETS
   - SIGMETS
   - RADAR REPORTS

FLIGHT PLANNING 12

As soon as the VFR pilot gets involved in studying for his instrument rating, he finds out how really disorganized his flying has been. The slip-shod methods of getting from one place to another during his strictly VFR days lack the precision and dependability required for IFR flights.

The secret of good flight planning is the organized flight planning and log sheets (Figure 98) and a methodical procedure for completing them in a minimum amount of time. Your first exercises in flight planning may seem unnecessarily time consuming and discouraging. However, as you gain experience you will find this important phase of an IFR flight becoming more routine. Remember, the airline pilot spends approximately one hour in flight planning prior to takeoff even though he has flown the same route many times. It is emphasized that the student or low-time instrument pilot should spend at least one hour in planning a flight in actual IFR weather and at least one-half hour in planning a simulated IFR flight in VFR weather.

As in previous chapters on basic instruments, radio procedures and weather briefing, emphasis will be placed on an ORGANIZED STEP-BY-STEP PROCEDURE for flight planning based on the use of flight planning and log sheets. These steps are:
- Assemble equipment and charts.
- Initial route planning using chart information and check NOTAMS.
- Weather check and evaluation.
- Complete flight planning sheets.

After filing flight plan with ATC, the in-flight bookkeeping consists of filling in the ACTUAL columns and making in-flight changes as required.

The above outlined steps are further explained in the following paragraphs:
- ASSEMBLE EQUIPMENT AND DATA
  - COMPUTER — A standard aeronautical computer for calculating true airspeed and fuel consumption and solving wind vector problems is a necessity.
  - CHARTS — Enroute Low Altitude (Radio Facility) Charts and Approach Procedure (AL) Charts appropriate to route of flight.
  - FLIGHT PLANNING AND LOG SHEETS — It is considered imperative, at least for the student or low time instrument pilot, to use complete and detailed forms as shown in Figure 98 suitable for use with a full sized clipboard. Abbreviated forms should not be used until considerable experience has been accumulated.
  - CLIPBOARD — Use a standard, full-sized clipboard for holding in your lap.
  - AIRPLANE FLIGHT MANUAL — For airspeed, cruising altitude and fuel consumption data.
- INITIAL ROUTE PLANNING

  Using Enroute Low Altitude (Radio Facility) charts, fill out the Flight Planning and Log sheets with all available data such as:
  - Route (obtain preferred route from AIM). Plan route to VOR/VORTAC at destination.
  - Radio ranges and frequencies or any other compulsory checkpoints such as intersections.
  - Distance between check points in nautical miles.
  - Magnetic courses of the airway.
  - Variation.
  - Minimum Enroute Altitude (MEA).
  - Look up Notices to Airmen (NOTAMS) and other pertinent data in the Airmans Information Manual (AIM).

  Do this as far ahead of time as possible, preferably the night before an early morning flight. See Figure 98 for an example of a Flight Planning and Log Sheet filled out with these data.

- WEATHER CHECK AND EVALUATION

  Follow procedures as outlined in chapter 11, Weather Briefing. Evaluate this information relative to your airplane, your equipment, your flying capability and weather minimums at destination and alternate. Obtain wind velocity and direction and air temperature at all altitudes encompassing your intended cruising altitude, for use in completing the Flight Planning and Log sheets as indicated below.

DATE OCT 20 TYPE ACFT. C182 NO. 123XY PILOT MLR

TIME OFF	TIME DOWN

	RANGE	FREQ	ROUTE	M C	TC	WIND DIR./VEL.	T H	VAR	M H	DIST.	MEA	ALT. CRUISE TEMP.	IAS/TAS	ESTIMATE G S	ESTIMATE LEG TIME	ESTIMATE ETA	ACTUAL G S	ACTUAL LEG TIME	ACTUAL ATA
FROM	AIRPORT																		
TO	CUBA	MEM 115.5	V9W	341	346			5E		20		CLIMB	120		:10				
FROM	CUBA			341	346	270	338		333	23		6000	150	159	:09				
TO	MAW	111.2	V9W	011	016	20	009	5E	004	50	2500	+5	164	168	:18				
FROM	MAW																		
TO	FAM	115.7	V9	342	347	280/20	341	5E	336	69	3000	6000/0	150/163	154	:27				
FROM	FAM																		
TO	STL	117.4	V9	346	351	280/20	345	5E	340	72	3100	6000/0	150/163	156	:28				
FROM															1:32				
TO																			
FROM																			
TO																			
ALTERNATE FROM	STL	117.4																	
TO	VLA	114.3	V14	072	076	275/18	074	4E	070	63	2500	5000/+2	150/160	177	:21				
FROM	VLA																		
TO	HUF	111.8	V14	071	074	270/15	073	3E	070	92	2400	5000/+2	150/160	174	:32				
									TOTALS						:53				

FUEL ANALYSIS

TANK	TIME ON	TIME OFF
L		
R		

FUEL PLAN

FUEL TO DEST.	18.5
FUEL TO ALT.	10.5
45 MIN. RESV.	9.0
FUEL REQD.	28.0
FUEL AT DEPT.	40.0
EXTRA FUEL	12.0

	DEPART.	DEST.	ALT.
NAME	METRO	LAMBERT	HULMAN
TWR. FREQ.	118.3	118.5	118.3
DEPT. CONT.	119.7	119.9	
APP. CONT.	125.8	126.5	123.8
GRD. CONT.	121.9	121.9	121.9
FIELD ELEV.	331	571	585

ATC CLEARANCE

POSITION REPT.

IDEN.	POSITION	TIME	ALT.	INST. FLT. PLAN	ETA NEXT FIX	NAME SUC. FIX

Fig. 98 A completed flight planning and log sheet. After take-off the "ETA" and "Actual" columns are filled in as the flight progresses.

FEDERAL AVIATION AGENCY

FLIGHT PLAN

Form Approved. Budget Bureau No. 04-R072.3

1. TYPE OF FLIGHT PLAN: FVFR ☐ VFR ☐ XX IFR ☐ DVFR

2. AIRCRAFT IDENTIFICATION: N123XY

3. AIRCRAFT TYPE/SPECIAL EQUIPMENT 1/: C-182

4. TRUE AIRSPEED: 163 KNOTS

5. POINT OF DEPARTURE: MEM

6. DEPARTURE TIME: PROPOSED (Z) 0800 ACTUAL (Z)

7. INITIAL CRUISING ALTITUDE: 6000

8. ROUTE OF FLIGHT: V9W MAW V9 STL

9. DESTINATION (Name of airport and city): LAMBERT FIELD STL

10. REMARKS

11. ESTIMATED TIME EN ROUTE: HOURS 1 MINUTES 32

12. FUEL ON BOARD: HOURS 3 MINUTES 20

13. ALTERNATE AIRPORT(S): HULMAN HUF

14. PILOT'S NAME: M.L. REED

15. PILOT'S ADDRESS AND TELEPHONE NO. OR AIRCRAFT HOME BASE: MEMPHIS METRO

16. NO. OF PERSONS ABOARD: 4

17. COLOR OF AIRCRAFT: RED WHITE

18. FLIGHT WATCH STATIONS

CLOSE FLIGHT PLAN UPON ARRIVAL

1/ SPECIAL EQUIPMENT SUFFIX
A — DME & 4096 Code transponder
B — DME & 64 Code transponder
D — DME
L — DME & transponder—no code
T — 64 Code transponder
U — 4096 Code transponder
X — Transponder—no code

FAA Form 7233—1 (4-66) FORMERLY FAA 398 0052-027-8000

Fig. 99 Completed flight plan for the IFR flight shown in Fig. 98.

- COMPLETE PLANNING AND LOG SHEET

   Based on weather data, your airplane's performance capability and direction of flight, decide on your cruising altitude. Using temperature data, compute true airspeed. Using wind data, compute true heading, magnetic heading, ground speed and leg time. Complete fuel plan to destination and alternate. Again, check the AIM for NOTAMS, airport data, VOR's out of service and any other information affecting your flight. Figure 98 shows a completed Flight Planning and Log Sheet.

   This completed Flight Planning and Log sheet contains practically all the information needed for the entire flight on one sheet. However, charts and the AIM should be carried along on the flight for possible changes in routing.

The next steps involve filing the Flight Plan (see Figure 99) with the control tower or an FSS at least 30 minutes prior to intended takeoff. After filing the Flight Plan (probably by phone), conduct pre-flight check of your airplane and equipment. Also, be sure to check your VOR by means of a VOT if available on the airport.

After take-off, fill in ETA to first radio check point. Revise data as necessary enroute, as your ATA is compared to your ETA. With good initial planning, revisions can be made by estimation only without use of the computer.

USE OF THE COMPUTER

Don't let the magnitude of the computer handbook that comes with the computer scare you. The important problems you should be able to solve easily are:
- True airspeed (TAS) from indicated airspeed (IAS), flight altitude and temperature at altitude.
- Time, speed and distance problems.
- Fuel consumption.
- Basic wind vectors in order to find ground speed and true heading when wind velocity and direction, true course and true airspeed are known.

The Enroute Low Altitude (Radio Facility) charts provide distance between compulsory reporting points (solid triangle ▲), usually VOR/VORTAC stations, in NAUTICAL MILES. Also, wind velocity is always presented in KNOTS. It is best to complete all your calculations, including true airspeed (TAS), indicated airspeed (IAS) and ground speed (GS) in NAUTICAL MILES and KNOTS.

Most winds aloft forecasts provide air temperatures in degrees CELSIUS (Centigrade) at the respective altitude levels. If temperature at altitude is unavailable, a good rule of thumb is that temperature decreases 2° Celsius or 3 1/2° Fahrenheit per 1000 feet. Remember however, that surface temperatures supplied by the Weather Bureau are in degrees Fahrenheit, whereas temperatures at altitude are presented in degrees Celsius. For purposes of calculating true airspeed from indicated airspeed, always use degrees Celsius.

Enroute Low Altitude (Radio Facility) charts present all airways by means of MAGNETIC COURSES. However, since wind direction is always presented in TRUE directions and TRUE airspeed is used, all wind vector calculations should use TRUE course, TRUE airspeed, and TRUE wind direction. Thus, true course must be obtained from magnetic course (charts show airway magnetic courses) by ADDING easterly variation or SUBTRACTING westerly variation. Again, after obtaining true heading on the computer, subtract easterly (or add westerly) variation to obtain MAGNETIC heading (MH). Confusing? Refer to the example planning and log sheet and work out a few problems and it will all clear up.

PREFERRED ROUTES AND CRUISING ALTITUDES

For IFR flight planning purposes, routing should be arranged in accordance with the PREFERRED ROUTES published in AIM and at cruising altitudes of even or odd thousands of feet according to direction of flight.

It is emphasized that these routes and altitudes are for PLANNING purposes only. Generally ATC attempts to assign routes and altitudes as filed. However, ATC can assign routes and altitudes different from the preferred routes and altitudes of even or odd thousands of feet according to direction of flight.

SUMMARY

The point to remember in an instrument flight is to PLAN AHEAD. Thorough flight planning on the ground cannot be overemphasized. Remember, during IFR weather only the professionals are flying. Even though you may only have a private certificate with an instrument rating, you will be treated as a professional. Keep in mind that you are among the Boeing 707's and Douglas DC-8's. There are a minimum of three pilots in the cockpit. They have four engines, dual VOR, dual ADF, autopilot, dual instrumentation and radar. You may be flying an airplane with one pilot, one engine, one VOR, one ADF, one set of instruments, no autopilot, and no radar. So, do a thorough job of flight planning! Also, during an actual IFR flight obtain a co-pilot if possible, to assist you in communications, computing ETA's and in-flight planning.

OTHER CONSIDERATIONS

Besides IFR navigation and planning as discussed above, a pilot must be thoroughly familiar with other aspects of flight planning pertinent to any flight. Weight and balance, use of performance curves, knowledge of the airplane's performance limitations, density altitude computations, oxygen requirements, and any other items as specified in the Airplane Flight Manual must be considered as a part of IFR or any other flight planning.

APPENDIX

THE ATC TRANSPONDER
Primary and Secondary Radar

A "Primary" radar system depends on "skin paint" or echo return from the aircraft structure, on a radar scope for identification. "Secondary" radar relies on the exchange of electronic signals between a ground radar beacon antenna (interrogator) and an aircraft transponder. "Secondary" radar is also known as the Air Traffic Control Radar Beacon System (ATCRBS) or Secondary Surveillance Radar. Secondary radar has these advantages:
- It reinforces the radar target
- It allows rapid target identification
- It extends radar coverage.

Secondary radar is usually slaved with the primary surveillance radars, a common pedestal supporting both antennae.

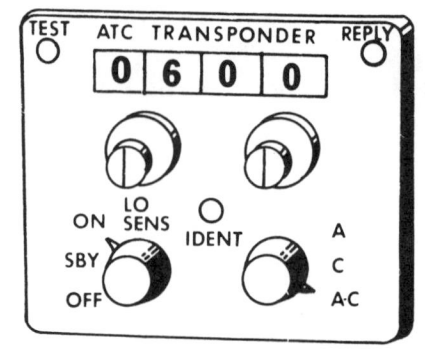

Fig. A-1 Transponder control panel.

THE TRANSPONDER

Use of secondary radar requires installation of a transponder in the aircraft. The ground equipment transmits an ultra-high frequency (UHF) pulsed signal on 1030 MHz to the aircraft transponder which receives the signal, interprets it, and replies by transmitting a coded signal on 1090 MHz to the ground receiver. This unit, in turn, decodes the signal and causes it to appear on the radar scope in a distinct pattern, normally two short parallel lines. The interrogator transmits *only* on 1030 MHz and the transponder replies *only* on 1090 MHz. Mode and code changes are made by varying the time interval between pulsed signals, not by frequency change. The transponder operates on "line of sight," therefore, range can be increased by climbing to a higher altitude. Another factor bearing on transponder operation is the attitude of the aircraft. In a bank, a part of the aircraft structure may block signals from the interrogator.

"MODES"

Presently there are six "Modes." Modes 1 and 2 are used exclusively by the military services. Mode A in the civil system is the same as military Mode 3 and is used exclusively for air traffic control. It is commonly designated Mode A/3. Mode B is also used for air traffic control in other countries. Mode C is used for automatic altitude reporting and requires additional aircraft equipment. Mode D is still unassigned. Most transponders installed in general aviation have Modes "A," "C," and "A-C" as shown on the illustration.

"CODES"

The first Mode A/3 system utilized 64 codes, however, equipment utilizing 4096 codes is being rapidly phased into the system. As there are no 8's or 9's used, the numerical value of the codes range from 0000 to 7777 (from 00 to 77 in the 64 code system.) The pilot of a civil aircraft should *never* operate his transponder on Code 0000. This is reserved for North American Air Defense (NORAD) use. Code 7700 is the emergency code and means MAYDAY to the ATC controller. Do not switch through 7700 when changing codes; this causes a momentary false alarm.

THE "IDENT" BUTTON

Should a controller be in doubt concerning your identity, he will tell you to "Ident." You press the "Ident" button, thereby transmitting a Special Position Identification pulse (SPI.) The space between the parallel lines of your target on the radar scope will then fill in, identifying you unmistakably. Transmit this signal only when so instructed by the controller to avoid mistaken identification with another aircraft.

"LOW SENSITIVITY" FUNCTION

As the range between the radar beacon and the transponder decreases, frequently the interrogating and replying signals will be too strong and cause the target on the scope to enlarge. Upon observing this the controller can reduce the target to normal size by having you switch to "Low Sensitivity." At some installations "side lobe

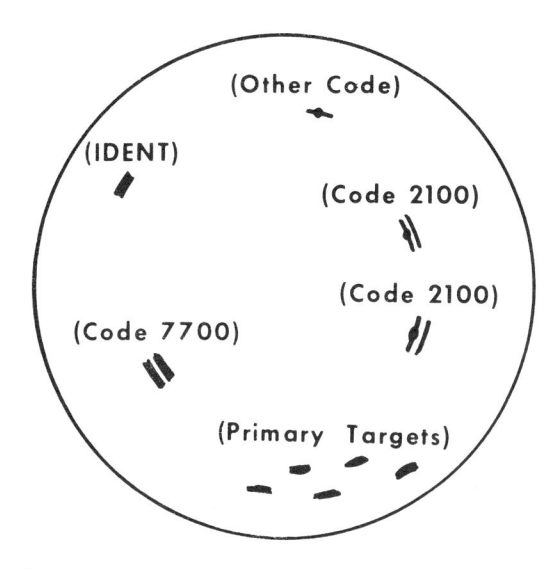

Fig. A-2 A typical radar scope display showing primary targets (aircraft with no transponder), an "Ident" reply, an aircraft experiencing a two-way radio failure (Code 7700), an aircraft with any other code and two aircraft with Code 2100 since (in this example) the controller wished to display all Code 2100 replies different from other coded replies or primary targets.

suppression" (SLS) has been implemented. This is an electronic device which maintains normal target size as range decreases.

"STANDBY" FUNCTION

A controller may ask you to "Squawk Standby" if he wishes to have your transponder stop replying to interrogation. He uses this means to selectively clear his scope.

OPERATING A TRANSPONDER

At a specified point on the aircraft checklist, the transponder is turned to the "Standby" position, and the internal circuitry of the set is checked by operating the "Test" switch. On an IFR flight, set in the code specified by ATC. On a VFR flight, set in code 1200 if operating below 10,000 feet, if at or above 10,000 feet, set in code 1400. If your transponder is the 64 code type, disregard the last two numerals, e.g., if the code assigned is 2100, set in code 21. Just prior to takeoff, switch from "Standby" to "On." Upon arrival, the controller may tell you to "Stop Squawk" or switch off the transponder. If you are not so instructed, turn the transponder off as soon as practicable after landing.

REQUIREMENTS FOR A TRANSPONDER

A transponder is desirable for all IFR flights. A transponder is required by FAR 91.97 when operating in a positive control area. Positive control airspace is depicted on enroute high altitude charts (for use at and above 18,000 ft. MSL.) Also, a transponder is required when operating in certain terminal control areas (TCAs) in accordance with FAR 91.24.

Should the pilot of an aircraft equipped with a coded radar beacon transponder experience a loss of two-way radio capability the pilot should:

(1) adjust his transponder to reply on Mode A/3, code 7700 for a period of 1 minute.

(2) then change to code 7600 and remain on 7600 for a period of 15 minutes or the remainder of the flight, whichever occurs first.

(3) repeat steps 1 and 2, as practicable.

Pilots should understand that they may not be in an area of radar coverage. Also many radar facilities are not presently equipped to display automatically code 7600 and will interrogate 7600 only when the aircraft is under direct radar control at the time of radio failure. However, replying on code 7700 first increases the probability of early detection of a radio failure condition.

RADAR BEACON PHRASEOLOGY

Air traffic controllers will use the following phraseology when referring to operation of the Air Traffic Control Radar Beacon System (ATCRB). Instructions by air traffic control refer only to Mode A/3 or Mode C operations and do not affect the operation of the transponder on other Modes.

SQUAWK (number) — Operate radar beacon transponder on designated code in Mode A/3.

IDENT — Engage the "IDENT" feature.

SQUAWK (number) AND IDENT — Operate transponder on specified code in Mode A/3 and engage the "IDENT".

SQUAWK LOW/NORMAL — Operate transponder on low or normal sensitivity as specified. Transponder is operated in "NORMAL" position unless ATC specified "LOW" ("ON" is used instead of "NORMAL" as a master control label on some

127

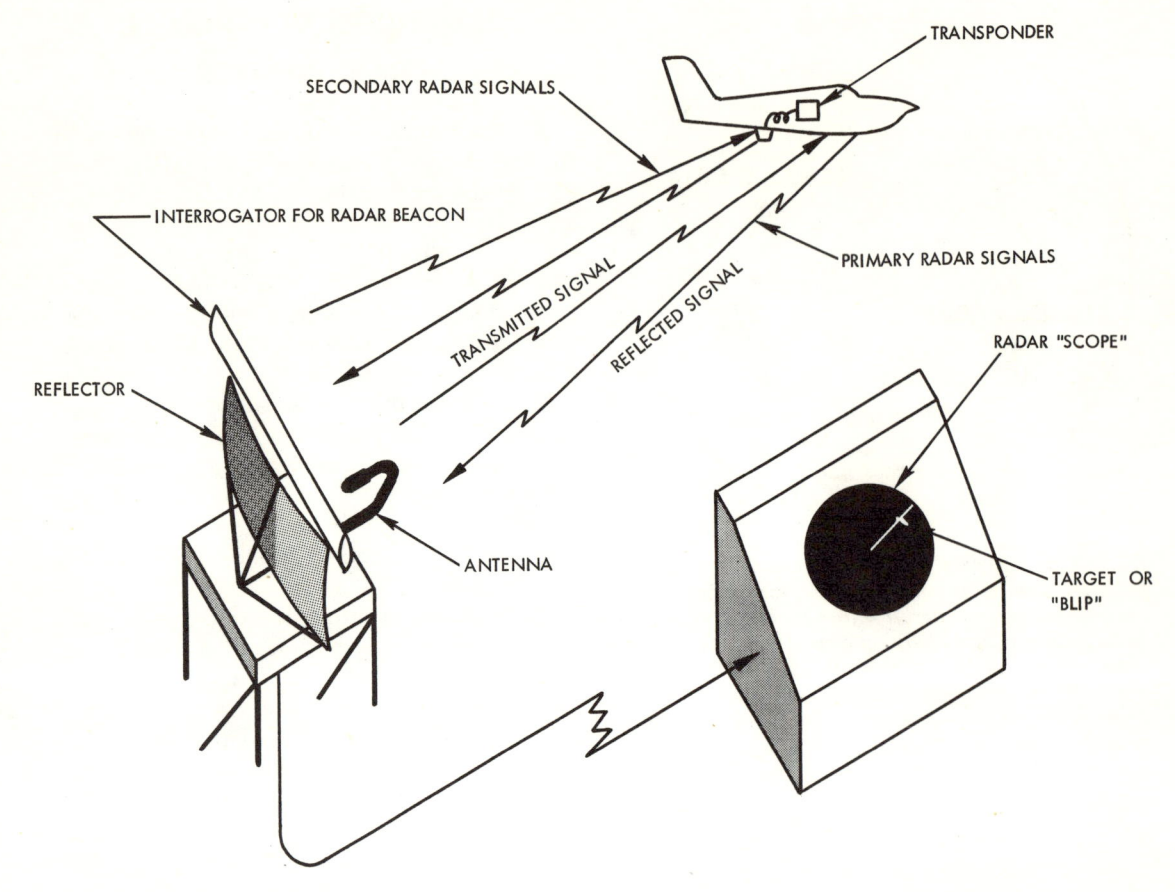

Fig. A-3 Radar is based on the "echo" principle. A transponder reinforces the return signal for a sharper "blip".

types of transponders.)

SQUAWK ALTITUDE — Activate MODE C with automatic altitude reporting.

STOP ALTITUDE SQUAWK — Turn off altitude reporting switch and continue transmitting MODE C framing pulses. If your equipment does not have this capacity, turn off MODE C.

STOP SQUAWK — Switch off transponder.

SQUAWK MAYDAY — Operate transponder in the emergency position. (Mode A Code 7700.)

AIRSPACE AND AIRPORTS

UNCONTROLLED AIRSPACE

Uncontrolled airspace is that portion of the airspace that has not been designated as continental control area, control area, control zone, terminal control area, or transition area and within which ATC has neither the authority nor the responsibility for exercising control over air traffic.

If visibility and/or distance from clouds in uncontrolled airspace is less than the minimums specified in FAR 91.105 (and shown in the table), flight must be conducted in accordance with IFR requirements regarding pilot certification and aircraft equipment. IFR flight within uncontrolled airspace does not require an ATC clearance or an IFR flight plan.

CONTROLLED AIRSPACE

Controlled airspace consists of those areas designated as Continental Control Area, Control Area, Control Zones, Terminal Control Areas and Transition Areas, within which some or all aircraft may be subject to Air Traffic Control.

CONTINENTAL CONTROL AREA

The continental control area consists of the airspace of the 48 contiguous States, the District of Cloumbia, and some portions of Alaska, but does not include:

- The airspace less than 1,500 feet above the surface of the earth; or
- Prohibited and restricted areas, other than restricted area military climb corridors and the restricted areas listed in FAR Part 71.

CONTROL AREAS

Control areas consist of the airspace designated as Federal airways, Additional Control Areas, and Control Area Extensions, but do not include the Continental Control Area. Unless otherwise designated, control areas also include the airspace between a segment of a main VOR airway and its associated alternate segments.

POSITIVE CONTROL AREA

Positive control area is airspace at and above 18,000 feet MSL, wherein aircraft are required to be operated under Instrument Flight Rules. For operations within positive control areas, aircraft must be:

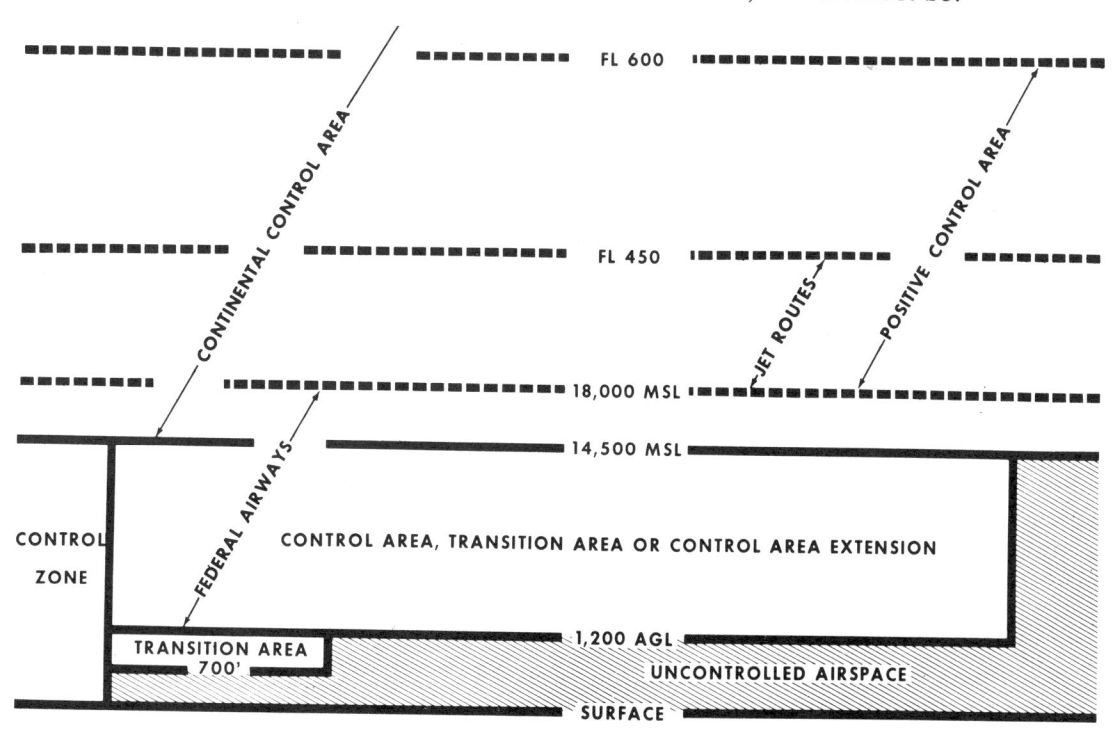

Fig. A-4 Vertical extent of airspace segments.

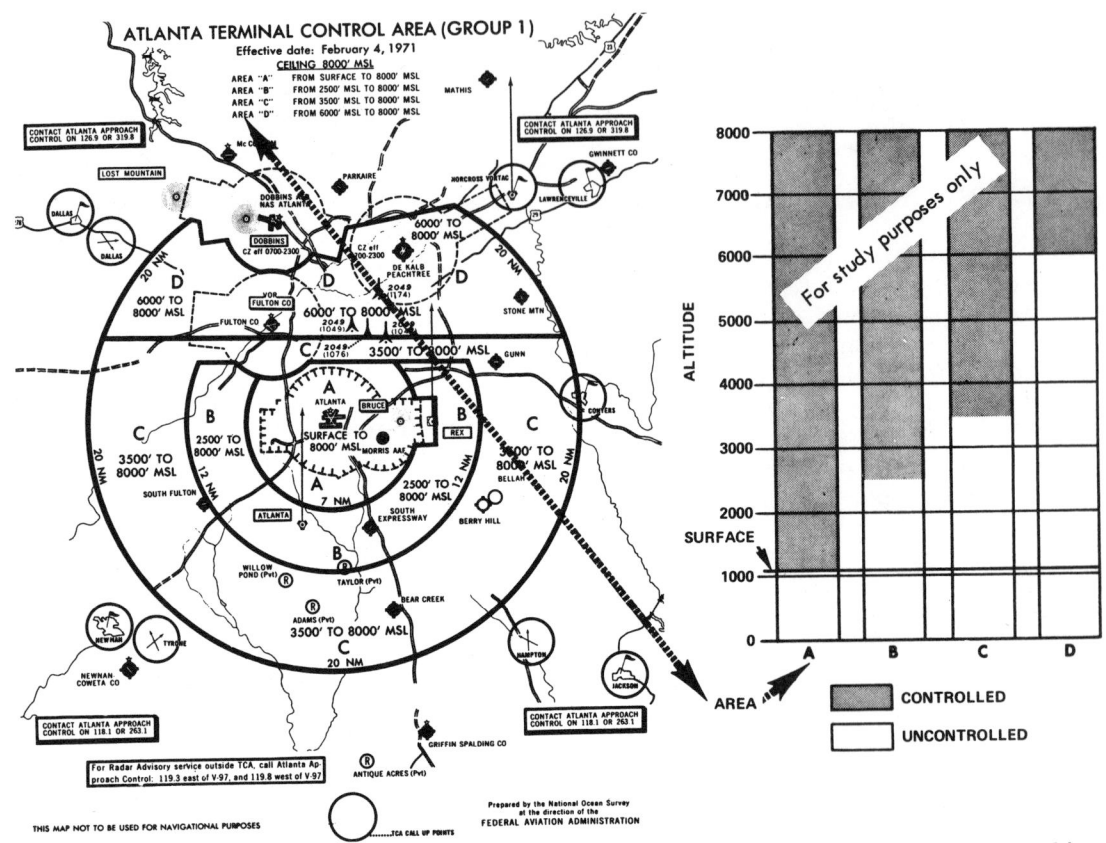

Fig. A-5 A Terminal Control Area (TCA) is designated for certain high density traffic airports to safely accommodate a variety of air traffic.

- Operated under IFR at specified FL assigned by ATC.
- Equipped with instruments and equipment required for IFR operations and flown by a pilot rated for instrument flight;
- Equipped with a transponder;
- Radio equipped to provide direct pilot/controller communication on the frequency specified by ATC for the area concerned.

ATC may authorize deviations from the above requirements for operation in a positive control area. In the case of in-flight failure of a radar beacon transponder, ATC may immediately approve operation within a positive control area.

TRANSITION AREAS

A Transition Area is controlled airspace extending upward from 700 feet or more above the surface when designated in conjunction with an airport for which an instrument approach procedure has been prescribed; or from 1,200 feet or more above the surface when designated in conjunction with airway route structures or segments. Unless specifically stated otherwise, transition areas terminate at the base of overlying controlled airspace.

Transition areas are designated to contain IFR operations in controlled airspace during portions of the terminal operation and while transitioning between the terminal and en route environment.

CONTROL ZONES

Controlled airspace which extends upward from the surface and terminates at the base of the continental control area. Control Zones that do not underlie the continental control area have no upper limit. A control Zone may include one or more airports and is normally a circular area with a radius of 5 statute miles and any extensions necessary to include instrument departure and arrival paths.

Control zones are depicted on charts (for example — on the sectional charts the zone is outlined by a broken blue line) and if a control zone is effective only during certain hours of the day, this fact will also be noted on the charts.

TERMINAL CONTROL AREA

A Terminal Control Area (TCA) consists of controlled airspace extending upward from the surface or higher to specified altitudes, within which all aircraft are subject

IFR ALTITUDES/FLIGHT LEVELS—UNCONTROLLED AIRSPACE
COURSES ARE MAGNETIC

Outside Controlled Airspace

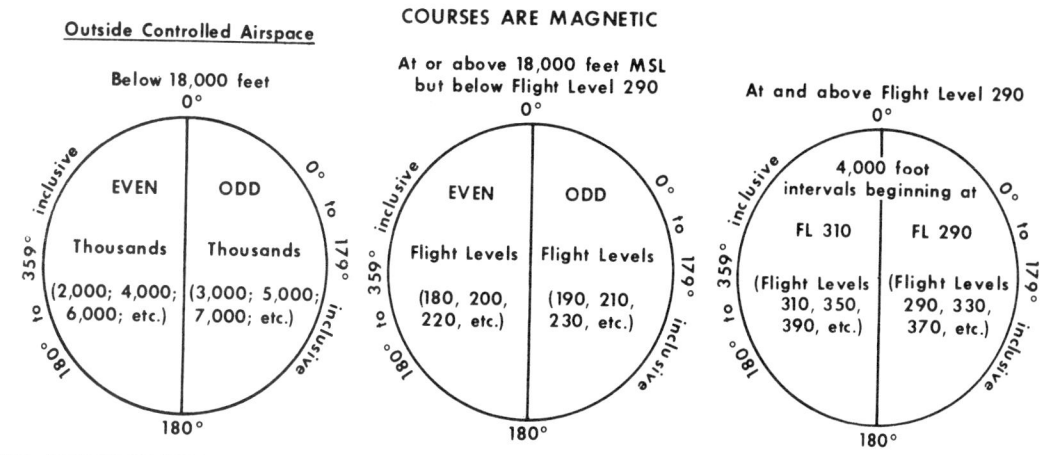

Below 18,000 feet: 0° to 179° inclusive — ODD Thousands (3,000; 5,000; 7,000; etc.); 180° to 359° inclusive — EVEN Thousands (2,000; 4,000; 6,000; etc.)

At or above 18,000 feet MSL but below Flight Level 290: 0° to 179° inclusive — ODD Flight Levels (190, 210, 230, etc.); 180° to 359° inclusive — EVEN Flight Levels (180, 200, 220, etc.)

At and above Flight Level 290: 4,000 foot intervals beginning at FL 290 (Flight Levels 290, 330, 370, etc.) for 0° to 179° inclusive; FL 310 (Flight Levels 310, 350, 390, etc.) for 180° to 359° inclusive

VFR ALTITUDES/FLIGHT LEVELS—CONTROLLED AND UNCONTROLLED AIRSPACE
COURSES ARE MAGNETIC

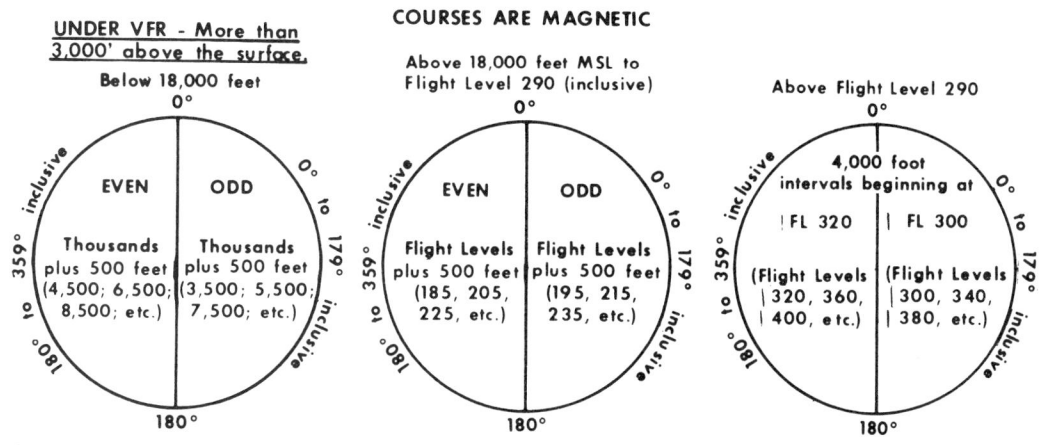

UNDER VFR - More than 3,000' above the surface.

Below 18,000 feet: 0° to 179° inclusive — ODD Thousands plus 500 feet (3,500; 5,500; 7,500; etc.); 180° to 359° inclusive — EVEN Thousands plus 500 feet (4,500; 6,500; 8,500; etc.)

Above 18,000 feet MSL to Flight Level 290 (inclusive): 0° to 179° inclusive — ODD Flight Levels plus 500 feet (195, 215, 235, etc.); 180° to 359° inclusive — EVEN Flight Levels plus 500 feet (185, 205, 225, etc.)

Above Flight Level 290: 4,000 foot intervals beginning at FL 300 (Flight Levels 300, 340, 380, etc.) for 0° to 179° inclusive; FL 320 (Flight Levels 320, 360, 400, etc.) for 180° to 359° inclusive

Fig. A-6 Chart showing IFR altitudes/flight levels in uncontrolled airspace and VFR altitude/flight levels in controlled and uncontrolled airspace. Pilots operating IFR within controlled airspace will fly at an altitude/flight level assigned by ATC.

MINIMUM VISIBILITY AND DISTANCE FROM CLOUDS—VFR IN UNCONTROLLED AIRSPACE

ALTITUDE	FLIGHT VISIBILITY	DISTANCE FROM CLOUDS
1200 feet or less above the surface (regardless of MSL altitude)	*1 statute mile	Clear of clouds
More than 1200 feet above the surface, but less than 10,000 feet MSL	1 statute mile	500 feet below 1,000 feet above 2,000 feet horizontal
More than 1200 feet above the surface and at or above 10,000 feet MSL	5 statute miles	1,000 feet above 1,000 feet below 1 mile horizontal

* Helicopters may operate with less than 1 mile visibility, outside controlled airspace at 1200 feet or less above the surface, provided they are operated at a speed that allows the pilot adequate opportunity to see any air traffic or obstructions in time to avoid collisions.

Fig. A-7 Minimum visibility and distance from clouds for VFR flight in controlled airspace. If conditions are lower than the above, an instrument rating is required of a pilot.

MINIMUM VISIBILITY AND DISTANCE FROM CLOUDS—VFR IN CONTROLLED AIRSPACE

ALTITUDE	FLIGHT VISIBILITY	DISTANCE FROM CLOUDS
1,200 feet or less above the surface (regardless of MSL altitude)	3 statute miles	500 feet below 1,000 feet above 2,000 feet horizontal
More than 1200 feet above the surface but less than 10,000 feet MSL	3 statute miles	500 feet below 1,000 feet above 2,000 feet horizontal
More than 1200 feet above the surface and at or above 10,000 feet MSL	5 statute miles	1,000 feet above 1,000 feet below 1 mile horizontal

In addition to the above, when operating within a control zone beneath a ceiling, the ceiling must not be less than 1,000 feet. If the pilot intends to land or takeoff or enter a traffic pattern within a control zone, the ground visibility must be at least 3 miles at that airport. If ground visibility is not reported at the airport, 3 miles flight visibility is required. (FAR 91.105)

Fig. A-8 Minimum visibility and distance from clouds for VFR flight in controlled airspace. If conditions are lower than the above, flight in accordance with IFR is required by the FAR

to operating rules and pilot and equipment requirements specified in Part 91.90 of the FAR's. Each such location is designated as a Group I or Group II terminal control area, and includes at least one primary airport around which the TCA is located.

A TCA is set up for certain high density airports to accommodate safely a wide variety of traffic. However, to a pilot on an IFR flight plan, the existance of a TCA makes little or no difference.

IFR ALTITUDES/FLIGHT LEVELS

Pilots operating IFR within controlled airspace will fly at an altitude/flight level assigned by ATC. When operating IFR within controlled airspace with an altitude assignment of "VFR-ON-TOP", an altitude/flight level appropriate for VFR flight is to be flown. (FAR 91.121) VFR-ON-TOP is not permitted in certain airspace such as positive control airspace, active Intensive Student Jet Training Areas, certain Restricted Areas, etc. Consequently, IFR flights operating VFR-ON-TOP will avoid such airspace.

VFR REQUIREMENTS

Minimum flight visibility and distance from clouds have been prescribed in FAR 91.109.

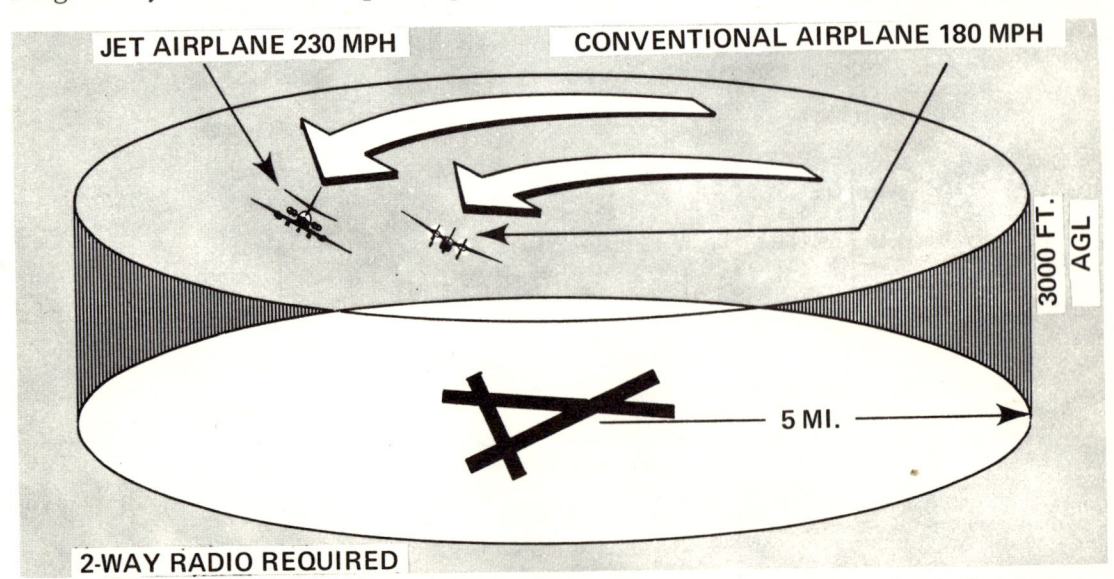

Fig. A-9 An airport traffic area has communications requirements and a speed restriction. To be in effect an airport traffic area requires an operating control tower.

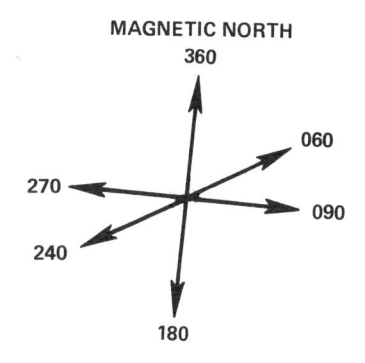

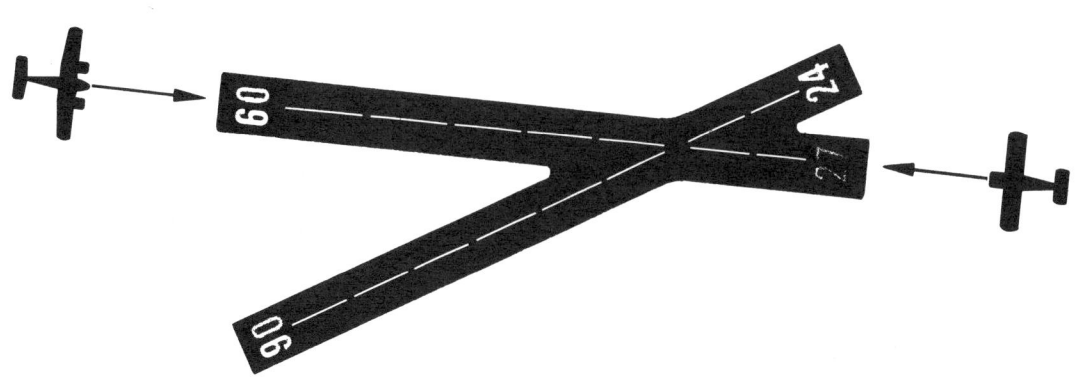

Fig. A-10 Runways are numbered in accordance with their magnetic direction. The twin-engine airplane is headed 090 degrees and is landing on runway 9 while the single-engine airplane, headed 270 degrees, is landing on runway 27.

AIRPORT TRAFFIC AREA

The dimensions of an Airport Traffic Area are shown in the figure. To a pilot operating on an IFR flight plan, an Airport Traffic Area has little or no effect except possibly a speed limit.

AIRPORTS

RUNWAY MARKINGS

A hard surface runway is normally given a number corresponding to its magnetic direction as determined from the approach end (see Figure A-10). The runway number is the magnetic direction of the runway to the nearest 10 degrees with the last zero left off. For example, the twin-engine airplane in Figure A-10, is approaching runway nine (its actual direction may not be exactly 090 degrees). The single-engine airplane in Figure A-10 is approaching runway two-seven. Occasionally, airports may have two (or even three) parallel runways. In addition to the basic number, the letters "L", "C" (in rare cases) or "R" will also become part of the runway number.

Basic runways, used for operation under Visual Flight Rules (VFR) are normally centerline marked as shown in Figure A-10. Instrument runways have additional markings

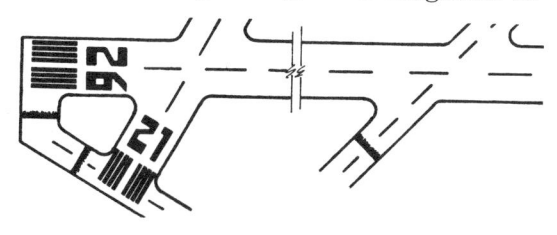

Fig. A-11 Non-precision instrument runway markings.

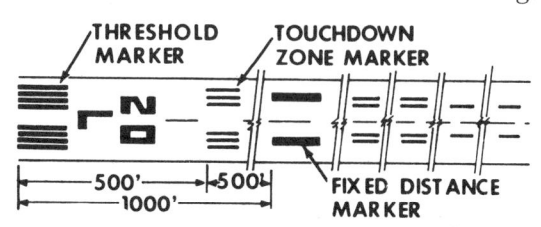

Fig. A-12 Precision instrument runway markings.

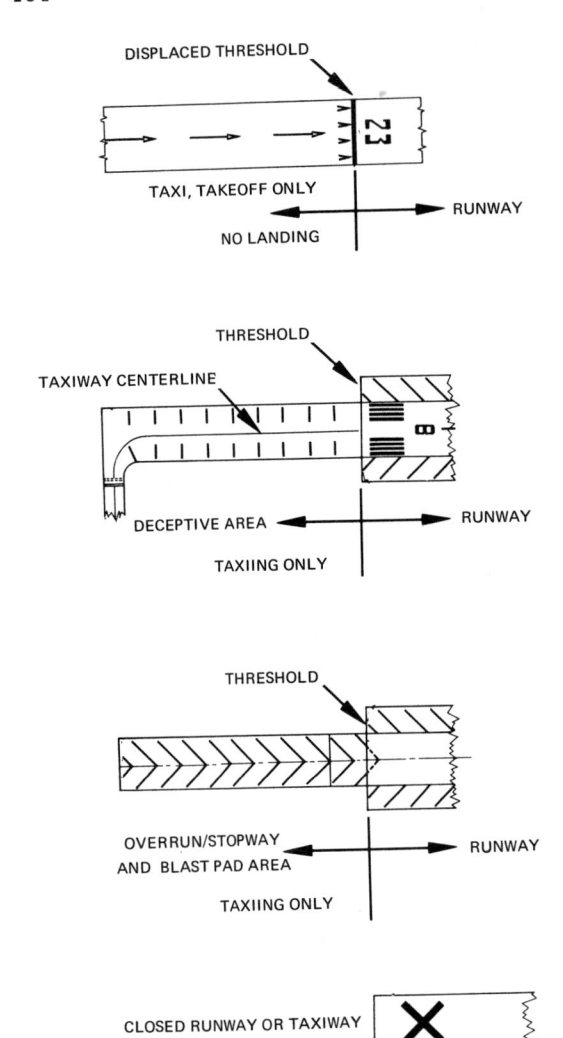

Fig. A-13 Various runway end configurations.

to assist pilots in conducting a visual landing from an instrument approach during adverse weather conditions.

Instrument runways are of two types, non-precision and precision.
- Non-precision markings are shown in Figure A-11. These consist of basic markings (runway number and centerline plus threshold markings as in Figure A-13). Non-precision marked runways are intended for landings from non-precision instrument approaches such as the VOR and ADF (or NDB) approaches.
- Precision runways are served by ILS or PAR approach systems which provide glide slope information for very low visibility approaches and landings. Markings include touchdown zone marking, fixed distance marking, plus side stripes. See Figure A-12.

The beginning of the part of the runway suitable for landing is called the "threshold." Normally, this is the beginning of the pavement as shown in Figure A-10. However, some runways have a "displaced threshold" shown in Figure A-13, whereby a portion of pavement precedes the landing portion. This area cannot be used for landing but may be used for taxiing and takeoff.

Unusuable areas for both takeoff and landing, but suitable for taxiing only, as shown in Figure A-13, are:
- Deceptive areas.
- Overrun/stopway and blast areas.
- Some runway shoulders as marked.

AIRPORT LIGHTING

Rotating beacon lights are installed at most lighted airports to assist pilots in locating the airport at night. The beacon rotates at a constant speed which produces the visual effect of flashes at regular intervals. Lighted land airports are indicated by alternate white and green flashes. Military airport beacons also flash alternately white and green, but are differentiated from Civil beacons by dual peaked (two quick) white flashes between the green flashes.

DAYLIGHT BEACON OPERATION indicates that the ground visibility in the control zone is less than three miles and/or the ceiling is less than 1000 feet and that a traffic clearance is required for landings and take-offs and flight in the traffic pattern.

FLASHING LIGHTS OUTLINING THE TETRAHEDRON during hours of darkness also indicates that the ground visibility is less than three miles and/or the ceiling is less than 1000 feet. However, *all tetrahedrons (or other traffic indicators) are not equipped with flashing lights.* This should not be the only means used to determine weather conditons.

RUNWAY LIGHTS are white and may be of variable intensity. Threshold lights are green. Taxiway lights are blue of relatively low intensity; see Figure A-14. Obstructions or hazards at and around the airport are marked with red lights. A displaced threshold is also marked with red lights.

You may find the following additional lighting at airports with approved instrument approaches (see Figure 58, Chapter 6, The Instrument Approach).
- Instrument approach light system extending some distance from the approach end of the instrument runway. In some cases, it also includes a condenser-discharge flashing light sys-

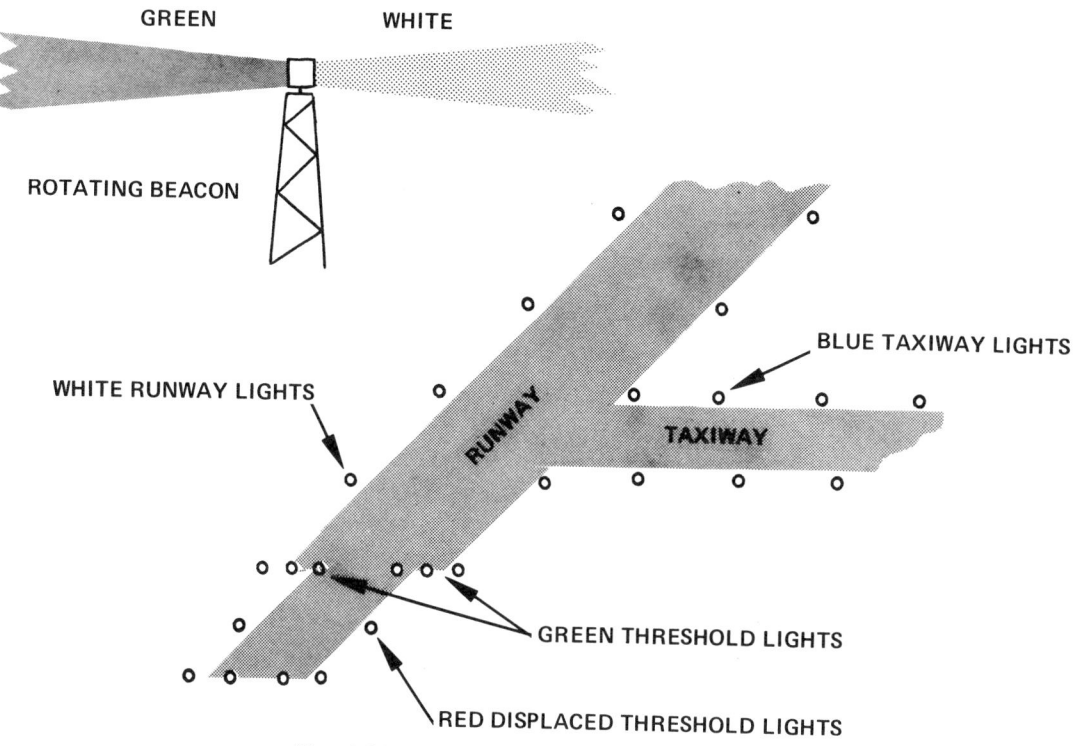

Fig. A-14 Typical airport lighting installation.

tem.
- Runway end identifier lights (REIL) are flashing lights installed at many airports to provide rapid and positive identification of the approach end of a particular runway.
- HIRL, High intensity runway edge lights installed on instrument runways. The lights are white, except the last 2000 feet which are amber.
- TDZ/CL, Touchdown Zone/ centerline lights. A rather complex white and red lighting system installed on the centerline of some instrument runways.

Operation of approach light systems and runway lighting is controlled by the control tower. At some locations the FSS may control the lights where there is no control tower in operation.

Pilots may request that lights be turned on, off, or that the intensity be increased or

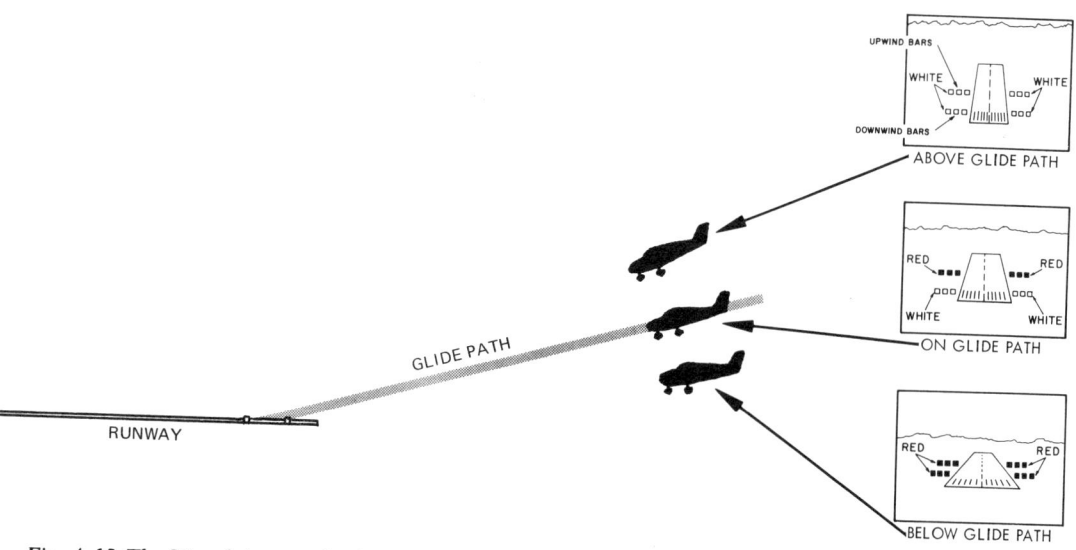

Fig. A-15 The Visual Approach Slope Indicator (VASI) provides a visual glide slope assuring obstruction clearance both day and night.

decreased. The HIRL, and the instrument approach lights have intensity controls which can be adjusted to meet pilot's requests. The sequence flashing lights do not have intensity controls, but can be turned on or off at pilot's request.

VISUAL APPROACH SLOPE INDICATOR (VASI)

The Visual Approach Slope Indicator (VASI) is a ground device which uses lights to define a predetermined visual glide path during the approach to a runway. As soon as the VASI lights are visible on final approach — day or night — a pilot receives the same information by visual reference that the glide slope unit of the Instrument Landing System (ILS) provides electronically. Once the principles and color code of the lighting system are understood, flying the VASI is as simple as looking out through the windshield and establishing and maintaining the proper rate of descent to stay on the glide slope.

A series of focused lights using red and white filters are installed on each side of the runway near the approach end. As shown in figure 15, if the airplane is on the glide path, the pilot sees a row of red lights above a row of white lights on both sides of the runway. If the pilot is above the glide path, only white lights will be seen; however, if below the glide path only red lights are visible.

Some airports serving long-bodied aircraft have 3-bar VASI's which provides two visual glide paths to the same runway. The first glide path encountered is the same as provided by the standard FAA VASI. The second glide path is about ½ degree higher that the first and is designed for the use of pilots of long-bodied aircraft.

COMPLEX INSTRUMENT AND NAVIGATION SYSTEMS

The basic instrument and navigation systems, normally installed in single-engine and light twin-engine aircraft, have been previously discussed. As the professional pilot steps up into higher performance aircraft, he will encounter more complex instrument and navigation systems. Although these systems are complex mechanically and electronically, they are designed to ease the job of piloting. These advanced systems are briefly discussed herein to familiarize the instrument pilot with them; however, no detailed description or instructional data are presented.

Fig. A-16 A radio magnetic indicator (RMI).

RADIO MAGNETIC INDICATOR (RMI)

The radio magnetic indicator or RMI allows the pilot to use three or more separate displays at all times, simultaneously shown on one three-inch diameter panel mounted instrument.

- The compass card, actuated by a slaved gyro source, rotates as the aircraft turns and indicates the aircraft's magnetic heading.
- The magnetic bearing TO a VOR (or VORTAC) is continuously displayed by a double-barred pointer.
- A single-barred pointer is an ADF needle which presents the magnetic bearing to the selected low frequency facility.

The tail of the double-barred indicator tells you the radial you are on, and the tail of the single-barred indicator tells you your magnetic bearing from a low frequency station. Some RMI installations have selector switches which permit the pilot to use both indicators in conjunction with dual VOR receivers or both indicators as ADF needles. When used with area navigation equipment, the RMI can be set up to indicate either the bearing to the "waypoint" or to the VOR/DME station used to establish the "waypoint".

INTEGRATED FLIGHT DIRECTOR SYSTEM

The flight director system enables the pilot to fly his aircraft with the computed precision of an autopilot. The system graphically consolidates navigational and attitude information and presents computed steering commands for the pilot to follow on two indicators. With this system, the pilot is relieved of the exacting tasks of interpreting a multiplicity of instruments. The flight director system can also provide the inputs for an autopilot. During autopilot mode, the two indicators may be used to monitor the aircraft performance while flown by the autopilot.

Cockpit instrumentation consists of:
- Flight Director Indicator. (Also called Steering Horizon, Attitude Director Horizon and Director Indicator, and Horizon Flight Director Indicator.)
- Course Indicator. (Also called Horizontal Situation Display, Pictorial Navigation Indicator, and various other combinations of these words.)

FLIGHT DIRECTOR INDICATOR

The flight director indicator displays aircraft attitude in roll and pitch against an artificial horizon; glide slope, localizer, and

Fig. A-17 The flight director (upper) and the course indicator are the cockpit components of an integrated flight director system. (Collins FD-108)

speed deviations on moving bars against fixed scales; and integrated steering commands. The command bar is positioned by signals from the flight steering computer. To satisfy a command, the pilot flys the fixed aircraft reference to align with the movable command bar.

COURSE INDICATOR

The course indicator provides a pictorial presentation of aircraft displacement relative to VOR radials and localizer or localizer and glide slope beam centers. It also presents aircraft heading reference with respect to magnetic north.

RADIO ALTIMETER (ABSOLUTE ALTIMETER, RADAR ALTIMETER, GROUND AVOIDANCE RADAR)

A barometric altimeter measures air pressure in order to determine altitude. When flying well above the terrain, the barometric altimeter is a satisfactory altitude indicating instrument. However, when flying instrument approaches down to 100 foot or less decision height such as required during category II or III approaches, an accurate height indication above the ground is necessary.

The radio altimeter system measures altitude by sending out a very short-duration burst of energy and measures the time required for this energy to reach the ground and be reflected back to the aircraft (radar principle). A computer converts this round trip travel time into altitude above the ground for presentation on a cockpit indicator.

During low approach and landing maneuvers, the system measures terrain clearance from about 3000 feet to touchdown. It can also supply altitude information to integrated flight systems, autopilot and flare computors as well as displaying altitude on an indicator.

Fig. A-18 A radio altimeter.

ENCODING ALTIMETER

An encoding altimeter displays the aircraft altitude to the pilot on a standard face. In addition, however, it transmits electrical

Fig. A-19 An encoding altimeter.

signals in accordance with the altitude indication, to the aircraft transponder "C" channel (see "The ATC Transponder" in this Appendix). Thus the aircraft's altitude information is transmitted to the ground Air Traffic Control System where it is displayed on the radar scope ((see the Automated Radar Terminal System (ARTS) in this Appendix)).

AREA NAVIGATION SYSTEMS

Area navigation is a system of navigation which allows a pilot to fly a selected course to a predetermined point without the need to overfly ground-based navigation facilities. Doppler radar, inertial navigation systems, and course line computers are all classified as Area Navigation Systems.

Doppler radar and inertial navigation systems acquire their data without the need for any reference outside the airplane such as radio aids, earth landmarks, or celestial bodies. The course line computer, however, is based on azimuth and distance information generated by the present VORTAC system.

COURSE LINE COMPUTER RNAV

The system which the pilot is most likely to encounter is the course line computer. This system is based on azimuth and distance information generated by the present VORTAC system. The advantages of VORTAC area navigation stem from the ability of the airborne computer to, in effect, locate the VORTAC wherever convenient, if it is in reception range. Although the term RNAV, by definition, applies to all forms of area navigation, it is commonly applied to the VORTAC system of area navigation.

RNAV (based on course line computer) is a method of navigation that permits point-to-point navigation of aircraft without the need for flight over the station. Without RNAV, most aircraft using VORTAC facilities fly straight courses from one station to another. The resulting convergence or "funneling" of traffic over the station limits the number of routes between points. Using RNAV, pilots are able to fly accurate straight-line courses between geographical points without having to dogleg between VORTACs. On a flight of even moderate length, a significant reduction of enroute time results. "Course Line Computer" RNAV is based on the ground navigation system (VORTAC) already in place — a system that can be used for VORTAC radial navigation by aircraft having conventional omni and DME equipment, and for area navigation by aircraft having airborne course line computers.

In order to fly RNAV (based on course line computer), an aircraft must have area navigation equipment installed. A typical airborne system consists of a waypoint selector, a guidance display and a vector analog computer. The computer is the heart of the system. For most systems, the guid-

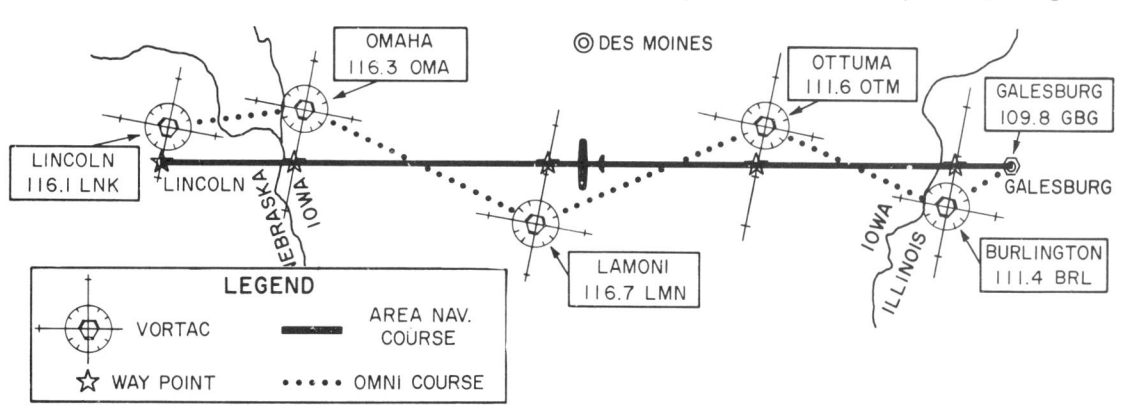

Fig. A-20 Area navigation course versus omni course.

ance display is the same CDI used for conventional VORTAC navigation. The waypoint selector/RNAV computer is used to select either the "VOR DME" mode or the "RNAV" mode.

The FAA defines a "waypoint" as ..."a predetermined geographical position used for route-definition and/or progress-reporting purposes that is defined relative to a VORTAC station position." Waypoints are also defined by latitude and longitude coordinates for the use of airborne self-contained systems not dependent on VORTAC inputs. With his course line computer, the pilot effectively moves or off-sets the VORTAC to a desired location. He creates a "phantom station" by setting the distance and the bearing of the waypoint from a convenient VORTAC, in the appropriate windows of the "waypoint selector" or "off-set control".

Once the waypoint has been established, it becomes, in effect, a VORTAC station. By means of the CDI and DME, the pilot tracks to the waypoint.

CATEGORY II INSTRUMENT APPROACH

Instrument approaches and landings are classified by "category" or progressively advanced levels of operation and increasingly complex airborne and ground equipment. These categories are:

CATEGORY I	Not less than 200 feet decision height, and not less than 2400 feet RVR (Runway Visual Range).
CATEGORY II	Below 200 feet, down to 100 feet decision height, and less than 2400 feet, and as low as 1200 feet RVR.
CATEGORY III a	0 feet decision height, and 700 feet RVR minimums
CATEGORY III b	0 feet decision height, and 150 feet RVR minimums.
CATEGORY III c	0 feet decision height and 0 feet RVR minimums.

Category I is in effect at major airports equipped with an Instrument Landing System (ILS). The airplane must be instrument equipped in accordance with FAR 91.33 and discussed in Chapter 2 of this manual. The pilot must hold an instrument rating as defined in FAR 61.65.

For Category II operation, however, additional airport, airplane, and pilot requirements must be met. For example, the airplane must be equipped with dual instrument and ILS systems. Also, a radar altimeter is required in some cases. These systems must meet rigid FAA requirements and approval, and must be maintained in accordance with a rigid maintenance program.

A pilot authorized for Category II approaches must have experience requirements in excess of those for an instrument rating. Also, a special oral and flight test is required.

AUTOMATED RADAR TERMINAL SYSTEM (ARTS III)

In a terminal area not equipped with ARTS III, it is the air traffic controller's responsibility to maintain a mental association between a target on the radar scope, the target's identification, altitude, velocity, etc.

The presentation on the radar scope of an ARTS III system consists of a target plus an alpha-numerics (letters and numbers) tag. The controller's identification symbol is also displayed at the target's reported position.

The basic ARTS III radar and beacon equipment provide a 55 nautical mile radius of coverage for each terminal area. This complex task of surveillance of the terminal airspace is accomplished with the use of beacon and primary radar at the site. The beacon subsystem acquires data from transponder-equipped aircraft that systematically report their beacon identity and altitude (if aircraft is equipped with an encoding altimeter). The transmitted altitude data is measured in 100 feet increments.

The beacon data is fed into a computer system which provides a target on the air traffic controller's radar scope along with identification, altitude and speed displays.

FEDERAL AVIATION REGULATIONS

The Federal Aviation Regulations (FAR) as presented herein, pertain ONLY to the instrument rating and instrument flight. Also, information pertinent to fixed wing aircraft only is presented. Rotorcraft and lighter-than-air requirements are not included.

FAR are presented in two parts:
- Part 61 - Certification; Pilots and Flight Instructors (Instrument pilot information only is included)
- Part 91 - General Operating and Flight Rules (again, sections pertaining to instrument flight only are included)

PART 61 CERTIFICATION: PILOTS AND FLIGHT INSTRUCTORS

Subpart A—General

§ 61.3 Requirements for certificates, rating, and authorizations.

(a) *Pilot certificate.* No person may act as pilot in command or in any other capacity as a required pilot flight crewmember of a civil aircraft of United States registry unless he has in his personal possession a current pilot certificate issued to him under this Part. However, when the aircraft is operated within a foreign country a current pilot license issued by the country in which the aircraft is operated may be used.

(c) *Medical certificate.* Except for free balloon pilots piloting balloons and glider pilots piloting gliders, no person may act as pilot in command or in any other capacity as a required pilot flight crewmember of an aircraft under a certificate issued to him under this Part, unless he has in his personal possession an appropriate current medical certificate issued under Part 67 of this chapter.

(e) *Instrument rating.* No person may act as pilot in command of a civil aircraft under instrument flight rules, or in weather conditions less than the minimum prescribed for VFR flight unless—

(1) In the case of an airplane, he holds an instrument rating or an airline transport pilot certificate with an airplane category rating on it;

(f) *Category II pilot authorization.*

(1) No person may act as pilot in command of a civil aircraft in a Category II operation unless he holds a current Category II pilot authorization for that type aircraft or, in the case of a civil aircraft of foreign registry, he is authorized by the country of registry to act as pilot in command of that aircraft in Category II operations.

(h) *Inspection of certificate.* Each person who holds a pilot certificate, flight instructor certificate, medical certificate, authorization, or license required by this Part shall present it for inspection upon the request of the Administrator, an authorized representative of the National Transportation Safety Board, or any Federal, State, or local law enforcement officer.

§ 61.5 Certificates and ratings issued under this Part.

(b) The following ratings are placed on pilot certificates (other than student pilot) where applicable:

(6) Instrument ratings (on private and commercial pilot certificates only):

§ 61.33 Tests: general procedure.

Tests prescribed by or under this Part are given at times and places, and by persons, designated by the Administrator.

§ 61.35 Written test: prerequisites and passing grades.

(a) An applicant for a written test must—

(1) Show that he has satisfactorily completed the ground instruction or home study course required by this Part for the certificate or rating sought;

(2) Present as personal identification an airman certificate, driver's license, or other official document; and

(3) Present a birth certificate or other official document showing that he meets the age requirement prescribed in this Part for the certificate sought not later than 2 years from the date of application for the test.

(b) The minimum passing grade is specified by the Administrator on each written test sheet or booklet furnished to the applicant.

This section does not apply to the written test for an airline transport pilot certificate or a rating associated with that certificate.

§ 61.39 Prerequisites for flight tests.

(a) To be eligible for a flight test for a certificate, or an aircraft or instrument rating issued under this Part, the applicant must—

(1) Have passed any required written test since the beginning of the 24th month before the month in which he takes the flight test;

(2) Have the applicable instruction and aeronautical experience prescribed in this Part;

(3) Hold a current medical certificate appropriate to the certificate he seeks or, in the case of a rating to be added to his pilot certificate, at least a third-class medical certificate issued since the beginning of the 24th month before the month in which he takes the flight test;

(4) Except for a flight test for an airline transport pilot certificate, meet the age requirement for the issuance of the certificate or rating he seeks; and

(5) Have a written statement from an appropriately certificated flight instructor certifying that he has given the applicant flight instruction in preparation for the flight test within 60 days preceding the date of application, and finds him competent to pass the test and to have satisfactory knowledge of the subject areas in which he is shown to be deficient by his FAA airman written test report.

§ 61.43 Flight tests: general procedures.

(a) The ability of an applicant for a private or commercial pilot certificate, or for an aircraft or instrument rating on that certificate to perform the required pilot operations is based on the following:

(1) Executing procedures and maneuvers within the aircraft's performance capabilities and limitations, including use of the aircraft's systems.

(2) Executing emergency procedures and maneuvers appropriate to the aircraft.

(3) Piloting the aircraft with smoothness and accuracy.

(4) Exercising judgment.

(5) Applying his aeronautical knowledge.

(6) Showing that he is the master of the aircraft, with the successful outcome of a procedure or maneuver never seriously in doubt.

(b) If the applicant fails any of the required pilot operations in accordance with the applicable provisions of paragraph (a) of this section, the applicant fails the flight test. The applicant is not eligible for the certificate or rating sought until he passes any pilot operations he has failed.

(c) The examiner or the applicant may discontinue the test at any time when the failure of a required pilot operation makes the applicant ineligible for the certificate or rating sought. If the test is discontinued the applicant is entitled to credit for only those entire pilot operations that he has successfully performed.

§ 61.45 Flight tests: required aircraft and equipment.

(a) *General.* An applicant for a certificate or rating under this Part must furnish, for each flight test that he is required to take, an appropriate aircraft of United States registry that has a current standard or limited airworthiness certificate. However, the applicant may, at the discretion of the inspector or examiner conducting the test, furnish an aircraft of U.S. registry that has a current airworthiness certificate other than standard or limited, an aircraft of foreign registry that is properly certificated by the country of registry, or a military aircraft in an operational status if its use is allowed by an appropriate military authority.

(b) *Required equipment (other than controls).* Aircraft furnished for a flight test must have—

(1) The equipment for each pilot operation required for the flight test;

(2) No prescribed operating limitations that prohibit its use in any pilot operation required on the test;

(3) Pilot seats with adequate visibility for each pilot to operate the aircraft safely, except as provided in paragraph (d) of this section; and

(4) Cockpit and outside visibility adequate to evaluate the performance of the applicant, where an additional jump seat is provided for the examiner.

(c) *Required controls.* An aircraft (other than lighter-than-air) furnished under paragraph (a) of this section for any pilot flight test must have engine power controls and flight controls that are easily reached and operable in a normal manner by both pilots, unless after considering all the factors, the examiner determines that the flight test can be conducted safely without them. However, an aircraft having other controls such as nose-wheel steering, brakes, switches, fuel selectors, and engine air flow controls that are not easily reached and operable in a normal manner by both pilots may be used, if more than one pilot is required under its airworthiness certificate, or if the examiner determines that the flight can be conducted safely.

(d) *Simulated instrument flight equipment.* An applicant for any flight test involving flight maneuvers solely by reference to instruments must furnish equipment satisfactory to the examiner that excludes the visual reference of the applicant outside of the aircraft.

§ 61.47 Flight tests: status of FAA inspectors and other authorized flight examiners.

An FAA inspector or other authorized flight examiner conducts the flight test of an applicant for a pilot certificate or rating for the purpose of observing the applicant's ability to perform satisfactorily the procedures and maneuvers on the flight test. The inspector or other examiner is not pilot in command of the aircraft during the flight test unless he acts in that capacity for the flight, or portion of the flight, by prior arrangement with the applicant or other person who would otherwise act as pilot in command of the flight, or portion of the flight. Notwithstanding the type of aircraft used during a flight test, the applicant and the inspector or other examiner are not, with respect to each other (or other occupants authorized by the inspector or other examiner), subject to the requirements or limitations for the carriage of passengers specified in this chapter.

§ 61.49 Retesting after failure.

An applicant for a written or flight test who fails that test may not apply for retesting until after 30 days after the date he failed the test. However, in the case of his first failure he may apply for retesting before the 30 days have expired upon presenting a written statement from an authorized instructor certifying that he has given flight or ground instruction as appropriate to the applicant and finds him competent to pass the test.

§ 61.51 Pilot logbooks.

(a) The aeronautical training and experience used to meet the requirements for a certificate or rating, or the recent flight experience requirements of this Part must be shown by a reliable record. The logging of other flight time is not required.

(b) *Logbook entries.* Each pilot shall enter the following information for each flight or lesson logged:

(1) *General.*
   (i) Date.
   (ii) Total time of flight.
   (iii) Place, or points of departure and arrival.
   (iv) Type and identification of aircraft.

(2) *Type of pilot experience or training.*
   (i) Pilot in command or solo.
   (ii) Second in command.
   (iii) Flight instruction received from an authorized flight instructor.
   (iv) Instrument flight instruction from an authorized flight instructor.
   (v) Pilot ground trainer instruction.
   (vi) Participating crew (lighter-than-air).
   (vii) Other pilot time.

(3) *Conditions of flight.*
   (i) Day or night.
   (ii) Actual instrument.
   (iii) Simulated instrument conditions.

(4) *Instrument flight time.* A pilot may log as instrument flight time only that time during which he operates the aircraft solely by reference to instruments, under actual or simulated instrument flight conditions. Each entry must include the place and type of each instrument approach completed, and the name of the safety pilot for each simulated instrument flight. An instrument flight instructor may log as instrument time that time during which he acts as instrument flight instructor in actual instrument weather conditions.

(5) *Instruction time.* All time logged as flight instruction, instrument flight instruction, pilot ground trainer instruction, or ground instruction time must be certified by the appropriately rated and certificated instructor from whom it was received.

(d) *Presentation of logbook.*

(1) A pilot must present his logbook (or other record required by this section) for inspection upon reasonable request by the Administrator, an authorized representative of the National Transportation Safety Board, or any State or local law enforcement officer.

§ 61.57 Recent flight experience: pilot in command.

(e) *Instrument.*

(1) *Recent IFR experience.* No pilot may act as pilot in command under IFR, nor in weather conditions less than the minimums prescribed for VFR, unless he has, within the past 6 months—

   (i) In the case of an aircraft other than a glider, logged at least 6 hours of instrument time under actual or simulated IFR conditions, at least 3 of which were in flight in the category of aircraft involved, including at least 6 instrument approaches, or passed an instrument competency check in the category of aircraft involved.

(2) *Instrument competency check.* A pilot who does not meet the recent instrument experience requirements of subparagraph (1) of this paragraph during the prescribed time or 6 months thereafter may not serve as pilot in command under IFR, nor in weather conditions less than the minimums prescribed for VFR, until he passes an instrument competency check in the category of aircraft involved, given by an FAA inspector, a member of an armed force in the United States authorized to conduct flight tests, an FAA-approved check pilot, or a certificated instrument flight instructor. The Administrator may authorize the conduct of part or all of this check in a pilot ground trainer equipped for instruments or an aircraft simulator.

Subpart B—Aircraft Ratings and Special Certificates

§ 61.65 Instrument rating requirements.

(a) *General.* To be eligible for an instrument rating (airplane) or an instrument rating (helicopter), an applicant must—

(1) Hold a current private or commercial pilot certificate with an aircraft rating appropriate to the instrument rating sought;

(2) Be able to read, speak, and understand the English language; and

(3) Comply with the applicable requirements of this section.

(b) *Ground instruction.* An applicant for the written test for an instrument rating must have received ground instruction, or have logged home study in at least the following areas of aeronautical knowledge appropriate to the rating sought.

(1) The regulations of this chapter that apply to flight under IFR conditions, the Airman's Information Manual, and the IFR air traffic system and procedures;

(2) Dead reckoning appropriate to IFR navigation, IFR navigation by radio aids using the VOR, ADF, and ILS systems, and the use of IFR charts and instrument approach plates;

(3) The procurement and use of aviation weather reports and forecasts, and the elements of forecasting weather trends on the basis of that information and personal observation of weather conditions; and

(4) The safe and efficient operation of airplanes or helicopters, as appropriate, under instrument weather conditions.

(c) *Flight instruction and skill—airplanes.* An applicant for the flight test for an instrument rating (airplane) must present a logbook record certified by an authorized flight instructor showing that he has received instrument flight instruction in an airplane in the following pilot operations, and has been found competent in each of them:

(1) Control and accurate maneuvering of an airplane solely by reference to instruments.

(2) IFR navigation by the use of the VOR and ADF systems, including compliance with air traffic control instructions and procedures.

(3) Instrument approaches to published minimums using the VOR, ADF, and ILS systems (instruction in the use of the ADF and ILS may be received in an instrument ground trainer and instruction in the use of the ILS glide slope may be received in an airborne ILS simulator).

(4) Cross-country flying in simulated or actual IFR conditions, on Federal airways or as routed by ATC, including one such trip of at least 250 nautical miles, including VOR, ADF, and ILS approaches at different airports.

(5) Simulated emergencies, including the recovery from unusual attitudes, equipment or instrument malfunctions, loss of communications, and engine-out emergencies if a multiengine airplane is used, and missed approach procedures.

(d) *Instrument instruction and skill—(helicopter).* An applicant for the flight test for an instrument rating (helicopter) must present a logbook record certified to by an authorized flight instructor showing that he has received instrument flight instruction in a helicopter in the following pilot operations, and has been found competent in each of them:

(1) The control and accurate maneuvering of a helicopter solely by reference to instruments.

(2) IFR navigation by the use of the VOR and ADF systems, including compliance with air traffic control instructions and procedures.

(3) Instrument approaches to published minimums using the VOR, ADF, and ILS systems (instruction in the use of the ADF and ILS may be received in an instrument ground trainer, and instruction in the use of the ILS glide slope may be received in an airborne ILS simulator).

(4) Cross-country flying under simulated or actual IFR conditions, on Federal airways or as routed by ATC, including one flight of at least 100 nautical miles, including VOR, ADF, and ILS approaches at different airports.

(5) Simulated IFR emergencies, including equipment malfunctions, missed approach procedures, and deviations to unplanned alternates.

(e) *Flight experience.* An applicant for an instrument rating must have at least the following flight time as a pilot:

(1) A total of 200 hours of pilot flight time, including 100 hours as pilot in command, of which 50 hours are cross-country in the category of aircraft for which an instrument rating is sought.

(2) 40 hours of simulated or actual instrument time, of which not more than 20 hours may be instrument instruction by an authorized instructor in an instrument ground trainer acceptable to the Administrator.

(3) 15 hours of instrument flight instruction by an authorized flight instructor, including at least 5 hours in an airplane or a helicopter, as appropriate.

(f) *Written test.* An applicant for an instrument rating must pass a written test appropriate to the instrument rating sought on the subjects in which ground instruction is required by paragraph (b), of this section.

(g) *Practical test.* An applicant for an instrument rating must pass a flight test in an airplane or a helicopter, as appropriate. The test must include instrument flight procedures selected by the inspector or examiner conducting the test to determine the applicant's ability to perform competently the IFR operations on which instruction is required by paragraph (c) or (d) of this section.

PART 91
GENERAL OPERATING AND FLIGHT RULES

Subpart A—General

§ 91.3 Responsibility and authority of the pilot in command.

(a) The pilot in command of an aircraft is directly responsible for, and is the final authority as to, the operation of that aircraft.

(b) In an emergency requiring immediate action, the pilot in command may deviate from any rule of this subpart or of Subpart B to the extent required to meet that emergency.

(c) Each pilot in command who deviates from a rule under paragraph (b) of this section shall, upon the request of the Administrator, send a written report of that deviation to the Administrator.

§ 91.5 Preflight action.

Each pilot in command shall, before beginning a flight, familiarize himself with all available information concerning that flight. This information must include:

(a) For a flight under IFR or a flight not in the vicinity of an airport, weather reports and forecasts, fuel requirements, alternatives available if the planned flight cannot be completed, and any known traffic delays of which he has been advised by ATC.

(b) For any flight, runway lengths at airports of intended use, and the following takeoff and landing distance information:

(1) For civil aircraft for which an approved airplane or rotorcraft flight manual containing takeoff and landing distance data is required, the takeoff and landing distance data contained therein; and

(2) For civil aircraft other than those specified in subparagraph (1) of this paragraph, other reliable information appropriate to the aircraft, relating to aircraft performance under expected values of airport elevation and runway slope, aircraft gross weight, and wind and temperature.

§ 91.21 Flight instruction; simulated instrument flight and certain flight tests.

(a) No person may operate a civil aircraft that is being used for flight instruction unless that aircraft has fully functioning dual controls.

(b) No person may operate a civil aircraft in simulated instrument flight unless—

(1) An appropriately rated pilot occupies the other control seat as safety pilot;

(2) The safety pilot has adequate vision forward and to each side of the aircraft, or a competent observer in the aircraft adequately supplements the vision of the safety pilot; and

(3) Except in the case of a lighter-than-air aircraft, that aircraft is equipped with functioning dual controls.

(c) No person may operate a civil aircraft that is being used for a flight test for an airline transport pilot certificate or a class or type rating on that certificate, or for a Federal Aviation Regulation Part 121 proficiency flight test, unless the pilot seated at the controls, other than the pilot being checked, is fully qualified to act as pilot in command of the aircraft.

§ 91.23 Fuel requirements for flight in IFR conditions.

No person may operate a civil aircraft in IFR conditions unless it carries enough fuel (considering weather reports and forecasts, and weather conditions) to—

(a) Complete the flight to the first airport of intended landing;

(b) Fly from that airport to the alternate airport; and

(c) Fly thereafter for 45 minutes at normal cruising speed.

However, the requirement for fuel to fly from the first airport of intended landing to the alternate airport does not apply if Part 97 of this subchapter prescribes a standard instrument approach procedure for the first airport of intended landing and the weather conditions at that airport are forecast to be, from two hours before to two hours after the estimated time of arrival, a ceiling of at least 1,000 feet above the lowest MEA, MOCA, or altitude prescribed for the initial approach segment of the instrument approach procedure for the airport and visibility at least three miles, or two miles more than the lowest authorized landing minimum visibility, whichever is greater.

§ 91.24 ATC transponder equipment.

(a) *All airspace: U.S. registered civil aircraft.* For operations not conducted under Parts 121, 123, 127, or 135 of this chapter, ATC transponder equipment installed after January 1, 1974, in U.S. registered civil aircraft not previously equipped with an ATC transponder, and all ATC transponder equipment used in U.S. registered civil aircraft after July 1, 1975, must meet the performance and environmental requirements of any class of TSO–C74b or any class of TSO–C74c as appropriate, except that the Administrator may approve the use of TSO–C74 or TSO–C74a equipment after July 1, 1975, if the applicant submits data showing that such equipment meets the minimum performance standards of the appropriate class of TSO–C74c and environmental conditions of the TSO under which it was manufactured.

(b) *Controlled airspace: all aircraft.* Except for persons operating helicopters in terminal control areas at or below 1,000 feet AGL under the terms of a letter of agreement, and except for persons operating gliders above 12,500 feet MSL but below the floor of the positive control area, no person may operate an aircraft in controlled airspace, after the applicable dates prescribed in subparagraphs (b)(1) through (b)(4) of this paragraph, unless that aircraft is equipped with an operable coded radar beacon transponder having a Mode 3/A 4096 code capability, replying to Mode 3/A interrogation with the code specified by ATC, and is equipped with automatic pressure altitude reporting equipment having a Mode C capability that automatically replies to Mode C interrogations by transmitting pressure altitude information in 100-foot increments. This requirement applies—

(1) After July 1, 1974, in Group I Terminal Control Areas governed by § 91.90(a);

(2) After January 1, 1975, in Group II Terminal Control Areas governed by § 91.90(b);

(3) After January 1, 1975, in Group III Terminal Control Areas governed by § 91.90(c), except as provided therein; and

(4) After July 1, 1975, in all controlled airspace of the 48 contiguous States and the District of Columbia, above 12,500 feet MSL, excluding the airspace at and below 2,500 feet AGL.

(c) *ATC authorized deviations.* ATC may authorize deviations from paragraph (b) of this section—

(1) Immediately, to allow an aircraft with an inoperative transponder to continue to the airport of ultimate destination, including any intermediate stops, or to proceed to a place where suitable repairs can be made, or both; and

(2) On a continuing basis, or for individual flights, for operations not involving an inoperative transponder, in which cases the request for a deviation must be submitted to the ATC facility having jurisdiction over the airspace concerned at least four hours before the proposed operation.

§ 91.25 VOR equipment check for IFR operations.

(a) No person may operate a civil aircraft under IFR using the VOR system of radio navigation unless the VOR equipment of that aircraft—

(1) Is maintained, checked, and inspected under an approved procedure; or

(2) Has been operationally checked within the preceding ten hours of flight time and within ten days before flight, and was found to be within the limits of the permissible indicated bearing error set forth in paragraph (b) or (c) of this section.

(b) Except as provided in paragraph (c) of this section, each person conducting a VOR check under subparagraph (a)(2) of this section, shall—

(1) Use, at the airport of intended departure, an FAA operated or approved test signal or, outside the United States, a test signal operated or approved by appropriate authority, to check the VOR equipment (the maximum permissible indicated bearing error is plus or minus 4 degrees);

(2) If a test signal is not available at the airport of intended departure, use a point on an airport surface designated as a VOR system checkpoint by the Administrator or, outside the United States, by appropriate authority (the maximum permissible bearing error is plus or minus 4 degrees);

(3) If neither a test signal nor a designated checkpoint on the surface is available, use an airborne checkpoint designated by the Administrator or, outside the United States, by appropriate authority (the maximum permissible bearing error is plus or minus 6 degrees); or

(4) If no check signal or point is available, while in flight—

(i) Select a VOR radial that lies along the centerline of an established VOR airway;

(ii) Select a prominent ground point along the selected radial preferably more than 20 miles from the VOR ground facility and maneuver the aircraft directly over the point at a reasonably low altitude; and

(iii) Note the VOR bearing indicated by the receiver when over the ground point (the maximum permissible variation between the published radial and the indicated bearing is 6 degrees).

(c) If dual system VOR (units independent of each other except for the antenna) is installed in the aircraft, the person checking the equipment may check one system against the other in place of the check procedures specified in paragraph (b) of this section. He shall tune both systems to the same VOR ground facility and note the indicated bearings to that station. The maximum permissible variation between the two indicated bearings is 4 degrees.

(d) Each person making the VOR operational check as specified in paragraph (b) or (c) of this section shall enter the date, place, bearing error, and his signature in the aircraft log or other permanent record.

§ 91.32 Supplemental oxygen.

(a) *General.* No person may operate a civil aircraft of U.S. registry—

(1) At cabin pressure altitudes above 12,500 feet (MSL) up to and including 14,000 feet (MSL), unless the required minimum flight crew is provided with and uses supplemental oxygen for that part of the flight at those altitudes that is of more than 30 minutes duration;

(2) At cabin pressure altitudes above 14,000 feet (MSL), unless the required minimum flight crew is provided with and uses supplemental oxygen during the entire flight time at those altitudes; and

(3) At cabin pressure altitudes above 15,000 feet (MSL), unless each occupant of the aircraft is provided with supplemental oxygen.

§ 91.33 Powered civil aircraft with standard category U.S. airworthiness certificates; instrument and equipment requirements.

(a) *General.* Except as provided in paragraphs (c)(3) and (e) of this section, no person may operate a powered civil aircraft with a standard category U.S. airworthiness certificate in any operation described in paragraphs (b) through (f) of this section unless that aircraft contains the instruments and equipment specified in those paragraphs (or FAA approved equivalents) for that type of operation, and those instruments and items of equipment are in operable condition.

(b) *Visual flight rules (day).* For VFR flight during the day the following instruments and equipment are required:

(1) Airspeed indicator.
(2) Altimeter.
(3) Magnetic direction indicator.
(4) Tachometer for each engine.

(5) Oil pressure gauge for each engine using pressure system.

(6) Temperature gauge for each liquid-cooled engine.

(7) Oil temperature gauge for each air-cooled engine.

(8) Manifold pressure gauge for each altitude engine.

(9) Fuel gauge indicating the quantity of fuel in each tank.

(10) Landing gear position indicator, if the aircraft has a retractable landing gear.

(11) If the aircraft is operated for hire over water and beyond power-off gliding distance from shore, approved flotation gear readily available to each occupant, and at least one pyrotechnic signaling device.

(12) Except as to airships, approved safety belts for all occupants who have reached their second birthday. The rated strength of each safety belt shall be not less than that corresponding with the ultimate load factors specified in the current applicable aircraft airworthiness requirements considering the dimensional characteristics of the safety belt installation for the specific seat or berth arrangement. The webbing of each safety belt shall be replaced as required by the Administrator.

(c) *Visual flight rules (night).* For VFR flight at night the following instruments and equipment are required:

(1) Instruments and equipment specified in paragraph (b) of this section.

(2) Approved position lights.

(3) An approved aviation red or aviation white anticollision light system on all large aircraft, on all small aircraft when required by the aircraft's airworthiness certificate, and on all other small aircraft after August 11, 1972. Anticollision light systems initially installed after August 11, 1971, on aircraft for which a type certificate was issued or applied for before August 11, 1971, must at least meet the anticollision light standards of Parts 23, 25, 27, or 29, as applicable, that were in effect on August 10, 1971, except that the color may be either aviation red or aviation white. In the event of failure of any light of the anticollision light system, operations with the aircraft may be continued to a stop where repairs or replacement can be made.

(4) If the aircraft is operated for hire, one electric landing light.

(5) An adequate source of electrical energy for all installed electrical and radio equipment.

(6) One spare set of fuses, or three spare fuses of each kind required.

(d) *Instrument flight rules.* For IFR flight the following instruments and equipment are required:

(1) Instruments and equipment specified in paragraph (b) of this section and for night flight, instruments and equipment specified in paragraph (c) of this section.

(2) Two-way radio communications system and navigational equipment appropriate to the ground facilities to be used.

(3) Gyroscopic rate-of-turn indicator,

ALSO:
   SAFETY BELTS
   FLOTATION GEAR
      (OVER WATER FOR HIRE ONLY)
   POSITION LIGHTS
   LANDING LIGHT (FOR HIRE ONLY)
   ELECTRICAL ENERGY SOURCE
   SPARE FUSES
   GENERATOR (IFR ONLY)
   ANTI-COLLISION LIGHT (WHEN REQUIRED)

ADDITIONAL IFR REQUIREMENTS
(SHADED AREA)

LANDING GEAR POSITION INDICATOR
(RETRACTABLE LANDING GEAR)

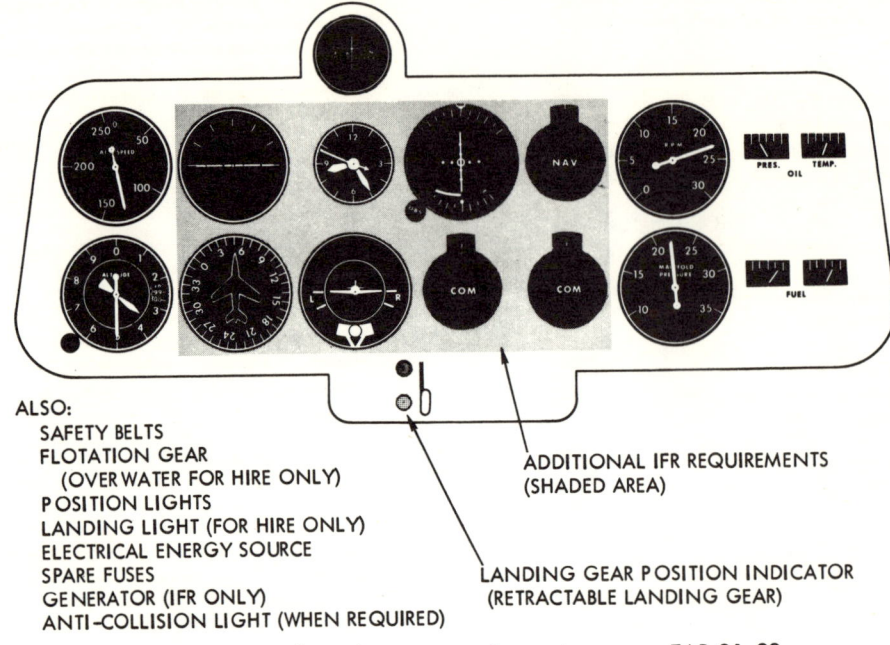

Instrument and equipment requirements----per FAR 91.33.
For IFR flight, additional gyro instrument, clock, generator,
two-way radio and navigation equipment, are required.

except on large aircraft with a third attitude instrument system usable through flight attitudes of 360° of pitch and roll and installed in accordance with § 121.305(j) of this title.

(4) Slip-skid indicator.

(5) Sensitive altimeter adjustable for barometric pressure.

(6) Clock with sweep-second hand.

(7) Generator of adequate capacity.

(8) Gyroscopic bank and pitch indicator (artificial horizon).

(9) Gyroscopic direction indicator (directional gyro or equivalent).

(e) *Flight at and above 24,000 feet MSL.* If VOR navigational equipment is required under subparagraph (d)(2) of this section, no person may operate a U.S. registered civil aircraft in the State of Alaska after March 31, 1968, in the State of Hawaii after April 30, 1967 or, in the 48 Contiguous States or in the District of Columbia, at and above 24,000 feet MSL, unless that aircraft is equipped with an approved distance measuring equipment (DME). When DME required by this paragraph fails at and above 24,000 feet MSL, each pilot shall notify ATC immediately, and may then continue operations at and above 24,000 feet MSL to the next airport of intended landing at which repairs or replacement of the equipment can be made.

§ 91.36 Data correspondence between automatically reported pressure altitude data and the pilot's altitude reference.

No person may operate any automatic pressure altitude reporting equipment associated with a radar beacon transponder—

(a) When deactivation of that equipment is directed by ATC; or

(b) Unless, as installed, that equipment was tested and calibrated to transmit altitude data corresponding within 125 feet (on a 95 percent probability basis) of the indicated or calibrated datum of the altimeter normally used to maintain flight altitude, with that altimeter referenced to 29.92 inches of mercury.

Subpart B—Flight Rules
GENERAL

§ 91.70 Aircraft speed.

(a) Unless otherwise authorized by the Administrator, no person may operate an aircraft below 10,000 feet MSL at an indicated airspeed of more than 250 knots (288 m.p.h.).

(b) Unless otherwise authorized or required by ATC, no person may operate an aircraft within an airport traffic area at an indicated airspeed of more than—

(1) In the case of a reciprocating engine aircraft, 156 knots (180 m.p.h.); or

(2) In the case of a turbine-powered aircraft, 200 knots (230 m.p.h.).

Paragraph (b) does not apply to any operations within a Terminal Control Area. Such operations shall comply with paragraph (a) of this section.

(c) No person may operate aircraft in the airspace beneath the lateral limits of any terminal control area at an indicated airspeed of more than 200 knots (230 m.p.h.).

However, if the minimum safe airspeed for any particular operation is greater than the maximum speed prescribed in this section, the aircraft may be operated at that minimum speed.

§ 91.75 Compliance with ATC clearances and instructions.

(a) When an ATC clearance has been obtained, no pilot in command may deviate from that clearance, except in an emergency, unless he obtains an amended clearance. However, except in positive controlled airspace, this paragraph does not prohibit him from cancelling an IFR flight plan if he is operating in VFR weather conditions.

(b) Except in an emergency, no person may, in an area in which air traffic control is exercised, operate an aircraft contrary to an ATC instruction.

(c) Each pilot in command who deviates, in an emergency, from an ATC clearance or instruction shall notify ATC of that deviation as soon as possible.

(d) Each pilot in command who (though not deviating from a rule of this subpart) is given priority by ATC in an emergency, shall, if requested by ATC, submit a detailed report of that emergency within 48 hours to the chief of that ATC facility

§ 91.77 ATC light signals.

ATC light signals have the meaning shown in the following table.

Color and type of signal	Meaning with respect to aircraft on the surface	Meaning with respect to aircraft in flight
Steady green	Cleared for takeoff	Cleared to land.
Flashing green	Cleared to taxi	Return for landing (to be followed by steady green at proper time).
Steady red	Stop	Give way to other aircraft and continue circling.
Flashing red	Taxi clear of runway in use.	Airport unsafe—do not land.
Flashing white	Return to starting point on airport.	Not applicable.
Alternating red and green.	Exercise extreme caution.	Exercise extreme caution.

§ 91.79 Minimum safe altitudes; general.

Except when necessary for takeoff or landing, no person may operate an aircraft below the following altitudes:

(a) *Anywhere.* An altitude allowing, if a power unit fails, an emergency landing without undue hazard to persons or property on the surface.

(b) *Over congested areas.* Over any congested area of a city, town, or settlement, or over any open air assembly of persons, an altitude of 1,000 feet above the highest obstacle within a horizontal radius of 2,000 feet of the aircraft.

(c) *Over other than congested areas.* An altitude of 500 feet above the surface, except over open water or sparsely populated areas. In that case, the aircraft may not be operated closer than 500 feet to any person, vessel, vehicle, or structure.

§ 91.81 Altimeter settings.

(a) Each person operating an aircraft shall maintain the cruising altitude or flight level of that aircraft, as the case may be, by reference to an altimeter that is set, when operating—

(1) Below 18,000 feet MSL, to—
(i) The current reported altimeter setting of a station along the route and within 100 nautical miles of the aircraft;

(ii) If there is no station within the area prescribed in subdivision (i) of this subparagraph, the current reported altimeter setting of an appropriate available station; or

(iii) In the case of an aircraft not equipped with a radio, the elevation of the departure airport or an appropriate altimeter setting available before departure; or

(2) At or above 18,000 feet MSL, to 29.92″ Hg.

(b) The lowest usable flight level is determined by the atmospheric pressure in the area of operation, as shown in the following table:

Current altimeter setting	Lowest usable flight level
29.92 (or higher)	180
29.91 thru 29.42	185
29.41 thru 28.92	190
28.91 thru 28.42	195
28.41 thru 27.92	200
27.91 thru 27.42	205
27.41 thru 26.92	210

(c) To convert minimum altitude prescribed under §§ 91.79 and 91.119 to the minimum flight level, the pilot shall take the flight-level equivalent of the minimum altitude in feet and add the appropriate number of feet specified below, according to the current reported altimeter setting:

Current altimeter setting	Adjustment factor
29.92 (or higher)	None
29.91 thru 29.42	500 feet
29.41 thru 28.92	1000 feet
28.91 thru 28.42	1500 feet
28.41 thru 27.92	2000 feet
27.91 thru 27.42	2500 feet
27.41 thru 26.92	3000 feet

§ 91.83 Flight plan; information required.

(a) Unless otherwise authorized by ATC, each person filing an IFR or VFR flight plan shall include in it the following information:

(1) The aircraft identification number and, if necessary, its radio call sign.

(2) The type of the aircraft or, in the case of a formation flight, the type of each aircraft and the number of aircraft, in the formation.

(3) The full name and address of the pilot in command or, in the case of a formation flight, the formation commander.

(4) The point and proposed time of departure.

(5) The proposed route, cruising altitude (or flight level), and true airspeed at that altitude.

(6) The point of first intended landing and the estimated elapsed time until over that point.

(7) The radio frequencies to be used.

(8) The amount of fuel on board (in hours).

(9) In the case of an IFR flight plan, an alternate airport, except as provided in paragraph (b) of this section.

(10) In the case of an international flight, the number of persons in the aircraft.

(11) Any other information the pilot in command or ATC believes is necessary for ATC purposes.

When a flight plan has been filed, the pilot

in command, upon cancelling or completing the flight under the flight plan, shall notify the nearest FAA Flight Service Station or ATC facility.

(b) Paragraph (a)(9) of this section does not apply if Part 97 of this subchapter prescribes a standard instrument approach procedure for the first airport of intended landing and the weather conditions at that airport are forecast to be, from two hours before to two hours after the estimated time of arrival, a ceiling of at least 1,000 feet above the lowest MEA, MOCA, or altitude prescribed for the initial approach segment of the instrument approach procedure for the airport and visibility at least three miles, or two miles more than the lowest authorized landing minimum visibility, whichever is greater.

(c) *IFR alternate airport weather minimums.* Unless otherwise authorized by the Administrator, no person may include an alternate airport in an IFR flight plan unless current weather forecasts indicate that, at the estimated time of arrival at the alternate airport, the ceiling and visibility at that airport will be at or above the following alternate airport weather minimums:

(1) If an instrument approach procedure has been published in Part 97 for that airport, the alternate airport minimums specified in that procedure or, if none are so specified, the following minimums:

(i) Precision a p p r o a c h procedure: ceiling 600 feet and visibility 2 statute miles.

(ii) Non-precision approach procedure: ceiling 800 feet and visibility 2 statute miles.

(2) If no instrument approach procedure has been published in Part 97 for that airport, the ceiling and visibility minimums are those allowing descent from the MEA, approach, and landing, under basic VFR.

§ 91.90 Terminal control areas.

(a) *Group I terminal control areas.*

(1) *Operating rules.* No person may operate an aircraft within a Group I terminal control area designated in Part 71 of this chapter except in compliance with the following rules:

(i) No person may operate an aircraft within a Group I terminal control area unless he has received an appropriate authorization from ATC prior to the operation of that aircraft in that area.

(ii) Unless otherwise authorized by ATC, each person operating a large turbine engine powered airplane to or from a primary airport shall operate at or above the designated floors while within the lateral limits of the terminal control area.

(2) *Pilot requirements.* The pilot in command of a civil aircraft may not land or take off that aircraft from an airport within a Group I terminal control area unless he holds at least a private pilot certificate.

(3) *Equipment requirements.* Unless otherwise authorized by ATC in the case of in-flight VOR, TACAN, or two-way radio failure; or unless otherwise authorized by ATC in the case of a transponder failure occurring at any time, [1] no person may operate an aircraft within a Group I terminal control area unless that aircraft is equipped with—

(i) An operable VOR or TACAN receiver (except in the case of helicopters);

(ii) An operable two-way radio capable of communicating with ATC on appropriate frequencies for that terminal control area; and

(iii) On and before the applicable dates specified in paragraphs (a) and (b)(1) of § 91.24, an operable coded radar beacon transponder having at least a Mode 3/A 64-code capability, replying to Mode 3/A interrogation with the code specified by ATC. On and before those dates, this requirement is not applicable to helicopters operating within the terminal control area, or to IFR flights operating to or from a secondary airport located within the terminal control area, or to IFR flights operating to or from an airport outside of the terminal control area but which is in close proximity to the terminal control area, when the commonly used transition, approach, or departure procedures to such airport require flight within the terminal control area. After the applicable dates specified in paragraphs (a) and (b)(1) of § 91.24, the applicable provisions of that section shall be complied with, notwithstanding the exceptions in this section.

(b) *Group II terminal control areas.*

(1) *Operating rules.* No person may operate an aircraft within a Group II terminal control area designated in Part 71 of this chapter except in compliance with the following rules:

(i) No person may operate an aircraft within a Group II Terminal Control Area unless he has received an appropriate authorization from ATC prior to operation of that aircraft in that area, except that, after the applicable dates in § 91.24 (b)(2), authorization is not required if the aircraft is VFR, is equipped as required by § 91.24(b), and does not land or take off within the terminal control area.

(ii) Unless otherwise authorized by ATC, each person operating a large turbine engine powered airplane to or from a primary airport shall operate at or above the designated floors while within the lateral limits of the terminal control area.

(2) *Equipment requirements.* Unless otherwise authorized by ATC in the case of in-flight VOR, TACAN, or two-way radio failure; or unless otherwise authorized by ATC in the case of a transponder failure occurring at any time, no person may operate an aircraft within a Group II terminal control area unless that aircraft is equipped with—

(i) An operable VOR or TACAN receiver (except in the case of helicopters);

(ii) An operable two-way radio capable of communicating with ATC on the appropriate frequencies for that terminal control area; and

(iii) On and before the applicable dates specified in paragraphs (a) and (b)(2) of § 91.24, an operable coded radar beacon transponder having at least a Mode 3/A 64-code capability, replying to Mode 3/A interrogation with the code specified by ATC. On and before those dates, this requirement is not applicable to helicopters operating within the terminal control area, or to VFR aircraft operating within the terminal control area, or to IFR flights operating to or from a secondary airport located within the terminal control area, or to IFR flights operating to or from an airport outside of the terminal control area but which is in close proximity to the terminal control area, when the commonly used transition, approach, or departure procedures to such airport require flight within the terminal control area. After the applicable dates in paragraphs (a) and (b)(2) of § 91.24, that section shall be complied with, notwithstanding the exceptions in this section.

(c) *Group III terminal control areas.* After the date specified in § 91.24(b)(3), no person may operate an aircraft within a Group III Terminal Control Area designated in Part 71 unless the applicable provisions of § 91.24(b) are complied with, except that such compliance is not required if two-way radio communications are maintained, within the TCA, between the aircraft and the ATC facility, and the pilot provides position, altitude, and proposed flight path prior to entry.

§ 91.97 Positive control areas and route segments.

(a) Except as provided in paragraph (b) of this section, no person may operate an aircraft within a positive control area or positive control route segment, designated in Part 71 of this chapter, unless that aircraft is—

(1) Operated under IFR at a specific flight level assigned by ATC;

(2) Equipped with instruments and equipment required for IFR operations;

(3) Flown by a pilot rated for instrument flight; and

(4) Equipped, when in a positive control area, with—

(i) A coded radar beacon transponder, having at least a Mode A (Military Mode 3) 64-code capability, replying to Mode 3/A interrogation with the code specified by ATC, except that, after the applicable dates specified in paragraphs (a) and (b)(3) of § 91.24, the applicable provisions of that section shall be complied with.

(ii) A radio providing direct pilot/controller communication on the frequency specified by ATC for the area concerned.

(b) ATC may authorize deviations from the requirements of paragraph (a) of this section. In the case of an inoperative transponder, ATC may immediately approve an operation within a positive control area allowing flight to continue, if desired, to the airport of ultimate destination, including any intermediate stops, or to proceed to a place where suitable repairs can be made, or both. A request for authorization to deviate from a requirement of paragraph (a) of this section, other than for operation with an inoperative transponder as outlined above, must be submitted at least four days before the proposed operation, in writing, to the ATC center having jurisdiction over the positive control area concerned. ATC may authorize a deviation on a continuing basis or for an individual flight, as appropriate.

VISUAL FLIGHT RULES

§ 91.105 Basic VFR weather minimums.

(a) Except as provided in § 91.107, no person may operate an aircraft under VFR when the flight visibility is less, or at a distance from clouds that is less, than that prescribed for the corresponding altitude in the following table:

(c) Except as provided in § 91.107, no person may operate an aircraft, under VFR, within a control zone beneath the ceiling when the ceiling is less than 1,000 feet.

(d) Except as provided in § 91.107, no person may take off or land an aircraft, or enter the traffic pattern of an airport, under VFR, within a control zone—

(1) Unless ground visibility at that airport is at least three statute miles; or

(2) If ground visibility is not reported at that airport, unless flight visibility during landing or take off, or while operating in the traffic pattern, is at least three statue miles.

(e) For the purposes of this section, an aircraft operating at the base altitude of a transition area or control area is considered

MINIMUM VISIBILITY AND DISTANCE FROM CLOUDS—VFR

Altitude	Flight visibility	Distance from clouds
1,200 feet or less above the surface (regardless of MSL altitude)—		
Within controlled airspace	3 statute miles	500 feet below. 1,000 feet above. 2,000 feet horizontal.
Outside controlled airspace	1 statute mile except as provided in § 91.105(b).	Clear of clouds.
More than 1,200 feet above the surface but less than 10,000 feet MSL—		
Within controlled airspace	3 statute miles	500 feet below. 1,000 feet above. 2,000 feet horizontal.
Outside controlled airspace	1 statue mile	500 feet below. 1,000 feet above. 2,000 feet horizontal.
More than 1,200 feet above the surface and at or above 10,000 feet MSL.	5 statute miles	1,000 feet below. 1,000 feet above. 1 mile horizontal.

to be within the airspace directly below that area.

§ 91.109 VFR cruising altitude or flight level.

Except while holding in a holding pattern of 2 minutes or less, or while turning, each person operating an aircraft under VFR in level cruising flight at an altitude of more than 3,000 feet above the surface shall maintain the appropriate altitude prescribed below:

(a) When operating below 18,000 feet MSL and—

(1) On a magnetic course of zero degrees through 179 degrees, any odd thousand foot MSL altitude +500 feet (such as 3,500, 5,500, or 7,500); or

(2) On a magnetic course of 180 degrees through 359 degrees, any even thousand foot MSL altitude +500 feet (such as 4,500, 6,500, or 8,500).

(b) When operating above 18,000 feet MSL to flight level 290 (inclusive), and—

(1) On a magnetic course of zero degrees through 179 degrees, any odd flight level +500 feet (such as 195, 215, or 235); or

(2) On a magnetic course of 180 degrees through 359 degrees, any even flight level +500 feet (such as 185, 205, or 225).

(c) When operating above flight level 290 and—

(1) On a magnetic course of zero degrees through 179 degrees, any flight level, at 4,000-foot intervals, beginning at and including flight level 300 (such as flight level 300, 340, or 380); or

(2) On a magnetic course of 180 degrees through 359 degrees, any flight level, at 4,000-foot intervals, beginning at and including flight level 320 (such as flight level 320, 360, or 400).

INSTRUMENT FLIGHT RULES

§ 91.115 ATC clearance and flight plan required.

No person may operate an aircraft in controlled airspace under IFR unless—

(a) He has filed an IFR flight plan; and

(b) He has received an appropriate ATC clearance.

§ 91.116 Takeoff and landing under IFR: general.

(a) *Instrument approaches to civil airports.* Unless otherwise authorized by the Administrator (including ATC), each person operating an aircraft shall, when an instrument letdown to an airport is necessary, use a standard instrument approach procedure prescribed for that airport in Part 97 of this chapter.

(b) *Landing minimums.* Unless otherwise authorized by the Administrator, no person operating an aircraft (except a military aircraft of the United States) may land that aircraft using a standard instrument approach procedure prescribed in Part 97 of this chapter unless the visibility is at or above the landing minimum prescribed in that Part for the procedure used. If the landing minimum in a standard instrument approach procedure prescribed in Part 97 is stated in terms of ceiling and visibility, the visibility minimum applies. However, the ceiling minimum shall be added to the field elevation and that value observed as the MDA or DH, as appropriate to the procedure being executed.

(c) *Civil airport takeoff minimums.* Unless otherwise authorized by the Administrator, no person operating an aircraft under Part 121, 123, 129, or 135 of this chapter may take off from a civil airport under IFR unless weather conditions are at or above the weather minimums for IFR takeoff prescribed for that airport in Part 97 of this chapter. If takeoff minimums are not prescribed in Part 97 of this chapter, for a particular airport, the following minimums apply to takeoffs under IFR for aircraft operating under those parts:

(1) Aircraft having two engines or less: 1 statute mile visibility.

(2) Aircraft having more than two engines: ½ statute mile visibility.

(d) *Military airports.* Unless otherwise prescribed by the Administrator, each person operating a civil aircraft under IFR into, or out of, a military airport shall comply with the instrument approach procedures and the takeoff and landing minimums prescribed by the military authority having jurisdiction on that airport.

(e) *Comparable values of RVR and ground visibility.*

(1) If RVR minimums for takeoff or landing are prescribed in an instrument approach procedure, but RVR is not reported for the runway of intended operation, the RVR minimum shall be converted to ground visibility in accordance with the table in subparagraph (2) of this paragraph and observed as the applicable visibility minimum for takeoff or landing on that runway.

(2)

RVR	Visibility (statute miles)
1600 feet	¼ mile
2400 feet	½ mile
3200 feet	⅝ mile
4000 feet	¾ mile
4500 feet	⅞ mile
5000 feet	1 mile
6000 feet	1¼ mile

(f) *Use of radar in instrument approach procedures.* When radar is approved at certain locations for ATC purposes, it may be used not only for surveillance and precision radar approaches, as applicable, but also may be used in conjunction with instrument approach procedures predicated on other types of radio navigational aids. Radar vectors may be authorized to provide course guidance through the segments of an approach procedure to the final approach fix or position. Upon reaching the final approach fix or position, the pilot will either complete his instrument approach in accordance with the procedure approved for the facility, or will continue a surveillance or precision radar approach to a landing.

(g) *Use of low or medium frequency simultaneous radio ranges for ADF procedures.* Low frequency or medium frequency simultaneous radio ranges may be used as an ADF instrument approach aid if an ADF procedure for the airport concerned is prescribed by the Administrator, or if an approach is conducted using the same courses and altitudes for the ADF approach as those specified in the approved range procedure.

(h) *Limitations on procedure turns.* In the

case of a radar initial approach to a final approach fix or position, or a timed approach from a holding fix, or where the procedure specifies "NOPT" or "FINAL", no pilot may make a procedure turn unless, when he receives his final approach clearance, he so advises ATC.

§ 91.117 Limitations on use of instrument approach procedures (other than Category II).

(a) *General.* Unless otherwise authorized by the Administrator, each person operating an aircraft using an instrument approach procedure prescribed in Part 97 of this chapter shall comply with the requirements of this section. This section does not apply to the use of Category II approach procedures.

(b) *Descent below MDA or DH.* No person may operate an aircraft below the prescribed minimum descent altitude or continue an approach below the decision height unless—

(1) The aircraft is in a position from which a normal approach to the runway of intended landing can be made; and

(2) The approach threshold of that runway, or approach lights or other markings identifiable with the approach end of that runway, are clearly visible to the pilot.

If, upon arrival at the missed approach point or decision height, or at any time thereafter, any of the above requirements are not met, the pilot shall immediately execute the appropriate missed approach procedure.

(c) *Inoperative or unusable components and visual aids.* The basic ground components of an ILS are the localizer, glide slope, outer marker, and middle marker. The approach lights are visual aids normally associated with the ILS. In addition, if an ILS approach procedure in Part 97 of this chapter prescribes a visibility minimum of 1800 feet or 2000 feet RVR, high intensity runway lights, touchdown zone lights, centerline lighting and marking and RVR are aids associated with the ILS for those minimums. Compass locator or precision radar may be substituted for the outer or middle marker. Surveillance radar may be substituted for the outer marker. Unless otherwise specified by the Administrator, if a ground component, visual aid, or RVR is inoperative, or unusable, or not utilized, the straight-in minimums prescribed in any approach procedure in Part 97 are raised in accordance with the following tables. Except as provided in subparagraph (c)(5) of this paragraph or unless otherwise specified by the Administrator, if a ground component, visual aid, or RVR is inoperative, or unusable or not utilized, the straight-in minimums prescribed in any approach procedure in Part 97 of this chapter are raised in accordance with the following tables. If the related airborne equipment for a ground component is inoperative or not utilized, the increased minimums applicable to the related ground component shall be used. If more than one component or aid is inoperative, or unusable, or not utilized, each minimum is raised to the highest minimum required by any one of the components or aids which is inoperative, or unusable, or not utilized.

(1) *ILS and PAR.*

Component or aid	Increase decision height	Increase visibility (statute miles)	Approach category
LOC[1]	ILS approach not authorized.		All.
GS	As specified in the procedure.		All.
OM, MM	50 feet	None	ABC.
OM, MM	50 feet	¼	D.
ALS	50 feet	¼	All.
SSALSR	50 feet	¼	ABC.
MALSR	50 feet	¼	ABC.

[1] Not applicable to PAR.

(2) *ILS with visibility minimum of 1,800 or 2,000 feet RVR.*

Component or aid	Increase decision height	Increase visibility (statute miles)	Approach category
LOC	ILS approach not authorized.		All.
GS	As specified in the procedure.		All.
OM, MM	50 feet	To ½ mile	ABC.
OM, MM	50 feet	To ¾ mile	D.
ALS	50 feet	To ¾ mile	All.
HIRL, TDZL, RCLS.	None	To ½ mile	All.
RCLM	As specified in the procedure.		All.
RVR	None	To ½ mile	All.

(3) *VOR, LOC, LDA, and ASR.*

Component or aid	Increase MDA	Increase visibility (statute miles)	Approach category
ALS, SSALSR, MALSR	None	½ mile	ABC.
SSALS, MALS, HIRL, and REIL	None	¼ mile	ABC.

(4) *NDB(ADF) and LFR.*

Component or aid	Increase MDA	Increase visibility (statute miles)	Approach category
ALS, SSALSR, MALSR	None	¼ mile	ABC.

(5) The inoperative component tables in subparagraphs (1) through (4) of this paragraph do not apply to helicopter procedures. Helicopter procedure minimums are specified on each procedure for inoperative components.

§ 91.119 Minimum altitudes for IFR operations.

(a) Except when necessary for takeoff or landing, or unless otherwise authorized by the Administrator, no person may operate an aircraft under IFR below—

(1) The applicable minimum altitudes prescribed in Parts 95 and 97 of this chapter; or

(2) If no applicable minimum altitude is prescribed in those Parts—

(i) In the case of operations over an area designated as a mountainous area in Part 95, an altitude of 2,000 feet above the highest obstacle within a horizontal distance of five statute miles from the course to be flown; or

(ii) In any other case, an altitude of 1,000 feet above the highest obstacle within a horizontal distance of five statute miles from the course to be flown.

However, if both a MEA and a MOCA are prescribed for a particular route or route segment, a person may operate an aircraft below the MEA down to, but not below, the MOCA, when within 25 statute miles of the VOR concerned (based on the pilot's reasonable estimate of that distance).

(b) *Climb.* Climb to a higher minimum IFR altitude shall begin immediately after passing the point beyond which that minimum altitude applies, except that, when ground obstructions intervene, the point beyond which the higher minimum altitude applies shall be crossed at or above the applicable MCA.

§ 91.121 IFR cruising altitude or flight level.

(a) *In controlled airspace.* Each person operating an aircraft under IFR in level cruising flight in controlled airspace shall maintain the altitude or flight level assigned that aircraft by ATC. However, if the ATC clearance assigns "VFR conditions-on-top," he shall maintain an altitude or flight level as prescribed by § 91.109.

(b) *In uncontrolled airspace.* Except while holding in a holding pattern of two minutes or less, or while turning, each person operating an aircraft under IFR in level cruising flight, in uncontrolled airspace, shall maintain an appropriate altitude as follows:

(1) When operating below 18,000 feet MSL and—

(i) On a magnetic course of zero degrees through 179 degrees, any odd thousand foot MSL altitude (such as 3,000, 5,000, or 7,000); or

(ii) On a magnetic course of 180 degrees through 359 degrees, any even thousand foot MSL altitude (such as 2,000, 4,000, or 6,000).

(2) When operating at or above 18,000 feet MSL but below flight level 290, and—

(i) On a magnetic course of zero degrees through 179 degrees, any odd flight level (such as 190, 210, or 230); or

(ii) On a magnetic course of 180 degrees through 359 degrees, any even flight level (such as 180, 200, or 220).

(3) When operating at flight level 290 and above, and—

(i) On a magnetic course of zero degrees through 179 degrees, any flight level, at 4,000-foot intervals, beginning at and including flight level 290 (such as flight level 290, 330, or 370); or

(ii) On a magnetic course of 180 degrees through 359 degrees, any flight level, at 4,000-foot intervals, beginning at and including flight level 310 (such as flight level 310, 350, or 390).

§ 91.123 Course to be flown.

Unless otherwise authorized by ATC, no person may operate an aircraft within controlled airspace, under IFR, except as follows:

(a) On a Federal airway, along the centerline of that airway.

(b) On any other route, along the direct course between the navigational aids or fixes defining that route.

However, this section does not prohibit maneuvering the aircraft to pass well clear of other air traffic or the maneuvering of the aircraft, in VFR conditions, to clear the intended flight path both before and during climb or descent.

§ 91.125 IFR, radio communications.

The pilot in command of each aircraft operated under IFR in controlled airspace shall have a continuous watch maintained on the appropriate frequency and shall report by radio as soon as possible—

(a) The time and altitude of passing each designated reporting point, or the reporting points specified by ATC, except that while the aircraft is under radar control, only the passing of those reporting points specifically requested by ATC need be reported;

(b) Any unforecast weather conditions encountered; and

(c) Any other information relating to the safety of flight.

§ 91.127 IFR operations; two-way radio communications failure.

(a) *General.* Unless otherwise authorized by ATC, each pilot who has two-way radio communications failure when operating under IFR shall comply with the rules of this section.

(b) *VFR conditions.* If the failure occurs in VFR conditions, or if VFR conditions are encountered after the failure, each pilot shall continue the flight under VFR and land as soon as practicable.

(c) *IFR conditions.* If the failure occurs in IFR conditions, or if paragraph (b) of this section cannot be complied with, each pilot shall continue the flight according to the following:

(1) *Route.*

(i) By the route assigned in the last ATC clearance received;

(ii) If being radar vectored, by the direct route from the point of radio failure to the fix, route, or airway specified in the vector clearance;

(iii) In the absence of an assigned route, by the route that ATC has advised may be expected in a further clearance; or

(iv) In the absence of an assigned route or a route that ATC has advised may be expected in a further clearance, by the route filed in the flight plan.

(2) *Altitude.* At the highest of the following altitudes or flight levels for the route segment being flown:

(i) The altitude or flight level assigned in the last ATC clearance received;

(ii) The minimum altitude (converted, if appropriate, to minimum flight level as prescribed in § 91.81(c)) for IFR operations; or

(iii) The altitude or flight level ATC has advised may be expected in a further clearance.

(3) [Revoked].

(4) *Leave holding fix.* If holding instructions have been received, leave the hold-

ing fix at the expect-further-clearance time received, or, if an expected approach clearance time has been received, leave the holding fix in order to arrive over the fix from which the approach begins as close as possible to the expected approach clearance time.

(5) *Descent for approach.* Begin descent from the en route altitude or flight level upon reaching the fix from which the approach begins, but not before—

(i) The expect-approach-clearance time (if received); or

(ii) If no expect-approach-clearance time has been received, at the estimated time of arrival, shown on the flight plan, as amended with ATC.

§ 91.129 Operation under IFR in controlled airspace; malfunction reports.

(a) The pilot in command of each aircraft operated in controlled airspace under IFR, shall report immediately to ATC any of the following malfunctions of equipment occurring in flight:

(1) Loss of VOR, TACAN, ADF, or low frequency navigation receiver capability.

(2) Complete or partial loss of ILS receiver capability.

(3) Impairment of air/ground communications capability.

(b) In each report required by paragraph (a) of this section, the pilot in command shall include the—

(1) Aircraft identification;

(2) Equipment affected;

(3) Degree to which the capability of the pilot to operate under IFR in the ATC system is impaired; and

(4) Nature and extent of assistance he desires from ATC.

Subpart C—Maintenance, Preventive Maintenance, and Alterations

§ 91.170 Altimeter system tests and inspections.

(a) No person may operate an airplane in controlled airspace under IFR unless, within the preceding 24 calendar months, each static pressure system and each altimeter instrument has been tested and inspected and found to comply with Appendix E of Part 43. The static pressure system and altimeter instrument tests and inspections may be conducted by—

(1) The manufacturer of the airplane on which the tests and inspections are to be performed;

(2) A certificated repair station properly equipped to perform these functions and holding—

(i) An instrument rating, Class I;

(ii) A limited instrument rating appropriate to the make and model altimeter to be tested;

(iii) A limited rating appropriate to the test to be performed;

(iv) An airframe rating appropriate to the airplane to be tested; or

(v) A limited rating for a manufacturer issued for the altimeter in accordance with § 145.101(b)(4) of this chapter;

or (3) A certificated mechanic with an airframe rating (static pressure system tests and inspections only).

(b) Revoked.

(c) No person may operate an airplane in controlled airspace under IFR at an altitude above the maximum altitude to which an altimeter of that airplane has been tested.

§ 91.177 ATC transponder tests and inspections.

(a) After January 1, 1974, no person may use an ATC transponder that is specified in [§ 91.24(a)], § 121.345(c), § 127.123(b), or § 135.143(c) of this chapter, unless, within the preceding 12 calendar months, that ATC transponder has been tested and inspected and found to comply with Appendix F of Part 43 of this chapter.

(b) The tests and inspections specified in paragraph (a) of this section may be conducted by—

(1) A certificated repair station properly equipped to perform those functions and holding—

(i) A radio rating, Class III;

(ii) A limited radio rating appropriate to the make and model transponder to be tested;

(iii) A limited rating appropriate to the test to be performed; or

(iv) A limited rating for a manufacturer issued for the transponder in accordance with § 145.101(b)(4) of this chapter; or

(2) A certificate holder authorized to perform maintenance in accordance with § 121.379 or § 127.140 of this chapter; or

(3) The manufacturer of the aircraft on which the transponder to be tested is installed, if the transponder was installed by that manufacturer.

Definitions and Abbreviations

"Alternate airport" means an airport at which an aircraft may land if a landing at the intended airport becomes inadvisable.

"Calibrated airspeed" means indicated airspeed of an aircraft, corrected for position and instrument error. Calibrated airspeed is equal to true airspeed in standard atmosphere at sea level.

"Category II operation", with respect to the operation of aircraft, means a straight-in ILS approach to the runway of an airport under a Category II ILS instrument approach procedure issued by the Administrator or other appropriate authority.

"IFR over-the-top", with respect to the operation of aircraft, means the operation of an aircraft over-the-top on an IFR flight plan when cleared by air traffic control to maintain "VFR conditions" or "VFR conditions on top".

"Indicated airspeed" means the speed of an aircraft as shown on its pitot static airspeed indicator calibrated to reflect standard atmosphere adiabatic compressible flow at sea level uncorrected for airspeed system errors.

"Instrument" means a device using an internal mechanism to show visually or aurally the attitude, altitude, or operation of an aircraft or aircraft part. It includes electronic devices for automatically controlling an aircraft in flight.

"Large aircraft" means aircraft of more than 12,500 pounds, maximum certificated takeoff weight.

"Positive control" means control of all air traffic, within designated airspace, by air traffic control.

"Precision approach procedure" means a standard instrument approach procedure in which an electronic glide slope is provided, such as ILS and PAR.

"RNAV way point (W/P)" means a predetermined geographical position used for route or instrument approach definition or progress reporting purposes that is defined relative to a VORTAC station position.

"Route segment" means a part of a route. Each end of that part is identified by—
(1) a continental or insular geographical location; or
(2) a point at which a definite radio fix can be established.

"Small aircraft" means aircraft of 12,500 pounds or less, maximum certificated takeoff weight.

"True airspeed" means the airspeed of an aircraft relative to undisturbed air. True airspeed is equal to equivalent airspeed multiplied by $(po/p)^{1/2}$.

"VFR over-the-top", with respect to the operation of aircraft, means the operation of an aircraft over-the-top under VFR when it is not being operated on an IFR flight plan.

Abbreviations and symbols.

In Subchapters A through K of this chapter:

"ALS" means approach light system.

"ASR" means airport surveillance radar.

"ATC" means air traffic control.

"CAS" means calibrated airspeed.

"CAT II" means Category II.

"CONSOL or CONSOLAN" means a kind of low or medium frequency long range navigational aid.

"DH" means decision height.

"DME" means distance measuring equipment compatible with TACAN.

"EAS" means equivalent airspeed.

"FAA" means Federal Aviation Administration.

"FM" means fan marker.

"GS" means glide slope.

"HIRL" means high-intensity runway light system.

"IAS" means indicated airspeed.

"ICAO" means International Civil Aviation Organization.

"IFR" means instrument flight rules.

"ILS" means instrument landing system.

"IM" means ILS inner marker.

"INT" means intersection.

"LDA" means localizer-type directional aid.

"LFR" means low frequency radio range.

"LMM" means compass locator at middle marker.

"LOC" means ILS localizer.

"LOM" means compass locator at outer marker.

"M" means mach number.

"MAA" means maximum authorized IFR altitude.

"MALS" means medium intensity approach light system.

"MALSR" means medium intensity approach light system with runway alignment indicator lights.

"MCA" means minimum crossing altitude.

"MDA" means minimum descent altitude.

"MEA" means minimum en route IFR altitude.

"MM" means ILS middle marker.

"MOCA" means minimum obstruction clearance altitude.

"MRA" means minimum reception altitude.

"MSL" means mean sea level.

"NDB(ADF)" means nondirectional beacon (automatic direction finder).

"NOPT" means no procedure turn required.

"OM" means ILS outer marker.

"PAR" means precision approach radar.

"RAIL" means runway alignment indicator light system.

"RBN" means radio beacon.

"RR" means low or medium frequency radio range station.

"RCLM" means runway centerline marking.

"RCLS" means runway centerline light system.

"REIL" means runway end identification lights.

"RVR" means runway visual range as measured in the touchdown zone area.

"SALS" means short approach light system.

"SSALS" means simplified short approach light system.

"SSALSR" means simplified short approach light system with runway alignment indicator lights.

"TACAN" means ultra-high frequency tactical air navigational aid.

"TAS" means true airspeed.

"TDZL" means touchdown zone lights.

"TVOR" means very high frequency terminal omnirange station.

"V_A" means design maneuvering speed.

"V_B" means design speed for maximum gust intensity.

"V_C" means design cruising speed.

"V_D" means design diving speed.

"V_{DF}/M_{DF}" means demonstrated flight diving speed.

"V_F" means design flap speed.

"V_{FC}/M_{FC}" means maximum speed for stability characteristics.

"V_{FE}" means maximum flap extended speed.

"VFR" means visual flight rules.

"V_H" means maximum speed in level flight with maximum continuous power.

"VHF" means very high frequency.

"V_{LE}" means maximum landing gear extended speed.

"V_{LO}" means maximum landing gear operating speed.

"V_{LOF}" means lift-off speed.

"V_{MC}" means minimum control speed with the critical engine inoperative.

"V_{MO}/M_{MO}" means maximum operating limit speed.

"V_{MU}" means minimum unstick speed.

"V_{NE}" means never-exceed speed.

"VOR" means very high frequency omnirange station.

"VORTAC" means collocated VOR and TACAN.

"V_R" means rotation speed.

"V_S" means the stalling speed or the minimum steady flight speed at which the airplane is controllable.

"V_{SO}" means the stalling speed or the minimum steady flight speed in the landing configuration.

"V_{S1}" means the stalling speed or the minimum steady flight speed obtained in a specified configuration.

"V_X" means speed for best angle of climb.

"V_Y" means speed for best rate of climb.

"V_1" means critical-engine-failure speed.

"V_2" means takeoff safety speed.

"$V_{2 min}$" means minimum takeoff safety speed.

SUMMARY - FEDERAL AVIATION REGULATIONS

The student instrument pilot must know the FAR pertaining to instrument flight as outlined below:

AIRMEN (FAR 61)
- Pilot certificates and ratings
- Pilot logs and flight time requirements
- Recency of experience

AIRCRAFT (FAR 91)
- Certificates, documents, inspections
- Equipment required
- Equipment accuracy checks

FLIGHT RULES (FAR 91)
- General operating rules
- General flight rules
- Visual flight rules
    - Basic minimums; control areas, control zones, continental control area, and outside controlled airspace
    - Special VFR
    - Cruising altitudes/flight levels
    - Flight plan requirements
    - Fuel requirements
- Altimeter setting
- Compliance with ATC clearance
- IFR operations outside controlled air space
- Takeoff and landing
- Minimum altitudes
- Cruising altitudes/flight levels
- Courses to be flown
- Radio communications
- Communications failure
- Equipment malfunction

What is IFR weather? Any time it's not VFR as defined in Figure A 7 and A 8. All major airports are included in a CONTROL ZONE. Therefore weather minimums of 1000 foot ceiling and 3 miles visibility apply. Conditions LESS than these require the airport to operate under IFR rules. During the daytime, IFR conditions at the airport are indicated by continuous operation of the rotating beacon. At night the lights on the wind "Tee" flash on and off.

FLIGHT PLANNING and Log Sheet

DATE _____ TYPE _____ AIRCRAFT _____ NO. _____ PILOT _____ TIME OFF _____ TIME DOWN _____

RANGE	FREQ	ROUTE		MC	TC	WIND DIR/VEL	TH	VAR	MH	DIST.	MEA	ALT/TEMP PRES/ALT	TAS/IAS	ESTIMATE GS	LEG TIME	ETA	ACTUAL GS	LEG TIME	ATA
		FROM	APT.																
		TO	HUF												06				
		FROM	HUF	V14								6000							
		TO	VLA																
		FROM	VLA	V14								6000							
		TO	STL																
		FROM	STL	V4								6000							
		TO	HLV																
		FROM	HLV	V4								6000							
		TO	MKC																
		FROM																	
		TO																	
		FROM	MKC	V12								6000							
		TO	EMP																
		FROM	EMP	V12								6000							
		TO	ICT																
										TOTALS			ATC CLEARANCE						

Use IND winds from HUF to VLA
Use STL winds from VLA to HLV
Use MKC winds from MKC to EMP
Use ICT winds from EMP to ICT

FUEL ANALYSIS

TANK	TIME ON	TIME OFF
L		
R		

FUEL PLAN

FUEL TO DEST.	
FUEL TO ALT.	
45 MIN. RESV.	
FUEL REQD.	
FUEL AT DEPT.	
EXTRA FUEL	

(Use for Worksheet)

SAMPLE WRITTEN EXAMINATION

The FAA instrument pilot written examination is a 50 question test using multiple choice answers. In order to provide a different examination for those taking a retest after failure, the FAA has more than one examination. In an attempt to include greater coverage, the following sample examination contains 70 questions even though the FAA test contains only 50 questions.

The FAA examination can be taken at any of the FAA District Offices as well as some Flight Service Stations. You will be supplied all charts and data. You must bring your own computer. It is generally permissible to bring any other aid you would normally use for flying, such as your own flight planning and log sheets. However, always show the FAA personnel in charge the equipment or material you intend to use.

Read each question carefully. Questions requiring calculations should be carefully prepared and computed accurately. The FAA instrument written examination will contain some questions which pertain to any flight, such as weight and balance calculations. Thus, you should thoroughly review these basic data.

This test is based on an instrument flight from Hulman Field, Terre Haute, Indiana to Kansas City, Municipal Airport, Kansas City, Missouri. Your take-off is scheduled for the morning of April 3. You will be flying a single-engine aircraft with two passengers.

Prior to the flight, you review some of the fundamentals of, and regulations and procedures pertaining to, instrument flying. Also, you complete your pre-flight planning. The night before your flight, you collect and review the necessary charts and fill in the Flight Planning and Log Sheet as far as possible.

The first test questions pertain to a review of instrument flying and procedures and pre-flight planning:

1. Prior to making this flight, you must have acquired, in the last six months, total instrument time of at least:
   1 – 6 hours, not more than 3 hours of which may have been in an approved synthetic instrument trainer.
   2 – 2 hours, all of which must have been in an aircraft.
   3 – 6 hours, all of which may have been in approved synthetic trainer.
   4 – 6 hours, not more than 3 hours of which must have been in an aircraft of the type and model used for the flight.

2. Unless aircraft and equipment are maintained under an approved continuous maintenance and inspection program, regulations require that VOR receiver accuracy checks be made within the preceeding:
   1 – 10 hours of flight or within 10 days before flight.
   2 – 10 days.
   3 – 10 hours of flight and within 10 days before flight.
   4 – 10 flight hours only.

3. From the list below, select the discrepancies that MUST be corrected prior to takeoff for the flight proposed in this examination.
   A – Vertical speed indicator indicates 250 feet per minute rate of descent.
   B – Generator is charging below minimum limit.
   C – Clock sweep second hand is inoperative.
   D – DME is inoperative.
   E – Ball-bank indicator is stuck in center of the race.
   F – Altimeter setting dial indicates +.03 inch Hg higher than current altimeter setting when altimeter is set at field elevation.
   1 – B, C, E
   2 – B, C, D
   3 – D, E, F
   4 – A, B, C

4. For an IFR flight from an airport located outside controlled airspace, a flight plan must be filed and an ATC clearance obtained prior to:
   1 – takeoff
   2 – takeoff if weather is below VFR minimums
   3 – entering IFR weather conditions
   4 – entering controlled airspace.

5. Your airplane has two VOR receivers. When checking their accuracy against each other, the maximum allowable variation between the indicated bearings is:
   1 – 4 degrees on the ground or 6 degrees in flight.
   2 – 6 degrees on the ground and in flight

3 — 4 degrees on the ground and in flight
4 — 6 degrees on the ground or 4 degrees in flight.

6. When encountering turbulence or moderate or severe updrafts and downdrafts, the pilot should:
1 — maintain a relatively constant attitude
2 — maintain a reasonably steady airspeed and altitude
3 — maintain an airspeed of 1.5 V_{so} or greater
4 — maintain a constant power setting.

7. Which of the following items must be reported to ATC, without request, by aircraft operating under Instrument Flight Rules?
A — Time leaving an assigned holding fix or point
B — Completion of procedure turn on final approach
C — Arrival at a newly assigned altitude
D — Inflight malfunction of VOR, ADF or marker beacon receiver capability affecting the flight.
E — Time and altitude reaching an assigned holding fix
F — Vacating an assigned altitude for a newly assigned altitude
G — Weather conditions — IFR or VFR
1 — A, C, D, G
2 — A, D, E, F
3 — B, C, E, G
4 — A, B, D, F

8. An alternate airport is not required on an IFR flight plan if your destination airport has a forecast ceiling, from two hours before to two hours after your ETA, of at least:
1 — 1000 feet above circling minimums
2 — 1000 feet above the lowest MEA, MOCA, or initial approach altitude
3 — 1000 feet above the highest initial approach altitude
4 — 1000 feet above straight in minimums

9. With reference to flight altitude, the term "cruise" is sometimes used in clearances. This term:
1 — indicates to the pilot that he is authorized to descend from the assigned altitude at his discretion without obtaining further ATC clearance.
2 — has the same meaning as "maintain."
3 — indicates to the pilot that he may climb to his assigned cruising altitude and remain there until receiving ATC clearance to descend
4 — is normally used for long range flights in high density traffic areas.

10. An IFR clearance issued by ATC provides:
1 — sufficient separation between aircraft in controlled airspace
2 — authorization to proceed under specified traffic conditions within controlled airspace
3 — that you will not violate any Federal Aviation Regulations
4 — the pilot with assurance that he will not collide with other aircraft in controlled airspace

11. A pilot may request an altitude assignment of "VFR CONDITIONS ON TOP" when filing an IFR flight plan. If ATC issues him such a clearance:
1 — the pilot can select an altitude of his choice or change altitude if in VFR conditions, rather than specific ATC assigned altitudes
2 — separation is guaranteed from all traffic
3 — the pilot is required to fly specific altitudes assigned by ATC
4 — the pilot can fly through clouds.

12. The practice flight in this examination is from Terre Haute, Indiana, to Kansas City, Missouri. If you wanted to make an intermediate stop at St. Louis to pick up an additional passenger, the best procedure to use in filing your flight plan in order to avoid undue delay in obtaining your ATC clearance would be:
1 — File one flight plan at HUF to include a stop at St. Louis
2 — File a flight plan for the entire flight and request "center" to amend your clearance after takeoff
3 — File two separate flight plans before takeoff at HUF
4 — File three separate flight plans at HUF: HUF to STL, STL to MKC and MKC to ICT

13. Assuming that all three airplanes in the illustration below are making coordinated turns, which of the following statements is completely accurate?

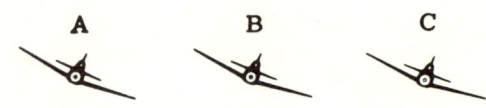

A B C
Bank 20° Bank 20° Bank 20°
TAS 100 mph TAS 150 mph TAS 200 mph

1 — Airplanes A, B, and C will have equal rates of turn, but airplane C will have the largest radius of turn.
2 — Airplane A will have one-half the rate of turn and one-half the radius of turn of airplane C.
3 — Airplane C will have a lesser rate of turn and a greater radius of turn than airplane A.
4 — Airplane B will have a greater rate of turn and a greater radius of turn than airplane A.

14. The illustration below depicts the turn-and-bank indications during three separate turns made at the same true airspeed. Three of the following statements regarding these turns are false. Which one is true?

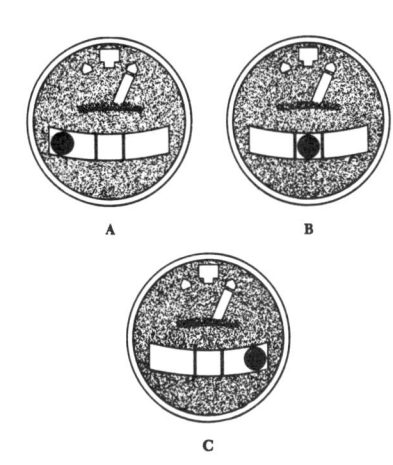

1 — Angle of bank is greatest in turn A.
2 — Rate of turn is greatest in turn A.
3 — Angle of bank is least in turn A, rate of turn is the same as B and C.
4 — Angle of bank is the same in all turns, rate of turn is greatest in turn C.

15. Transponder Mode A/3, Code 7600 is used:
1 — To alert ATC that you are in an emergency condition.
2 — When operating below 10,000 feet MSL.
3 — To alert ATC that you have experienced a loss of two-way radio capability.
4 — When operating above 10,000 feet MSL.

16. For IFR flights, the altimeter should be adjusted for:
1 — true altitude
2 — pressure altitude
3 — density altitude
4 — indicated altitude.

17. One of the following statements is true regarding the setting of an altimeter.
1 — When flying below 14,500 feet, the altimeter should be set to 29.92 in. Hg.
2 — Altimeter settings are only necessary when flying IFR.
3 — The altimeter should be set to the current reported altimeter setting of the nearest FSS within 100 NM of the aircraft, regardless of the flight altitude.
4 — When the altimeter is set to the current local altimeter setting, the indicated altitude does not necessarily show the correct altitude for the airplane's position.

18. You can depart from an airport in uncontrolled airspace under IFR conditions. In this case, you must:
1 — file an IFR flight plan by telephone to an FSS before takeoff.
2 — maintain VFR until you obtain an IFR clearance.
3 — obtain an ATC clearance before takeoff.
4 — remain outside of controlled airspace until you have obtained an IFR clearance.

19. According to FAR you can fly in actual instrument weather conditions in uncontrolled airspace, provided:
1 — you have an instrument rating and an ATC clearance.
2 — you have an instrument rating.
3 — you do not need either an instrument rating or an ATC clearance.
4 — you need an ATC clearance only.

20. Pilot flight records are:
1 — required to be kept for all flight time
2 — not required
3 — required to be kept for all instrument flight time
4 — are required to be kept only for proof of experience for any pilot rating or certificate and to meet recent flight experience requirements.

21. As defined by FAR, controlled airspace includes which of the following?
A — Control areas
B — Continental control area
C — Control zones
D — Transition areas.
1 — B, C
2 — A, B, D
3 — A, B, C, D
4 — B, C, D.

22. A reliable indication of carburetor icing,

in a nonsupercharged engine equipped with a constant speed propeller, is:
1 — a drop in RPM
2 — an increase in cylinder head temperature
3 — an increase in exhaust temperature
4 — a drop in manifold pressure.

23. The terms used to report the "degree" of turbulence should be known by, and mean the same to, all pilots. To the list of terms below (A, B, C, and D) match the corresponding appraisal of the "degree" of turbulence (E, F, G, and H).
A — Light
B — Moderate
C — Severe
D — Extreme
E — Aircraft is violently tossed about
F — Unsecured objects move about
G — Loose objects remain at rest
H — Unsecured objects are tossed about
1 — A-F; B-H
2 — B-F; C-E
3 — C-H; D-E
4 — D-H; A-G

24. Which of the following statements are true regarding fronts?
A — They are always found in troughs of low pressure.
B — They form only between air masses of different temperature and/or moisture content.
C — Fronts always slope over the colder air.
D — Fronts always produce hazardous flying weather.
1 — A and B only
2 — A, B, and C
3 — A, B, C, and D
4 — B and D only.

25. Refer to the surface frontal diagram below. A pilot maintaining a straight track from A to C at approximately 3000 feet above the surface would expect to correct heading to the:

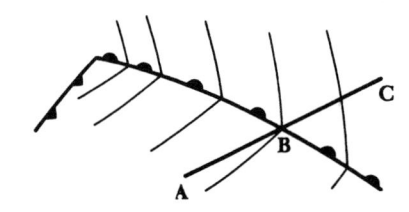

1 — right after noting a rise in OAT (outside air temperature) at point B.
2 — right after noting a drop in OAT between points B and C.
3 — left after noting a rise in OAT between points B and C.
4 — right after noting a drop in OAT between points A and B.

26. Using the illustration below, assume that you are flying westbound in the cold air mass and encounter freezing rain at position "A." Select from the procedures listed below the ones that would reduce structural ice accumulation to a minimum.

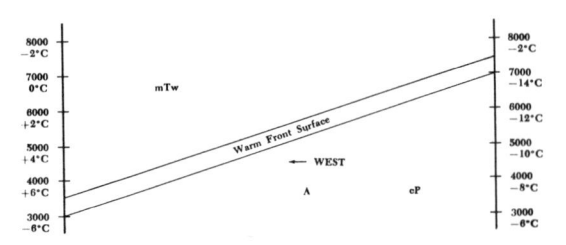

A — Descend to a lower altitude.
B — Remain at the same altitude and reduce airspeed.
C — Remain at the same altitude and increase airspeed.
D — Climb into the warm air.
E — Fly a heading that will allow you to penetrate the front at a right angle.
1 — D and E
2 — C only
3 — B only
4 — A and E

27. Which of the following are necessary for the development of a thunderstorm?
A — Stable air
B — Unstable air
C — High moisture content
D — A lifting force
E — A front
1 — B, C and D
2 — B and E only
3 — A, C and D
4 — B and D only.

28. Which of the following statements are correct regarding structural icing.
A — Rime ice spreads rapidly as a rough granular sheet.
B — Rime ice is more difficult to remove than clear ice when de-icer equipment is used.
C — Clear ice is most likely to form between 0° C. and −10° C.
D — Clear ice tends to take the shape of the structural form.
E — Rime ice is more hazardous than clear ice.
F — Rime ice is more likely to form in cumulus clouds rather than stratiform clouds.
1 — A, B, C, D, E and F.
2 — A, B, C, D and E.

3 — B, C and F.
4 — C and E.

29. To maintain the same course after passing through a front (in the northern hemisphere) a heading correction to the right is necessary:
   1 — regardless of the direction of flight and type of front.
   2 — only when flying in an easterly direction.
   3 — only when flying from warm air to cold air.
   4 — only when passing through a cold front.

30. Which of the following statements are true regarding fronts (northern hemisphere):
   A — They only form between air masses of different temperatures and/or moisture content.
   B — Fronts always produce hazardous flying weather.
   C — The flight hazards encountered in cold fronts are distinctly different from those encountered in warm fronts.
   D — Fronts always slope over the colder air.
   1 — A, B, C, D.
   2 — A, D.
   3 — A, B, D.
   4 — C, D.

The following questions pertain more directly to the flight from Terre Haute, Indiana, to Kansas City, Missouri. All necessary weather data, charts, airplane specifications, and supplementary information are in the section following this examination.

31. The estimated time enroute from take-off to MKC VORTAC is nearest to which of the following?
   1 — 2 hours, 14 minutes
   2 — 2 hours, 6 minutes
   3 — 2 hours, 19 minutes
   4 — 3 hours, 26 minutes

32. The quantity of fuel required by regulations for this flight is:
   1 — 53 gallons
   2 — 43 gallons
   3 — 39 gallons
   4 — 29 gallons

33. Compass heading for the leg from STL to HLV is calculated to be:
   1 — 273
   2 — 278
   3 — 277
   4 — 275

34. With load as specified below, and assuming average fuel consumption of 12.5 gallons per hour, how long could you hold at MKC before proceeding to your alternate?

   Empty weight
      (4 gallons unusable fuel included) 1776
   Oil   22
   Pilot and passenger   350
   Rear seat passenger   200
   Baggage   132
   Fuel — to 2900 lbs. max. gross wt.
   1 — 1 hour, 22 minutes
   2 — 2 hours, 12 minutes
   3 — 2 hours, 29 minutes
   4 — 3 hours, 17 minutes

35. The example of loading specified below is unlikely, but such a situation is possible and used for the purpose of illustration. Determine the actual C.G. location (arm or inches aft of datum) and by reference to the loading envelope (chart showing approved C.G. range and weight), determine whether or not the C.G. location is within limits.

	Weight	ARM	Moment
Empty weight	1776	83.6	148,474
Oil	22	28.0	616
Fuel - 30 gals. (inboards)	180	90.0	16,200
Fuel - 30 gals. (outboards)	180	95.0	17,100
Pilot	150	84.8	
Passengers - 2 (rear seats)	392	120.5	
Baggage	200	142.0	28,400

   1 — 92.5 and out of limits
   2 — 92.5 and within limits
   3 — 93.4 and out of limits
   4 — 93.4 and within limits.

36. The stability and performance characteristics of an airplane will vary with load distribution, and this could be particularly important during instrument flight. Which of the following statements concerning the effects of load distribution is correct?
   1 — Loading toward the forward C.G. limit will improve performance (rate of climb and airspeed).
   2 — Loading toward the rearward C.G. limit will improve longitudinal stability.
   3 — Loading toward the rearward C.G. limit will improve stall characteristics.
   4 — Loading toward the forward C.G. limit will increase the stall speed.

37. Based on weather reports and forecasts,

you can expect the following during your flight:
1 — Moderate to locally heavy icing in precipitation.
2 — No icing.
3 — Light to moderate icing over central Missouri.
4 — Icing only if you encounter precipitation.

38. Although you filed for 5000 feet, you expect to be "VFR on Top" for:
1 — flight legs through Illinois
2 — flight legs through Missouri
3 — no part of your flight
4 — the entire flight.

39. Upon your arrival at Kansas City, you can expect:
1 — ceiling of 800 feet and 3 miles visibility
2 — ceiling of 1000 feet and 7 miles visibility
3 — ceiling of 1500 feet and 7 miles visibility
4 — ceiling of 2000 feet and 7 miles visibility.

40. Which of the following statements are true of Weather Depiction Charts?
A — The information from which the chart is made is approximately 1½ hours old when the chart reaches the weather station.
B — Solid contour lines enclose areas of ceilings below 1000 feet and/or visibilities below 3 miles.
C — Areas where instrument surface weather conditions exist can be easily identified.
D — Scalloped lines enclose areas of ceilings 1000 to 5000 feet and visibilities 3 miles or greater.
1 — A, B, C, and D
2 — A, B, and C
3 — B, C, and D
4 — A and D only.

41. Which of the statements below correctly describe a portion of the weather "picture" shown on the 1300Z Weather Depiction Chart?
1 — An area of low, thin stratus cloudiness extends from the Dakotas southeastward through Arkansas.
2 — Ceilings along the route from HUF to MKC are above 400 feet and visibilities are 3 miles or more.
3 — Skies in northeastern Iowa, northeastern Illinois, and most of Indiana, are overcast with ceilings above 5000 feet.
4 — Skies in eastern Kansas and western Missouri are mostly overcast with ceilings below 1000 feet and visibilities below 3 miles in rain showers.

42. The Prognostic Chart will be available for your weather briefing. Which of the following statements regarding this chart are true?
A — Valid time for this *predicted* situation is 0000Z, April 4 (CST-1800, April 3).
B — The precipitation shown in the North Central States is continuous rain.
C — A broken area of rain showers and thunderstorms is expected in an area southeast of Kansas City.
D — The low pressure area centered in southern Iowa is expected to continue moving eastward at 15 knots.
E — The area in eastern Colorado and western Kansas is expected to be mostly clear with light surface winds.
1 — A, B, C, D and E
2 — A and B only
3 — B and C only
4 — C and D only.

43. From the 1500Z (0900CST) hourly surface weather report for MKC, you can determine that —
1 — the reported ceiling is 800 feet MSL
2 — surface wind is reported from the NNE at 10 mph
3 — the last portion of the report concerns NOTAM information
4 — multiple cloud layers are reported.

44. Comparison of the 1400Z and 1500Z hourly surface weather reports for MKC indicates that the —
1 — temperature/dewpoint spread has increased
2 — barometric pressure has risen
3 — ceiling has lifted
4 — visibility has improved.

45. Comparison of the 1400Z and 1500Z hourly surface weather reports for ICT indicates that —
1 — there has been no improvement
2 — the ceiling has remained the same
3 — visibility has increased
4 — the weather has improved slightly.

46. Review of the terminal forecast for Kansas City indicates that for the period of your arrival —
1 — light rain showers are likely
2 — occasional light drizzle may be expected
3 — occasional light rain showers are forecast
4 — the ceiling is forecast to be 2000 feet.

47. Considering the radio equipment installed in your airplane and the airplane performance, an approach to runway 18 at Kansas City airport using chart AL-213 (ILS Rwy 18), will require:
1 — DH of 1137 feet and 1 mile visibility
2 — 700 foot ceiling and 1 mile visibility
3 — MDA of 1260 feet and 1 mile visibility
4 — MDA of 1400 feet and mile visibility

48. Which of the following statements regarding the "Restrictions to Enroute Navigation Aids" is true?
1 — One of the enroute navigation aids required for your flight is affected by a restriction.
2 — The restrictions are published in the *Airman's Information Manual* one time only.
3 — The restrictions are due to inadequate or unreliable azimuth information.
4 — The restrictions apply only to VHF facilities (VOR/VORTAC).

49. From the Kansas City Municipal Airport listing in the Airport/Facility Directory, determine which of the following statements are correct.
A — The longest runway is 18-36; 7000 feet.
B — The instrument runway is equipped with High Intensity Runway Lights.
C — Runway Visual Range is provided for runway 18.
D — Your initial contact with approach control should be made on 118.9 MHz.
E — The back course of the ILS is unusable.
F — The minimum descent altitude for a precision approach to runway 18 is 1150 MSL.
1 — A, B, C, D, E, and F
2 — A, B, D, E, and F
3 — B, C, and E
4 — A, E, and F.

50. Based on the Wichita ILS — Rwy 19 instrument approach procedure chart, which of the following statements are true?
A — The procedure turn is standard
B — The procedure turn is non-standard.
C — When flying the localizer inbound to runway 19, you must correct towards the needle.
D — Since the back course is usable, use of glide slope is permitted.
E — Without radar, simultaneous reception of both ILS and VOR is required.
1 — A and E only
2 — B, C, and E
3 — B and E only
4 — B and D only.

51. The two factors which determine the aircraft approach categories on the instrument approach procedure charts are:
1 — Stall speed and maximum landing weight
2 — Stall speed and gross weight
3 — Stall speed and number of engines
4 — Maneuvering speed and gross weight

52. You are taxiing out for takeoff on runway 23 and expect to make a left turn to the HUF VORTAC. Which of the examples below shows good planning for use of your radio equipment?

1 — Communications   121.9 and 118.3
    VOR   111.8 and 111.8
    DME   111.8
    ADF   245

2 — Communications   121.9 and 118.3
    VOR   111.8 and 114.3
    DME   111.8
    ADF   362

3 — Communications   118.3 and 118.3
    VOR   111.8 and 109.7
    DME   111.8
    ADF   362

4 — Communications   118.3 and 123.8
    VOR   111.8 and 111.8
    DME   109.7
    ADF   333.2

53. You receive your clearance over Hulman ground control frequency after being cleared to runway 23. Which of the following is correct?
1 — ATC CLEARS BON AIR FOUR TWO TWO SIX BRAVO TO THE KANSAS CITY MUNICIPAL AIRPORT AS FILED. MAINTAIN SIX THOUSAND. RADAR VECTOR TO VICTOR FOURTEEN. DEPARTURE CONTROL FREQUENCY IS ONE TWO THREE POINT EIGHT.
2 — ATC CLEARS BON AIR FOUR TWO TWO SIX BRAVO TO THE KANSAS CITY MUNICIPAL AIRPORT AS FILED. MAINTAIN SIX THOUSAND. TURN LEFT AFTER TAKEOFF. PROCEED DIRECT TO TERRE HAUTE VORTAC BEFORE PROCEEDING ON COURSE.
3 — ATC CLEARS BON AIR FOUR TWO TWO SIX BRAVO TO THE KANSAS CITY MUNICIPAL AIRPORT AS FILED. MAINTAIN SIX THOUSAND. CONTACT TOWER ON ONE ONE EIGHT POINT

THREE AFTER TAKEOFF FOR RADAR VECTOR TO VICTOR FOURTEEN.

4 — ATC CLEARS BON AIR FOUR TWO TWO SIX BRAVO TO THE KANSAS CITY MUNICIPAL AIRPORT AS FILED. CONTACT DEPARTURE CONTROL ON TWO THREE NINE POINT ZERO FOR RADAR VECTOR TO VICTOR FOURTEEN.

54. Which of the following illustrations of VOR receiver indications could represent your position approximately 2 minutes after departure?

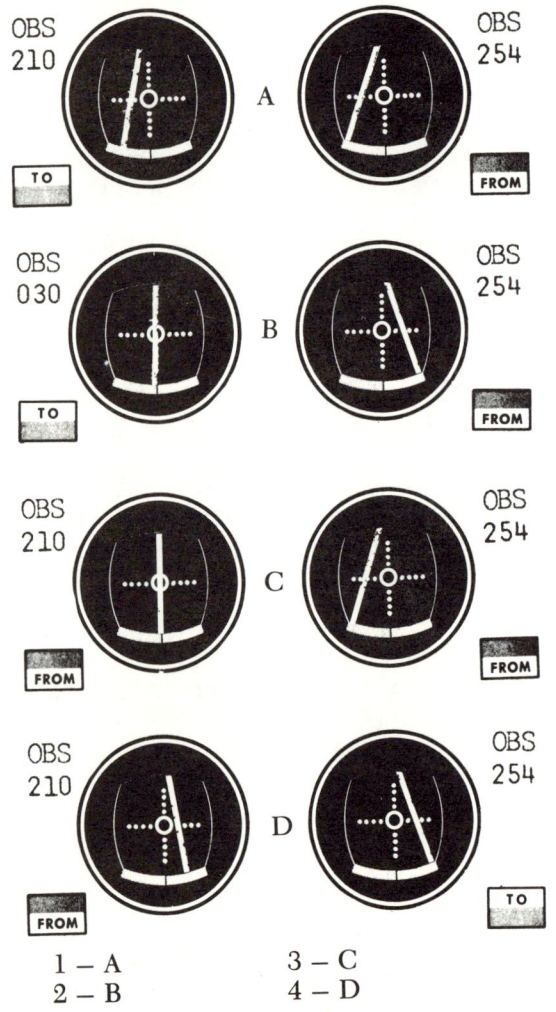

1 — A   3 — C
2 — B   4 — D

55. You cross HUF VORTAC at 1010 CST at 6000 feet and proceed on course. Your ETA for your next compulsory reporting point for a non-radar environment is:

1 — 1014   3 — 1042
2 — 1026   4 — 1046

56. After leaving HUF VORTAC on course, you are advised by ATC that you are in radar contact. At a point approximately 40 miles from HUF, you are instructed to contact Kansas City center on 134.6 MHz. Your reply to this call should be:

1 — "KANSAS CITY CENTER THIS IS BON AIR FOUR TWO TWO SIX BRAVO, SIX THOUSAND ESTIMATING VANDALIA AT FOUR SIX, ST LOUIS, OVER."

2 — "KANSAS CITY CENTER THIS IS BON AIR FOUR TWO TWO SIX BRAVO, SIX THOUSAND ESTIMATING VANDALIA AT FOUR SIX, OVER."

3 — "KANSAS CITY CENTER, BON AIR FOUR TWO TWO SIX BRAVO AT SIX THOUSAND, OVER."

4 — "KANSAS CITY CENTER, BON AIR FOUR TWO TWO SIX BRAVO ON ONE THREE FOUR POINT SIX, OVER."

57. Soon after leaving HUF VORTAC along V14, you cross Casey intersection. This intersection is based on the 033 radial from Bible Grove on 109.9 MHz. Bible Grove is a

1 — VORTAC station controlled by Vandalia FSS.
2 — VOR station controlled by Vandalia FSS.
3 — VOR station controlled by Bible Grove FSS.
4 — VORTAC station controlled by Bible Grove FSS.

58. After departing HUF VORTAC along V14, you find that a 5 degree wind correction angle to the left is required to maintain course. If you tuned to Mattoon (MTO) radio beacon, which of the instrument indications below represents the ADF indication upon arrival over CASEY intersection. Use a magnetic bearing from MTO to Casey intersection of 138 degrees.

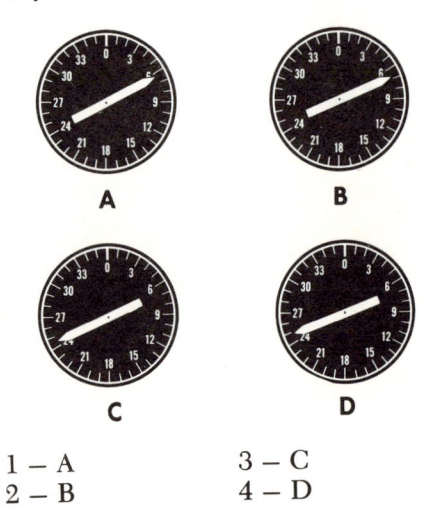

1 — A   3 — C
2 — B   4 — D

59. Along V14 between HUF and VLA VORTAC's the
    1 – MEA is 2400 feet and MOCA is 2000 feet.
    2 – MOCA is 2400 feet and MEA is 2000 feet.
    3 – Minimum flight altitude is 4000 feet for IFR westbound.
    4 – MRA is 2400 feet and MEA is 2000 feet.

60. While flying near St. Louis, you tuned one of your VHF navigational receivers to 110.3 MHz. Which of the following statements are correct?
    A – Scheduled weather broadcasts are available.
    B – This is a VORTAC station.
    C – This is a VOR station.
    D – DME is available.
    E – Identification is I-STL.
    1 – A and B only.
    2 – A, B, D, and E.
    3 – A, C, D, and E.
    4 – D and E only.

61. After passing Hallsville, you are advised that you are in radar contact and receive the following clearance:
BON AIR 4226 BRAVO – CLEARED TO THE MISSOURI CITY INTERSECTION – DESCEND TO AND MAINTAIN 5000.
Which of the following statements regarding this clearance is true?
    1 – Pilot readback of this clearance is not required.
    2 – Holding instructions should have been issued with this clearance.
    3 – You are expected to descend immediately and as rapidly as possible to 5000 feet.
    4 – It is an indication that your flight will be delayed.

62. You crossed HLV VORTAC at 1140 CST. Your ETA for Missouri City intersection is:
    1 – 1200 CST   3 – 1215 CST
    2 – 1228 CST   4 – 1219 CST

63. Soon after crossing Hallsville VORTAC, ATC advises that radar contact has been temporarily lost and requests a position report over Malta intersection. The minimum altitude to comply with this request is:
    1 – 2300 feet   3 – 4000 feet
    2 – 3500 feet   4 – 2600 feet.

64. A DME fix located near Malta intersection (approximately one-half way between HLV and MKC VORTAC's) is:
    1 – 57 nautical miles from HLV when tuned to HLV.
    2 – 46 nautical miles from HLV when tuned to HLV.
    3 – 57 nautical miles from MKC when tuned to MKC.
    4 – 58 nautical miles from MKC when tuned to MKC.

65. If you arrive at Missouri City and have not received further clearance because of frequency congestion, you should –
    1 – hold in a nonstandard holding pattern in the direction from which you approached the fix.
    2 – continue on your route and stand by for further clearance.
    3 – hold in a standard holding pattern in the direction from which you approached the fix.
    4 – continue on your route and immediately request further clearance.

66. If you were cleared from Missouri City intersection for an ILS approach to Kansas City airport without radar vectoring, you would have to proceed under your own navigation. This would be accomplished by:
    1 – Plotting the course from Missouri City intersection to the outer marker and flying the computed heading until your 3-lite marker indicated that you were over the outer marker.
    2 – Tuning your ADF to 75 MHz and proceeding directly to the outer marker.
    3 – Tuning your ADF to 219 KHz and proceeding directly to the LOM.
    4 – Tuning your ADF to 201 KHz and proceeding directly to the LMM.

67. By reference to the approach procedure chart and the aircraft specifications, select the statements which are true for your approach at MKC.
    A – Missed approach point is runway threshold.
    B – Time from LOM to LMM, considering the headwind component, is approximately 4 minutes 9 seconds.
    C – MDA for ILS approach if Bluff FM is received, is 1260 MSL.
    D – Missed approach point is at the middle marker.

    1 — A, B, C and D   3 — C and D
    2 — B, C and D   4 — A only

68. The Compass Locator at the Outer

Marker on the Kansas City ILS Instrument Approach chart has a frequency of —

1 — 75 MHz
2 — 201 KHz
3 — 219 KHz
4 — 219 MHz.

69. What is the MEA for the transition route from Missouri City intersection to the outer marker? (ILS Rwy 18.)

1 — 3358 feet
2 — 2500 feet
3 — 3100 feet
4 — 2600 feet

70. After passing the LOM (assuming no compass deviation), the instrument indications below show the aircraft —

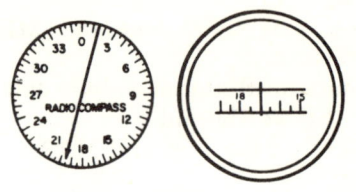

1 — on course.
2 — right of course.
3 — left of course.
4 — left of course and correcting for left drift.

ANALYSIS OF ANSWERS TO SAMPLE EXAMINATION QUESTIONS

1 — (1) FAR 61.57.

2 — (3) FAR 91.25.

3 — (1) FAR 91.33.

4 — (4) FAR 91.115.

5 — (3) FAR 91.25.

6 — (1) See Chapter 3. The air-speed indicator and altimeter are pressure instruments and will fluctuate rapidly. By maintaining a constant *attitude* with reference to the artificial horizon and a constant power setting, the airspeed and altitude will average out without undue stresses on the airplane. During severe turbulence, a power setting in accordance with the airplane's maneuvering speed should be used.

7 — (2) See Chaper 8; also see FAR 91.129.

8 — (2) FAR 91.83 (b).

9 — (1) Most clearances require a pilot to "maintain" a specified altitude. This requires ATC permission (clearance) to change altitudes. The term "cruise" may be used for short range and/or flights in low traffic density areas, instead of "maintain." Thus, the pilot can begin descent and begin an approach at his destination without further clearance. See Chapter 8.

10 — (2) An ATC clearance does *not* guarantee that no FAR are violated. This is a pilot responsibility. Also, the clearance does not assure that no collision with other aircraft will occur in controlled airspace inasmuch as VFR conditions may exist somewhere along the route. Therefore other aircraft may be in the same airspace, unknown to ATC. Remember, ATC *does not* know whether the weather conditions are IFR or VFR. Thus the only correct answer is: an ATC clearance provides "authorization to proceed under specified traffic conditions within controlled airspace." See Chapter 8.

11 — (1) An IFR clearance of "VFR on top" allows the pilot to select his own altitude. However, he must now strictly observe VFR flight rules, that is the proper altitude according to the direction of flight must be maintained according to the VFR odd or even thousand plus 500 feet requirement. Also, "see and be seen" applies. ATC cannot guarantee separation from any other traffic. A new clearance must be obtained from ATC in order to fly through clouds.

12 — (3) The best choice would be to file two flight plans at your point of departure and request FSS to relay the second flight plan to your stopover point. This will provide minimum delay in obtaining clearance from the stopover point.

13 — (3) For a specific angle of bank an increase in airspeed will produce a greater radius of turn and a lesser rate of turn. See page 17, Chapter 3.

14 — (3) Turn A is a skidding (underbanked)

turn. Turn C is a slipping (overbanked) turn. Since the turn needle is at the same position for all three turns, the rate of turn is the same for all. See page 16, Chapter 3.

15 — (3) See Appendix, "The ATC Transponder.

16 — (4) In order to assure proper vertical separation of IFR traffic, ATC expects all aircraft to use *indicated* altitude. This is the altitude read directly on the altimeter face when the proper altimeter setting is set into the barometric pressure window. This is not necessarily the true altitude. See Chapter 2.

17 — (4) According to FAR 91.81 when flying at or above 18,000 feet MSL, the altimeter shall be set at 29.92 inches of mercury. Below 18,000 feet the altimeter shall be set to the current local altimeter setting. As previously explained, these *indicated* altitudes are not necessarily true altitudes.

18 — (4) FAR 91.115, requires an IFR clearance only if operating in controlled airspace.

19 — (2) According to FAR 91.115 you need an ATC Clearance only when operating in controlled airspace. According to FAR 91.105, no person shall operate an aircraft VFR when weather conditions are below VFR minimums as specified in FAR 91.105. Thus the only *legal* requirement for operating in IFR weather in uncontrolled airspace is an instrument rating.

20 — (4) FAR 61.51.

21 — (3) See Appendix, "Airspace and Airports". Also see the "Glossary of Aeronautical Terms" in the Appendix.

22 — (4) Cylinder and exhaust temperatures will decrease, and RPM will not change during the early stages of ice development. Manifold pressure will usually drop in this situation. Refer to your private or commercial text books.

23 — (3) See the chart "Turbulence Reporting Criteria Table" in "Excerpts from the Airman's Information Manual", in the Appendix.

24 — (2) Only alternate "D" is false. See Chapter 9.

25 — (2) When flying in the northern hemisphere, pilots can expect to make a heading change to the right after crossing a frontal surface. Because of the frontal slope, the change from warmer to colder air will occur somewhere between B and C in this example. See Chapter 9.

26 — (1) Freezing rain is certain evidence of warmer air above. Perpendicular penetration of the front will reduce the time of exposure to the ice. Perhaps the best procedure of all, not mentioned here, would be to turn around.

27 — (1) See Chapter 9.

28 — (1) See Chapter 9.

29 — (1) In the northern hemisphere, circulation is clockwise around a high pressure area and counterclockwise around a low pressure area (see Chapter 9.) A front forms in a trough of low pressure, thus the pressure is higher on both sides of the front. Above about 1500 feet above the ground, the wind flows parallel to the isobars and shifts direction at the frontal surface. Thus a heading correction to the right is always required when passing through a front. Sketch a diagram of a front showing the isobars. Now draw a line perpendicular to the front line representing the airplane's flight path to illustrate the example.

30 – (2) See Chapter 9
Depending on many factors, fronts do not always produce hazardous flying weather. In fact, if both air masses have a low moisture content, little or no cloudiness may occur.

31 – (3) See completed flight planning and log sheet.

32 – (1) See completed flight planning and log sheet.

33 – (4) Magnetic heading from the flight planning and log sheet is 273 degrees. Compass correction card data shows a correction of +2 degrees. Thus the compass heading is 275 degrees for this leg.

34 – (1)

Step 1 – Maximum allowable	
gross weight	2900 lbs.
Weight at loading specified	2480 lbs.
Available for fuel	420 lbs.
420 lbs. at 6 lbs. per gallon	70 gal.

Step 2 — Usable fuel 70 gal.
Fuel required 53 gal.
Extra fuel 17 gal.
Step 3 — 17 gal. @ 12.5 g.p.h. = 1 hour and 22 minutes.

35 — (3)
Step 1 — Moments for pilot and passengers are 12,720 and 47,236 respectively.
Step 2 — Total moment of 270,746, divided by maximum gross weight of 2900, equals 93.4, which is out of limits according to the "Approved C.G. Range and Weight" Chart.

36 — (4) The changes in characteristics caused by changes in C.G. location are minor, unless the forward or aft C.G. limit is exceeded. Alternate 1 is false because a forward C.G. increases the weight that the wing must carry, and increases the drag from the "up" elevator required. Alternates 2 and 3 are false because the desirable pitch down tendency has been decreased. Alternate 4 is correct because of the increased wing loading; the stalling angle of attack is reached at a higher airspeed.

37 — (2) Obtain icing information from the Area Forecast. Icing is predicted to occur in precipitation above freezing level. Freezing levels for your flight are predicted to occur at altitudes higher than your cruising altitude along your route of flight.

38 — (3) Obtain "top" information from the Area Forecast. Where tops are forecast, they are above your cruising altitude along your route of flight.

39 — (1) At an expected departure time of 1000 CST (1600Z) you would arrive at MKC at 1219 CST (1819 Z). The terminal forecast for MKC between 0500 CST (1100Z) and 1500 CST (2100Z) shows ceiling of 800 feet overcast, visibility 3 miles in fog.

40 — (1) These are items of primary importance and should be known by all pilots. See Chapter 10.

41 — (3) There is no way of determining from the chart that the cloudiness is thin stratus. The general rain situation indicates nimbostratus, which would be several thousand feet thick. There are no rain showers reported in Kansas or Missouri.

42 — (1) Prognostic Charts are prepared for 12, 24, and 48 hour "valid times." The valid time expressed in Greenwich Mean Time (z) is the hour for which the prediction applies. The 12, 24, or 48 refers to the time interval between weather data collection time and valid time. Study this Chart and, if possible, discuss its use with a weatherman.

43 — (3) Ceiling is 800 measured (above ground). Surface wind is 110° at 10 knots. Only one cloud layer is reported. Arrows denote NOTAM information.

44 — (3) Ceiling has lifted from measured 700 overcast to measured 800 overcast.

45 — (4) Ceiling has increased, temperature/dewpoint spread has increased, pressure has risen.

46 — (2) Forecast 800 overcast, visibility 3 miles, fog, occasional light drizzle. See question 39.

47 — (3) Your airplane has a localizer and a marker beacon receiver but no glide slope; therefore, only a non-precision approach can be made. Your marker beacon receiver, however, can pick up the Bluff fan marker, therefore the straight-in minima for the localizer approach to runway 18 are 1260-1. These data are available in the "Minima" box on the Kansas City airport chart AL-213, Rwy 18.

48 — (3) All restrictions refer to areas of inadequate or unreliable signals.

49 — (2) All except C are true. RVR values are not provided, only RVV.

50 — (3) This is a back course approach which requires corrections *away* from the needle when approaching the runway (Chaper 6). Glide slope *cannot* be used for a back course approach. In order to determine position along the approach path (without radar) simultaneous reception of both ILS and VOR is required. The first turn of the procedure turn is to the right which is non-standard.

51 — (1) See Chapter 6.

52 — (1) Monitor ground control while taxiing out, unless otherwise directed.

(Rule out answers 3 and 4 because they do not provide this.) The number 2 communications set may be tuned to the tower frequency for ease in making the communications change at the appropriate time. DO NOT tune both communications sets to the same frequency.

If IFR weather conditions exist for the climbout, it would be wise to have one of the navigation receivers tuned to the ILS localizer frequency — this would be a big help if some emergency required an early return. For the climbout, however, (in VFR conditions) both navigation receivers could be tuned to HUF VORTAC — one of them set to the magnetic course of V14 and the other used to track to the station during the departure. The ADF tuned to the LOM for runway 5 would provide helpful information if a return was necessary.

It would not be wise to tune the second VOR receiver to VLA (as in alternate answer 2) because it won't be needed until you are well established enroute.

53 — (2) Only answer number 2 is correct. Hulman Field has no radar facility.

54 — (2) The aircraft would probably have just completed a left turn (as required by the clearance) and proceeding towards the VORTAC. The left indicator shown in the figure would therefore be centered on a 030 degree bearing to the station. The right indicator's OBS is set for the magnetic course of V14.

55 — (4) Your next compulsory reporting point (non-radar environment) is VLA (solid triangle on the chart). Estimated flying time for this leg is 36 minutes, thus your ETA for VLA is 1046 CST.

56 — (3) Since you are in a radar environment, the controller sees your position on the radar scope. Therefore, no position report or time estimate is required. The controller cannot determine altitude, however; therefore, this should be given in the initial contact.

57 — (2) The symbol for Bible Grove indicates that it is a VOR not a VORTAC. Also, the information box shows that it is controlled by Vandalia FSS.

58 — (2) The answer you want is the relative bearing from the aircraft to the station; that is, the number on the dial the ADF needle points to. First, obtain the reciprocal of the bearing from the station. This is 138 plus 180 or 318 degrees. Relative bearing then is 318 degrees minus 249 degrees (magnetic heading of 254 degrees minus 5 degrees wind correction angle), or 069 degrees. If you don't want to reason it out, remember this formula: magnetic heading of aircraft plus relative bearing to station equals magnetic bearing to station (MH + RH = MB to station). See page 52, Chapter 5.

59 — (1) See chart symbols and Chapter 8. The minimum enroute altitude (MEA) is determined by the higher of the two: (1) minimum altitude for continuous radio reception and (2) minimum altitude for obstruction clearance. In this case 2400 feet is the MEA since this altitude is required for continuous radio reception. The MOCA (minimum obstruction clearance altitude) is also given for emergency information. The MOCA is 2000 feet in this case.

60 — (4) This is the ILS localizer frequency for St. Louis therefore no scheduled weather broadcasts are given on this frequency.

61 — (1) There is no requirement to read back enroute clearances. You may simply "Roger" if you are sure you understand and have copied correctly. If you are not sure, you are expected to read back or ask for a repeat. Alternate 3 is wrong because descents (or climbs) through the last 1000 feet to assigned altitude should be made at the rate of 500 feet per minute. Alternates 2 and 4 are wrong because clearances similar to this one are often issued without holding instructions, when there is no likelihood that holding will be necessary.

62 — (4) The distance from HLV to Missouri City intersection is 101 miles. At an estimated ground speed of 157 knots, ETA for Missouri City is 1219 CST.

63 — (2) Refer to the chart symbols. The flag with an "R" indicates that a minimum altitude is necessary in order to receive all applicable radio signals. In this case the MRA is 3500 feet.

64 — (1) Refer to the chart symbols. The encircled mileage indicates the equivalent DME fix for Malta intersection.

65 — (3) Your last clearance specified Missouri City as a clearance limit. Therefore,

except in an emergency, you cannot proceed beyond Missouri City without further ATC clearance. Since holding is a means of "stopping" an aircraft, alternate number 3 is the only correct answer.

66 – (3) The only means of navigating a direct course to the LOM requires tracking (or homing) by means of ADF. The LOM frequency in this case is 219 KHz.

67 — (2) The aircraft being used for this flight has no glide slope receiver. At a groundspeed of 68 knots, time from LOM to LMM is 4 minutes 9 seconds. Alternate "C" can be determined as correct by reference to the chart. Alternate "D" can also be determined as correct by reference to the chart.

68 — (3) The compass locator at the outer marker is a low/medium frequency radio beacon operating on 344 KHz. See the ILS approach chart for Kansas City Airport.

69 — (4) Alternates 1, 2, and 3 are incorrect. Refer to the plan view of the chart.

70 – (1) Magnetic bearing of the localizer course is 185; aircraft heading is 15 degrees left. ADF needle indicates that the aircraft is on course. In a no wind condition these indications could also show that the aircraft was crossing the course at a 15 degree angle.

NOTE: The questions presented in this sample written test pertain directly to instrument flying. The FAA written test, however, may contain questions applicable to any flight such as: weight and balance problems, density altitude calculations, oxygen requirements, accelerate-stop distance and other airplane performance calculations using airplane performance charts. It is recommended that you review thoroughly these items in your basic private or commercial text books.

DATE APR. 3 TYPE ACFT BON AIR NO. 4226B PILOT YOUR NAME

	RANGE	FREQ	ROUTE	MC	TC	WIND DIR/VEL	TH	VAR	MH	DIST.	MEA	ALT. CRUISE TEMP	IAS/TAS	ESTIMATE GS	LEG TIME	ETA	ACTUAL GS	LEG TIME	ATA
FROM	APT.												110		06				
TO	HUF	111.8																	
FROM	HUF		V14	254	257	250/20	256	3E	253	92	2400	6000/+14	155/173	153	36				
TO	VLA	114.3																	
FROM	VLA		V14	254	258	240/18	256	4E	252	63	2500	6000/+18	155/174	157	24				
TO	STL	117.4																	
FROM	STL		V4	277	282	240/18	278	5E	273	78	2700	6000/+18	155/174	160	29				
TO	HLV	115.4																	
FROM	HLV		V4	270	277	215/27	269	7E	262	115	3500	6000/+11	155/172	157	44				
TO	MKC	112.6																	
FROM															2HRS 19 MIN.				
TO																			
FROM	MKC	112.6	V12	223	231	220/25.5	229	8E	221	94	2900	6000/+11	155/172	147	38				
TO	EMP	112.8																	
FROM	EMP		V12	234	243	220/25.5	240	9E	231	71	3100	6000/+11	155/172	149	29 / 1HR 07 MIN				
TO	ICT	113.8																	

FUEL ANALYSIS FUEL PLAN @ 12.5 GPH TOTALS ATC CLEARANCE

TANK	TIME ON	TIME OFF
L		
R		

FUEL TO DEST. 29.0
FUEL TO ALT. 14.0
45 MIN. RESV. 9.5
FUEL REQD. 52.5
FUEL AT DEPT.
EXTRA FUEL

	DEPART.	DEST.	ALT.
NAME			
TWR. FREQ.			
DEPT. CONT.			
APP. CONT.			
GRD. CONT.			
FIELD ELEV.			

POSITION REPT.

IDEN.	POSITION	TIME	ALT.	INST. FLT. PLAN	ETA NEXT FIX	NAME SUC. FIX

FLIGHT PLAN

FEDERAL AVIATION AGENCY

Form Approved.
Budget Bureau No. 04-R072.3

1. TYPE OF FLIGHT PLAN
- FVFR
- VFR
- XX IFR
- DVFR

2. AIRCRAFT IDENTIFICATION: N4226B

3. AIRCRAFT TYPE/SPECIAL EQUIPMENT 1/: BonAir/D

4. TRUE AIRSPEED (KNOTS):

5. POINT OF DEPARTURE: HUF

6. DEPARTURE TIME
- PROPOSED (Z): 1600
- ACTUAL (Z):

7. INITIAL CRUISING ALTITUDE: 6000

8. ROUTE OF FLIGHT: HUF V14 STL V4 MKC

9. DESTINATION (Name of airport and city): Kansas City Municipal

10. REMARKS:

11. ESTIMATED TIME EN ROUTE: HOURS / MINUTES

12. FUEL ON BOARD: HOURS / MINUTES

13. ALTERNATE AIRPORT(S): Wichita Municipal

14. PILOT'S NAME: Your Name

15. PILOT'S ADDRESS AND TELEPHONE NO. OR AIRCRAFT HOME BASE:

16. NO. OF PERSONS ABOARD: 4

17. COLOR OF AIRCRAFT: Red and White

18. FLIGHT WATCH STATIONS:

CLOSE FLIGHT PLAN UPON ARRIVAL

1/ SPECIAL EQUIPMENT SUFFIX
- A — DME & 4096 Code transponder
- B — DME & 64 Code transponder
- D — DME
- L — DME & transponder—no code
- T — 64 Code transponder
- U — 4096 Code transponder
- X — Transponder—no code

TURBULENCE REPORTING CRITERIA TABLE

EXCERPTS FROM AIRMAN'S INFORMATION MANUAL

Intensity	Aircraft Reaction	Reaction Inside Aircraft	Reporting Term Definition
LIGHT	Turbulence that momentarily causes slight, erratic changes in altitude and/or attitude (pitch, roll, yaw). Report as *Light Turbulence;* * **or** Turbulence that causes slight, rapid and somewhat rhythmic bumpiness without appreciable changes in altitude or attitude. Report as *Light Chop.*	Occupants may feel a slight strain against seat belts or shoulder straps. Unsecured objects may be displaced slightly. Food service may be conducted and little or no difficulty is encountered in walking.	Occasional—Less than 1/3 of the time. Intermittent—1/3 to 2/3. Continuous—More than 2/3. NOTE—Pilots should report location(s), time (GMT), intensity, whether in or near clouds, altitude, type of aircraft and, when applicable, duration of turbulence.
MODERATE	Turbulence that is similar to Light Turbulence but of greater intensity. Changes in altitude and/or attitude occur but the aircraft remains in positive control at all times. It usually causes variations in indicated airspeed. Report as *Moderate Turbulence;* * **or** Turbulence that is similar to Light Chop but of greater intensity. It causes rapid bumps or jolts without appreciable changes in aircraft altitude or attitude. Report as *Moderate Chop.*	Occupants feel definite strains against seat belts or shoulder straps. Unsecured objects are dislodged. Food service and walking are difficult.	Duration may be based on time between two locations or over a single location. All locations should be readily identifiable. Example: a. Over Omaha, 1232Z, Moderate Turbulence, in cloud, Flight Level 310, B707.
SEVERE	Turbulence that causes large, abrupt changes in altitude and/or attitude. It usualy causes large variations in indicated airspeed. Aircraft may be momentarily out of control. Report as *Severe Turbulence.**	Occupants are forced violently against seat belts or shoulder straps. Unsecured objects are tossed about. Food service and walking are impossible.	b. From 50 miles south of Albuquerque to 30 miles north of Phoennx, 1210Z to 1250Z, occasional Moderate Chop, Flight Level 330, DC8.
EXTREME	Turbulence in which the aircraft is violently tossed about and is practically impossible to control. It may cause structural damage. Report as *Extreme Turbulence.**		

* High level turbulence (normally above 15,000 feet ASL) not associated with cumuliform cloudiness, including thunderstorms, should be reported as CAT (clear air turbulence) preceded by the appropriate intensity, or light or moderate chop.

AIRCRAFT DATA

Specifications

BON AIR 4226B

4-place, single engine, typical of present general aviation aircraft.

Calibrated Airspeeds	(knots)
Climb (cruise climb)	110
Cruise	155
Approach (final)	75
Stall	53

De-icing—Anti-Icing

None

Baggage Compartment	(lbs.)
Maximum	200

Fuel Capacity	(gals.)
Total—4 tanks	90
Inboards 60 (4 gals. unusable)	
Outboards 30	

Oil Capacity	(gals.)
	3

Weight and Balance

Item	Weight	Arm	Moment
Empty weight (includes unusable fuel)	1776	83.6	148,474
Oil 3 gals		28.0	
Fuel 56.0 gals inboard tanks		90.0	
Fuel 30.0 gals outboard tanks		95.0	
Pilot and passenger		84.8	
2 passengers (rear seats)		120.5	
Baggage		142.0	

Weights	(lbs.)
Max. gross	2900
Empty (as equipped)	1776
Useful load	1124

Fuel Consumption	(gals.)
Per hour	12.5

Radio Communications and Navigation Equipment

VHF Communications
 (Dual—90 and 360 channel)
VOR/LOC (Dual—no glide slope)
ADF   Marker beacon receiver   DME

Compass Correction Card

FOR (MH)	0	30	60	90	120	150	180	210	240	270	300	330
STEER (CH)	0	28	54	88	120	152	179	210	240	272	300	330

APPROVED C.G. RANGE AND WEIGHT

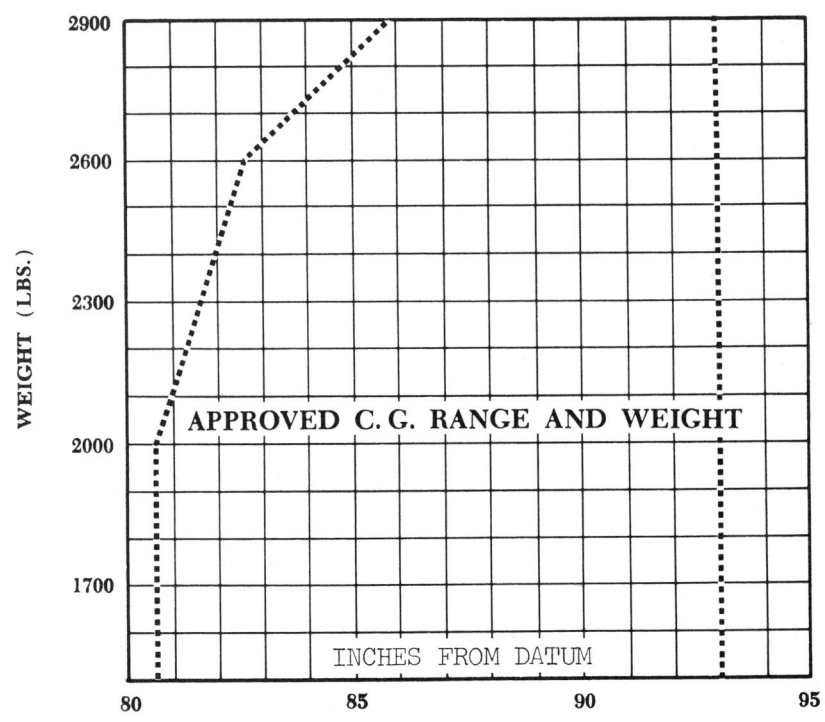

WEIGHT (LBS.) vs INCHES FROM DATUM

LEGEND ENROUTE LOW ALTITUDE – U.S.
For use up to but not including 18,000' MSL

Amdt 9

VOR RWY 23

AL-608 (FAA)

HULMAN FIELD
TERRE HAUTE, INDIANA

HULMAN APP CON
123.8 397.2
HULMAN TOWER
118.3 239.0
GND CON
121.9 348.6

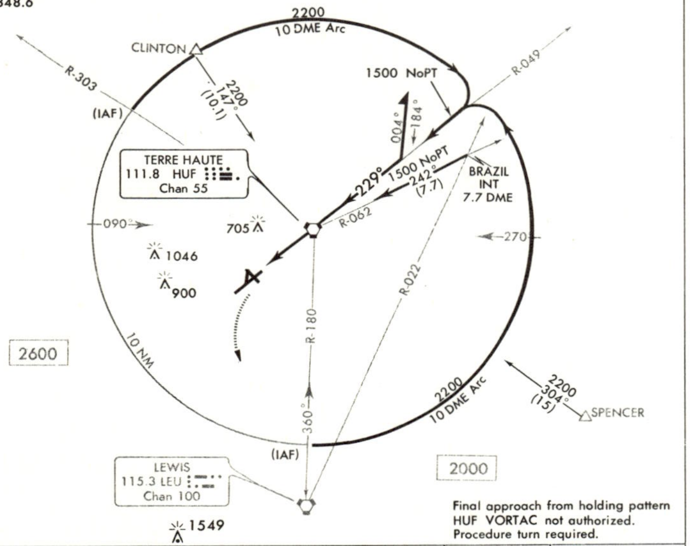

Final approach from holding pattern HUF VORTAC not authorized. Procedure turn required.

MISSED APPROACH
Climbing left turn to 2500 direct to LEU VORTAC .

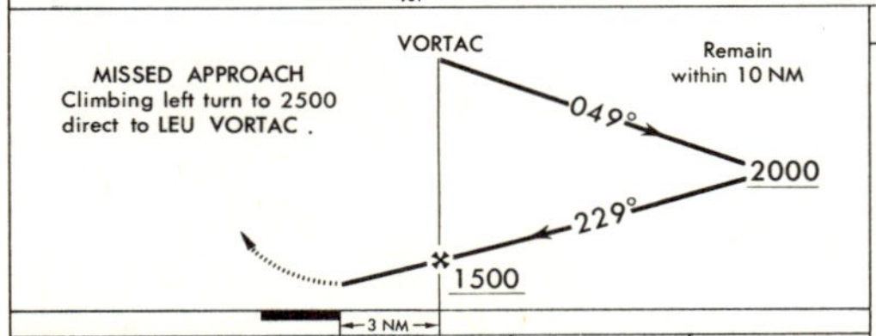

CATEGORY	A	B	C	D
S-23	920-3/4 338 (400-3/4)			920-1 338 (400-1)
CIRCLING	980-1 395 (400-1)	1040-1 455 (500-1)	1040-1½ 455 (500-1½)	1140-2 555 (600-2)

ELEV 585

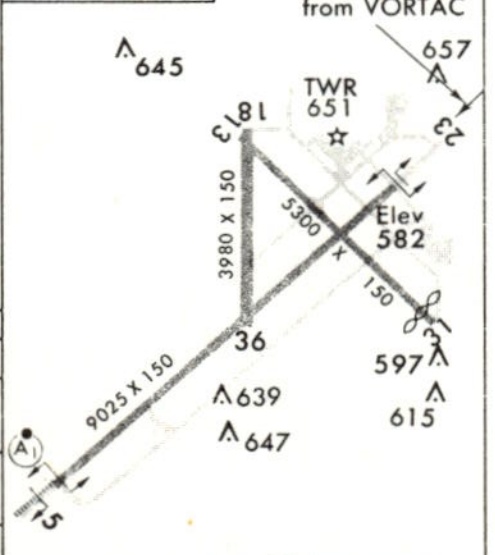

Rwy 31 ldg 4585'

MIRL Rwy 13-31
HIRL Rwy 5-23

FAF to MAP 3 NM					
Knots	60	90	120	150	180
Min:Sec	3:00	2:00	1:30	1:12	1:00

Amdt 12

ILS RWY 5

AL-608 (FAA)

HULMAN FIELD
TERRE HAUTE, INDIANA

HULMAN APP CON
123.8 397.2
HULMAN TOWER
118.3 239.0
GND CON
121.9 348.6

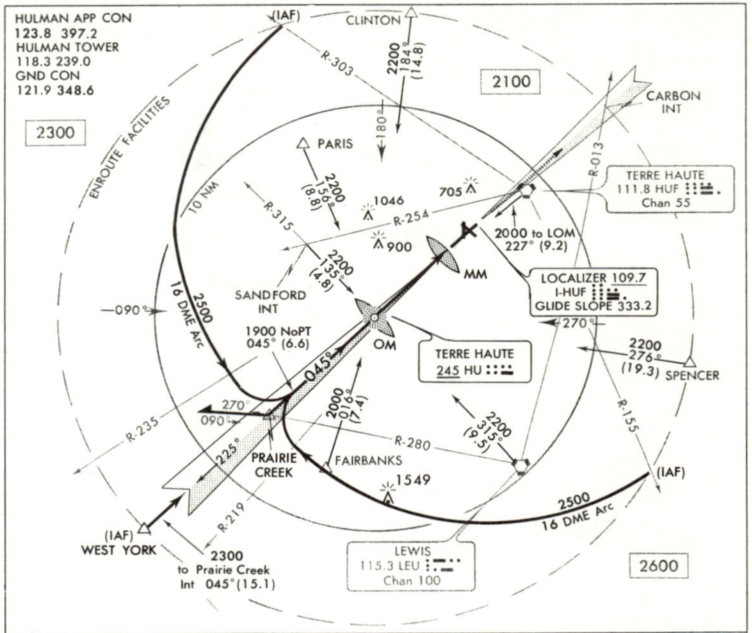

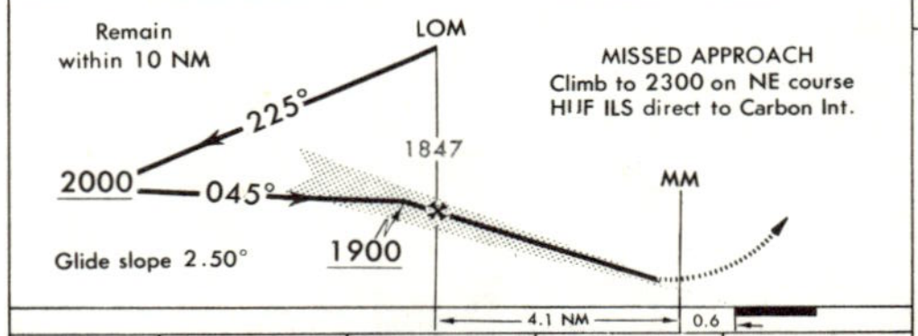

MISSED APPROACH
Climb to 2300 on NE course HUF ILS direct to Carbon Int.

CATEGORY	A	B	C	D
S-ILS 5	773-½ 200 (200-½)			
S-LOC 5	920-½ 347 (400-½)			920-3/4 347 (400-3/4)
CIRCLING	980-1 395 (400-1)	1040-1 455 (500-1)	1040-1½ 455 (500-1½)	1140-2 555 (600-2)

ELEV 585 | Rwy 31 ldg 4585'

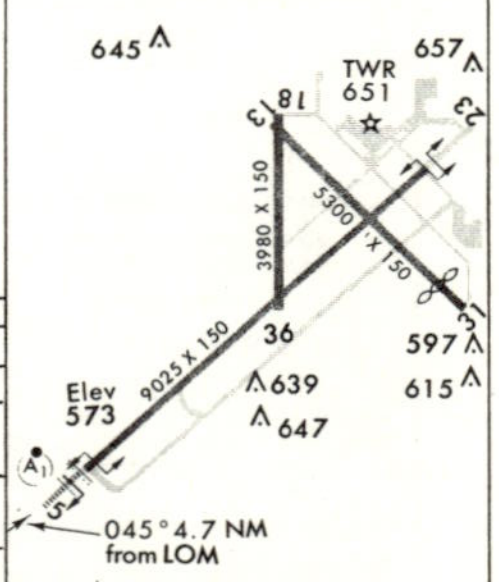

MIRL Rwy 13 - 31
HIRL Rwy 5-23

FAF to MAP 4.7 NM					
Knots	60	90	120	150	180
Min:Sec	4:42	3:08	2:21	1:53	1:34

39°27'N-87°18'W

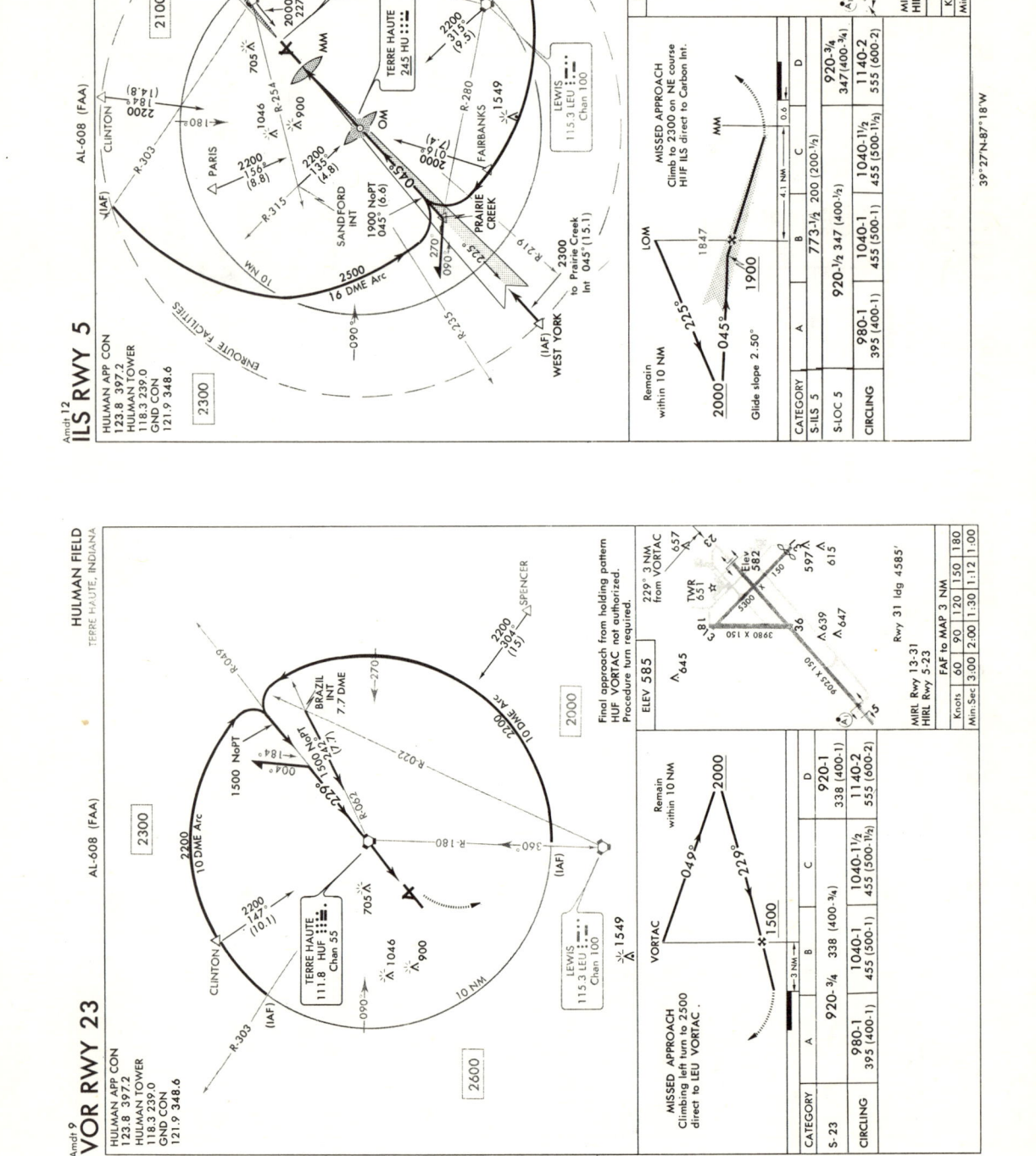

LOC BC RWY 19L

AL-987 (FAA)

WICHITA MUNI
WICHITA, KANSAS

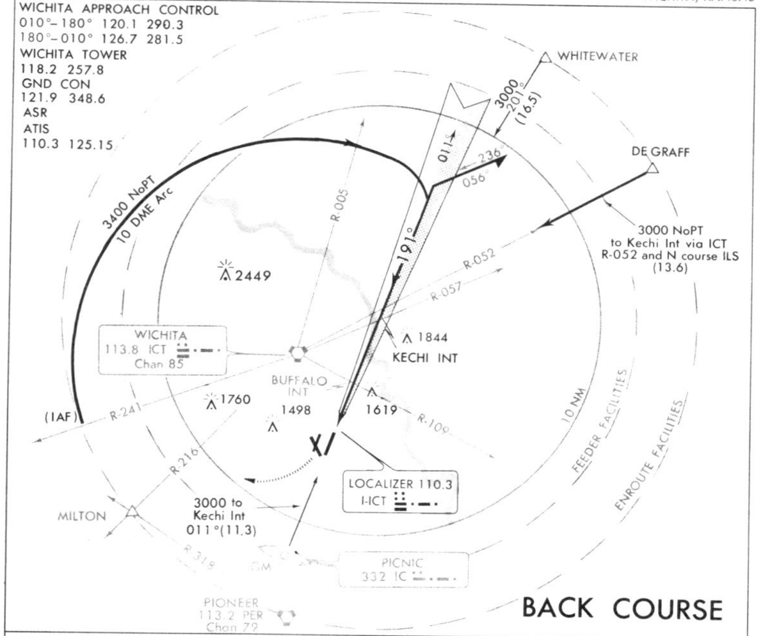

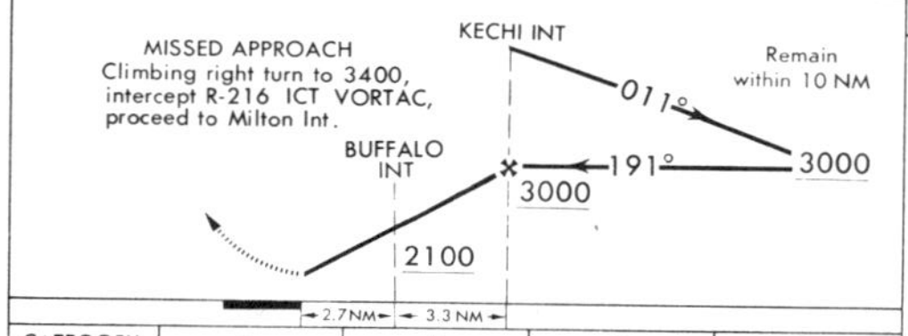

CATEGORY	A	B	C	D
S-19L	1700-¾ 382(400-¾)			1700-1 382 (400-1)
CIRCLING	1740-1 408(500-1)	1800-1 468 (500-1)	1800-1½ 468 (500-1½)	1900-2 568 (600-2)

Dual VOR receivers or Radar required.

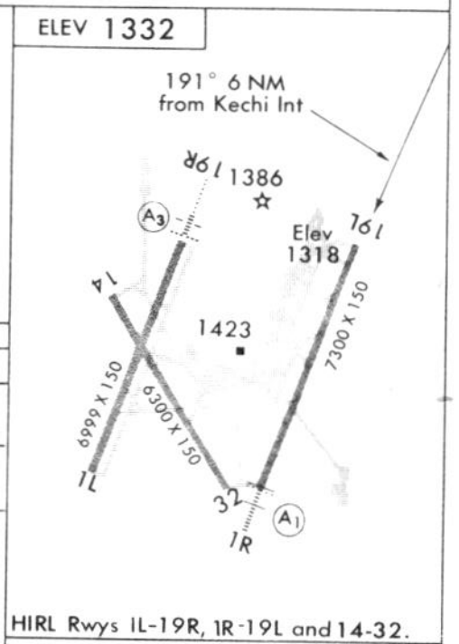

FAF to MAP	NM				
Knots	60	90	120	150	180
Min:Sec	6:00	4:00	3:00	2:24	2:00

ILS RWY 18

AL-213 (FAA)

KANSAS CITY MUNI
KANSAS CITY, MISSOURI

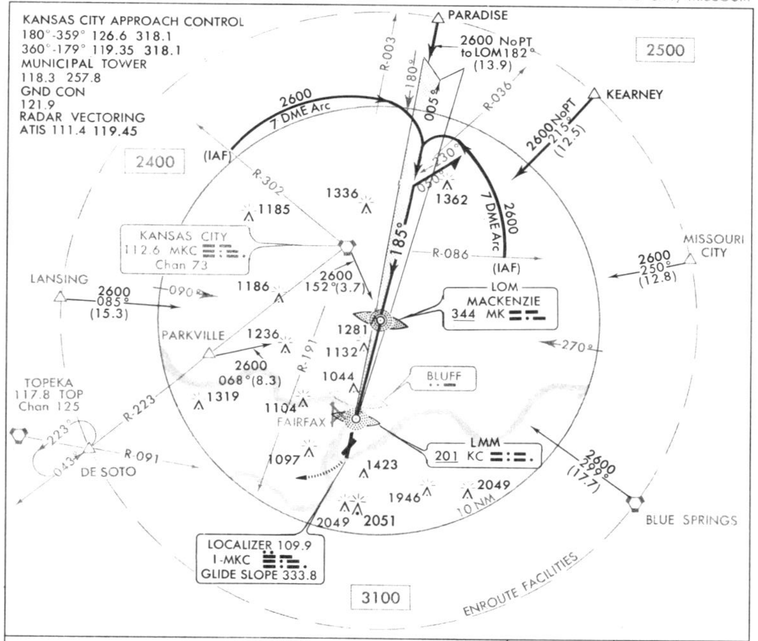

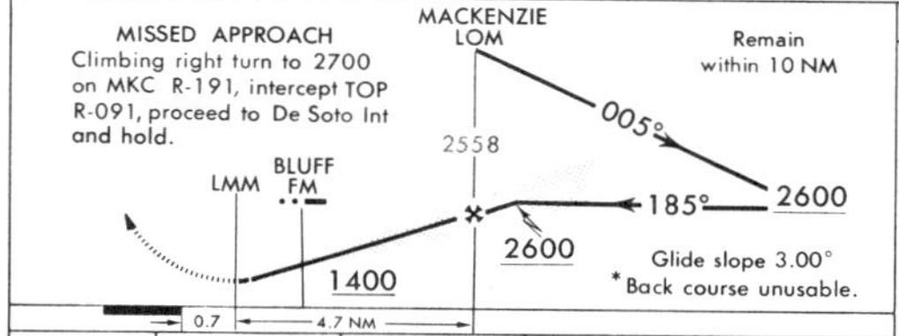

CATEGORY	A	B	C	D
S-ILS 18*	1137-1 379 (400-1)			
S-LOC 18*	1400-1 642 (700-1)			
CIRCLING	1400-1 642 (700-1)		1400-1½ 642 (700-1½)	1400-2 642 (700-2)
FM MINIMA				
S-LOC 18*	1260-1 502 (600-1)			

* Sliding scale not authorized. Inoperative table does not apply to SALS and HIRL Rwy 18.

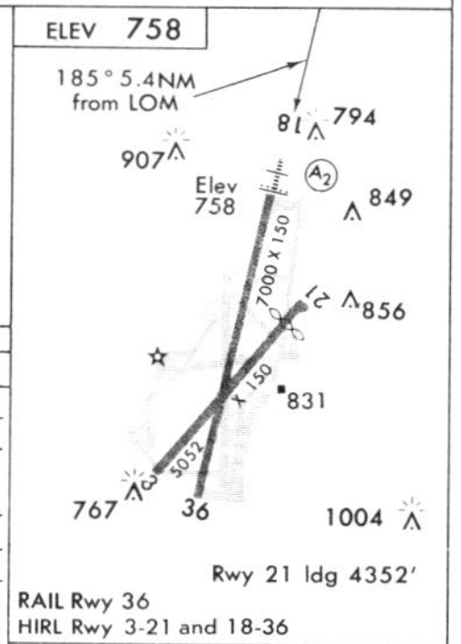

FAF to MAP 4.7 NM					
Knots	60	90	120	150	180
Min:Sec	4:42	3:08	2:21	1:53	1:34

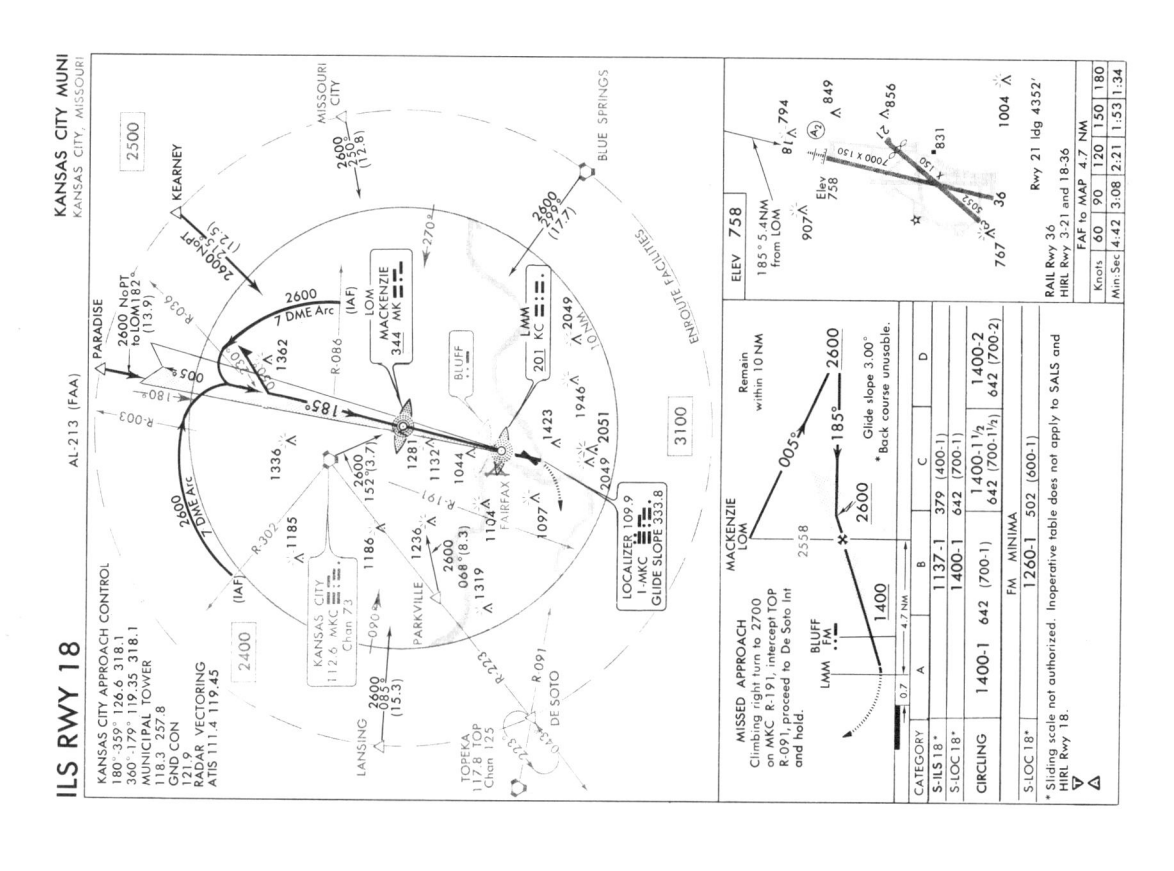

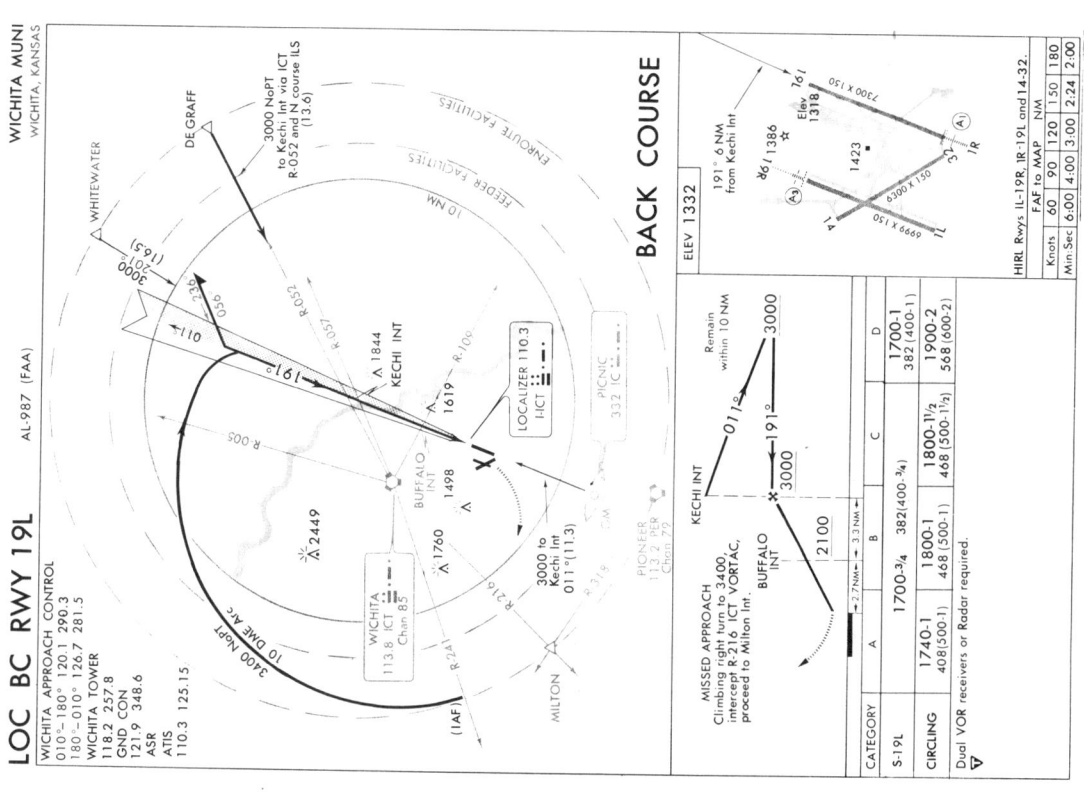

A/G VOICE COMMUNICATIONS

Civil Aerodromes with terminal control A/G voice communications are listed below. Aerodromes located within the limits of the ten Area Charts are listed with the specific Area Chart. Frequencies transmit and receive unless otherwise noted. An asterisk (*) follows those tower frequencies also used for approach control. Values defining sectors are outbound radials from the facility. Chart panel identification letter is shown to right of listing. For additional communications data, refer to appropriate supplemental publications.

ASHLAND BOYD CO Huntington App Con—118.5 122.5R E

BI-STATE PARKS Scott App and Dep Con—124.7 B

BLUE GRASS Lexington App Con—119.1 117.0T 110.1T E
Lexington Twr—121.1 122.4R* Lexington Gnd Con—121.9

BOWMAN Standiford Dep Con—119.0 D
Standiford App Con—124.5 120.5 120.3
Twr—119.5 126.2* 122.4R Gnd Con—121.9

CAPITAL Twr—121.3* 122.5R Gnd Con—121.9 B
Springfield App Con—118.6 112.7T 109.5T

CHEROKEE VILLAGE B
Memphis Center App and Dep Con—127.4

CINCINNATI Dep Con—121.0 122.7R D-E
Lunken Twr—118.7 126.2* 122.4R Lunken Gnd Con—121.9
App Con—119.7 124.7 122.7R

CIVIC MEM St Louis Dep Con—119.9 B
St Louis App Con—126.5 (059°-238°) 118.1 (239°-058°) 126.2
123.7
Alton Twr—121.1 122.5R Alton Gnd Con—121.7

COLUMBUS Indianapolis Dep Con—121.1 D
Indianapolis App Con—119.3 (220°-044°) 118.1 (045°-219°)
126.2 122.5R 118.5 116.3T

DANVILLE Greensboro Dep Con—124.6 G
Greensboro App Con—118.5 122.5R 120.9 116.2T

DECATUR App Con—118.9 C
Twr—118.9* 122.5R Gnd Con—121.9

DRESS MEM Evansville App Con—119.4 109.9T C
Evansville Twr—118.7* 122.5R* Evansville Gnd Con—121.9

GREATER CINCINNATI Cincinnati Gnd Con—121.7 D-E
Cincinnati App Con—119.7 124.7
Cincinnati Twr—118.3 126.2* 122.7R*
Cincinnati Dep Con—121.0 122.7R VOT 108.4

GREENBRIER F
Roanoke App and Dep Con—120.2 122.1R 108.4T

GREENSBORO-HIGH PT.-WINSTON SALEM REGIONAL G
Greensboro App Con—118.5 120.9 116.2T
Greensboro Dep Con—124.6 Greensboro Gnd Con—121.9
Greensboro Twr—119.1 126.2 122.5R*

HAMILTON INC E
Cincinnati App Con—119.7 126.2 124.7 122.7R

HENDERSON Evansville App Con—119.4 118.7 C

HOPEWELL Richmond App Con—119.0 H

HOPKINSVILLE-CHRISTIAN CO C
Campbell App Con—118.1 134.1

HULMAN App Con—123.8 C
Twr—118.3* 122.5R* Gnd Con—121.9

HUNTINGBURG D
Evansville App Con—119.4 125.8 118.7

HUNTINGTON DOWNTOWN F
Huntington App Con—118.5 122.5R

INDIANAPOLIS MUNI/WEIR COOK D
Indianapolis App Con—118.1 (045°-219°) 119.3 (220°-044°)
118.5 116.3T 109.3T
Indianapolis Twr—120.9 126.2* 122.5R* VOT 109.0
Indianapolis Gnd Con—121.9 Indianapolis Dep Con—121.1

KANAWHA Charleston App Con—119.2 F
Charleston Twr—120.3 126.2 122.4R VOT 111.0
Charleston Gnd Con—121.9 Charleston Dep Con—124.1

LAMBERT-ST LOUIS St Louis Gnd Con—121.9 B
St Louis App Con—118.1 (239°-058°) 126.5 (059°-238°)
123.7
St Louis Twr—118.5 126.2* 122.7R 118.95
St Louis Dep Con—119.9 VOT 111.0

LAWRENCEVILLE Richmond App Con—119.9 G
Richmond Dep Con—118.2

LYNCHBURG MUNI-PRESTON GLENN G
Lynchburg App Con—118.0 Lynchburg Gnd Con—121.9
Lynchburg Twr—120.7 122.5R*

MADISONVILLE Evansville App Con—119.4 125.8 C

McGHEE-TYSON Knoxville App Con—123.9 116.4T E
Knoxville Gnd Con—121.9 Knoxville Dep Con—120.2
Knoxville Twr—118.7 126.2 122.5R* VOT 112.0

MERCER CO Roanoke App and Dep Con—120.2 F

METTEL Dayton App Con—118.0 D
Dayton Dep Con—119.9

MIAMI UNIVERSITY Cincinnati Dep Con—121.0 122.7R D
Cincinnati App Con—119.7 126.2 124.7 122.7R

NASHVILLE METROPOLITAN Gnd Con—121.9 D
Twr—119.1 126.2 122.5R* Dep Con—118.4
App Con—120.6 124.0 109.9T VOT 112.0

NEW RIVER VALLEY F
Roanoke App and Dep Con—120.2

NORFOLK Twr—121.1 122.5R H
App Con—125.35 125.7 Gnd Con—121.9
Dep Con—118.5 126.8

OUTLAW Campbell App Con—118.1 134.1 C

OWENSBORO-DAVIESS CO C
Evansville App Con—125.8 122.5R 108.6T

PATRICK HENRY Norfolk App Con—125.7 H
Norfolk Dep Con—118.5 126.8 Gnd Con—121.9
Twr—118.7 122.4R

RALEIGH CO MEM F
Charleston App and Dep Con—124.1 126.2

RALEIGH DURHAM G
Raleigh App Con—125.3 120.6 Gnd Con—121.9
Twr—119.3 126.2 122.5R* Raleigh Dep Con—124.8 120.6

RICHARD E. BYRD Richmond Dep Con—118.2 H
Richmond App Con—119.0 119.9
Richmond Twr—119.5 126.2* 122.5R*
Richmond Gnd Con—121.9 VOT 110.8

ROANOKE G
App Con—126.9 109.0T Twr—118.3 122.5R 120.2*
Gnd Con—121.9 Dep Con—126.0 120.2 109.0T

ROBINSON Hulman App Con—123.8 118.3 C

ROCKY MOUNT Raleigh Dep Con—124.8 120.6 G
Raleigh App Con—125.3 122.5R 120.6

SMITH-REYNOLDS Greensboro Dep Con—124.6 F
Greensboro App Con—118.5 122.5R 120.9 116.2T
Winston-Salem Twr—118.7 126.2 122.7R
Winston-Salem Gnd Con—121.7

SPIRIT OF ST LOUIS B
St Louis App Con—126.5 (059°-238°) 118.1 (239°-058°) 126.2
123.7
Twr—118.3 122.5R Gnd Con—121.7

SPRINGFIELD Twr—119.9 122.5R* A
App Con—125.8 116.9T 109.9T Gnd Con—121.9

STANDIFORD D
App Con—124.5 120.5 Twr—120.3* 126.2* 122.7R
Gnd Con—121.7 Dep Con—119.0 VOT 111.0

TRI-CITY F
App Con—118.4 (046°-244°) 125.6 (245°-045°) 114.6T
Twr—119.5 126.2* 122.5R* Gnd Con—121.7
Dep Con—118.4 (046°-244°) 125.6 (245°-045°) 126.2

TRI-STATE Huntington App Con—118.5 F
Huntington Twr—120.9 122.4R*
Huntington Gnd Con—121.9

VPI Roanoke App and Dep Con—120.2 F

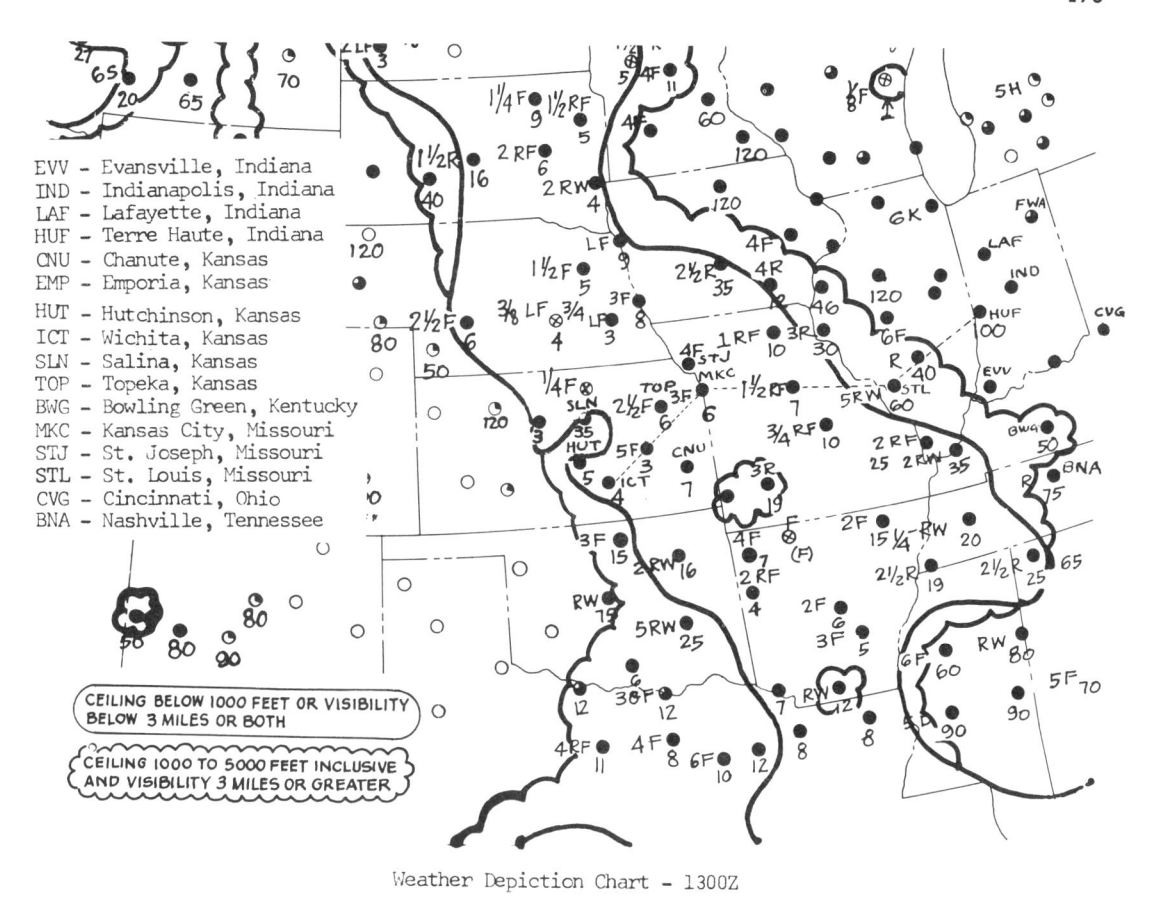

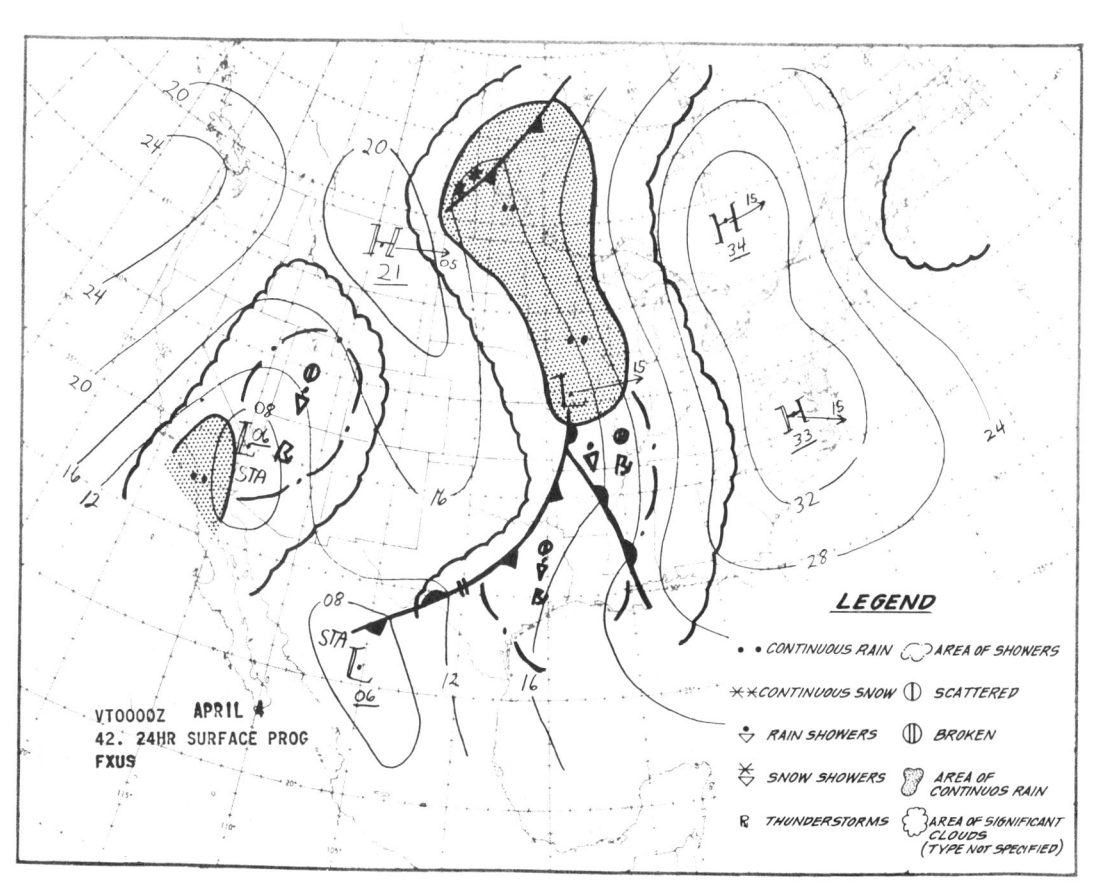

EVV - Evansville, Indiana
IND - Indianapolis, Indiana
LAF - Lafayette, Indiana
HUF - Terre Haute, Indiana
CNU - Chanute, Kansas
EMP - Emporia, Kansas
HUT - Hutchinson, Kansas
ICT - Wichita, Kansas
SLN - Salina, Kansas
TOP - Topeka, Kansas
BWG - Bowling Green, Kentucky
MKC - Kansas City, Missouri
STJ - St. Joseph, Missouri
STL - St. Louis, Missouri
CVG - Cincinnati, Ohio
BNA - Nashville, Tennessee

CEILING BELOW 1000 FEET OR VISIBILITY BELOW 3 MILES OR BOTH

CEILING 1000 TO 5000 FEET INCLUSIVE AND VISIBILITY 3 MILES OR GREATER

Weather Depiction Chart - 1300Z

VT0000Z APRIL 4
42. 24HR SURFACE PROG
FXUS

LEGEND
•• CONTINUOUS RAIN   AREA OF SHOWERS
** CONTINUOUS SNOW   ⊕ SCATTERED
▽ RAIN SHOWERS   ⦷ BROKEN
✷ SNOW SHOWERS   AREA OF CONTINUOUS RAIN
R THUNDERSTORMS   AREA OF SIGNIFICANT CLOUDS (TYPE NOT SPECIFIED)

Surface prognostic chart.

HOURLY SURFACE WEATHER REPORTS

SA 25031400 (some stations omitted)
LAF	E60 ⊕ 8K 152/48/36/1708/001
HUF	E50 ⊕ 10RW 121/51/47/1806/996
IND	E80 ⊕ 8HF 113/49/38/1510/996
EVV	A30 ⊕ 5RF 115/52/48/1308/994
CVG	E100 ⓦ 10K 119/50/37/1308/998
BNA	M9 ⊕ 5RW 115/56/50/1110/994
STL	M7 ⊕ 3RF 132/53/50/1006/993
MKC	M7 ⊕ 3F 149/44/41/1013/995 → MKC ↘ 2/100A 3/150A 4/30A

SA 30031400 (some stations omitted)

TOP	M5 ⊕ 21/2F 136/46/44/1209/992/CIG RGD
STJ	A7 ⊕ 3F 41/40/1110G17/996/ 28V36/LGT TURBC 23 DC3
ICT	S M5 ⓦ 9 ⊕ 8 102/56/55/1314/983/RE44 → ICT ↘ 11/1810 3/23AN
HUT	E3 ⊕ 7 55/52/1312/982
EMP	E3 ⊕ 2F 129/48/46/1414/990
CNU	S B6 ⊕ 4L-F 123/49/49/1212/989/TE40 RWE 45 T MOVD SE

SA 25031500 (some stations omitted)

LAF	E50 ⊕ 7K 120/ 50/38/1607/998
HUF	E40 ⊕ 10RW--078/52/49/1805/997
IND	E60 ⊕ 8HF 078/51/39/1410/997
EVV	A25 ⊕ 5RF 113/53/49/1408/996
CVG	E100 ⊕ 10K 078/52/38/1207/997
BNA	M8 ⊕ 4RW 142/57/51/1108/995
BWG	M9 ⊕ 4RW 144/56/51/1109/995
STL	M6 ⊕ 3RF 115/54/51/1006/994
MKC	M8 ⊕ 3F 141/45/42/1110/993

SA 30031500 (some stations omitted)

TOP	M6 ⊕ 3F 130/48/45/1210/990/CIG RGD
STJ	M7 ⊕ 3F 44/41/1210G16/996
ICT	S 6 ⓦ M9 ⊕ 8 103/58/56/1414/984/ 000 16// → ICT ↘ 11/1810 3/2AN 4/210
HUT	E5 ⊕ 3F 56/54/1514/982
EMP	W1X1/4F 116/49/49/1410/986/ 002
CNU	S B2 ⊕ 3F 124/51/51/1513/989/LEO3RWB03E42/ 805

TERMINAL FORECAST

FT03 1045

STL 031111 C60⊕5RW. 14Z C6⊕2RF. 05Z IFR..
EVV 031111 C80⊕10. 14Z C40⊕5RF. 17Z C25⊕3RF
 20Z C8 2RF. 05Z IFR..
IND 031111 C100①10. 15Z C50⊕10. 18Z C30⊕5.
 05Z MVFR..
HUF 031111 C100①10. 14Z C60⊕10. 17Z C25⊕4RW.
 05Z MVFR..
CVG 031111 100①15. 15Z C100①10K. 05Z VFR..

FT03 1045

STJ 031111 C8⊕3F 1210 OCNL L-. 20Z C10①20⊕7
 OCNL RW-. 05Z VFR..
TOP 031111 C8⊕3F 1210 OCNL L-. 20Z C10①20⊕7
 1615 OCNL RW-. 00Z 20①C25①2010.
 05Z VFR..
MKC 031111 C8⊕3F 1112 OCNL L-. 21Z C10①20⊕7
 1612 OCNL RW-. 02Z 15 C20 7 1810.
 05Z VFR..
ICT 03111 5①C10⊕ 1415 OCNL C5① TILL 17Z.
 20Z C10①20⊕ 1815. 00Z 20①C50① 2012.
 05Z VFR..

AREA FORECAST

FA MCK 031245
07C-18C SAT
CNTRL AND SRN ILL MO EXCP NWN PORTION CLDS AND WX. CIGS ERN ILL
ABV 50 LWG TO 30-50 FORNN. CIGS WRN ILL 10-50 LWG TO LESS THAN 10
FORNN. LOW CIGS AND POOR VSBY C4-10 1-3R-F WITH OCNL RW - ERN
ILL AND MO DURG ENTR PD. TOPS OF CLDS 200+ASL.

ICG. MDT TO LCLY HVY ICGICIP ABV FRZG LVL. FRZG LVL 70 CNTRL MO
AND ILL WL LFT TO 90 DURG DA.

TURBC. LGT TO MDT OVR CNTRL MO.

OTLK. 18C SAT-07C SUN. LW CIGS AND VSBY CONTG DURG NGT BUT CLRG
FM WRN MO. GNDFG FRMG DURG NGT IN CLRG SECS WRN MO.

WINDS ALOFT FORECAST

12-18Z

LVL	3000	5000FT	7000FT	10000FT
IND	2215	2419+16	2621	2625+06
STL	2114	2316+20	2520	2625+10
MKC	2026	2126+13	2228	2228+04

RESTRICTIONS TO ENROUTE NAVIGATION AIDS

Radio Facility Restrictions are cited until cancelled by the Associated Station.

ILLINOIS

- CHICAGO O'HARE VORTAC: VOR unusable 060–072°, 160–190°, 290–305° and 340–360°, and 145–153° beyond 18 nmi. DME unusable 004–014°, 138–156°, 170–218°, 250–255°, 285–315°, and 340–350°.
- CHICAGO HEIGHTS VORTAC: VOR unusable 330–350° beyond 20 mi below 8,000' MSL.

INDIANA

- BLOOMINGTON VOR: VOR unusable 025–045° beyond 30 mi below 4,000' MSL.
- FORT WAYNE VORTAC: VOR unusable 044–062° below 14,500 MSL.
- KNOX VOR: VOR unusable 045–135° beyond 37 mi.
- MUNCIE VOR: VOR unusable 115–210° beyond 30 NM below 2500' MSL.

KANSAS

- MANHATTAN VOR: VOR unusable beyond 10 NM 260–282° below 5500' MSL.

MISSOURI

- JEFFERSON CITY VOR: VOR unusable beyond 20 NM 040–105° and 140–285°; unusable below 4000' beyond 20 mi 285–040° and 105–140°; unusable below 4000' 0–20 mi 040–105° and 140–285°.
- MARYLAND HEIGHTS VORTAC: VOR unusable 150–210° beyond 35 mi below 3.500' MSL. DME unusable 150–215° beyond 30 mi below 3,500' MSL.
- RIVERSIDE VOR: VOR unusable in following areas: 125–170°, 252–260° and 300–310° all distances and altitudes; all other azimuths beyond 15 mi below 2,400' MSL.

Part 3–A—NOTICES TO AIRMEN

This part is issued every 14 days and is primarily designed to supplement Part 3 of the AIM. It contains appropriate notices from the daily NOTAM Summary, Airmen Advisories, new or revised Oil Burner Routes and other items considered essential to flight safety.

NOTE: Data preceded by a checkmark (✓) are considered permanent and will usually be cited only once. Such information should be noted on charts and records. Temporary information is normally carried twice unless re-submitted.

NOTE: Data are arranged in alphabetical order by State (and within the State by City or locality).

NEW OR REVISED DATA: New or revised data are indicated by underlining the first line of the affected item. The new information is not necessarily limited to the underlined portion, which is used only to attract attention to the new insert.

ILLINOIS

BLOOMINGTON, NORMAL ARPT: Rn~~ men & eqpmt at int 3-21 and 11 ~~. First 3700' rnwy 29 usable, rn~~ ~~ 500' SE of int rnwys 3-21 and 11-29 ~~ 11-19 length 4400', lgtg avbl.
CHICAGO, HINSDALE ARPT: New rnwy 4-22 clsd til Dec 1, constr.
CHICAGO MIDWAY ARPT: Rnwy 13R A/LS inop.
CHICAGO MIDWAY ARPT TWR: REIL rnwy 22L inop.
CHICAGO O'HARE INTL ARPT: RVR rollout end rnwy 14L and T/D end rnwy 32R, 27R to be opernl aprxly Oct 31. Rnwy 14L-32R clsd ngts btwn 0300–1200Z until aprxly Nov 15—installation of ctr line and T/D zone lgtg.
CHICAGO/WHEELING/, PALWAUKEE ARPT: 150' dsplcd thr SE end rnwy 30R. 4300' avbl lndg day/ngt 30R, and tkof 12L day/ngt.
GRAYSLAKE, CAMPBELL ARPT: Extension on SW end of rnwy 6-24 under constr UFN.
✓LOMBARD, YORK TOWNSHIP ARPT: Rnwy lgts dcmsnd. Rnwy 1 apch restrictd by street lgt 25' high 100' from rnwy end. Arpt remains clsd to transient acft.
MONTICELLO, MONTICELLO AVIATION INC ARPT: One N-S 3960' turf rnwy—south one quarter clsd until aprxly Jun 1, 1968, reseeding.
PEORIA, GREATER PEORIA ARPT TWR: ILS G/S rnwy 30 shutdown UFN—rnwy constr.

PLAINFIELD ARPT: Clsd to transient acft UFN.
QUINCY MUNI BALDWIN FLD: Rnwy lgts rnwy 17-35 inop UFN.
STREATOR AIR SER~~ICE ARPT: Rnwy 9-27 hard sfc clsd UFN ~~ open and lgtd.

INDIANA

~~ORD, GRISSOM MUNI ARPT: UFN rnwy 13-31 has soft shoulders.

KANSAS

NEWTON MUNI ARPT: Rotg bcn inop UFN.
STILWELL, STILWELL-MISSION ROAD ARPT: Clsd til aprxly March 1, 1968.

MISSOURI

✓BROOKFIELD MEML ARPT: Rnwy 9-27 realigned to 7-25.
✓CAPE GIRARDEAU MUNI ARPT: "New" rnwy 10-28 now open, apsh, 6500', rnwy 2-20 open for ngt operns.
CARUTHERSVILLE MEML ARPT: Constr on rnwy 18-36 (extension on S end) until aprxly Mar 1, 1968; at present, 2400' avbl with low int rnwy lgts operg dusk-dawn on 1000' N end.
KANSAS CITY, MID-CONTINENT INTL ARPT: WIP until aprxly Apr 1968, rnwy and txwy constr. Rnwy 36—1000' tmpry dsplcd thr apch end intmtly dalgt VFR conditions UFN. Rnwy 9-27 constr continues until aprxly Dec 1.
✓KANSAS CITY MUNI ARPT: Rnwy 17-35 permly clsd, usable as txwy.
MOSBY ARPT: Clsd UFN.
ST JOSEPH, ROSECRANS MEML ARPT: First 500' rnwy 22 apch clsd UFN. Usable length both directions 5600'.

EXCERPTS FROM AIRMAN'S INFORMATION MANUAL

Airport Directory

LEGEND

LOCATION

The airport location is given in nautical miles (to the nearest mile) and direction from center of referenced city.

ELEVATION

Elevation is given in feet above mean sea level and is based on highest usable portion of the landing area. When elevation is sea level, elevation will be indicated as "00." When elevation is below sea level, a minus sign (−) will precede the figure.

RUNWAYS

The runway surface length, and weight bearing capacity are listed for the longest instrument runway or sealane, or the longest active landing portion of the runway or strip, given to the nearest hundred feet, using 70 feet as the division point, i.e., 1468 feet would be shown as "14"; 1474 feet would be shown as "15". Runways lengths prefixed by the letter "H" indicates that runways are hard surfaced (concrete; asphalt; bitumen, or macadam with a seal coat). If the runway length is not prefixed, the surface is sod, clay, etc. The total number of runways available is shown in parenthesis. (However, only hard surfaced runways are counted at airfields with both hard surfaced and sod runways.)

RUNWAY WEIGHT BEARING CAPACITY

Add 000 to figure following S, T, TT and MAX for gross weight capacity, e.g., (S-000).
- S–Runway weight bearing capacity for aircraft with single-wheel type landing gear. (DC-3), etc.
- T–Runway weight bearing capacity for aircraft with twin-wheel type landing gear. (DC-6), etc.
- TT–Runway weight bearing capacity for aircraft with twin-tandem type landing gear. (707), etc.

Quadricycle and twin-tandem are considered virtually equal for runway weight bearing considerations, as are single-tandem and twin-wheel.

A blank space following the letter designation is used to indicate the runway weight bearing capacity to sustain aircraft with the same type landing gear, although definite figures are not available, e.g., (T-). Omission of weight bearing capacity indicates information unknown. Footnote remarks are used to indicate a runway with a weight bearing greater than the longest runway.

SEAPLANE BASE FACILITIES

A number preceding the parenthetical designation, indicates the number (quantity) available.

Beaching gear, consisting of the quantity and type of beaching gear available.

The number (quantity) if available, of Mooring Buoys (MB) and Crash Boats (CB) available.

LIGHTING

B: Rotating Light (Rotating beacon). (Green and white, split-beam and other types.) Omission of **B** indicates rotating light is either not available or not operating standard hours (sunset-sunrise).

NOTE.—Code lights are not codified, and are carried in Remarks.

L: Field Lighting (when code **L4-7** is indicated, lighting **4, 5, 6, 7** is available). An asterisk (*) preceding an element indicates that it operates on prior request only (by phone call, telegram or letter). Where the asterisk is not shown, the lights are in operation or available sunset to sunrise or by request (radio call). L by itself indicates temporary lighting, such as flares, smudge pots, lanterns.

1—Strip lights or portable runway lights (electrical)
2—Boundary
3—Runway Floods
4—Low Intensity Runway
5—Medium Intensity Runway
6—High Intensity Runway
7—Instrument Approach (neon)
8A, B, or C—High Intensity Instrument Approach

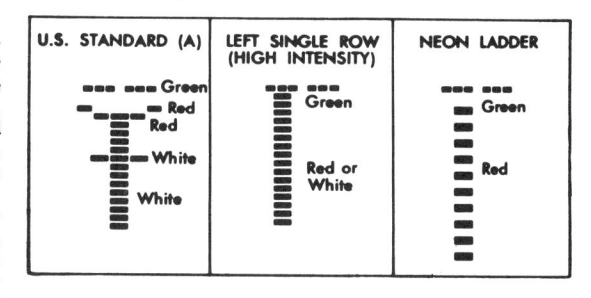

U.S. STANDARD (A)	LEFT SINGLE ROW (HIGH INTENSITY)	NEON LADDER
Green / Red / White / White	Green / Red or White	Green / Red

9—Sequence Flashing Lights (3,000' out unless otherwise stated)
10—Visual Approach Slope Indicator (VASI)
11—Runway end identification lights (threshold strobe) REIL
12—Short approach light systems (SALS)
13—Runway alignment lights (RAIL)
14—Runway centerline
15—Touchdown zone

Because the obstructions on virtually all lighted fields are lighted, obstruction lights have not been included in the codification.

SERVICING

- **S1:** Storage.
- **S2:** Storage, minor airframe repairs.
- **S3:** Storage, minor airframe and minor powerplant repairs.
- **S4:** Storage, major airframe and minor powerplant repairs.
- **S5:** Storage, major airframe and major powerplant repairs.

FUEL

- **F1** 80 oct., at least.
- **F2** 80/87 oct., or lower.
- **F3** 91/96 oct., or lower.
- **F4** 100/130 performance rating, or lower.
- **F5** 115/145 performance rating, or lower.

TURBINE FUELS

- **TP–1** 650 turbine fuels for civil jets.
- **JP–1** (Kerosene), JP–3, JP–4, JP–5.

DAYLIGHT SAVING TIME

Daylight Saving Time runs from the last Sunday in April to the last Sunday in October. All states in conterminous United States except Kentucky and Michigan will go on Daylight Saving Time. At the time this publication goes to press no information is available for Puerto Rico and Virgin Islands.

AIRPORT DIRECTORY

OTHER

§ Notam Service is provided. Applicable only to airports with established instrument procedures or high volume VFR activity (as described in FAA Notice 7930.1).

AOE—Airport of Entry.

VASI—Visual Approch Slope Indicator, applicable runway provided.

RVV—Runway Visibility Value, applicable runway provided.

RVR—Runway Visual Range, applicable runway provided.

TPA—Traffic Pattern Altitude—This information is provided for only those airports without a 24-hour operating control tower or FSS. Directions of turns are indicated only when turns of the pattern(s) are to the right (non-standard). TPA data are related to the runway listed under the tabulated airport information. Generally, only one altitude is listed; however, one of conventional aircraft and one for high performance aircraft. They are shown in this manner, TPA 8/15-R (increments of 100 feet). The higher figure being the higher performance aircraft altitude.

FSS—The name of the associated FSS and/or combined station/tower (CS/T) is shown in all instances. When the FSS is located on the named airport, "on fld" is shown following the FSS name. When the FSS can be called through the local telephone exchange, (Foreign Exchange) at the cost of a local call, it is indicated by "(LC)" (local call) with the phone number immediately following the name of the FSS, i.e., "FSS: WICHITA (LC481-5867)." When an Interphone line exists between the field and the FSS, it is indicated by "(DL)" (direct line) immediately following the name of the FSS, i.e., "FSS: OTTO (DL)."

The availability of a VHF/DF at a FSS is indicated by the letters VHF/DF. For service, contact FSS on standard frequencies.

AIRPORT REMARKS

(£) Indicates that an air traffic control tower and/or an instrument landing system are associated with the airport. For specific details see the Airport/Facility Directory in Part 3 of the Airman's Information Manual.

"**Fee**" indicates landing charges for private or non-revenue producing aircraft. In addition, fees may be charged for planes that remain over a couple of hours and buy no services, or at major airline terminals for all aircraft.

"**Rgt tfc 13–31**" indicates right turns should be made on landings and takeoffs on runways 13 and 31.

Remarks—data is confined to operational items affecting the status and usability of the airport, traffic patterns and departure procedures

Obstructions.—Because of space limitations only the more dangerous obstructions are indicated. Natural obstructions, such as trees, clearly discernible for contact operations, are frequently omitted. On the other hand, all pole lines within at least 15:1 glide angle are indicated.

UNICOM

A private aeronautical advisory communications facility operated for purposes other than air traffic control, transmits and receives on one of the following frequencies:

- **U1**—122.8 for Landing Areas (except heliports) without an ATC Tower or FSS;
- **U2**—123.0 for Landing Areas (except heliports) with an ATC Tower or FSS;
- **U3**—123.05 for heliports.

EXCERPTS FROM AIRMAN'S INFORMATION MANUAL

AIRPORT LEGEND

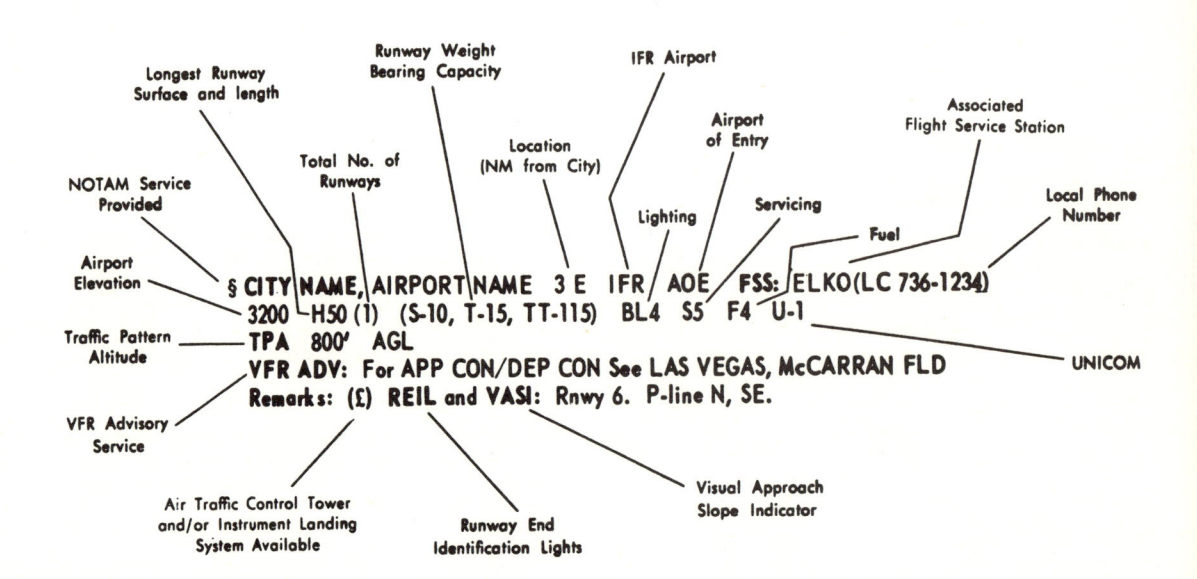

§ CITY NAME, AIRPORT NAME 3 E IFR AOE FSS: ELKO(LC 736-1234)
3200 H50 (1) (S-10, T-15, TT-115) BL4 S5 F4 U-1
TPA 800' AGL
VFR ADV: For APP CON/DEP CON See LAS VEGAS, McCARRAN FLD
Remarks: (£) REIL and VASI: Rnwy 6. P-line N, SE.

Labels:
- NOTAM Service Provided
- Longest Runway Surface and length
- Total No. of Runways
- Runway Weight Bearing Capacity
- Location (NM from City)
- IFR Airport
- Airport of Entry
- Lighting
- Servicing
- Fuel
- Associated Flight Service Station
- Local Phone Number
- Airport Elevation
- Traffic Pattern Altitude
- VFR Advisory Service
- Air Traffic Control Tower and/or Instrument Landing System Available
- Runway End Identification Lights
- Visual Approach Slope Indicator
- UNICOM

AIRPORT/FACILITY DIRECTORY

INDIANA

TERRE HAUTE
§**HULMAN FIELD** *IFR* 5E   **FSS:** TERRE HAUTE on Fld
585 H90/5-23(3) (S-50, T-65, TT-100) BL5,6 S3 F12,18,34
RVV: Rnwy 5
Remarks: J-bar/A-gear rnwy 5-23. 1254' overrun NE end rnwy 5. Rnwy 18-36 clsd to acft over 25,000 lbs.
Tower 118.3 122.5R   **Gnd Con** 121.9
  App Con 123.8 122.5R 118.3
Tfc Info Ctc App Con on 123.8
ILS 109.7 I-HUF Apch Brg 045° **LOM:** 245/HU
Terre Haute (L) **BVORTAC** 111.8/HUF 229° 3.0NM to fld.
Terre Haute **RBn MHW** 245/HU 045° 4.7 NM to rnwy 5.
Remarks: LOM is MHW.

KANSAS

§**WICHITA MUNI** *IFR* 5SW   **FSS:** WICHITA on Fld
1332 H73/1-19(2) (S-100, T-188, TT-350) BL6,8A,9 S5 F5, JP1 U2   **RVR:** Rnwy 1
Remarks: 1079' (2444' MSL) and 1064 (2431' MSL) twr 9NM NNW.
Tower 119.5   **Gnd Con** 121.9
ATIS[1] 110.3
Radar Services: (BCN)
  Wichita App Con 120.1 120.6 134.1 125.7 122.7R 113.8T
  Wichita Dep Con 124.5 113.8T
Tfc Info Ctc App Con on 120.1
ASR Rnwys 1, 32 Ceil 400 Vsby 1 mi Min Alt 1732.
  Rnwy 14 Ceil 500 Vsby 1 mi Min Alt 1832.
  Rnwy 19 Ceil 600 Vsby 1 mi Min Alt 1932.
ILS 110.3 I-ICT Apch Brg 011° **LOM:** 332/IC
(H) BVORTAC 113.8/ICT 162° 4.3 NM to rnwy 14.
RBn H-SAB 332●/IC 011° 4.1 NM to rnwy 1
Remarks: LOM is H-SAB. [1]Operates 0700-2300 lcl time.

MISSOURI

§**KANSAS CITY MUNI** *IFR* 4N   **FSS:** KANSAS CITY on Fld
758 H70/18-36(3) (S-100, T-185, TT-350) BL4,6,8A,9,11,13 S5 F4, JP1 U2 **RVV:** Rnwy 18 **REIL:** Rnwy 36
Remarks: Overrun each end rnwy 18-36. S 3270' rnwy 35 usable daylight hrs only. Rnwy 17 clsd. 1042 (2094' MSL) twr 3.5NM S and 1023' (1946' MSL) twr 4.5NM ESE. Lead-in lgts rnwy 36.
Tower 118.3 126.2 122.7R 121.1 111.4T   **Gnd Con** 121.9
‡**Clrnc Del:** 121.9
ATIS: 111.4
Radar Services: (BCN)
  App Con 118.9[1] 126.2 121.1[2] 112.6T 109.9T
  Dep Con 118.1
Tfc Info Ctc App Con
PAR Rnwy 18 Ceil 400 Vsby 1 mi Min Alt 1158.
ILS[3] 109.9 I-MKC Apch Brg 185° BC unusable **LOM:** 219/MK
(H) BVORTAC 112.6/MKC 171° 8.7NM to fld.
  Riverside (T) VOR 111.4/RIS on fld.
  VHF/DF Ctc twr.

MISSOURI—Continued

Remarks: Acft approaching from 001-180° use 118.9 and/from 179°-360° 121.1. Radar advisories avbl. [1]E sector. [2]W sector. ASR apch not auth. [3]Glide slope unusable below 1014' MSL. Front crs unusable beyond 20 NM. Back course unusable.
VOT: 108.6.

KANSAS CITY
§**MID-CONTINENT INTL** *IFR* 15NW   **FSS:** KANSAS CITY
1011 H90/18-36(1) (S-100+, T-185, TT-350) BL6,8A,9
RVR: Rnwy 36
Remarks: Attended 0800-1700 daily.
Tower 120.7   Gnd Con 121.8
Radar...
              .. 118.9[1] 126.2 121.1[2]
  109.9T   **Kansas City Dep Con** 118.1
Tfc Info Ctc Kansas City App Con.
ILS 110.5 I-MCI Apch Brg 005°   **LOM:** 359/MC
RBn H-SAB 359●/MC 005° 4.4 to rnwy 36.
Remarks: [1]E sector. [2]W sector. LOM is H-SAB.

ST. LOUIS
§**LAMBERT-ST LOUIS** *IFR* 10NW **FSS:** ST. LOUIS on Fld
571 H100/12R-30L(4) (S-100, T-200, TT-400) BL4,6,8A,9,12 S5 F5, JP1, JP5 U2 **RVR:** Rnwy 24
Remarks: U.S. Customs lndg rgts arpt (3 hr advance notice rqrd). 476' displaced threshold rnwy 12R, 9542' avbl lndg day/ngt. Full length 10,018' abl lndg/tkof day/ngt rnwy 30L and tkof day/ngt rnwy 12R.
St. Louis Tower 118.5 126.2 122.7R   **Gnd Con** 121.9
‡**Clrnc Del** 119.5
ATIS[4]: 110.3 109.7
Radar Services: (BCN)
  St. Louis App Con 126.5[1] 123.7 118.1[2]
  117.4T   **St. Louis Dep Con** 119.9
Tfc Info Ctc St. Louis App Con.
PAR[3] Rnwy 24 Ceil 200 Vsby ½ mi Min Alt 771.
ASR Rnwys 6, 17, 24, 30L, 35 Ceil 500 Vsby 1 Min Alt 1071.
  Rnwys 12L, 30R Ceil 500 Vsby 1½ mi Min Alt 1071.
  Rnwy 12R Ceil 400 Vsby 1 mi Min Alt 971.
ILS 110.3 I-STL Apch Brg 238° **LOM:** 404/ST
  109.7 I-LMR Apch Brg 117° **LOM:** 338/LM
St. Louis (H) BVORTAC 117.4/STL 138° 8.0NM to fld.
St. Louis RBn H-SAB 338●/LM 117° 5.3 NM to fld.
Remarks: [1]Southeast arrivals. [2]Northwest arrivals. [3]Radar monitoring of instrument apchs only at pilot's request. LOM is H-SAB. [4]Opers 0600-2400 lcl.   **VOT:** 111.0

§ **SPIRIT OF ST. LOUIS** 20W   **FSS:** ST. LOUIS (DL)
462 H51/7-25(1) (S-33, T-50, TT-80) BL6 S5 F4 JP1
Remarks: Special Air Traffic Rules—Part 93, Subpart G in effect. Rgt tfc rnwy 7. When twr clsd tkoff W only, lndgs not authorized.
Tower[1] 118.3 122.5R **Gnd Con** 121.7
St. Louis App Con 126.5[2] 118.1[3]
VFR/ADV Ctc App Con St. Louis, Lambert-St. Louis.
Remarks: [1]Opers 0700-2400 lcl time. [2]Southeast arrivals. [3]Northwest arrivals.

185

EXERPTS FROM AIRMANS INFORMATION MANUAL

GREENWICH MEAN OR "Z" TIME

All aviation operations are conducted using Greenwich Mean (GMT) or "Z" ("Zebra") time. In addition, all aviation information including weather reports is also based on "Z" time. Conversion of local time to 24 hour clock time, thence to Z time is sometimes confusing unless an organized approach is set up. Use of daylight saving time adds to the confusion.

The following table has been set up to simplify and illustrate the conversion procedure considering the standard time zones of the United States.

Time Zones	Pacific	Mountain	Central	Eastern
Local A.M.	9:00	10:00	11:00	12:00
24 hr. Clock	0900	1000	1100	1200
For Z add	+8	+7	+6	+5
Z	1700	1700	1700	1700

Time Zones	Pacific	Mountain	Central	Eastern
Local P.M.	9:00	10:00	11:00	12:00
24 hr. Clock (+12)	2100	2200	2300	2400 (0000)
For Z add	+8	+7	+6	+5
Subtract 24 if over 2400	2900 −24	2900 −24	2900 −24	2900 −24
Z (next day)	0500	0500	0500	0500

FREQUENTLY USED WORD CONTRACTIONS

A

about	ABT
above	ABV
above ground level	AGL
above sea level	ASL
across	ACRS
acting	ACTG
active	ACTV
advance	ADVN
advise	ADZ
advisory	ADVY
affect	AFCT
after	AFT
after dark	AFDK
afternoon	AFTN
again	AGN
ahead	AHD
aircraft	ACFT
air mass	AMS
airport	ARPT
airway	AWY
aloft	ALF
along	ALG
alternate	ALTN
altitude	ALT
amount	AMT
analysis	ANLYS
approach	APCH
around	ARND
atmospherics	SFERICS
average	AVG

B

backing	BCKG
become	BCM
before	BFR
before dark	BFDK
begin, began	BGN
behind	BHND
below	BLO
beneath	BNTH
better	BTR
between	BTN
beyond	BYD
blizzard	BLZD
border	BDR
boundary	BNDRY
break	BRK
brief	BRF
broken	BRKN
build	BLD

C

ceiling	CIG
center	CNTR
central	CNTRL
change	CHG
clear	CLR
clear air turbulence	CAT
clear or scattered clouds and visibility greater than 10 miles	CAVU
cloud	CLD
coast	CST

FREQUENTLY USED WORD CONTRACTIONS (Con't.)

condition	COND
confine	CFN
considerable	CSDRBL
continue	CONT
cover	CVR

D

daybreak	DABRK
daylight	DALGT
decrease	DCR
deep	DP
deepening	DPNG
degree	DEG
delay	DLA
dense	DNS
develop	DVLP
diffuse	DFUS
diminish	DMSH
dissipate	DSIPT
distant	DSNT
district	DIST
ditto	DO
downslope	DNSLP
drift	DRFT
drizzle	DRZL
during	DURG

E

elsewhere	ELSW
ending	ENDG
entire	ENTR
evening	EVE
except	EXCP
expect	EXPC
extensive	EXTSV
extreme	EXTRM

F

falling	FLG
feet; foot; Fort	FT
filling	FILG
flurry	FLRY
follow	FLW
forecast	FCST
forenoon	FORNN
forward	FWD
freeze	FRZ
frequent	FQT
from	FM
frontal passage	FROPA
frontal surface	FROSFC
frost	FRST
frozen	FRZN
further; farther	FTHR

G

general	GEN
gradual	GRDL
ground	GND
ground fog	GNDFG

H

hailstones	HLSTO
half	HLF
hear, here, hour	HR
heavy	HVY
height	HGT
high	HI
however	HWVR
hundred	HND
hurricane	HURCN

I

icing	ICG
icing in clouds	ICGIC
icing in precipitation	ICGIP
icing in clouds, in precipitation	ICGICIP
immediate	IMDT
important	IMPT
improve	IPV
increase	INCR
indefinite	INDEF
indicate	INDC
information	INFO
intense	INTS
intensify	INTSFY
interior	INTR
intermittent	INTMT
isolated	ISOLD

J

jet stream	JTSTR

K

knot or knots	KT

L

later	LTR
layer	LYR
level	LVL
light	LGT
likely	LKLY
limit	LMT
little	LTL
little change	LTLCG
local	LCL
lower	LWR

M

maritime	MRTM
maximum	MAX
mean sea level	MSL
middle	MID
midnight	MIDN
mile or miles	MI
minimum	MIN
mixed	MXD
moderate	MDT
morning	MRNG
mountain	MTN
move	MOV

N

nautical mile or miles	NMI
night	NGT
numerous	NMRS

O

obscure	OBSC
observe	OBS
occasional	OCNL
occlude	OCL
occluded front	OCFNT
occlusion	OCLN
occur	OCR

FREQUENTLY USED WORD CONTRACTIONS (Con't.)

off shore	OFSHR
on shore	ONSHR
other	OTR
outlook	OTLK
over	OVR
overcast	OVC
overrun	OVRN

P

partly	PTLY
passing, passage	PSG
period	PD
persist	PRST
portion	PTN
position	PSN
possible	PSBL
precipitation	PCPN
prevail	PVL
prognostic; prognosis, progress	PROG

R

ragged	RGD
rapid	RPD
reach	RCH
region	RGN
remain	RMN
repeat	RPT
restrict	RESTR
retard	RTRD
return	RTRN
ridge	RDG
rising	RSG
rough	RUF
route	RTE

S

scattered	SCTD
second; section	SEC
sector	SCTR
several	SVRL
severe	SVR
shallow	SHLW
shift	SHFT
shower	SHWR
sleet	SLT
slight	SLGT
slope	SLP
slow	SLO
small	SML
smoke	SMK
smooth	SMTH
snow	SNW
solid	SLD
somewhat	SMWHT
spread	SPRD

squall	SQAL
squall line	SQLN
stable	STBL
steady	STDY
storm	STM
strong	STG
surface	SFC
system	SYS

T

temperature	TEMP
temporary	TMPRY
tendency	TNDCY
terminal	TRML
terrain	TRRN
thereafter	THRFTR
thick	THK
thin	THN
thousand	THSD
through	THRU
throughout	THRUT
thunder	THDR
thundershower	TSHWR
thunderstorm	TSTM
today	TDA
tomorrow	TMW
tonight	TNGT
top of overcast	TOVC
topping	TPG
toward	TWD
trough	TROF
turbulence	TURBC

U

unrestricted	UNRSTD
unstable	UNSTBL
until	TIL
upper	UPR
upslope	UPSLP

V

valley	VLY
variable	VRBL
veer	VR
visibility	VSBY

W

warm	WRM
wave	WV
weak	WK
weaken	WKN
weather	WX or WEA
widely	WDLY
will	WL
wind	WND

EXCERPTS FROM AIRMAN'S INFORMATION MANUAL

GLOSSARY OF AERONAUTICAL TERMS

ADVISORY SERVICE—Advice and information provided by a facility to assist pilots in the safe conduct of flight and aircraft movement.

AIR DEFENSE IDENTIFICATION ZONE (ADIZ)—The area of airspace over land or water within which the ready identification, the location, and the control of aircraft are required in the interest of national security. For operating details see ADIZ procedures.

AIR NAVIGATION FACILITY (NAVAID)—Any facility used in, available for use in, or designed for use in aid of air navigation, including landing areas, lights, any apparatus or equipment for disseminating weather information, for signaling, for radio direction-finding, or for radio or other electronic communication, and any other structure or mechanism having a similar purpose for guiding or controlling flight in the air or the landing or takeoff of aircraft.

AIRPORT ADVISORY AREA—The area within five statute miles of an uncontrolled airport on which is located a Flight Service Station so depicted on the appropriate Sectional Aeronautical Chart.

AIRPORT ADVISORY SERVICE—A terminal service provided by a Flight Service Station located at an airport where a control tower is not operating.

AIRPORT INFORMATION DESK (AID)—A local airport unmanned facility designed for pilot self-service briefing, flight planning and filing of flight plans.

AIRPORT SURFACE DETECTION EQUIPMENT (ASDE)—Radar equipment specifically designed to detect all principal features on the surface of an airport, including vehicular traffic, and to present the entire picture on a radar indicator console in the control tower. ASDE has a maximum range of four miles, though its 16 inch diameter scope usually displays an area of only one mile radius about the control tower.

AIRPORT SURVEILLANCE RADAR (ASR)—Radar providing position of aircraft by azimuth and range data without elevation data. It is designed for a range of 50 miles. Used for Terminal approach and departure control.

AIRPORT TRAFFIC CONTROL SERVICE—Air traffic control service provided by an airport traffic control tower for aircraft operating on the movement area and in the vicinity of an airport.

AIRPORT TRAFFIC CONTROL TOWER (TOWER)—A facility providing airport traffic control service.

AIRPORT TRAFFIC AREA—Unless otherwise specifically designated (FAR Part 93), that airspace with a horizontal radius of five statute miles from the geographical center of any airport at which a control tower is operating, extending from the surface up to, but not including, an altitude of 3,000 feet above the elevation of the airport.

AIR ROUTE SURVEILLANCE RADAR (ARSR)—Long range radar which increases the capability of ATC for handling heavy en route traffic. An ARSR site is usually located at some distance from the ARTCC it serves. Range, approximately 200 NM.

AIR ROUTE TRAFFIC CONTROL CENTER (CENTER)—A facility established to provide air traffic control service to aircraft operating on an IFR flight plan within controlled airspace and principally during the en route phase of flight.

AIR TRAFFIC—Aircraft operating in the air or on an airport surface, exclusive of loading ramps and parking areas.

AIR TRAFFIC CLEARANCE (CLEARANCE)—An authorization by air traffic control for the purpose of preventing collision between known aircraft, for an aircraft to proceed under specified traffic conditions within controlled airspace.

AIR TRAFFIC CONTROL RADAR BEACON SYSTEM (ATCRBS)—See RADAR.

AIR TRAFFIC CONTROL SERVICE (CONTROL)—A service provided for the purpose of promoting the safe, orderly, and expeditious flow of air traffic, including airport, approach, and enroute air traffic control service.

ALERT AREA—Airspace which may contain a high volume of pilot training activities or an unusual type of aerial activity.

ALTITUDE RESERVATION (ALTRV)—Airspace utilization under prescribed conditions, normally employed for the mass movement of aircraft or other special user requirements which cannot otherwise be accomplished. ALTRV's are approved by the appropriate FAA facility.

APPROACH CONTROL FACILITY—A terminal facility (CIFRR, CS/T, RAPCON, RATCF, Tower, etc.) providing approach control service.

APPROACH CONTROL SERVICE—Air traffic control service provided by an approach control facility for arriving and departing VFR/IFR aircraft and, on occasion, tower en route control service.

APPROACH FIX—The fix from or over which final approach (IFR) to an airport is executed.

APPROACH GATE—That point on the final approach course which is 1 mile from the approach fix on the side away from the airport or 5 miles from the landing threshold, whichever is farther from the landing threshold.

APPROACH SEQUENCE—The order in which aircraft are positioned while awaiting approach clearance or while on approach.

ARC—The track over the ground of an aircraft flying at a constant distance from a navaid by reference to distance measuring equipment.

AREA NAVIGATION INSTRUMENT APPROACH—Instrument approach procedures based on area navigation capability and identified by the prefix RNAV followed by the procedure number.

AREA NAVIGATION (RNAV)—A method of navigation that permits aircraft operations on any desired course within the coverage of station-referenced navigation signals or within the limits of self-contained system capability.

AREA NAVIGATION (RNAV) ROUTE, DESIGNATED—An RNAV route, based on the current high altitude or low altitude VOR/DME coverage, as designated by the Administrator and published in FAR's 71 and 75.

AREA NAVIGATION (RNAV) ROUTE, ESTABLISHED—A predefined enroute segment, arrival or departure route (including RNAV SIDS and STARS).

AREA NAVIGATION TRANSITION ROUTE—Transition routes based on area navigation, within or between route structures, from the en route environment to the initial approach fix or from departure to the en route structure.

AUTOMATIC TERMINAL INFORMATION SERVICE (ATIS)—The continuous broadcast of recorded noncontrol information in selected high activity terminal areas. Its purpose is to improve controller effectiveness and to relieve frequency congestion by automating the repetitive transmission of essential but routine information.

BROADCAST—Transmission of information for which an acknowledgement is not expected.

CARDINAL ALTITUDES OR FLIGHT LEVELS—"Odd" or "even" thousand-foot altitudes or flight levels. Examples: 5000, 6000, 7000, FL 250, FL 260, FL 270.

CEILING—The height above the earth's surface of the lowest layer of clouds or obscuring phenomena that is reported as "broken," "overcast," or "obscuration" and not classified as "thin" or "partial."

CENTRAL ALTITUDE RESERVATION FACILITY (CARF)—An Air Traffic Service facility established to conduct the volume of coordination, planning and approval of special user requirements under the altitude reservation concept.

CLEAR AIR TURBULENCE (CAT)—Turbulence encountered in

air where no clouds are present; more popularly applied to high-level turbulence associated with wind shear; often encountered in the vicinity of the jet stream.

CLEARANCE LIMIT—The fix to which an aircraft is issued an air traffic clearance.

CLOSED TRAFFIC—Successive landing/takeoff/low approach operations without exiting or re-entering the traffic pattern. (Effective July 1, 1974.)

CODES—The numbers assigned to the multiple pulse reply signals transmitted by ATCRBS and SIF transponders.

CONSOLAN—A low frequency, long-distance navaid used principally for transoceanic navigation.

CONTACT APPROACH—An approach wherein an aircraft on an IFR flight plan, operating clear of clouds with at least one mile flight visibility and having received an air traffic control authorization, may deviate from the prescribed instrument approach procedure and proceed to the airport of destination by visual reference to the surface.

CONTERMINOUS U.S.—Forty-eight states and the District of Columbia.

CONTINENTAL U.S.—The 49 States located on the continent of North America and the District of Columbia.

CONTROLLED AIRSPACE—Airspace designated as continental control area, control area, control zone, terminal control area, or transition area, within which some or all aircraft may be subject to air traffic control. (See Chapter 3.)

COURSE—The intended direction of flight in the horizontal plane. Also a leg of an L/MF range.

CRUISE—A word used in an ATC clearance to authorize a pilot to conduct flight at any altitude from the MEA/MOCA up to and including the altitude specified in the clearance. The pilot may level off at any intermediary altitude within this block of airspace. Climb/descent within the block is to be made at the discretion of the pilot. However, once the pilot starts descent and reports leaving an altitude in the block he may not return to that altitude without additional ATC clearance. Further, it is approval for the pilot to proceed to and make an approach at destination airport and can be used in conjunction with:

a. An airport clearance limit at locations with an approved/prescribed instrument approach procedure. The FARs require that if an instrument letdown to an airport is necessary the pilot shall make the letdown in accordance with an approved/prescribed instrument approach procedure for that airport, or

b. An airport clearance limit at locations that are within/below/outside controlled airspace and without an approved/prescribed instrument approach procedure. Such a clearance is NOT AUTHORIZATION for the pilot to descend under IFR conditions below applicable MEA/MOCA nor does it imply that ATC is exercising control over aircraft in uncontrolled airspace; however, it provides a means for the aircraft to proceed to destination airport, descend and land in accordance with applicable FARs governing VFR flight operations. Also, this provides search and rescue protection until such time as the IFR flight plan is closed.

CRUISING ALTITUDE—A level determined by vertical measurement from mean sea level.

DECISION HEIGHT (DH)—The height, specified in MSL, above the highest runway elevation in the touchdown zone at which a missed approach shall be initiated if the required visual reference has not been established. This term is used only in procedures where an electronic glide slope provides the reference for descent, as in ILS or PAR.

DENSITY ALTITUDE—Altitude as determined by pressure altitude and existing ambient temperature. In standard atmosphere, density and pressure altitude are equal. For a given pressure altitude, the higher the temperature, the higher the density altitude. (For hazards of—See Mountain Flying in Chapter 5. Good Operating Practices)

DEPARTURE CONTROL—A function of approach control providing service for departing IFR aircraft and on occasion, VFR aircraft.

DISCRETE FREQUENCY—A frequency assigned a particular function.

DISTANCE MEASURING EQUIPMENT (DME)—Equipment (airborne and ground) used to measure, in nautical miles, the distance of an aircraft from a navaid.

DME FIX—A geographical position determined by reference to a navaid which provides distance and azimuth information and defined by a specified distance in nautical miles and a radial in degrees magnetic from that aid.

DISTANT EARLY WARNING IDENTIFICATION ZONE (DEWIZ)—An identification zone of defined dimensions extending upwards from the surface, in the Dew Line in Canada, and around the entire coastal area of Alaska. (See Security Control of Air Traffic in Chapter 4.)

DME SEPARATION—Spacing of aircraft in terms of distance determined by reference to distance measuring equipment (DME).

EMERGENCY LOCATOR TRANSMITTER (ELT)—A radio transmitter, attached to the aircraft structure, which operates from its own power source on 121.5 MHz and 243 MHz, transmitting a distinctive downward swept audio tone for homing purposes, and is designed to function without human action after an accident.

EN ROUTE AIR TRAFFIC CONTROL SERVICE—Air traffic control service provided aircraft on an IFR flight plan, generally by centers, when these aircraft are operating between departure and destination terminal areas.

EN ROUTE FLIGHT ADVISORY SERVICE (Flight Watch)—Is a service specifically designed to provide the pilot with timely weather information pertinent to his type of flight intended, route of flight and altitude.

EXPECTED APPROACH CLEARANCE TIME (EAC)—The time at which it is expected that an arriving aircraft will be cleared to begin approach for a landing.

EXPECTED FURTHER CLEARANCE TIME (EFC)—The time at which it is expected that additional clearance will be issued to an aircraft.

FINAL APPROACH FIX—The fix from or over which final approach (IFR) to an airport is executed.

FINAL APPROACH—IFR—The flight path of an aircraft which is inbound to the airport on an approved final instrument approach course, beginning at the final approach fix and extending to the airport or the point where circling for landing or missed approach is executed.

FINAL APPROACH—VFR—A flight path of a landing aircraft in the direction of landing along the extended runway centerline from the base leg to the runway.

FINAL CONTROLLER—That controller providing final approach guidance utilizing radar equipment.

FIX—A geographical position determined by visual reference to the surface by reference to one or more radio navaids, by celestial plotting, or by another navigational device.

FIXED-WING SPECIAL IFR OPERATIONS—Aircraft operating in accordance with a waiver and a Letter of Agreement within control zones specified in FAR 93.113 by IFR qualified pilots in IFR equipped aircraft and by pilots of agricultural and industrial aircraft.

FLIGHT LEVEL (FL)—A level of constant atmospheric pressure related to a reference datum of 29.92 inches of mercury. Each is stated in three digits that represent hundreds of feet. For example, FL 250 represents a barometric altimeter indication of 25,000 feet. FL 255 indicates 25,500 feet.

FLIGHT PLAN—Specified information relating to the intended flight of an aircraft that is filed orally or in writing with an air traffic control facility.

FLIGHT SERVICE STATION (FSS)—A facility operated by the FAA to provide flight assistance service.

FLIGHT VISIBILITY—The average forward horizontal distance from the cockpit of an aircraft in flight at which prominent unlighted objects may be seen and identified by day and prominent lighted objects may be seen and identified by night.

FLIP—Flight Information Publication.

FORMATION FLIGHT—More than one aircraft which, by prior arrangement between the pilots, operate as a single aircraft with regard to navigation and position reporting. (Ref: FAR 91.65). Separation between aircraft within the formation is the responsibility of the flight leader and the pilots of the other aircraft in the flight. This includes transition periods when aircraft within the formation are maneuvering to attain separation from each other to effect individual control and during join-up and breakaway.

    1. A *standard formation* is one in which a proximity of no more than one mile laterally or longitudinally and within 100 feet vertically from the flight leader is maintained by each wingman.

    2. *Non-standard formations* are those operating under any of the following conditions.

      a. When the flight leader has requested and ATC has approved other than standard formation dimensions.

      b. When operating within an authorized Altitude Reservation (ALTRV) or under the provisions of a Letter of Agreement.

      c. When the operations are conducted in airspace specifically designated for a special activity.

GROUND VISIBILITY—Prevailing horizontal visibility near the earth's surface as reported by the U.S. National Weather Service or an accredited observer.

HEIGHT ABOVE AIRPORT (HAA)—Indicates the height of the MDA above the published airport elevation. This is published in conjunction with circling minimums.

HEIGHT ABOVE TOUCHDOWN (HAT)—Indicates the height of the DH or MDA above the highest elevation in the touchdown zone. This is published in conjunction with straight-in minimums.

HERTZ (Hz)—Cycle per second.

HOLDING—A predetermined maneuver which keeps an aircraft within a specified airspace while awaiting further clearance.

HOLDING FIX—A specified fix used as a reference point in establishing and maintaining the position of an aircraft while holding.

"IDENT" FEATURE—The special feature in ATCRBS equipment and the "I/P" feature in certain SIF equipment used to distinguish one displayed select code from other codes.

IFR CONDITIONS—Weather conditions below the minimum prescribed for flight under VFR.

INITIAL APPROACH—"Initial approach" is the segment (of a standard instrument approach procedure) between the initial approach fix and the intermediate fix or the point where the aircraft is established on the intermediate course of final approach course.

INITIAL APPROACH ALTITUDE—Means the altitude (or altitudes, in High Altitude Procedures) prescribed for the initial approach segment of an instrument approach.

INLAND SAR REGION—The area in which the USAF, through the Aerospace Rescue and Recovery Service (ARRS), exercises the SAR coordinating function. It includes all of the inland area within the conterminous U.S., except the waters under jurisdiction of the U. S. Coast Guard for SAR purposes. The ARRS has divided the Inland Region into three sub-regions and a rescue coordination center in each sub-region executes coordination responsibilities.

INTENSIVE STUDENT JET TRAINING AREA—Airspace which contains the intensive training activities of military student jet pilots and in which restrictions are imposed on IFR flight.

INTERROGATOR—The ground-based surveillance radar beacon transmitter-receiver which scans in synchronism with a primary radar, transmitting discrete radio signals which repetitiously request all transponders, on the mode being used, to reply. The replies received are then mixed with the primary radar video to be displayed on the same plan position indicators. **"I/P" FEATURE**—(See "IDENT" feature.)

JET ADVISORY SERVICE—The service provided certain civil aircraft while operating within radar and nonradar jet advisory areas. Within radar jet advisory areas, civil aircraft receiving this service are provided radar flight following, radar traffic information, and vectors around observed traffic. In nonradar jet advisory areas, civil aircraft receiving this service are afforded standard IFR separation from all other aircraft known to ATC to be operating within these areas.

JET ROUTES—A high altitude route system at 18,000 feet MSL to Flight Level 450 inclusive. Jet routes are predicated on high altitude navigational aids." (For operating procedures applicable to this system, see En Route.)

JOINT USE RESTRICTED AREA—A restricted area within which IFR and/or VFR flight operations may be authorized by the controlling agency (a FAA facility) when not in use by the using agency.

LIMITED REMOTE COMMUNICATIONS OUTLET (LRCO)—An unmanned satellite air/ground communications facility operated as an LRCO-A, using the voice channel of the VOR transmission, and a receiver; or, an LRCO-B, a separate facility with transmit and receive capability. Both types effectively extend the service area of the controlling FSS.

LOCALIZER-TYPE DIRECTIONAL AID (LDA)—A facility of comparable utility and accuracy to a localizer but which is not part of a complete ILS and will not be aligned with the runway.

MARITIME SAR REGION—The area in which the U. S. Coast Guard exercises the SAR coordinating function. It includes the territories and possessions of the U. S. (except the Canal Zone and the inland region of Alaska) and areas of the high seas designated in the National SAR Plan. The USCG has divided the Maritime Region into sub-regions and a rescue coordination center in each sub-region exercises coordination responsibilities.

MAXIMUM AUTHORIZED ALTITUDE (MAA)—The highest altitude on a Federal airway, jet route, area navigation low or high route, or other direct route for which a MEA is designated in F.A.R. Part 95 at which adequate reception of navigation aid signals is assured.

MILES—As used in this publication, Miles means nautical miles unless otherwise specified, and means statute miles in conjunction with visibility.

MINIMUM CROSSING ALTITUDES (MCA)—The lowest altitudes at certain radio fixes at which an aircraft must cross when proceeding in the direction of a higher minimum en route IFR altitude.

MINIMUM DESCENT ALTITUDE (MDA)—Means the lowest altitude, expressed in feet above mean sea level, to which descent is authorized on final approach or during circling-to-land maneuvering in execution of a standard instrument approach procedure where no electronic glide slope is provided.

MINIMUM EN ROUTE IFR ALTITUDE (MEA)—The altitude in effect between radio fixes which assures acceptable navigational signal coverage and meets obstruction clearance requirements between those fixes. The MEA prescribed for a Federal airway or segment thereof, area navigation low or high route, or other direct route, applies to the entire width of the airway, segment or route between the radio fixes defining the airway, segment or route.

MINIMUM HOLDING ALTITUDE (MHA)—The lowest altitude prescribed for a holding pattern which assures navigational signal coverage, communications, and meets obstruction clearance requirements.

MINIMUM OBSTRUCTION CLEARANCE ALTITUDE (MOCA)—The specified altitude in effect between radio fixes on VOR/LF airways, off-airway routes or route segments, which meets obstruction clearance requirements for the entire route segment and which assures acceptable navigational signal coverage only within 22 nautical miles of a VOR.

MINIMUM RECEPTION ALTITUDE (MRA)—The lowest altitude required to receive adequate signals to determine specific VOR/VORTAC/TACAN fixes.

MINIMUM VECTORING ALTITUDE (MVA)—The lowest altitude,

expressed in feet above mean sea level, that aircraft will be vectored by a radar controller. This altitude assures communications, radar coverage, and meets obstruction clearance criteria.

MODE—The number or letter referring to the specific pulse spacing of the signal transmitted by an interrogator.

MOVEMENT AREA—The runways, taxiways, and other areas of an airport which are used for taxiing, takeoff, and landing of aircraft, exclusive of loading ramps and parking areas.

NATIONAL AIRSPACE SYSTEM (NAS)—The common system of air navigation and air traffic control encompassing communications facilities, air navigation facilities, airways, controlled airspace, special use airspace, and flight procedures authorized by Federal Aviation Regulations for domestic and international aviation.

NATIONAL SEARCH AND RESCUE PLAN—An interagency agreement whose purpose is to provide for the effective utilization of all available facilities in all types of search and rescue missions.

NON-PRECISION APPROACH PROCEDURE—means a standard instrument approach procedure in which no electronic glide slope is provided.

NOTICE TO AIRMEN—A notice identified either as a NOTAM or Airmen Advisory containing information concerning the establishment, condition, or change in any component of, or hazard in, the National Airspace System, the timely knowledge of which is essential to personnel concerned with flight operations.

(1) *NOTAM*. A Notice to Airmen in message form requiring expeditious and wide dissemination by telecommunications means.

(2) *Airmen Advisory*. A Notice to Airmen normally only given local dissemination, during preflight or in-flight briefing, or otherwise during contact with pilots.

OPTION APPROACH—An approach conducted and requested by a pilot which will result in a touch-and-go, missed approach, low approach, stop-and-go, and/or full stop landing. (Effective July 1, 1974.)

OUTER FIX—A fix in the destination terminal area, other than the approach fix, to which aircraft are normally cleared by an air route traffic control center or an approach control facility, and from which aircraft are cleared to the approach fix or final approach course.

OVERSEAS SAR REGION—Overseas unified command areas, including the inland area of Alaska, which are not included within the Inland Region or Maritime Region as defined by the National SAR Plan.

PARALLEL OFFSET ROUTE—A desired parallel track to the left or right of the parent designated or established airway/route.

PROHIBITED AREA—Airspace of defined dimensions identified by an area on the surface of the earth within which flight is prohibited.

RADAR (RADIO DETECTION AND RANGING)—A device which, by measuring the time interval between transmission and reception of radio pulses and correlating the angular orientation of the radiated antenna beam or beams in azimuth and/or elevation, provides information on range, azimuth and/or elevation of objects in the path of the transmitted pulses.

Radar beacon (secondary radar)—A radar system in which the object to be detected is fitted with cooperative equipment in the form of a radio receiver/transmitter (transponder). Radio pulses transmitted from the searching transmitter/receiver (interrogator) site are received in the cooperative equipment and used to trigger a distinctive transmission from the transponder. This latter transmission rather than a reflected signal, is then received back at the transmitter/receiver site.

RADAR ADVISORY—The term used to indicate that the provision of advice and information is based on radar observation. (See Advisory Service)

RADAR CONTACT—The term air traffic controllers use to indicate that an aircraft is identified on the radar display and that radar service can be provided until radar identification is lost or radar service is terminated, and that when the aircraft is informed of "radar contact" it automatically discontinues reporting over compulsory reporting points.

RADAR FLIGHT FOLLOWING—The general observation of the progress of identified aircraft targets sufficiently to retain their identity or the observation of the movement of specific radar targets.

RADAR IDENTIFICATION—The process of ascertaining that a radar target is the radar return from a particular aircraft.

RADAR SERVICE—A term which encompasses one or more of the following services based on the use of radar which can be provided by a controller to a pilot of a radar-identified aircraft.

Radar Separation—Radar spacing of aircraft in accordance with established minima.

Radar Navigation Guidance—Vectoring aircraft to provide course guidance.

Radar Monitoring—The radar flight following of aircraft, whose primary navigation is being performed by the pilot, to observe and note deviations from its authorized flight path airway, or route. As applied to the monitoring of instrument approaches from the final approach fix to the runway, it also includes the provision of advice on position relative to approach fixes and whenever the aircraft proceeds outside the prescribed safety zones.

RADAR SURVEILLANCE—The radar observation of a given geographical area for the purpose of performing some radar function.

RADAR VECTOR—A heading issued to an aircraft to provide navigational guidance by radar.

RADIAL—A radial is a magnetic bearing extending from a VOR, VORTAC, or TACAN.

RANDOM AREA NAVIGATION ROUTE—Direct flight, based on area navigation capability, between waypoints defined in terms of degree-distance fixes or offset from published or established routes/airways at a specified distance and direction.

REMOTE COMMUNICATIONS OUTLET (RCO)—An unmanned satellite air-to-ground communications station remotely controlled, providing UHF and VHF transmit and receive capability to extend the service range of the FSS.

REPORTING POINT—A geographical location in relation to which the position of an aircraft is reported.

RESCUE COORDINATION CENTER (RCC)—A primary search and rescue (SAR) facility suitably staffed by supervisory personnel and equipped for coordinating and controlling SAR operations in a region, sub-region, or sector as defined by the National SAR Plan.

RESTRICTED AREA—Airspace of defined dimensions identified by an area on the surface of the earth within which the flight of aircraft, while not wholly prohibited, is subject to restrictions.

ROLLOUT RVR—The RVR readout values obtained from RVR equipment located nearest the runway end.

ROUTE—A defined path, consisting of one or more courses, which an aircraft traverses in a horizontal plane over the surface of the earth. (See JET ROUTES)

RUNWAY REFERENCE POINT (RRP)—The point on the runway where the effective visual glide slope intercepts the runway surface.

SEARCH AND RESCUE FACILITY—A facility responsible for maintaining and operating a search and rescue service to render aid to persons and property in distress.

SELECT CODE—That code displayed when the ground interrogator and the airborne transponder are operating on the same mode and code simultaneously.

SEPARATION—Spacing of aircraft to achieve their safe and orderly movement in flight and while landing and taking off.

SEPARATION MINIMA—The minimum longitudinal, lateral, or vertical distances by which aircraft are spaced through the application of air traffic control procedures.

SHORT TAKE OFF AND LANDING (STOL) AIRCRAFT—An aircraft which has the capability of operating from a STOL runway in accordance with applicable airworthiness and operating regulations.

SHORT TAKE OFF AND LANDING (STOL) RUNWAY—A runway specifically designated and marked for STOL operations.

SPECIAL VFR CONDITIONS (SPECIAL VFR MINIMUM WEATHER CONDITIONS)—Weather conditions which are less than basic VFR weather conditions and which permit flight under Visual Flight Rules.

SPECIAL VFR OPERATIONS—Aircraft operating in accordance with clearances within control zones in weather conditions less than the basic VFR weather minima.

STANDARD INSTRUMENT DEPARTURE (SID)—A preplanned coded air traffic control IFR departure routing, preprinted for pilot use in graphic and textual or textual form only.

STANDARD TERMINAL ARRIVAL ROUTE (STAR)—A preplanned coded air traffic control IFR arrival routing, preprinted for pilot use in graphic and textual or textual form only.

STRAIGHT-IN APPROACH—IFR—An instrument approach wherein final approach is begun without first having executed procedure turn.

STRAIGHT-IN APPROACH—VFR—Entry of the traffic pattern by interception of the extended runway centerline without executing any other portion of the traffic pattern.

SURVEILLANCE APPROACH—An instrument approach conducted in accordance with directions issued by a controller referring to the surveillance radar display.

SURVIVAL RADIO EQUIPMENT—A self-buoyant, water resistant, portable emergency radio signaling device which operates from its own power source on 121.5 and/or 243 MHz, preferably on both emergency frequencies, transmitting a distinctive downward swept audio tone for homing purposes, which may or may not have voice capability, and which is capable of operation by unskilled persons. This type equipment is agreed upon internationally for extended overwater operations and is presently required for air carriers engaged in extended overwater operations.

THRESHOLD CROSSING HEIGHT (TCH)—The height of the straight line extension of the visual or electronic glide slope above the runway threshold.

TOUCHDOWN RVR—The RVR readout values obtained from RVR equipment serving the runway threshold.

TRACK—The flight path of an aircraft over the surface of the earth.

TRAFFIC INFORMATION–RADAR—Information issued to alert an aircraft to any radar targets observed on the radar display which may be in such proximity to its position or intended route of flight to warrant its attention.

TRAFFIC PATTERN—The traffic flow that is prescribed for aircraft landing at, taxiing on, and taking off from an airport. The usual components of a traffic pattern are upwind leg, crosswind leg, downwind leg, base leg, and final approach.

TRANSFER OF CONTROL—That action whereby the responsibility for the provision of separation to an aircraft is transferred from one controller to another.

TRANSPONDER—The airborne radar beacon receiver-transmitter which automatically receives radio signals from all interrogators on the ground, and which selectively replies with a specific reply pulse or pulse group only to those interrogations being received on the mode to which it is set to respond.

VERTICAL TAKE OFF AND LANDING (VTOL) AIRCRAFT—An aircraft which has the capability of vertical takeoff and landing. These aircraft include, but are not limited to, helicopters.

VFR CONDITIONS—Basic weather conditions prescribed for flight under Visual Flight Rules.

VISIBILITY, PREVAILING—The horizontal distance at which targets of known distance are visible over at least half of the horizon. It is normally determined by an observer on or close to the ground viewing buildings or other similar objects during the day and ordinary city lights at night. Under low visibility conditions the observations are usually made at the control tower. Visibility is REPORTED IN MILES AND FRACTIONS OF MILES in the Aviation Weather Report. If a single value does not adequately describe the visibility, additional information is reported in the "Remarks" section of the report.

VISIBILITY, RUNWAY VISIBILITY VALUE (RVV)—The visibility determined for a particular runway by a transmissometer, a photoelectric device calibrated in terms of a human observer. A meter in the control tower provides a continuous indication of the visibility (reported in miles or fractions of miles) for the runway. RVV is used in lieu of prevailing visibility in determining minimums for a particular runway. This program is gradually being replaced by RVR at transmissometer locations.

VISIBILITY, RUNWAY VISUAL RANGE (RVR)—An instrumentally derived value, based on standard calibrations, that represents the horizontal distance a pilot will see down the runway from the approach end; it is based on the sighting of either high intensity runway lights or on the visual contrast of other targets—whichever yields the greater visual range. RVR, in contrast to prevailing or runway visibility, is based on what a pilot in a moving aircraft should see looking down the runway. RVR is horizontal, AND NOT SLANT, visual range. It is based on the measurement of a transmissometer made near the touchdown point of the instrument runway and is REPORTED IN HUNDREDS OF FEET. RVR provides an additional operating minimum at fields equipped with specified navigational aids. For example, at the present time the RVR minimum at Newark is 2400 ft. [in combination with a decision height (DH) of 211' MSL] for both takeoffs and landings regardless of the reported ceiling and visibility.

VISUAL APPROACH—An approach wherein an aircraft on an IFR flight plan, operating in VFR conditions under the control of a radar facility and having an air traffic control authorization, may deviate from the prescribed instrument approach procedure and proceed to the airport of destination by visual reference to the surface.

VOT (VOR TEST SIGNAL)—A ground facility which emits a test signal to check VOR receiver accuracy. System is limited to ground use only.

WARNING AREA—Airspace which may contain hazards to nonparticipating aircraft in international airspace.

WAYPOINT—A predetermined geographical position used for route definition and/or progress reporting purposes that is defined relative to a VORTAC station position. Two subsequently related waypoints define a route segment.

WEATHER ADVISORY—In aviation forecast practice, an expression of hazardous weather conditions not predicted in the area forecast, as they affect the operation of air traffic and as prepared by the NWS.

FLIGHT TEST GUIDE

INSTRUMENT PILOT Airplane . . .

PREFACE

Part 61 (revised) of Federal Aviation Regulations, effective November 1, 1973, establishes a new concept of pilot training and certification requirements. To provide a transition to these revised requirements, Part 61 (revised) permits the applicant, for a period of 1 year after the effective date, to meet either the previous requirements or those contained in the revised part. AC 61-17B, *Instrument Pilot Airplane Flight Test Guide*, dated 1972, outlines the previous requirements.

This flight test guide, AC 61-56, has been prepared by Flight Standards Service of the Federal Aviation Administration to assist the applicant and his instructor in preparing for the flight test for the Instrument Pilot Airplane Rating under Part 61 (revised). It contains information and guidance concerning the pilot operations, procedures, and maneuvers relevant to the flight test required for the Instrument Rating. A suggested flight test checklist is included for the convenience of those who may find such a checklist useful.

In addition to providing help to the applicant and his instructor, this guide will be useful to FAA Inspectors and designated pilot examiners in the conduct and standardization of flight tests.

GENERAL INFORMATION

PILOT TRAINING AND CERTIFICATION CONCEPT

Part 61 of the Federal Aviation Regulations has been revised and upgraded to reflect the complexity of the modern aircraft as well as its operating environment. In the past, airman certification requirements could be met by training a student to pass a written test and then to demonstrate his ability to perform predetermined flight training maneuvers during a flight test. Rather than merely duplicating on the flight test the maneuvers used for training, the new training and certification concept requires that the applicant receive instruction in and demonstrate his competency in *all pilot operations* listed in pertinent sections of the Part 61 (revised).

A pilot operation, as used herein, is a group of related procedures and maneuvers involving skills and knowledge required to safely and efficiently function as a pilot. The specific procedures and maneuvers used to teach the pilot operations are not listed in Part 61 (revised). Instead, the instructor is permitted to select procedures and maneuvers from FAA-approved training publications pertinent to the certificate or rating sought. The instructor indicates by logbook endorsement that the applicant has demonstrated competency in all the required pilot operations and considers him qualified to pass the flight test. On the flight test, the examiner[1] selects the proce-

---

[1] The word "examiner" is used hereafter in this guide to denote either the Federal Aviation Administration Inspector or designated pilot examiner who conducts an official flight test.

dures and maneuvers to be performed by the applicant to show competency in each required pilot operation.

The procedures and maneuvers appropriate to the Instrument Pilot Airplane rating are contained in *Instrument Flying Handbook, AC 61-27B; Airman's Information Manual;* and *Civil Use of U.S. Government Approach Procedure Charts, AC 90-1A.*

USE OF THIS GUIDE

The pilot operations in this flight test guide, indicated by Roman numerals, are required by § 61.65 of Part 61 (revised). This guide is intended only to outline appropriate pilot operations and the minimum standards for the performance of each procedure or maneuver which will be accepted by the examiner as evidence of the pilot's competency. It is not intended that the applicant be tested on every procedure or maneuver within each pilot operation, but only those considered necessary by the examiner to determine competency in each pilot operation. Throughout the flight test, certain procedures or maneuvers may be evaluated separately or in combination with other procedures or maneuvers.

When, in the judgment of the examiner, certain demonstrations are impractical, competency may be determined by oral testing.

This guide contains an **Objective** for each required pilot operation. Under each pilot operation, pertinent procedures or maneuvers are listed with **Descriptions** and **Acceptable Performance Guidelines.**

1. The **Objective** states briefly the purpose of each pilot operation required on the flight test.

2. The **Description** provides information on what may be asked of the applicant regarding the selected procedure or maneuver. The procedures or maneuvers listed have been found most effective in demonstrating the objective of that particular pilot operation.

3. The **Acceptable Performance Guidelines** include the factors which will be taken into account by the examiner in deciding whether the applicant has met the objective of the pilot operation. The airspeed, altitude, and heading tolerances given represent the minimum performance expected in good flying conditions. However, consistently exceeding these tolerances before corrective action is initiated or prematurely descending below DH or MDA, is indicative of an unsatisfactory performance. Any procedure or action, or the lack thereof, which requires the intervention of the examiner to maintain safe flight will be disqualifying.

In the event the applicant takes the instrument pilot flight test and the commercial pilot flight test simultaneously, the maneuvers selected by the examiner for each may be combined and evaluated together, where practicable.

GENERAL PROCEDURES FOR FLIGHT TESTS

The ability of an applicant for an instrument pilot airplane rating to perform the required pilot operations is based on the following:

1. Completing a checklist for instrument flight operations appropriate to the airplane and equipment used.

2. Performing procedures and maneuvers within the airplane's performance capabilities and limitations, including use of the airplane's systems.

3. Performing emergency procedures and maneuvers appropriate to the airplane used.

4. Piloting the airplane with smoothness and accuracy.

5. Exercising judgment.

6. Applying his aeronautical knowledge.

7. Showing that he is master of the aircraft, with the successful outcome of a procedure or maneuver never seriously in doubt.

If the applicant fails any of the required pilot operations, he fails the flight test. The examiner or the applicant may discontinue the test at any time when the failure of a required pilot operation makes the applicant ineligible for the certificate or rating sought. If the test is discontinued, the applicant is entitled to credit for only those entire pilot operations that he has successfully performed.

FLIGHT TEST PREREQUISITES

An applicant for the instrument pilot airplane flight test is required by revised § 61.39 of the Federal Aviation Regulations to have: (1) passed the Instrument Pilot Airplane Written Test within 24 months before the date he takes the flight test; (2) the applicable instruction and aeronautical experience prescribed in Part 61 (revised); (3) at least a third class medical certificate issued within the past 24 months; and (4) a written statement from a certificated instrument flight instructor certifying that he has given the applicant flight instruction in preparation for the flight test within 60 days preceding the date of application, and finds him competent to pass the flight test and to have a satisfactory knowledge of the subject areas in which he is shown to be deficient by his airman written test report.

AIRPLANE AND EQUIPMENT REQUIREMENTS FOR FLIGHT TEST

The applicant is required by revised § 61.45 to provide an airworthy airplane for the flight test. This airplane must be capable of, and its operating limitations must not prohibit, the pilot operations required on the flight test. Flight instruments required are those appropriate for controlling the airplane in instrument conditions. Appropriate flight instruments are considered to be those outlined in FAR Part 91 for flight under instrument flight rules. The required radio equipment is that necessary for communications with ATC and for the performance of VOR, ADF, and ILS (glide slope and localizer) approaches unless the applicant makes prior arrangements to demonstrate ADF or ILS approaches, or both, in an instrument ground trainer.

The instrument ground trainer used for the demonstration of ADF and ILS approaches must have at least: (1) the flight instruments required by FAR Part 91 for flight under instrument flight rules; (2) a means for simulating ADF or ILS approaches (including a marker beacon), as appropriate; (3) a means for simulating radio communications with ATC; (4) separately operating rudder, aileron, and elevator controls; (5) a means for simulating the effect of various wind conditions; and (6) a means for recording the simulated flight path.

PILOT OPERATIONS
Procedures/Maneuvers

I. MANEUVERING BY REFERENCE TO INSTRUMENTS

Objective

To determine that the applicant can safely and accurately maneuver the airplane in instrument conditions.

Procedures/Maneuvers

A. Straight-and-Level Flight

1. Description The applicant may be asked to demonstrate straight-and-level flight with changes in airspeed and airplane configuration. He will be expected to maintain altitude and heading and to accurately control airspeed.

2. Acceptable Performance Guidelines The applicant's performance shall be evaluated on the basis of his ability to maintain altitude within ±100 ft., heading within ±10°, and airspeed within ±10 kts. of that assigned.

B. Turns

1. Description The applicant may be asked to demonstrate heading changes using various means to determine rate and amount of turn. He should perform these turns in level, climbing, and descending flight. This may also include changes in airspeed and airplane configuration. Turns for this demonstration may be selected from the following:

    a. Standard rate turns.
    b. Timed turns.
    c. Turns to predetermined headings.
    d. Magnetic compass turns.
    e. Steep turns.

2. Acceptable Performance Guidelines The applicant's performance shall be evaluated on the basis of his ability to complete turns within ±10° of desired headings. He shall maintain altitude within ±100 ft. and airspeed within ±10 kts. of that assigned.

C. Climbs and Descents

1. Description The applicant may be asked to demonstrate changes of altitude including:

    a. Constant airspeed climbs and descents.
    b. Rate climbs and descents.
    c. Climbs and descents to predetermined altitudes and headings.

The examiner may request that the above demonstrations be performed in various airplane configurations.

2. Acceptable Performance Guidelines The applicant's performance shall be evaluated on his ability to maintain airspeed within ±10 kts. and vertical rate within ±200 ft. per minute of that desired. Level-offs and rollouts shall be completed within ±100 ft. and ±10° of the altitude and heading assigned.

II. IFR NAVIGATION

Objective

To determine that the applicant can safely and efficiently navigate in instrument conditions in the National Airspace System in compliance with Instrument Flight Rules and ATC clearances and instructions.

Procedures/Maneuvers

A. Time, Speed, and Distance

1. Description The applicant may be asked to demonstrate preflight and inflight computations to determine ETE, ETA, wind correction angle, and groundspeed.

2. Acceptable Performance Guidelines The applicant's performance shall be evaluated on the basis of his ability to make accurate and timely computations.

B. VOR Navigation

1. Description The applicant may be asked to demonstrate:

    a. Intercepting a VOR radial at a predetermined angle.
    b. Tracking on a selected VOR radial.
    c. Determinating position using intersecting VOR radials.

2. Acceptable Performance Guidelines The applicant's performance shall be evaluated on the basis of his accuracy in determining his position by means of cross bearings, his interception procedures, and his ability to maintain orientation and the assigned flight path.

C. ADF Navigation

1. Description The applicant may be asked to use ADF for homing, intercepting, and tracking predetermined radio bearings to and from non-directional beacons, and for determining position by use of cross bearings.

2. Acceptable Performance Guidelines The applicant's performance shall be evaluated on the basis of his accuracy in determining his position by means of cross bearings, his interception procedures, and his ability to maintain orientation and the assigned track.

D. Navigation by ATC Instructions

1. Description The applicant may be asked to show that he can comply with ATC instructions and procedures. This includes navigation by adherence to radar vectors and specific instructions for headings and altitude changes.

2. Acceptable Performance Guidelines Evaluation of the applicant's performance shall be based on his promptness and accuracy in reponding to and complying with

ATC navigation instructions.

III. INSTRUMENT APPROACHES

Objective

To determine that the applicant can execute safe and accurate instrument approaches to published minimums under instrument conditions.

Procedures/Maneuvers

A. VOR Approach

1. Description The applicant may be requested to demonstrate a published VOR approach procedure.

2. Acceptable Performance Guidelines The applicant shall descend at the proper rate to the MDA so as to arrive at a position from which a normal landing approach can be made, straight-in or circling, as appropriate. Deviations of more than ±10 kts. from the desired approach speed shall be disqualifying. Errors in altitude of more than 100 ft. below prescribed altitudes during the initial approach or descending below the MDA prior to the examiner reporting the runway environment in sight, shall be disqualifying. If a circling approach is made, exceeding the radius of turn dictated by published visibility minimums or descending below the MDA prior to reaching a position from which a normal approach to the landing runway can be made, shall also be disqualifying.

B. ILS Approach

1. Description The applicant may be requested to demonstrate a published ILS approach procedure.

2. Acceptable Performance Guidelines As directed by the examiner, the applicant shall descend on a straight-in approach to the DH, or on a circling approach to the MDA, arriving at a position from which a normal landing approach can be made straight-in or circling, as appropriate. Deviations of more than ±10 kts. from the desired approach speed shall be disqualifying. Errors in altitude of more than 100 ft. below prescribed altitudes during the initial approach, full scale deflection of the CDI or the glide slope indicator after glide slope interception, or descending below the DH or MDA prior to the examiner reporting the runway environment in sight, shall be disqualifying. If a circling approach is made, exceeding the radius of turn dictated by published visibility minimums or descending below the MDA prior to reaching a position from which a normal approach to the landing runway can be made, shall also be disqualifying.

C. Localizer Approach

1. Description The applicant may be requested to demonstrate a published localizer approach, or an ILS (back course) approach procedure.

2. Acceptable Performance Guidelines The applicant shall descend at the proper rate to the MDA so as to arrive at a position from which a normal landing approach can be made, straight-in or circling, as appropriate. Deviations of more than ±10 kts. from the desired approach speed shall be disqualifying. Errors in altitude of more than 100 ft. below prescribed altitudes during the initial approach, full scale deflection of the CDI, or descending below the MDA prior to the examiner reporting the runway environment in sight, shall be disqualifying. If a circling approach is made, exceeding the radius of turn dictated by published visibility minimums or descending below the MDA prior to reaching a position from which a normal approach to the landing runway can be made, shall also be disqualifying.

D. ADF Approach

1. Description The applicant may be requested to demonstrate an ADF approach using a published NDB (non-directional beacon) approach procedure.

2. Acceptable Performance Guidelines The applicant shall descend at the proper rate to the MDA so as to arrive at a position from which a normal landing approach can be made, straight-in or circling, as appropriate. Deviations of more than ±10 kts. from the desired approach speed shall be disqualifying. Errors in altitude of more than 100 ft. below prescribed altitudes during the initial approach, or descending below the MDA prior to the examiner reporting the runway environment in sight, shall be disqualifying. If a circling approach is made, exceeding the radius of turn dictated by published visibility minimums or descending below the MDA prior to reaching a position from which a normal approach to the landing runway can be made, shall also be disqualifying.

IV. CROSS–COUNTRY FLYING[2]

Objective

To determine that the applicant can competently conduct en route and terminal operations within the National Airspace System in instrument conditions, using radio aids and complying with ATC instructions.

Procedures/Maneuvers

A. Selection of Route

1. Description The applicant may be asked to select a route for a 250 nautical mile IFR flight, based on information contained in the *Airman's Information Manual*, *En route Charts, Instrument Approach Procedure Charts*, and other appropriate sources of information. This includes facilities for all departures and arrivals.

2. Acceptable Performance Guidelines The applicant's performance shall be evaluated on his ability to obtain and apply pertinent information for the selection of a suitable route. Failure to determine current status and usability of facilities shall be disqualifying.

B. Procurement and Analysis of Weather Information

1. Description The applicant may be

---

[2] The examiner may ask the applicant to plan an IFR cross–country flight and set out on course. The flight may be continued only long enough for the examiner to determine the applicant's competence in IFR cross–country flying.

asked to procure and analyze weather reports and forecasts pertinent to his proposed flight. This information should provide (1) forecast weather conditions at destination, (2) the basis for selecting an alternate airport, and (3) the basis for selecting a route to avoid severe weather.

2. Acceptable Performance Guidelines The applicant shall correctly analyze the weather reports and forecasts and understand their significance to the proposed flight. Failure to recognize conditions which would be hazardous to his flight shall be disqualifying.

C. Development of Flight Log

1. Description The applicant may be asked to develop a flight log for the proposed flight. This log should include at least the en route courses, estimated ground speeds, distances between checkpoints, estimated time between checkpoints (ETEs), and amount of fuel required. On the basis of his log, the applicant is expected to prepare an IFR flight plan for the examiner's review.

2. Acceptable Performance Guidelines The applicant's performance shall be evaluated on the completeness and accuracy of his flight log and flight plan.

D. Aircraft Performance and Limitations

1. Description The applicant may be asked to apply the information contained in the airplane flight manual or manufacturer's published recommendations to determine the aircraft performance capabilities and weight and balance limitations.

2. Acceptable Performance Guidelines The applicant's performance shall be evaluated on his proper application of aircraft performance and loading data in the conduct of the proposed flight.

E. Aircraft Systems and Equipment

1. Description The applicant may be asked to explain the use of the instruments, avionic equipment, and any special system installed in the airplane used, including indications of malfunctions and limitations of these units.

2. Acceptable Performance Guidelines The applicant's performance shall be evaluated on his knowledge of the instruments and equipment which are installed in the airplane used for the flight test.

F. Preflight Check of Instruments and Equipment

1. Description Prior to takeoff, the applicant may be asked to perform a systematic operational check of engine instruments, flight instruments, and avionic equipment. All equipment should be appropriately set for his departure clearance.

2. Acceptable Performance Guidelines The applicant's performance shall be evaluated on the thoroughness and accuracy of his checks and procedures. Failure to properly check and set instruments and equipment shall be disqualifying.

G. Maintaining Airways or ATC Routes (see Pilot Operation II).

H. Use of Radio Communications

1. Description The applicant may be asked to demonstrate the use of two-way radio voice communication procedures for reports, ATC clearances, and other instructions. Radio communications may be simulated at the discretion of the examiner.

2. Acceptable Performance Guidelines The applicant's performance shall be evaluated on the basis of his use of proper frequencies, correct phraseology, and the conciseness, clarity, and timeliness of his transmissions. Acceptance of clearances based on facilities or frequencies not appropriate to the equipment being used or to the aircraft performance capabilities, shall be disqualifying.

I. Holding Procedures

1. Description The applicant may be directed, by ATC or the examiner, to hold in either a standard or a non-standard pattern at a specified fix. He should make a proper entry as described in the *Airman's Information Manual*, remain within protected airspace, apply adequate wind correction, and accurately time the pattern so as to leave the fix at the time specified.

2. Acceptable Performance Guidelines The applicant's performance shall be evaluated on his compliance with instructions, and his entry procedure, orientation, accuracy and timing. Deviations of more than ± 100 ft. from the prescribed altitude or more than ± 10 kts. from holding airspeed shall be disqualifying.

J. Instrument Approach Procedures (see Pilot Operation III).

V. EMERGENCIES

Objective

To determine that the applicant can promptly recognize and take appropriate action for abnormal or emergency conditions and equipment malfunctions while in instrument conditions.

Procedures/Maneuvers

A. Recovery from Unusual Attitudes

1. Description The examiner may place the airplane in unusual flight attitudes which may result from vertigo, wake turbulence, lapse of attention, or abnormal trim conditions. The applicant should recover and return to the original altitude and heading. For this demonstration, the examiner may limit the use of flight instruments by simulating malfunctions of the attitude indicator and heading indicator.

2. Acceptable Performance Guidelines Evaluation shall be based on the promptness, smoothness, and accuracy demonstrated. All maneuvering shall be conducted within the operating limitations for the airplane used. Any loss of control which makes it necesary for the examiner to take over to avoid exceeding any operating limitation of the airplane shall be disqualifying.

B. Equipment or Instrument Malfunctions

1. Description The applicant may be

asked to demonstrate the emergency operation of the retractable gear, flaps, and the electrical, fuel, deicing, and hydraulic systems if operationally practical. Emergency operations such as the use CO_2 pressure for gear extension, or the discharge of a pressure fire extinguisher system will be *simulated only*. Occasionally, during the performance of flight maneuvers described elsewhere in this guide, the examiner may simulate a partial or complete loss of flight instruments, navigation instruments, or equipment.

2. Acceptable Performance Guidelines The applicant shall respond to emergency situations in accordance with procedures outlined in the manufacturer's published recommendations. The applicant's performance shall be evaluated on the basis of his competency in maintaining aircraft control, his knowledge of the emergency procedures, the judgment he displays, and the accuracy of his operations.

C. Loss of Radio Communications

1. Description The examiner may simulate loss of radio communications. The applicant should know the actions required pertaining to altitudes, routes, holding procedures, and approaches.

2. Acceptable Performance Guidelines Evaluation shall be based on the applicant's knowledge of, and compliance with, the pertinent procedures required by Part 91 of the *Federal Aviation Regulations* and the emergency procedures outlined in the *Airman's Information Manual*. An explanation or simulation of the proper procedures for loss of radio communications is acceptable.

D. Engine–Out Procedures (Multiengine Airplane)

1. Description The applicant may be asked to demonstrate his ability to positively and accurately maneuver the airplane after one engine has been throttled to simulate the drag of a feathered propeller, or with one propeller feathered, as agreed upon by the applicant and examiner. Feathering of a propeller for flight test purposes will be performed only under such conditions and at such altitudes and positions that a safe landing can readily be accomplished if an emergency develops or difficulty is encountered in unfeathering.

2. Acceptable Performance Guidelines Evaluation shall be based on the applicant's ability to promptly identify the inoperative engine, and to follow the procedures outlined in the manufacturer's published recommendations. In cruising flight, the applicant shall maintain his heading and altitude within $\pm 20°$ and ± 100 ft. If the airplane is incapable of maintaining altitude with an engine inoperative under existing circumstances, the applicant shall maintain an airspeed within ± 5 kts. of the engine-out best rate-of-climb speed.

During approaches, the applicant shall promptly correct any deviation from the desired flight path.

Any loss of control that makes it necessary for the examiner to take over, or any attempt at prolonged flight contrary to the single-engine operating limitations of the airplane, shall be disqualifying.

E. Missed Approach Procedures

1. Description At any time during an instrument approach, the applicant may be asked to execute the missed approach procedure depicted on the approach chart being used. If the examiner does not specifically ask for the missed approach but he fails to report the runway in sight at the DH or MDA, the applicant should immediately initiate the missed approach procedure as described on the chart, or as directed by ATC.

2. Acceptable Performance Guidelines The evaluation shall be based on the applicant's timely and correct execution of the missed approach procedure.

F. ASR (Airport Surveillance Radar) Approach

1. Description The applicant may be requested to demonstrate an ASR approach procedure as directed by ATC or simulated by the examiner to the published straight-in or circling MDA.

2. Acceptable Performance Guidelines The applicant shall descend at the proper rate to the MDA so as to arrive at a position from which a normal landing approach can be made, straight-in or circling, as appropriate. Deviations of more than ±10 kts. from the desired approach speed shall be disqualifying. Errors in altitude of more than 100 ft. below prescribed altitudes during the initial approach, or descending below the MDA prior to the examiner reporting the runway environment in sight, shall be disqualifying. If a circling approach is made, exceeding the radius of turn dictated by published visibility minimums or descending below the MDA prior to reaching a position from which a normal approach to the landing runway can be made, shall also be disqualifying.

APPLICANT'S FLIGHT TEST GUIDE CHECKLIST

(Suggested)

APPOINTMENT WITH INSPECTOR OR EXAMINER: Name _____

Time/Date _____

PROPERLY CERTIFICATED AIRPLANE WITH DUAL CONTROLS

☐ View-Limiting Device
☐ Aircraft Documents:
  Airworthiness Certificate
  Registration Certificate
  Operating Limitations
☐ Aircraft Maintenance Records:
  Airworthiness Inspections
  Static System and Altimeter Check
☐ FCC Station License

PERSONAL EQUIPMENT

☐ Current Charts
☐ Computer and Plotter
☐ Flight Plan Form
☐ Flight Logs

PERSONAL RECORDS

☐ Pilot Certificate
☐ Medical Certificate
☐ Signed Recommendation
☐ Written Test Results
☐ Logbook
☐ Notice of Disapproval
  (if applicable)
☐ Approved School Graduation Certificate
  (if applicable)
☐ FCC Radiotelephone Operator Permit
☐ Examiner's Fee
  (if applicable)

INDEX

A

Acceleration Error 12
ADF methods and procedures 48
Advection 89, 90
Advection fog 90
Aerodrome symbols 59
Air mass thunderstorm 95
Aircraft approach categories 66
Aircraft attitude 7, 13
Aircraft power 13, 14, 15, 16, 19, 20, 21
Airman's Information
   Manual (AIM) 121, 123, 169, 173, 182, 183, 184,
                    185, 189, 190, 191, 192, 193
AIRMET 113, 114, 115, 117, 120
Airport/facility directory 185
Airports 129, 133, 134, 135, 183, 184
Airport Surveillance
   Radar (ASR) 33, 56, 58, 63, 64, 66, 67, 70, 189
Air Route Surveillance Radar (ARSR) 33, 189
Air Route Traffic Control
   Center (ARTCC) 78, 79, 80, 81, 85, 189
Air Traffic Control Radar Beacon
   System (ARTCBS) 128, 189, 192
Airspeed indicator 8, 9
Airspeed system 9
Airspeed, types of 9
Air Traffic Control (ATC) 78, 81, 84, 85, 86
Airways system 78, 79
Alternate airport 56, 66, 67, 146, 149, 150, 155
Altimeter 8, 9, 138, 139, 147, 148, 155
Altimeter errors 9, 10
Altocumulus clouds 91, 93
Altostratus clouds 91, 93
Aneroid 9, 88
Antenna 29, 128
Anticyclone 88
Approach charts 56, 58, 59, 62, 63, 64, 65, 68, 69, 70,
                 71, 72, 73, 74, 75, 76, 121
Approach control 79, 81, 85, 189
Approach lighting 32, 64, 67, 134, 135
Area forecasts 102, 110, 111, 115, 117, 119, 120
ARSR 33, 189
ARTCC 78, 79, 80, 81, 85, 189
ARTC center 78, 79, 80, 81, 189
Artificial horizon ...8, 10, 11, 13, 14, 15, 17, 18, 23, 14, 148
ARTSIII 141
ASR 56, 58, 63, 64, 66, 67, 70, 189
ATCRBS 128, 189, 192
ATIS 64, 189
Atmospheric pressure 88
Attitude control 7, 13
Attitude indicator ..8, 10, 11, 13, 14, 15, 17, 18, 23, 24, 148
Attitude instrument flying 7
Automatic Direction Finding
   (ADF) 31, 48, 49, 50, 51, 52, 53, 54, 55, 56, 57, 58, 60, 64
Automatic Terminal Information Service (ATIS) ...64, 189
Aviation weather
      forecasts . 102, 108, 109, 110, 111, 112, 113, 115, 117, 120
Aviation weather reports ..106, 107, 108, 115, 117, 119, 110

B

Back course 60, 61, 63, 64
Bank control 13, 16, 17, 22, 23
Barometers 88
Basic flight maneuvers 12
Bearing, ADF 31, 48, 51, 52, 53, 55
Bearing, VOR 28, 35, 37, 47

C

Calibrated airspeed 155
Calibrated leak 10
Categories of turbulence intensity 173
Category II operations 56, 141, 142, 153, 155
CDI . 29, 30, 35, 36, 37, 41, 42, 43, 44, 45, 46, 47, 54, 58, 60
Ceiling 63, 66, 91, 103, 107, 108, 109, 110, 111, 189
Celsius (Centigrade) temperature scale 87
Checklist, weather 120
Circling approach 58, 68, 69, 70, 71, 72, 73
Cirrocumulus clouds 91
Cirrostratus clouds 91
Clearance delivery frequency 81
Clearances 79, 81, 82, 85, 148, 152, 190
Clear ice 95, 98
Climbs and descents 14, 15, 16, 19, 21, 22
Clouds 90, 91, 92, 93, 94, 95, 96, 97, 98, 99, 100, 101
Clouds with extensive vertical development 91
Codes, Transponder 126, 127, 128, 190
Cold front 99, 100, 101
Commercial Broadcast Stations 26, 34, 48
Communications 26, 85, 154
Compass 8, 11, 12
Compass correction card 12
Compass errors 12
Compass locator, outer marker (LOM) 31, 32, 33, 34, 48, 59
Compulsory reports 85
Condensation nuclei 88
Contact approach 190
Continental control area 129
Controlled airspace 129, 190
Control zone 129, 130
Convection 89, 90
Course Deviation Indicator (CDI)
   29, 30, 35, 36, 37, 41, 42, 43, 44, 45, 46, 47, 54, 58, 60
Course interception
   VOR 37, 38
   ADF 51
Course-Line Computer (CLC) 139
Course selector 29
Cross-checking the instruments 18, 24
Cruise clearance 190
Cumuliform clouds 90, 91, 93, 94, 95
Cumulonimbus clouds 91, 94
Cumulus clouds 90

D

Decision height (DH) 63, 64, 67, 69, 190
Density altitude 124, 190

Departure control 79, 81, 190
Depiction charts, weather 102, 103, 115, 120
Descents 15, 16, 21, 58, 84
Deviation 12
Dew point 90, 107
Differential pressure instruments 9
Directional gyro 8, 10, 11, 18
Directional indicators 11
Displaced threshold 134, 135
Dissipating stage 96
Distance Measuring Equipment (DME) 28, 30, 31, 190
Downdrafts 96
Drizzle 107

E

Earth's atmosphere 87
Effects of air stability and instability 87
Errors, altimeter 9, 10
Enroute low altitude charts 78, 121
Enroute reports 84
Emergency frequency 28

F

Facsimile charts 102
False glide slope 32, 60
Fahrenheit temperature scale 87
Fan marker 31
Final approach 56, 62, 77, 84, 86, 190
Flight instruments 8, 9, 10, 11, 12, 147, 148
Flight plan 80, 121, 122, 123, 149, 150, 190
Flight planning 121, 122, 123, 124
Flight Service Station 28, 78, 81, 85, 116, 117, 118, 119, 120, 190
Fog 90, 94, 103, 107
Forecasts, aviation weather
    102, 108, 109, 110, 111, 112, 113, 115, 117, 120
Freezing level 110, 111
Frequencies
  26, 27, 28, 29, 30, 31, 32, 33, 34, 85, 117, 118, 119, 122, 126
Fronts and frontal
    systems 90, 95, 98, 99, 100, 101, 102, 105, 111, 117
Frontal thunderstorms 95

G

Glide slope (path) 32, 34, 58, 60, 61, 63, 64
Glide slope indicator 30
Glossary of aeronautical terms 189
Greenwich Mean Time (GMT) 186
Gyroscopic flight instruments 8, 10, 11

H

Hail 95, 96
Heading 11, 18, 22, 28, 35, 36, 37, 41, 44, 48, 50, 51, 52, 53, 54
Heading indicators 11, 18
Heights of clouds 91, 93, 94
High clouds 91
Height Above Touchdown (HAT) 63, 64, 191
Holding 41, 42, 43, 44, 45, 46, 47, 54, 55, 56, 60, 61, 65, 82, 191
Holding pattern entry 45, 46, 47
Homing, ADF 31, 48, 49, 53, 55, 60
Horizon, artificial ..8, 10, 11, 13, 14, 15, 17, 18, 23, 24, 148
Hourly sequence reports...103, 106, 107, 108, 115, 117, 120

I

Icing, accretion rate 97, 98
Icing, types of 98
IFR altitudes/flight levels 84, 85, 131
ILS approach
  31, 32, 34, 56, 58, 59, 60, 61, 63, 67, 68, 69, 70, 75, 76, 156
Indicated airspeed 9, 123, 156
Indicated altitude 10
Initial approach 56, 57, 69, 191
Inoperative components and visual aids 66, 67, 153
Instrument approach 32, 56-77, 79
Instrument flight rules (IFR) ..152, 153, 154, 155, 156, 191
Instrument Landing System (ILS)
  31, 32, 34, 56, 58, 59, 60, 61, 63, 67, 68, 69, 70, 75, 76, 156
Intensities of turbulence 173
Intercept angle 38, 51
Interrogator 126, 191
Isobars 88

J

Jet route system 78, 79, 191

L

Landing minimums 57, 58, 63, 64, 66, 67, 68, 69, 70, 71
Lapse rates 87
Level turns 16, 17, 18, 22, 23, 25
Light signals 149
Lighting, airport 64, 134, 135
Lighting system, approach 64, 134, 135, 156
Lightning 96
Listening watch 85
Localizer 32, 33, 34, 59, 60, 61, 63, 64, 65, 68, 69, 75
Logbooks 143, 144
Low altitude enroute charts 78, 79, 121, 175
Low clouds 91, 93, 94
Low stratus clouds 91, 93, 94
Low/medium frequencies 26, 28, 117, 118

M

Magnetic compass 8, 11, 12
Magnetic direction indicators 8, 11, 12
Maneuvers required for instrument flight
    test 25, 144, 145, 196, 197
Marker beacon 31, 32, 33, 34, 65, 175
Mature stage 96
Mercury barometer 88
Middle clouds 91
Middle marker 31, 32, 61, 156
Minimum Descent Altitude (MDA) 63, 64, 69, 156, 191
Minimum Enroute Altitude (MEA) ..84, 153, 156, 173, 191
Minimum Crossing Altitude (MCA) 84, 156, 175, 191
Minimum Descent Altitude (MDA) . 63, 64, 69, 71, 156, 191
Minimum Obstruction Clearance
    Altitude (MOCA) 84, 156, 175, 191
Minimum Reception Altitude (MRA) 84, 156, 175, 191
Minimums, landing 57, 58, 63, 64, 66, 67, 68, 69, 70, 71
Missed approach 56, 59, 65, 68, 69, 70, 71, 73, 85
Mode, transponder 126, 127, 128, 192
Moisture content 87, 90

N

National Weather Service (NWS) 102, 117, 119
Nautical mile 123

Navigation, flight planning 121, 122, 123
Navigation, radio 7, 26-55
Nimbostratus clouds 94
Non-Directional Radio
    Beacon (NDB) 31, 34, 56, 64, 65, 66, 67
Non-precision approach 63, 70, 71, 192
Non-precision instrument runway 133
Non-standard holding pattern 42
Non-standard procedure turn 41
Non-standard temperature 10
Northerly turning error 12
Notices to Airmen (NOTAM) 121, 192

O

Obstructions to visibility 87, 107, 109
Occluded fronts 99, 100
Omni bearing selector (OBS) 29
Omnirange 28
Outer marker 31, 32, 33, 57, 59, 61, 156
Oxygen requirements 124, 147

P

Partial panel flying 18, 19, 20, 21, 22, 25
Pilot's Automatic Telephone
    Weather Answering Service (PATWS) 117, 118
Pilot weather reports (PIREPS) 114, 115, 117, 119, 120
Pitch attitude 13, 19
Pitot-static system 9
Pitot tube 9
Position reports 84, 85, 86
Positive control area 129
Precipitation 95
Precision approach 63, 67, 68, 69, 156
Precision Approach Radar (PAR) 33, 34, 57, 58, 63, 66, 67, 156
Precision instrument runway 133, 134
Preflight action 116, 121, 143
Procedure turns 40, 45, 56, 57, 62, 65, 69, 71, 77
Prognostic charts 105, 106, 120

R

Radar 33, 34, 56, 70, 85, 103, 104, 126, 127, 128, 192
Radar principles 126, 127, 128
Radar summary charts 103, 104
Radial 28, 35, 192
Radio beacon 31, 34, 48
Radio Magnetic Indicator (RMI) 74, 75, 137
Radio Navigation and approach
    procedures test 144, 145, 197, 198
Ram pressure 9
Rate of climb 15, 19
Rate of climb indicator 8, 10
Rate of descent 16, 19
Rate-of-turn 16, 17
Rate-of-turn indicator 8, 10, 12, 16
Recovery from unusual attitudes 22, 23, 25, 200
Rigidity in space 10
Rime ice 95, 98
RNAV 139, 140
Route of flight 82, 84
Runway lighting 134, 135
Runway markings 133, 134
Runway Visual Range (RVR) 64, 193

S

Saturated air 90
Scheduled weather broadcasts 118, 119
Sea level pressure 88
Sectors, ARTC 78, 85
Separation 78, 81, 84, 192
Setting the altimeter 9, 10, 149
Sequence reports 106, 107, 108, 117
Sigmets 102, 113, 114, 116, 117, 120
Skid indication 10
Sky waves, radio 28
Slant range 30, 31
Slip indication 10
Speed, holding 41, 77
Speed limits 132, 133
Squawk 127, 128
Stacking 60, 61
Stalls 23, 25
Standard atmospheric pressure 88
Standard holding pattern 41
Standard Instrument Departure (SID) charts 82, 83
Standard rate turn 16, 17, 18, 21, 22, 37, 41, 44
Standard Terminal Arrival Route (STAR) charts 82, 83, 193
Static pressure 9
Stationary fronts 99
Station passage 30, 36
Station pressure 88
Steep turns 23, 25, 197
Straight and level flight 14, 19, 196
Straight-in approach 56, 58, 193
Stratocumulus clouds 91, 93, 94
Stratus clouds 94
Structural icing 97, 98
Surface weather charts 102
Surveillance radar 33, 79, 192, 193

T

TACAN 27, 28, 156
Takeoff minimums 66
Taxiway lighting 135
Telephone weather briefing 117, 118
Teletype reports 106
Temperature 87
Temperature scales 87
Temperature inversion 88
Terminal Control Area (TCA) 131, 150
Terminal forecast 102, 108, 109, 110, 115, 117, 120
Test, instrument flight 142, 143, 144, 145, 194-202
Test, instrument written 142, 159, 196
Threshold, runway 133, 134
Thunderstorms 95, 96, 97
Time-distance check 47
Timed turns 21, 22
To-From indicator 29
Tower, control 78, 79, 81
Tracking, ADF 48, 49, 50, 51
Tracking, VOR 36, 37
Traffic separation 78, 81, 84, 192
Transcribed Weather Broadcast (TWEB) 117, 118
Transponder 33, 34, 126, 127, 128, 193
Trimming the aircraft 13, 14, 15, 16, 19, 21, 22
True airspeed 9, 123, 156
Turbulence reporting criteria table 173
Turn and bank indicator 8, 10, 16, 22
Turn coordinator 10

Turn, standard rate 16, 17, 18, 21, 22, 37, 41, 44
Two-way radio communications failure 154

U

Uncontrolled airspace 128
Updrafts 96
Upslope wind 90
Unusual attitudes 22, 23, 25

V

Variation 121, 122, 123
Vertical speed indicator 8, 9, 14
Vertigo 7
Very high frequency omnidirectional range (VOR) 28
VFR altitudes/flight levels 131, 152
Victor airways 28, 78
VHF frequency band 26, 28
VHF omnirange 28
Visibility 56, 58, 63, 66, 67, 95, 103, 107, 193
Visibility/distance from clouds, VFR 131, 132, 151
Visual approach 193
Visual Approach Slope indicator (VASI) 135, 136
Visual Flight Rules (VFR) 151, 152

VOR classes 30
VOR, methods and procedures 35-48
VOR receiver check 30, 146, 147
VORTAC 27, 28

W

Warm front 99, 100, 101
Waypoint 139, 140, 193
Weather, aviation 87-120
Weather briefing 116, 117, 118, 119, 120, 121
Weather broadcasts 118, 119
Weather charts 102, 103, 104, 105, 106, 117, 120
Weather depiction charts 102, 103, 104
Weather forecasts 102, 108, 109, 110, 111, 112, 113, 117, 120
Weather radar 103, 104, 105
Weight and balance 124
Winds aloft forecasts 112, 113, 117, 120, 123
Word contractions 186, 187, 188

Z

Zebra (Z) Time 186
Z marker 31, 32

This is to Certify That

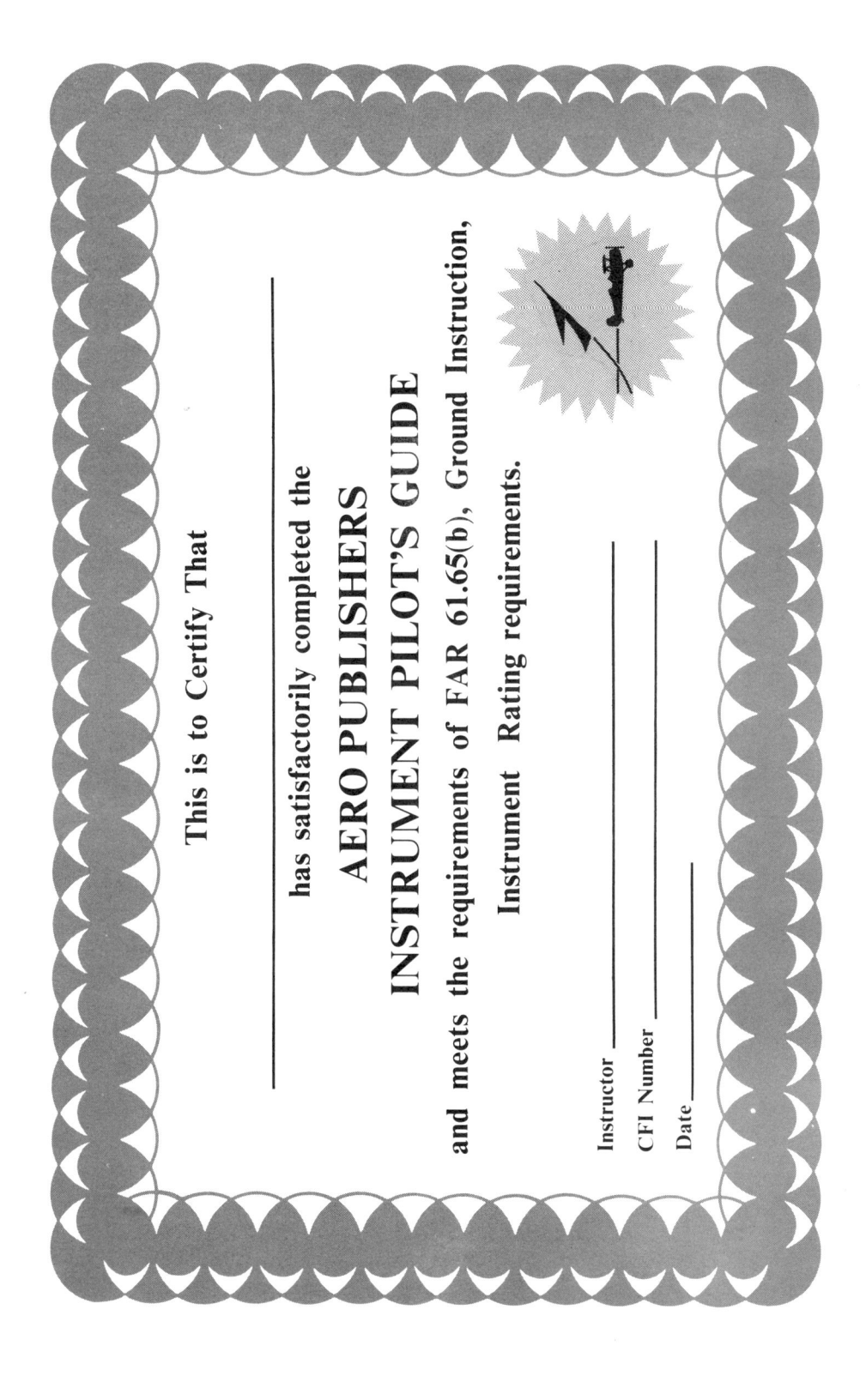

_____

has satisfactorily completed the

**AERO PUBLISHERS
INSTRUMENT PILOT'S GUIDE**

and meets the requirements of FAR 61.65(b), Ground Instruction, Instrument Rating requirements.

Instructor _____
CFI Number _____
Date _____